AF568137

REPRODUCTIVE DISEASES

ENCYCLOPAEDIA OF ANIMAL DISEASES-I

REPRODUCTIVE DISEASES

By

Ashok Kumar

Dept. of Zoology
Bundelkhand University
Campus Department
Jhansi (India)

DISCOVERY PUBLISHING HOUSE PVT. LTD.
NEW DELHI-110 002

Published by:
Namit Wasan
DISCOVERY PUBLISHING HOUSE PVT. LTD.
4383/4B, Ansari Road, Darya Ganj
New Delhi-110 002 (India)
Phone : +91-11-23279245; 23253475; 43596065
E-mail : discoverybooksindia@gmail.com
discoverypublishinghouse@gmail.com
namitwasan9@gmail.com
web : www.discoverypublishinggroup.com

Edition: **2020**

ISBN: 978-81-8356-206-5 (Set)

ISBN: 978-81-8356-282-9

Reproductive Diseases

Printed at:
Infinity Imaging Systems
Delhi

PREFACE

The **Reproductive Diseases** has been carefully compiled and edited to meet the long felt needs of increasingly large number of those who have to deal with the different aspects of human diseases in colleges, universities and research institutes. It provides a stimulating and important new view of interaction between animals and pathogens causing diseases. The objective is to introduce to students the essential principles for understanding various aspects of diseases. Most of diseases constitute the largest part of human pathology and are the primary cause of death. Hence, special importance is given to the study of such diseases.

The book is intended to acquaint students of various fields involved directly or indirectly with the major principles of human diseases. The book may be helpful as well to practitioners and those engaged in medical research.

In the preparation of this book large number of books and research papers have been consulted. So no authenticity is claimed.

The author wishes to express his deepest appreciation to the many people who have contributed in one way or the other to the preparation of this title.

The author expresses his gratitude to Mr. Wasan and staff of M/s Discovery Publishing House for their whole hearted co-operation in the publication of this book.

The author tried hard to be accurate and upto date in statement and realises the impossibility of completely avoiding errors therefore, the author will greatly appreciate having his attention called to any questionable statement.

Author

Contents

Chapter 1 1—36

MALE SEXUAL ORGANS

Embryology of the Reproductive Organs, The Testes, Histology, Function, The Scrotum, Function, Accessory Tubules, Epididymis, Ductus Deferens, Accessory Sex Glands, Ampullary Glands, Vesicular Glands, Prostate Glands, Bulbo-urethral Glands, The Bulbar Gland, Paraprostate Glands, The Prostatic Utricle, Urethral Glands, Preputial Glands, Inguinal Glands, Physiological and Environmental Factors which Influence Accessory Sex Structures, The Urethra, The Penis and Accessory Structures, The Penis, The Prepuce, Reproductive Organs of Various Species and Groups, The Opossum, Soricidae, Vespertilionidae, Subhuman Primates, Mustelidae, Canidae, Felidae, Lagomorpha, Sciuridae, Caviidae

Chapter 2 37—71

FORMATION OF MALE SEX CELLS

Spermatogenesis, Spermiogenesis, The Testicular Environment, Spermatophore, The Semen, Spermatozoa, Development of Sperm, Metabolism of Sperm, Survival of Sperm in vitro, Seminal Plasma, Function of Seminal Plasma, Chemical Composition of Seminal Plasma, Influence of the Female Reproductive Tract on Sperm, Sperm Transport, Prefertilization Changes of Sperm, Viability of Sperm in Female Reproductive Tract

Chapter 3 72—118

FEMALE SEXUAL ORGANS

Embryology, Gonads, Reproductive Ducts, Urogenital Sinus,

Ovary, Development of Ovarian Follicles, Formation of Eggs, Atresia and Degeneration, Corpus Luteum Formation, The Oviduct, Ligaments, Ovarian Bursa, Fimbriae and Infundibulum, Ampulla and Isthmus, Uterotubal Junction, Oviductal Eggs, Structure and Ultrastructure, Transport of Eggs, Fertilizable Life and Aging of Eggs, The Uterus, Uterine Structure, Uterine Functions, Biochemical Aspects of Uterus, The Cervix, The Vagina, The External Genitalia, Mammary Glands

Chapter 4 119—147

FORMATION OF FEMALE SEX CELLS

Oogenesis, Folliculogenesis, Atresia, Ovulation in Mammals, Ovulation in Nonmammalian Vertebrates, Induced Ovulation, Unilateral Ovulation, Estrus or Heat, Menstruation and Menopause, The Corpus Luteum, Preservation of the Corpus Luteum, Accessory Corpora Lutea

Chapter 5 148—171

COPULATORY ORGANS

Holdfast Mechanisms, Male Copulatory Organs, Female Genitalia, Accessory Glands, Originating in the Sperm Duct or Oviduct, Originating from the Urogenital Canal, Originating in the Integument, Devices for the Care of Eggs and Young, Degenerate and Rudimentary Organs, Periodicity in Reproduction

Chapter 6 172—189

PREGNANCY FAILURE

Occurrence, Medical Considerations, Evaluation of the Problem, Investigation, The Initial Interview, Fundamental Tests, Ovulation, Ovulation Defects, Sperm, Evaluation, Seminal Insufficiency, Artificial Insemination, Cervicalo Mucus, Tubal Function, The Enduaietriudi

Chapter 7 190—196

ABNORMAL VAGINAL DISCHARGE

Leukorrhea, Source and Character of Genital Discharges, Vulva, Vagina, Cervix, Uterine Body, Tubes, Causes, Constitutional, Endocrine Disorders, Inflammations of Any Part of the Genital Canal, Diagnosis of cause of Leukorrhea, Treatment

Chapter 8 197—220

VULVULAR DISEASES

Circulatory Diseases, Inflammations, Diseases of Bartholin's Gland, Inflammation (Bartholin Adenitis), Chronic Bartholinitis, Tumors, Ulcerative Lesions, Simple Acute Ulcer (Lipschiitz), Chancroid (Soft Chancer, Ulcus Molle), Syphilis, Chancer, Secondary Lesions-Condyloma Latum, Tertiary Syphilis-Gumma and Syphilitic Ulcer, Granuloma Inguinale, Lymphopathia Venereum (Lymphogranuloma), White Lesions of the Vulva, Absence of Pigment or Depigmenation, Increased Keratinization (Hyperkeratosis), Pruritus Vulvae, Local Causes, General Causes, Benign Tumors of the Vulva, Cystic, Solid, Cystic, Carcinoma of the Vulva, Treatment of Vulvar Cancer, Other Vulvar Malignancies, Urethra

Chapter 9 221—233

VAGINAL DISEASES

Vaginitis, Causes, Symptoms and Signs, Diagnosis of Nonspecific Form, Treatment, Trichomonas Vaginitis, Incidence, Symptoms, Diagnosis, Methods of Infection, Treatment, Mycotic Vaginitis (Fungous or Monial Vaginitis), Symptoms, Diagnosis, Methods of Infection, Treatment, Hemophilus vaginalis Vaginitis, Gonorrheal Vulvovaginitis in Children, Mode of Infection, Symptoms, Diagnosis, Treatment, Senile Vaginitis, Treatment, Emphysematous Vaginitis, Neoplasms of the Vagina, Benign Tumors, Malignant Tumors

Chapter 10 234—255

OVARIAN TUMORS

Histochemical Studies, Dysgeminoma, Incidence, Origin, Pathology, Clinical Characteristics, Treatment, Granulosa-Theca Cell Tumors, Histogenesis, Pathology of Granulosa Cell Tumors, Pathology of Thecoma, Luteinization of Granulosa-Theca Cell Tumors, Pregnancy Luteoma, Clinical characteristics of Granulosa-theca Tumors, Malignancy, Association of Endometrial Carcinoma with Feminizing Tumors, Treatment, Arrhenoblastoma and Adremal Ovarian Tumors, Arrhenoblastoma, Histogenesis, Pathology, Malignancy, Clinical Features, Treatment, Adrenal Tumors of the Ovary, Gynandroblastoma, Virilizing Hills Cell Tumors, Tumors with Functioning Matrix, Homology of Certain Ovarian and Testicular Tumors

Chapter 11 256—262

UTERINE TUMOR

Pathology and Classifications, Sarcomas, Leiomyosarcoma, Clinical Characteristics, Treatment

Chapter 12 263—278

OVARIAN CARCINOMA

Primary Solid Carcinoma of Ovary, Types, Gross Characteristics, Mesonephroma of the Ovary, Primary Cystic Carcinoma of Ovary, Primary Cystic Carcinoma of Ovary, Pseudomucinous Cystadenocarcinoma, Serous Cystadenocarcinoma, Secondary Carcinoma in Dermoid Cysts, Secondary of Metastatic Carcinoma of Ovary, Krukenberg Tumor, Extension of Ovarian Carcinoma, Clinical Characteristics of Ovarian Carcinoma, Ovarian Carcinoma in Pregnancy, Diagnosis, Prognosis, Treatment, Sarcoma of Ovary, Sarcoma of Ovary, Teratoma

Chapter 13 278—289

INFLAMMATORY GONADAL DISEASES

Etiology, Gonorrheal Type, Pathology, Acute Endometritis of Gonorrheal Type, Acute Salpingitis, Septic or Tyogenic Type, Acute Endometritis, Acute Salpingitis, Acute Ovaritis or Oophoritis, Acute Pelvic Peritonitis, Symptoms and Signs, Gonorrheal Form, Postpartum and Postabortive Types, Pyometra, Diagnosis, Gonorrheal Infection, Postpartum and Postabortive Infection, Differential Diagnosis, Acute Appendicitis, Acute Pyelitis, Suppurating Ovarian Cyst, Treatment, Surgery during Acute Stage

Chapter 14 290—299

CHRONIC GONADAL DISEASES

Chronic Endometritis, Subinvolution of Uterus, Chronic Salpingitis, Hydrosalpinx, Chronic Oophoritis and Perioophoritis, Symptoms of Chronic Pelvic Inflammatory Disease, Diagnosis, Differential Diagnosis, Treatment

Chapter 15 300—341

FAILURE OF MENSTRUATION

Incidence, Classification, Diagnosis and Treatment, Investigative

Procedures, Gonadotrophin Therapy, Clomiphene, Thyroid, Nutrition, Lesions of Central Origin; Neurogenic Lesions and Organic Brain Disease, Pituitary Amenorrhea, Psychogenic Amenorrhea, Lesions of Intermediate Origin, Chronic Disease, Metabolic Disease, Nutritional Amenorrhea, Disturbances of Steroid Excretion and Metabolism, LEsioins of Peripheral Origin, Ovarian, End Organs: Uterine and Vaginal Cryptomenorrhea, Physiological Amenorrhea, Delayed Puberty, Pregnancy and Postpartum Amenorrhea

INDEX 342—348

MALE SEXUAL ORGANS

The male reproductive system is associated with the urinary system from which it is partially derived. It consists of the following: (1) the primary sex organs which produce the sperm, i.e., the testes; (2) accessory sex glands which produce fluids that combine with and serve as a medium of transport for sperm during emission, i.e., the prostate, vesicular glands, bulbo-urethal glands, and lesser structures; (3) a series of ducts through which sperm and fluid are transported to the outside, i.e., the epididymis, ductus deferens, and urethra; and (4) the external genitalia, i.e., the penis and, in some forms, a scrotum. Embryonic development, anatomy, histology, and physiology of these structures will be discussed and species differences, will be illustrated.

EMBRYOLOGY OF THE REPRODUCTIVE ORGANS

The genital system arises from mesodermal mesenchyme to form bilateral *genital ridges* between the *mesonephros* and dorsal aorta. The genital ridges are covered with *germinal epithelium,* which is continuous with the mesothelium of the *coelomi* cavity. Into the germinal epithelium move primordial germ cells from either extraembryonic endoderm or from the *yolk sac. As* the genital ridge thickens and moves away from the mesonephros, it develops its own mesentery, the *mesorchium.* Germinal epithelium, including *primordial germ cells,* invaginates into the germinal ridge and forms *primary*

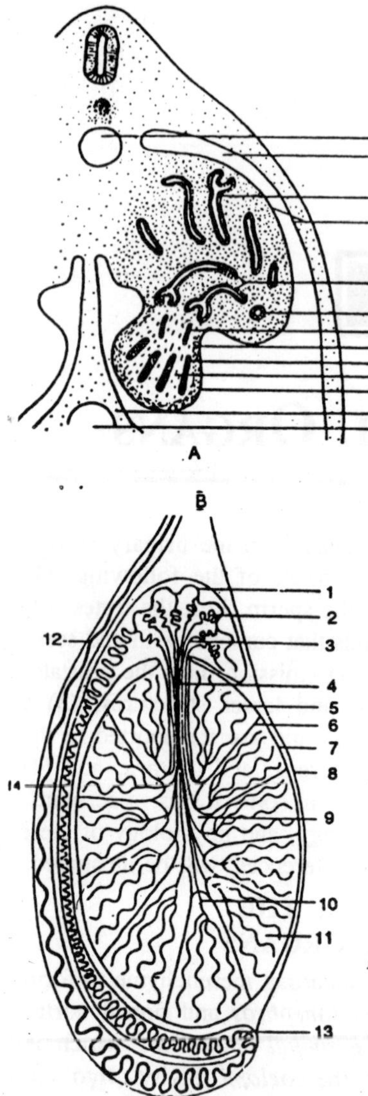

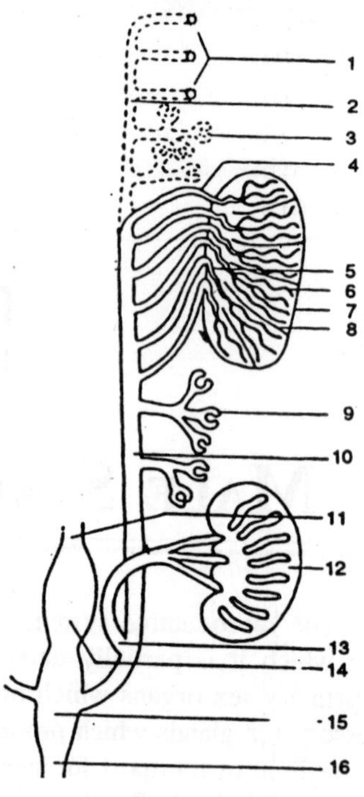

Fig. 1.1. Diagram of the development of the testis and accessory tubules.

A. *The urogenital ridge. (1) Dorsal aorta. (2) Coelom. (3) Mesonephric tubules. (4) Mesothelium. (5) Ductuli efferents. (6) Mesonephric duct. (7) Rete cord. (8) Tunica albuginea. (9) Sex cord. (10) Interstitial cells. (11) Germinal epithelium. (12) Mesentery. (13) Digestive tract.*

B. *The accessory tubules. (1) Pronephros. (2) Archinephrie duct. (3) Mesonephros. (4) Ductulus efferentes. (5) Rete tubule. (6) Seminiferous tubule. (7) Thnica albuginea. (8) Septulum. (9) Mesonephros. (10) Mesonephric duct. (11) Allantois. (12) Metanephros. (13) Metanephric tubule. (14) Bladder. (15) Urogenital sinus. (16) Cloaca.*

C. *The adult testis of the cat. (1) Duct of caput epididymis. (2) Lobule of epididymis. (3) Ductulus efferentes. (4) Rete tubules. (5) Tubuli contorti of seminiferous tubules. (6) Septulum. (7) Tunica albuginea. (8) Tunlea vaginalis. (9) Mediastium testis. (10) Tubuli recti of seminiferous tubules. (11) Interstitial tissue. (12) Ductus deferens. (13) Duct of cauda epididymis. (14) Corpus epididymis.*

sex cords which become continuous with *rete cords* derived from *mesenchyme.*

The structure, which has bisexual potencies, may then be termed a gonad. It consists of an outer cortes composed of mesenchyme; and a medulla composed of sex cords. rete cords, and mesenchyme. In the male, the gonad is *a testis* in which the primary sex cords and rete cords become hollow and from *seminiferous tubules* and *rete tubules,* respectively. The germinal epithelium regresses and becomes identical to other coelomic epithelium. The cortex differentiates into a connective tissue sheath, the *tunica albuginea.* Other mesenchymal cells differentiate into *interstitial cells.* Still others from a connective tissue framework of septula, which are continuous with the peripheral albuginea and the medial *mediastinum testis* in which the rete testis is located.

The septula divide the testis into *lobules,* each of which contains a number of seminiferous tubules.

As the metanephros develops and the mesonephros degenerates, certain tubules of the mesonephros undergo reduction; they remain functional as a connection between the rete tubules and the mesonephric portion of the Wolffian duct, and are known as the efferent duclules of the *epididymis.* The mesonephric duct loses its urinary function; the cranial portion undergoes extreme convolution and becomes the *ductus epididymis* while the caudal portion remains relatively straight and becomes the *ductus deferens.* The latter may expand into the *ampullary gland* cranial to its junction with the urethra; it may also develop an evagination just caudal to the ampullary gland, the vesicular gland.

A cyst lined with dolumnar epithelium, the *appendix epididymis, is* connected with the cranial end of the epididymis. *A paradidymis,* consisting of a group of blind tubules, is located in the spermatic cord just proximal to the cranial end of the epididymis. Both these structures are nonfunctional remnants of the mesonephros.

A groove parallel and lateral to the mesonephric duct develops in the urogenital ridge. The sides of the groove fold together and fuse to form the *Mullerian ducts.* Posteriorly, the genital ridges elevate, fold together, and fuse to form the median genital cord. In the process, the *Mullerian ducts* are brought into apposition and fuse. They end in a middorsal projection into the urogenital sinus, *Muller's tubercle.* The tubercle forms at the entrance of the Wolffian ducts and will become the adult *colliculus seminalis.* In the male, the anterior

Mullerian ducts degenerate; the posterior fused position remains as a midventral blind pouch, the *prostatic ulricle.* Epithelium from the urethra invades the pouch and replaces the original *Mullerian duct* epithelium.

During development of the testis, external genitalia also develop. *A urinary bladder* and *urogenital sinus* develop from the allantoic duct. The urogenital sinus and rectum open into a cloaca; the former two structures become separated on a frontal plane by a urorectal fold. A midventral genital tuberele develops cranial to the cloaca. Its posterior portion develops a urogenital groove which is bounded laterally by *urogenilal folds* and dorsally by a urogenital membrane. This membrane ruptures and provides an external opening for the urogenital sinus. The genital tubercle elongates into a phallus, the tip of which is a precursor of the *glans penis.* The urogenital folds fuse ventrally toward the glans the resulting lumen forms the quali*part* of the *urethra* which opens at the glans. The golds themselves develop into erectile tissue; they form the *corpus spongiosum* and glans distally, and expand to form the *bulbus penis* at the junction with the urethra. A fold of skin develops at the base of the glans, grows distally, and surrounds the glans. This is the prepuce.

Connective tissue in the dorsal side of the penis forms bilateral rods of erectile tissue, the *corpora cavernosa.* The corpora cavernosa fuse distally to varying degrees; proximally they diverge and form the *crura* which unite with the ischium on the respective sides. The crura thus unite the penis with the skeletal system. In some species an ectopic bone, the *baculurn or os penis,* develops between the two separate corpora or within the single corpus cavernosum.

Genital swellings develop lateral to the urogenital folds. In the male, these are destined to become the *scrotal swellings* from which will develop two *scrolal pouches.* The pouches are separated internally by a partition, the septum scroti; its external position is marked by the *scrotal raphe.*

In many species the testes descend into the scrotum during regression of the mesonephros. The mesonephros joins with the peritoneum of the scrotal swelling and meserchymal cells to form a connective tissue cord, the *gubernaculum testis,* between the testis and the serotal swelling. As soon as the gubernaculum forms, the peritoneum surrounding it evaginates into the body wall and thereby fòrms a lining for the scrotal pouches, the *scrotal sac.* Since formation of the gubernaculum precedes muscle formation, an *inguinal canal is* formed at the site of the evagination. The body lengthens, but the gubernaculum does not. As a result, the testis, with its associated tubules, blood vessels, and nerves, is drawn lateral to the ureter and into the scrotal sacs. The gubernaculum shortens, but this apparently is an effect, not a cause of testis descent.

As the testis descends into the scrotum, it becomes partly covered by a reflected fold of peritoneum, the *tunica vaginalis* in species in which the testes are seasonally withdrawn into the body, the inguinal canal remains open. If the testes remain permanently in the scrotum, the inguinal canal closes and the tunica vaginalis forms a closed sac with a *parietal layer* lining the scrotum and a visceral layer adjacent to the tunica albuginea of the testis. The two layers join at thc peritoneal fold, and it is here that blood vessels and nerves enter the testis.

THE TESTES

The primary sex organs, the *testes,* consist principally of an oval or pear-shaped mass of highly coiled tubules. They enlarge at sexual maturity, and in some species, maintain a practically constant size thereafter; in such species the male is capable of breeding at any time. In other species, the testes undergo alternate regression and enlargement and the male is capable of breeding only at certain periods.

Position of the testes is highly variable. In omnivores such as the opossum, carnivores and primates, they descend into the scrotum and remain there permanently. In bats, rats, and rabbits, the testes are carried within the abdominal cavity part of the year. During the breeding season the scrotum of bats and squirrels enlarges and the testes descend through the inguinal canal and enlarge. In other rodents and in rabbits, no true scrotum is formed and the testes lie in an inguinal pouch from which they may be withdrawn into thc abdominal cavity even when they are enlarged.

Histology

Each testis is surrounded by a capsule of collagenous fibers, the *tunica albuginea,* from which there is an extension, the *inediastinuin testis,* into the central portion of the testis. Membranes of more or less continuous connective tissue, the *septula, extend* from the tunica to the mediastinum and divide the testis into triangular lobules.

Within each lobule are several *seminiferous tubules* which are formed from branching of the sex cords. The highly coiled portion of the tubule near the tunica is the *tubuli contorli,* and the relatively straight portion near the mediastinum is the *tubuli recti.*

Each seminiferous tubule is surrounded by a basement membrane of collagenous fibers and lined with stratified epithelium. The epithelium consists of *spermatogenic cells* and *Sertoli's* or *sustentacular cells.* There are five morphologically distinguishable types of spermatogenic cells: spermatogonia, primary spermatocytes secondary, spermatocytes, spermatids and spermatozoa. They represent successive stages in the differentiation of mature male sex cells, and occur, in the order named, from the basement membrane, to which the spermatogonia are attached, to the lumen of the tubule. Sertoli's cells are attached to the basement membrane in spaces between spermatogonia, and there fore, are of irregular shape. They provide mechanical support and serve in the nutrition of spermatogenic cells.

Tubuli recti open into the rete testis. Two types of rate testes have been recognized, based upon their position within the testis: (1) a superficial type, present in man, rat, and mouse, and (2) an axial type found in the rabbit, guinea pig, cat, dog, and cattle.

In the rat, the rete testis may be divided into three parts: (1) the intertesticular, the largest part, is a single flattened tubule, with flattened pillars near the midline, which lies on the seminiferous tubules near the cranial pole.of the testis; (2) the intratunical rete, a transitional part of the intratesticular, which consists of a series of irregular passage ways running through the tunica albuginea; and (3) the extratesticular rete, an irregular subdivided cavity which is located on the eranial end of the testis, and which is joined by the ductuli efferentes near its most eranial extension. The intratesticular rete originates from the gonadal blastema, the extratesticular rete from the rete blastema which is derived from the mesonephros.

As found in the cat, the axial type of rete testis consists of a group of relatively straight tubules surrounded by connective tissue of the mediastinum and located approximately in the long axis of the testis. Tubules pass from the body of the testis at its proximal end and join ductuli efferentes which, in convoluted form, constitute part of the caput epididymis.

Rete testis tubules are lined with simple epithelium which rests upon a basement membrane that is adjacent to tissue of the mediastinum testis. Epithelial cells are squamous in the main cavity, but ctiboidal or low columnar near the tubulj recti and ductuli efferentes. The luminal surfaces have numerous microvilli and a few cells have a single cilium.

Interstitial cells of Leydig occur in clusters among the seminiferous tubules or in rows along blood vessels. They arise from cells which are indistinguishable from fibroblasts. In species with a cyclic reproductive function such as squirrels, the interstitial cells undergo atrophy and new cells differentiate the following breeding season. Pigment cells are present in some species, and, with atrophy of normal interstitial cells during sexual quiescence, become relatively more abundant and impart a dark brown color to the testis.

Function

The primary function of the testes is production of male sex cells. The function of the seminiferous tubules is controlled by interstitial-cell stimulating hormone from the adenohypophysis. The interstitial cells are the primary source of testosterone which, supplemented by testosterone produced by Sertoli's controls the size and secretory activity of accessory sex glands and the development of secondary sexual characteristics. The interrelationships are discussed in the section on accessory sex structures.

THE SCROTUM

The serotum is a thin pouch of skin, muscle, and elastic and collagenous connective tissue in which the testes lie. It is present in the opossum, cat, dog, ferrett, mink, squirrel, and ground squirrel. It is prepenial in the opossum, but postpenial in all other species. Usually the skin is devoid of hair. A medial ventral ridge, the scrotal raphe, marks the line of fusion of the embryonic genital swellings. Just beneath the skin is the *dartos tunic* which is composed of smooth muscle fibers and connective tissue; the tunic surrounds both testes individually, and medially the two tunics fuse to form an internal scrotal partition, the *septum scroti*. Dartos muscles unite with the skin at regular intervals.

Beneath the dartos tunic lie one or more layers composed of striated muscle and connective tissue. Usually this is considered to be a single layer, the cremaster fascia, which is a continuation of the internal oblique muscle into the scrotal pouch. The fascia forms a sheath around the spermatic cord. Under conditions of extreme hypertrophy of the human scrotum, two additional layers may be distinguished: (1) the *external spermalic fascia,* which is a pouch of the aponeurosis of the external oblique muscle; and (2) the internal *spermatic fascia,* which is a pouch of the aponeurosis of the transverse abdominis muscle. These two layers probably are present in subhuman primates.

The scrotum is lined with the parietal layer of the tunica vaginalis. This layer may be much attenuated, but is complete. Both the mesothelial cells, which constitute the tunica, and the macrophages lying within the tunica have phagocytic properties. In the opossum, this layer contains heavy deposits of melanin. The serotum of squirrels and ground squirrels also is pigmented.

Rabbits, bats and members of the Cricetidae and Muridae have an *inguinal pouch* rather then a scrotum. The pouch is formed by muscles and fascia of the body wall. In some species most of the pouch is partially devoid of hair; in others, only that part occupied by the epididymis is appreciably devoid of hair. In rats and mice the posterior portion is pigmented to varying degrees.

Function

Maintenance of the testes at the temperature which is optimum for sperm production is the function of the serotum. In most mammals, spermatogenesis takes place at less than body temperature. Contraction and relaxation of the dartos muscles raise and lower the testes with respect to the body, and their temperature is thereby regulated. In addition, the *pampiniform plexus,* which is formed by a network of veins as they leave the posterior border of the testes and pass up the spermatic cord, surrounds the convoluted testicular artery and serves as a thermoregulatory mechanism. Failure of a testis to descend into the scrotum results in a condition known as *cryptorchidism. A* bilaterally cryptorchid animal is sterile.

ACCESSORY TUBULES

Epididymis

The epididymis is a heavy cordlike structure, formed from highly coiled ducts, which closely adheres to the surface of the testis. It consists of there parts: (1) the *caput epididymis,* which lies at the end of the testis to which the spermatic cord is attached; (2) the *corpus epididymis* or central body; and (3) the *cauda epididymis,* which lies at the opposite pole of the testis from that occupied by the caput epididymis, and which joins the ductus deferens.

The *caput epididymis* consists in part of small lobes or cones formed from the highly convoluted *ducluti efferentes.* The apex of each cone is directed toward the mediastinum testis where the ductuli join tubules of the rete testis. Ductuli coalesce to from the single *ductus epididyinidis, which* is a highly convoluted duct that forms both corpus and caput epididymis.

Epithelium of the ductuli efferentes of a rodent, the nutria (*Moyocastor coypus*), has been described as composed of groups of tall cells alternating with short groups all being pseudostratified, ciliated columnar cells. Blebs of secretory material project from the free surface. This is quite similar to the description usually given for ductuli efferentes epithelium in man. In the cat, the epithelium is simple cuboidal with stereocilia on the free surface. Stereocilia are nonmotile, have neither basal bodies nor internal filaments, and are thought to be very long icrovilli. In the opossum, ductuli are lined with simple columnar-cells, some of which are ciliated and some nonciliated. These cells rest upon a thick basement membrane whichSissunderlain with variable amounts of smooth muscle and connective tissue. Ductuli of the rat and rabbit are lined with simple columnar cells, at least part of which have stereocilia.

The *ductus epididymidis* maintains a relatively constant diameter as it traverses the caput and corpus epididymis, but its diameter approximately doubles in the caudal region. It lies embedded in collagenous connective tissue throughout its entire length. In sexually active animals the caudal tubules show distinctly through the connective tissue sheath.

Two cell types, holocrine and principal cells, are present in the rat epididymis. Basal apical, and clear cells represent different stages of the holocrine cell cycle as it accumulates secretory products and degenerates. Principal and holocrine cells differ in their histochemical reaction.

Ductus epithelial cells have long stereocilia projecting from the surface. Cell height and length of stereocilia diminish in the corpus epididymis. The epithelium of the greatly distended cauda epididymis may be simple lower columnar or low cuboidal; the cells may be without stereocilia, but with blebs of secretory material extruding from the free surface. But epithelium, in contract to basal nuclei of other species, is characterized by centrally located nuclei throughout the length of the ductus epididymis.

Function. Ductuli efferentes retain the absorptive function of the mesonephric tubules from which they were derived. A large volume of fluid is transferred across the wall to the lumen of the seminiferous tubules; this fluid serves to move the sperm along the tubule to the ductus deferens. Excess fluid which is not required for propulsion of sperm in the ductus is resorbed by the ductuli efferentes, some of the cells of which have aggregations of canaliculi in the plasmalemma of the free surface. Movement of sperm is therefore more rapid in the ductuli efferentes than in the ductus epididymidis. The time required for movement of spern through the latter structure varies from 25 days in the guinea pig to 22 days in the rat under normal conditions, 7 to 10 days in freely mating rats, 10 days in the hamster, and 8 to 10 days in the rabbit.

The ductus epididymidis serves as a site for maturation and storage of spermatozoa as well as a vehicle for their transport. Changes in maturation of sperm as they pass through the ductus epididymidis have been thought to be temporal ones which were regulated by intrinsic factors, but Paufler and Foote demonstrated that extrinsic factors from the ductus epididymidis were required for development of functional spermatozoa. Spermatozoa which were isolated in the caput epididymis underwent morphological changes typical of normal maturation, but they had a low degree of fertility. Such spermatozoa never attained the motility of those from the cauda epididymis, and were completely nonmotile after 4 weeks. Spermatozoa in the cauda epididymis, the main reservoir, remained motile for 8 weeks and were as fertile as ejaculated spermatozoa. Thus, substances from the corpora and cauda epididymis are necessary for production and nourishment of fertile spermatozoa.

The epididymis produces enzymes. Localization of different enzymes in different parts of the epididymis and in certain epithelial cells of a given part, as well as counteraction of substances in the stroma and epithelium of a given part, have been demonstrated by Allen and Slater. PAS positive granules are produced by both principal and holocrine cells in the rat, hamster, and guinea pig. Activity of the epithelial cell is controlled by testicular hormones.

Ductus Deferens

The ductus deferens continues the canal of the epididymis as a highly convoluted tube parallel to the corpora epididymis; it gradually straightens as it leaves the epididymis, passes through the inguinal canal, loops around the ureter, and finally opens into the urethra at the colliculus seminalis. From the testes to where it loops around the ureter, the ductusdeferens, the testicular and epididymal blood and lymphatic vessels, and nerves constitute and spermatic cord. Near its junction with the urethra, *ampullary glands* may form as either tubes or crypts in the wall of the ductus or as distinct lobes. Beyond the ampullary gland an evagination, the *seminal vesicle,* forms in some species. A short, straight section of the ductus just distal to its junction with the seminal vesicle is the *ejaculatory duct.*

Epithelium of the ductus deferens is ciliated or has stereocilia in most species and is highly variable: stratified squamous in the eat; simple squamous near the epididymis to columnar with a layer in. basal cells in the area near the urethra in the guineing, high columnar with an incomplete layer of basal cells in the bat and opossum. The cells have centrally located nuclei in the bat, but greatly elongated basal ones in the opossum. Epithelium of the rabbit ductus is simple columnar; it may be folded to form crypts or tubules. The amount and proportion of elastic and collagenous tissue and smooth muscle varies from species to species. Most smooth muscle fibers are circularly arranged.

ACCESSORY SEX GLANDS

A high degree of development of the accessory sex glands is characteristic of the Mammalia. Some glands are derived from each of the germ layers and, on the basis of their origin, they may be classified as: (1) those derived from the lower ductus deferens and therefore, of mesodermal origin (ampullary glands and vesicular glands); (2) those derived from the endodermal part of the urogenital sinus (prostatic, membranous, and penile urethra); (3) those derived from the proximal ends of the Miillerian ducts (prostatic utricle); and (4) those derived from the ectoderm of the preputial or inguinal region (preputial glands and inguinal glands).

Products of these glands are combined with spermatozoa in the urethra to form the semen. There is much variation among species with respect to presence and degree of development of various glands and the chemical properties of their secretions.

Ampullary Glands

Ampullary glands *(ampullae ductus deferentis)* are highly variable structures formed from the ductus deferens near its junction with the urethra. The glands consist of tubules which are enclosed by a capsule of connective tissue and smooth muscle. Extensions of connective tissue from the capsule from septa between tubules. Smooth muscles are present in the anterior septa, but disappear as the ductus approaches the urethra. In strews and bats, smooth muscle is absent in both the ampullary capsule and the septa. Some tubules may coalesce, and folds of epithelium may project into the lumen of others. In some species there is no distinct wall for the lumen of the ductus deferens within the ampullary gland; rather, it is formed by the beginning of the tubular evagination.

In shrews and bate the lumen of the ductus deferens is distinct

TABLE 1.1. COMPARATIVE ANATOMY OF THE MALE REPRODUCTIVE STRUCTURES

Species	*Tesis*	*Ampullary Glands*	*Seminal Vesicles*	*Prostate Gland*	*Paraprostate Glands*	*Bulbo-urethral Glands*	*Baculum*	*Urethrat Glands*	*Bulbar Glands*	*Preputial Glands*	*Inguinal Glands*
Bat	3 × 2	4 × 15	A	5 × 3	A	1 × 1	F	F	A	A	A
Cat	14 × 8	A	A	5 × 2	A	4 × 3	F	A	A	A	A
Dog	40 × 30	F	A	25 × 16	A	A	F	A	A	A	A
Gerbil	14 × 9	6 × 5	20 × 12	9 × 7	A	6 × 4	F	F	A	A	A
Guinea pig	25 × 15	A	115 × 7	15 × 8	A	8 × 5	F	A	A	PD	A
Hamster	14 × 11	3 x 3	11 × 6	8 × 6	A	4 × 3	F	F	A	3 × 1	A
Mink	11 × 8	F	A	10 × 5	A	A	F	A	A	A	A
Mouse	6 × 4	2 × 1	13 × 4	4 × 4	A	3 × 2	F	F	A	6 × 5	A
Opossum	15 × 11	A	A	40 × 9	A	19 × 15	A	A	A	A	A
Rabbit-European	35 × 15	15 × 4	19 × 7	19 × 6	6 × 2	6 × 3	A	A	A	A	15 × 7
Rabbit-cottontail	35 × 17	F	A	25 × 6	A	6 × 2	A	A	A	A	10 × 4
Rat	20 × 12	4 × 4	20 × 10	13 × 10	A	5 × 3	F	F	A	16x4	A
Shrew	3 × 2	3 × 1	A	3 × 1.5	A	1 × 1	A	A	A	Diffuse	A
Squirrel-tree	30 × 12	F	7 × 4	28 × 8	A	13 × 13	F	A	10 × 7	A	A
Squirrel-ground	14 × 8	F	8 × 7	18 × 18	A	8 × 6	F	A	10 × 8	F	A
Subhuman-primate	10 ~c 7F	AF	14 x 7A	6 x 5F	A	A	F	A	A	Diffuse	A
Ferret	F	F	A	F	A	A	F	A	A	A	A

F-indicates that a functional gland is present, but was not measured; A-indicates that the structure does not occur; PD indicates that the gland is poorly developed.

and passes centrally through the ampullarium. In members of the families Cricetidae and Muridae, ampullary glands form distinct lobes from each ductus deferens. The lobes consist of ducts which pass through separately and are therefore embedded in the muscularis of the ductus deferens for a distance. Eventually portions of the duct walls form the lumen of the ductus deferens just anterior to the ejaculatory duct.

Although a few sperm may be found in tubules where they open into the ductus deferens, there is no indication that ampullary glands are a storage depot for sperm. They are true glands.

Vesicular Glands

Vesicular glands *(vesiculae seminales)* arise as evaginations of the ductus deferens.

Each consists of an elongated simple or branched tubule which is distended with fluid during the breeding season. The tubule may join with the ductus deferens to form the ejaculatory duct, or it may open independently into the urethra. The tubule wall consists of an inner mucous membrane, a medial layer of smooth muscle, and an external collagenous and elastic connective tissue layer.

In sexually potent animals, the tubule has a large central cavity filled with secretion into which folds of epithelium supported by delicate strands of connective tissue project. Union of the folds may produce small lateral erypts or subtubules. Compact glands are surrounded and divided into lobules by areolar connective tissue. Straight and curved glands are surrounded by variable proportions of smooth muscles and collagenous connective tissue.

Vesicular gland secretion varies from a viscous to gelatinous, usually clear or slightly yellowish, fluid; free epithelial cells may be present. It serves as a medium for transport of sperm. In combination with anterior prostate or, in some species, bulbo-urethral secretion, it coagulates. In some species the coagulant forms a *copulatory* or *vaginal plug* and prevents loss of the semen. The plug subsequently breaks down and the sperm are released into the vagina in a steady stream. The copulatory plug is necessary for fertilization in some species of rodents.

Prostate Glands

Prostate glands *(glandulae prostaticae)* are present in all members of Eutheria. They occur either as a mass of tissue, which may be lobulated to varying degrees, located at the ductus deferens-urethral junction; or they may be of the disseminate type, which extend along

TABLE 1.2. HISTOLOGY AND SECRETORY ACTIVITY OF MALE ACCESSORYSEX GLANDS AND URETHRA OF LABORATORY ANIMALS

Organ	*Epithelium*	*Properties of Secretion*
Ampullary glands	Simple, cuboidal, or columnar	Yellowish liquid containing ergothianeine, fructose, sialic acid, and phosphorus
Vesicular glands	Simple or pseudostratified columnar	White, yellowish or bluish fluid or gelatinous substance containing fructose, protein, citric acid, and ascorbie acid
Prostate gland	Simple or pseudostratified columnar	Colorless liquid containing fibrinolysin, fibrinogenase, diastase, carbonic anhydrase, amylase, vesiculase, fructose, citric aicd, free amino acids, and zinc
Paraprostate glands	Pseudostratified cuboidal or low columnar	No data
Bulbo-urethral glands	Simple columnar	Viscous fluid containing sialoprotein
Bulbar gland	Simple high columnar	Liquid which facilitates passage of bulbourethral secretion
Urethral glands	Simple cuboidal	Clear, watery fluid containing mucoprotein
Preputial glands	Stratified squamous	Contains 7-dehydrocholesterol
Prostatic urethra	Transitional	None
Membranouv and proximal spongy urethra	Stratified or pseudostratified columnar	None
Distal spongy urethra	Stratified squamous	None

the entire prostatic and most of the membranous urethra. Glands of the former type are encapsulated; they penetrate the urethral muscularis and open into the urethra by means of one pair to many ducts. They may form a single mass which is sub-divided by septa or they may form two or three pairs of distinct lobes. Designation of the lobes in quadrupeds has followed two systems of nomenclature. The first, modified from that used for man, designated anterior (ventral), middle, and posterior (dorsal). The second, designated anterior (cranial) middle, and posterior (caudal). A combination of the two systems has been used.

In some species, notably members of the family Cricetidae and Muridae, the anterior lobe of the prostate is elongated and closely appressed to the inner curvature of the vesicular glands; it is known as the coagulating gland. The "vasicular gland" of the European rabbit, which develops from a pair of dorsal evaginations of the urethra, is an homologous structure.

The prostate is a tubulo-alveolar or saccular gland. Saccular prostates have epithelial folds extending far into the lumen. Spherical globules of secretory products are released from the free surface and, during periods of high activity, the free surface is indistinguishable because of the presence of secretory globules. Three types of cells are present in the anterior prostate or the coagulating gland of the rabbit: (a) light cells, (b) dark cells, and (c) true basal cells. Only one cell type is present in the posterior lobe.

Differences in the staining reactions of the epithelium of the two lobes reflect differences in their secretions. In standard histological sections the lining of the anterior prostate of the rabbit and rat consists of cuboidal cells with oval hyperbasal nuclei, while the posterior prostate epithelium consists of columnar or high columnar cells with a round basal nucleus.

Nondisseminate prostates are surrounded by a capsule of collagenous and elastic fibers and smooth muscle. Tissue identical to the capsule forms the septa which subdivide the lobes into lobules. Trabeculae of connective tissue partially subdivide the lobules.

Glands of the disseminate type of prostate do not penetrate the urethral muscularis and the collecting ducts common to several glands radiate from the entire urethral circumference. Three regions are distinguishable in the disseminate prostate of the opossum, each with a characteristic epithelial lining the glands and a characteristic amount of connective tissue separating the glands.

Table 1.3. Anatomical Characteristics of Male Accessory Sex Glands of Laboratory Animals

Organ	*Anatomical characteristics*	*Species*
Ampullary glands	Spindle-shaped enlargement composed of branched tubular diverticulae which open by ducts on entire circumference of the ductus deferens	Dog Mink Rabbit
	A distinct, abrupt enlargement composed of branched, tubular diverticulae, the proximal ends of which form the lumen of the ductus deferens	Bats Shrews
	Distinct lobes projecting from the ductus deferens	Mice Rats
	Shallow diverticulae in wall of ductus deferens	Guinea pig
Vesicular glands	Simple or branched tubule which coils to form compact glands	Squirrels
	Simple, straight or curved tubules	Guinea pig
	Straight or curved spccules single and semibilobed bilateral structures	European rabbit Mice Rat
Prostate gland	Disseminate	Opossum
	semi-disseminate, bilobed	Cat
	non-disseminate, bilobed	Bat
	mas subdivided by septa	Dog Mink Some primates
	Two or three pairs of distinct lobes	Mice Rats
Bulbŏ-urethral glands	Three lobed	Opossum
	Single lobed	
	ducts opening into distal spongy urethra via the bulbar gland ahd penile duct	Squirrels
	ducts opening into the proximal spongy urethra	All others

Function

Prostate secretion serves as a medium for transport for sperm to the female. It stimulates motility in the sperm and also provides nourishment. In the rabbit the anterior lobe secretion is high in fructose and citric acid, while the posterior lobe secretion is mainly a protein with a large amount of fructose and some citric acid. Production of prostatic secretion is primarily controlled by the testosterone level, and secondarily, by nervous stimulation. Production may be relatively constant, or there may be periodic high peaks of production.

The coagulating fraction of anterior prostate secretion is known as *vesiculase*. Coagulation of vesicular gland fluid is a double reaction in which procoagulase from the vesicular gland combines with vesiculase to form the enzyme coagulase. Coagulase then combines with a protein fraction of vesicular gland secretion, coagulinogen, to form coagulated protein.

Bulbo-urethral Glands

Bulbo-urethral or Cowper's glands *(glandula bulbn-urethrales)* are a pair lying dorsal to the bulb to the penis and are partially or completely embedded in the bulbocavernosus muscle. Ducts may be short, as in the rabbit and cat, and the glands may appear as a projection on the dorsal side other urethra; or they may be long, as in the gerbil, squirrel, and guinea pig, with the glands located near the base of the tail.

The compound tubulo-alveolar glands resemble mucous glands and are surrounded by a capsule of connective tissue and striated muscle; the connective tissue forms septa and trabeculae which subdivide the glands. In squirrels (Sciurus) neither intrinsic nor extrinsic muscles completely surround the gland; intrinsic muscles occur as short interwoven bundles on the portion nearest the duct. Ducts may be lined with pseudostratified or stratified cuboidal epithelium.

The bulbo-urethral secretion is a milky white, mucus-like material; it is not a true mucus since it does not precipitate when treated with acetic acid. Long thought to be simply a lubricant, the secretion recently has been shown to contain a glucoprotein which undergoes a nonenzymatic, ionic reaction with a protein fraction of the vesicular glands to produce a coagulant in the rat, mouse, and hamster, but not in the guinea pig. The vesicular substrate upon which the bulbo-urethral secretion acts is different from that acted upon by the enzyme visiculase of the coagulating glands. Furthermore, the bulbo-urethral secretion reacts at an optimum at pH 5.9 in contrast to pH *7.4* for the coagulating gland enzyme. The foregoing reaction is probably responsible for formation of the vaginal plug in members of the genera *Sciurus and Citellus.*

The Bulbar Gland

The bulbar gland *(glanduli bulbi) is* confined to the Sciuridae and, in a modified form, in the Aplondontidae. The following description is based principally upon the foregoing publication. The gland is formed by fusion of the ducts of the bulbo-urethral glands; these ducts form the lateral lobescof the bulbar gland. Ducts of the median lobe and the lateral lobes)coalesee to form he penile duct which opens into the urethra at the ventral flexure of the penis. The glandular character of the bulbar epithelium gradually diminishes along the penile duct as it approaches its junction with the urethra.

The bulbar gland is located within the bulb of the corpus spongiosum. The gland is immediately surrounded by fibrous crectile tissue which constitutes part of the wall of the bulbo-urethral ducts and separates the two lateral lobes from the media lobe. The gland consists of complex folds. Secretion of the gland is thought to be liquid and to facilitate passage of the bulbo-urethral secretion through the penile duct.

Paraprostate Glands

Paraprostate, glands *(glandulac urethrales paraprostalicus)* develop as evaginations of the urethra of the European rabbit. There is dication of them in the North American cottontail. These glands have been described in detail by Berii and Krichesky. The following description is modified from their work.

The glands lie lateral to the urethra and ventral to the ampullae. In contrast to urethral glands, they lie outside the muscularis of the urethra. There are 3 to 8 glands on each side and each gland open lateral to the colliculus seminalis by an ejaculatory duct. The glands are tubulo-alveolar and resemble bulbo-urethral glands, but they lack striated muscle and have a greater amount of smooth muscle than the latter. Some paraprostates are indistinguishable from prostate glands.

The Prostatic Utricle

The prostatic utricle *(utriculus prostalicus) is* a small pouch commonly regarded as a persisting vaginal primordium which represents the fused posterior ends of the Mi llerian ducts. It lies on the dorsal wall of prostatic urethra and may be imbedded in the prostate. There is a single middorsal opening on the colliculus seminalis. The pouch is lined with epithelium in a manner similar to that of the prostate.

Urethral Glands

These *(glandulae urethrals)* are numerous small glands which lie within an areolar connective tissue layer between the epithelium and the muscularis of the prostatic and membranous urethra of certain bats. In *Corynorhinus,* they are simple tubulo-alveolar glands which open separately into the urethra; they are identical in staining reaction to bulbo-urethral glands.

In the hamster, compound tubulo-alveolar glands occur along the membranous and proximal penile urethra, where they partially penetrate the muscularis. Their staining reaction is much more basophilic than that of the bulbo-urethral glands.

Preputial Glands

Preputial or Tyson's glands *(glandulac preputiales)* are small, branched, and tubulo-alveolar. In rodents a pair of these glands lies on either side of the distal part of the penis and open into the preputial cavity near its orifice. In primates the glands are more diffuse and open at the base of the glans. The glands arise from evagination of preputial epithelium.

In the rat the glands are composed of two types of cells: (a) the squamous cells, which form a single layered wall and which later become stratified to form duct epithelium, and (b) the acinar cells, which accumulate fatty substance within their cytoplasm, fuse together, and disintegrate. In addition to the fatty substance, protein granules are also produced and released into the excretory duct when the cells degenerate. The holocrine secretion is called *smegma.*

Acinar cells do not regenerate and the glandular parenchyma gradually decreases with age. Connective tissue replaces the glandular parenchyma, so the gland does not decrease in size.

Inguinal Glands

These *(glandulae inguinales)* are present in rabbits as a pair of small compound tubulo-alveolar glands which lie between the skin and abdominal wall on either side of the penis. Each gland opens by a single duct into skin folds near the end of the prepuce. They do not contribute to the seminal fluid, but are sebaceous, odor-producing glands which are associated with sexual attraction. Socially dominant European rabbits have larger and more active glands than subordinate individuals. Castration during early life inhibits growth of the glands.

Physiological and Environmental Factors Which Influence Accessory Sex Structures

Among seasonal breeders the male may remain sexually potent throughout the year, as in some primates, the opossum, dog, and cat; or it may be active for several months, as in shrews, gray squirrels, and many mice; or it may be active for only a brief period as in bats, ground squirrels, and ferrets. Animals which belong to the first group may have one or two breedings per year. This is determined by the physiological condition of the female.

Reproductive organs of animals which are active during only part of the year undergo marked seasonal atrophy; and the testes, the accessory sex glands, and the ducts then regress to an essentially juvenile condition. Testes may decrease to less than ten percent and vesicular glands to less than five percent of their active weight. Histological, the atrophied organs show more connective tissue than juvenile organs. Grossly, atrophied tests appear light bluish rather than white or light pink, as in juvenile testes; and surface blood vessels are highly contorted in atrophied tests rather than straight as in juvenile organs.

Testis size is related to the diameter of the seminiferous tubules and to the interstitial cell mass. The former is regulated by follicle-stimulating hormone and the latter by interstitial cell stimulating hormone (ICSH), both of which are produced by the adenohypophysis. Testosterone controls development and function of accessory sex gland and tubules. Although some testosterone is produced by the adrenal cortex and by Sertoil's cells in the seminiferous tubules by far the greater portion is produced by the interstitial cells of the testis. Since it is commonly accepted without proof that endocrine function is correlated with endocrine mass, testis size and function should be closely correlated with size and function of the accessory sex structures. There is much evidence that this is indeed true.

Effects of Climate

Production of FSH and ISCH and, therefore, the period of sexual activity, are regulated by a number of factors such as day length, seasonal rains, presence of food, vitamin levels, and so on. Increased day length indirectly stimulates the adenohypophysis and initiates the breeding season in many rodents and other species; e.g., vespertilianid bats breed in the fall and viable sperm are carried in the female for 5 to 7 months before fertilization takes place. Still others, e.g., certain mustelids, breed in the fall, but the fertilized egg is not implanted until the following spring. In both these groups the stimulus for onset of enlargement of the male reproductive structures is decreased day length.

Stimulation of activity of reproductive structures by seasonal rains, as reported by Poole for the European rabbit in Australia, apparently is related to renewed vegetative growth. Some primates also become sexually active following seasonal rains.

Prolongation of the breeding season when food was unusually abundant has been demonstrated in North American mice (*Peromyscus*). The same phenomenon has been demonstrated for the field vole (*Microtus arvalis*) in Europe.

Ground squirrels estivate or hibernate during part of the year. They have a brief breeding season in the spring and the sexual organs then atrophy rapidly. Preparation for the next breeding season, in the form of initial enlargement of the sexual structures, begins before the animals become inactive in late summer or early fall. Restoration of the structures continues throughout the inactive period, but accelerates just before the animals resume activity. The stimulus for acceleration of development of the sexual structures is unknown. In many species it takes place when the animals are in burrow covered by several feet of snow.

Effects of Physiological Unbalance

An inverse relationship between size of sexual structures and population density of white mice has been reported. Testes, vesicular glands, and preputial glands decreased in size as population size. increased; confined populations of fixed size were used. Changes in size of reproductive organs were attributed to suppression of gonadotropic function, increased adrenocorticotropic function of the anterior pituitary, and a resultant decline in androgen output and testicular activity. Similar results have been reported for wild populations of various species.

Castration has long been known to cause atrophy of secondary sexual structures. This atrophy is reflected by both involution of the epithelium and loss of secretion from the glands and tubules. Treatment with testosterone will restore the structures to an active functional state and size. While regression of the rat vesicular gland is reflected in involution of the epithelium, regression of the hamster vesicular gland is caused mainly by loss of secretion; there is little or no involution of the epithelium. In the hamster, the bulbo-urethral glands are the most sensitive of the accessory glands to decreases in testosterone levels resulting from castration.

THE URETHRA

The common duct of the excretory and reproductive system, the urethra, serves as a vehicle for transport of spermatozoa and associated fluids to the end of the penis. It consists of three parts: the *pars prostatica, pars membranacea* and *pars spongiosa* or *pars cavernosa*. The portion from the bladder to the junction of the ductus deferens is formed from the primitive urethra which connected the embryonic bladder and the urogenital sinus. This portion is homologous to the entire female urethra.

The ductus deferens enters the urethra at a swelling on its dorsal wall, the *colliculus seminalis*. A single middorsal pouch, the *utriculus prostaticus,* may open on the colliculus. In some species, ducts of both the prostate and seminal vesicles also open on the colliculus.

That portion of the urethra from the colliculus seminalis to the base of the penis represents the persistent urogenital sinus, it is homologous to the female vestibule. The primitive urethra plus the most anterior part of the urogenital sinus constitute the adult membranous or muscular urethra.

The most distal part, the spongy or penile urethra, lies within the penis and is derived from the groove between the urogenital folds; it has no homologue in the female. Its opening at the end of the penis is the meatus or *external urethral orifice.* The bulbo-urethral glands and the urethral glands; the terminal part of the ejaculatory ducts of these glands has an epithelium similar to that portion of the urethra into which they open.

THE PENIS AND ACCESSORY STRUCTURES

The Penis

All mammals have a single intromittent or copulatory organ, the penis, for transfer of semen from male to female. It is located anterior to the scrotum in all Eutheria, but posterior to the scrotum in the opossum (Marsupialia). The penis consists principally of three cavernous (erectile) tissue bodies; they are as follows: (a) the right and left *corpora cavernosa penis,* which are located on the ventral side and which undergo varying degrees of fusion, and (b) the *corpus spongiosum* penis, which lies dorsal to, and in a groove of the corpora cavernosa.

Proximally the corpora cavernosa diverge as the *crura* and each crus becomes attached to the posterior ischium on its own side. Each corpus cavernosum is surrounded by a thick membrane, the *tunica albuginea,* which consists principally of collagenous bundles with an elastic fiber network. The cavernous spaces are subdivided by trabeculae which are formed from collagenous bundles, elastic fibers, and smooth muscles. The subdivisions are lined with endothelium which is continuous with the lining of associated blood vessels.

Before birth and during the first week of postnatal life of the rat, tissue of the corpora cavernosa is vascular, undifferentiated mesenchyme. Complete differentiation does not occur until the animal is sexually mature at about 60 days of age. Previous researchers had implied that differentiation took place early in embryonic development.

The corpus spongiosum is traversed by the urethra and, in most species, it is expanded at its distal end into a caplike structure, the *glans penis*. Its proximal end is enlarged into the *bulbus penis* which lies between the crura; it is here that the urethra enters the penis. Framework of the corpus spongiosum is similar to that of the corpora cavernosa; but its tunica albuginea is thinner and contains smooth muscle,. and the trabeculae contain more elastic fibers. The glans penis consists of an anastomosing network of large veins embedded in dense connective tissue. During sexual stimulation the subdivisions of cavernous tissue become filled with blood to the limit permitted by encasing connective tissue, and the organ becomes erect.

Many primates, carnivores, and rodents have the glans epithelium modified to form horny papillae. In the cat, these are well developed and the stratum corneum elongates into long spinelike structures. In the guinea pig they may be grouped in short rows parallel to the circumference of the penis. Spine length is correlated with andorgen level; the length increases as the andorgen level increases. These spines are the only known indicators of male hormone level in the cat.

A bone, the *os penis* or *baculum,* forms in the membrane between the unfused corpora cavernosa or in the sheath of the fused corpus of bats, dogs, mustelids, squirrels, members of the Cricetidae and Muridae and many subhuman primates. This bone adds rigidity to the penis. It enlarges and may change shape as the animal increases in age, and has been used as an indicator of age in studies of some wild species. The baculum of each species has a characteristic shape, and it and the glans penis both serve as diagnostic taxonomic structures in certain groups.

The Prepuce

In most species the penis normally is enclosed in a fold of. skin, the prepuce. In some primates the prepuce covers only the distal glans; in bats, the prepuce is free of the body wall; in the dog it lies in a fold of skin below the body wall; and, in other species, it lies immediately ventral to the body wall. The preputial cavity is lined with stratified squamous epithelium.

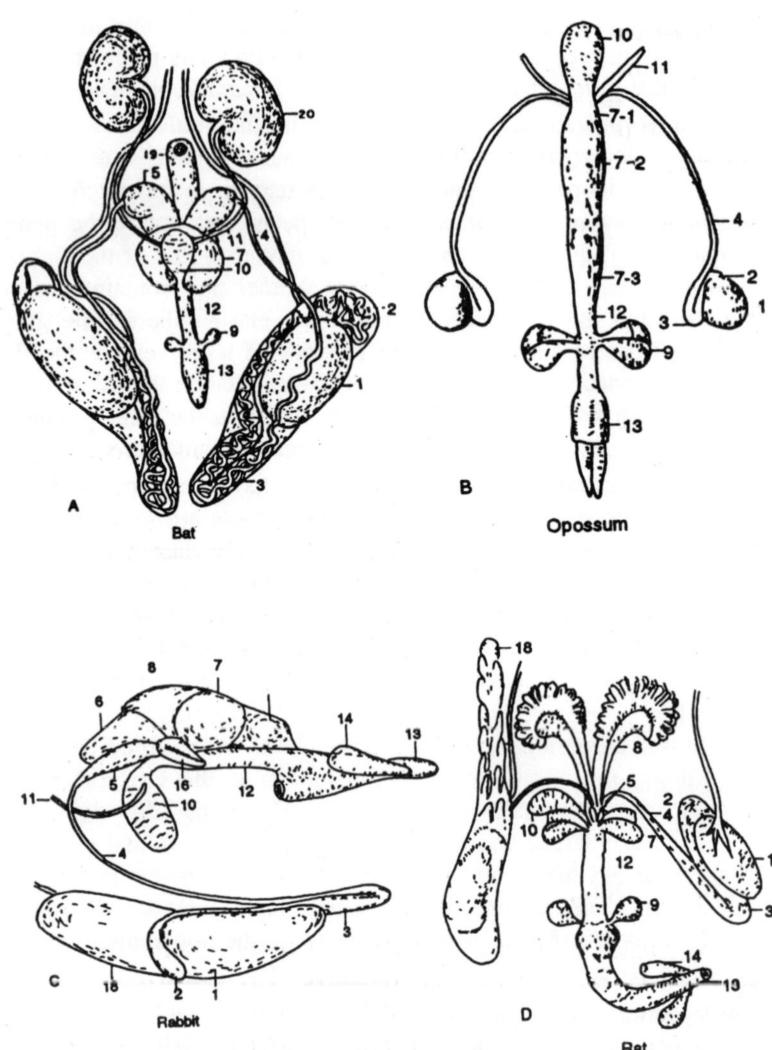

Fig. 1.2. Reproductive structures of the bat, opossum, European rabbit, and rat. (1) Testis. (2) Caput epididymis. (3) Cauda epididymis. (4) Ductus deferens, (5) Ampullary gland. (6) Vesicular gland. (7) Prostate gland. (8) Anterior lobe of prostate. (9) Bulbo-urethral gland. (10) Bladder. (11) Ureter. (12) Urethra. (13) Penis. (14) Preputial gland. (16) Paraprostate glands. (18) Fat body. (19) Rectum. (20) Kidney.

REPRODUCTIVE ORGANS OF VARIOUS SPECIES AND GROUPS

The Opossum

Opossums, *Didelphis marsupialis,* are unique in that the glans penis is cleft and the urethra continues as a groove on the inner surface of each half of the glans. Each glans is pointed and the urethral groove terminates some distance from the end. The edges of the groove in each half of the glans contact each other to form a functional tube. The preputial pouch opens just below the anus, so there is no cloaca. Opossums are sexually potent throughout the year and there is little seasonal variation in the secondary sexual structures of adults. The scrotum has a narrow neck and the tunica vaginalis is black. A single ductulus efferentes is present.

Soricidae

Shrews have the penis reflected anteriorly and then posteriorly, with the flexed portion lying between the skin and abdominal muscles. The glans is long and may account for one third of the total length of the organ in *Cryptotis parva.* Horny rings or ridges surround the entire glans of *Blarina;* but in *Cryptoti,* a closely related genus, the glans is smooth. Preputial glands "are diffuse and inconspicuous. The testes usually lie within the abdominal cavity, but many bulge into a shallow pouch which forms in the abdominal wall during the breeding season. Shrews breed from early spring to middle or later summer, depending upon environmental conditions. Tests and necessary glands atrophy following the breeding season.

Vespertilionidae

Many bats have a pendulous caudally directed penis with the thick prepuce completely separated from the body wall. The glans is small and not separated from the shaft by a constriction. A baculum is present in most species. Tests of sexually active animals lie in scrotal pouches which form in the interfemoral membrane posterior to the anus and lateral to the caudal vertebrae. The epididymis is highly developed and the caudal portion may be almost as large as the testes. The tunica vaginalis is darkly pigmented over the cauda epididymis. Bats are seasonal breeders; females are inseminated in the fall, but fertilization does not take place until the following spring.

Subhuman Primates

Reproductive organs of subhuman primates show much variation among families and among genera of the same family. Two superfamilies of the sub-order Anthropoidea will be considered: (1) Ceboidea or New World monkeys, which include the squirrel, the spider, and the howler monkeys; and (2) Cercopithecoidea or Old World monkeys, which include the rhesus monkey and baboon.

Ceboidea

These monkeys have a short, stout cylindrical penis, the glans of which projects from he prepuce; the entire organ projects from the anterior scrotum. Squirrel monkeys *(Saimiri* sp.) have cornified epithelial spines on the glans and distal stalk spider monkeys have black spines. A small baculum is present in squirrel monkeys, but is absent in spider monkeys. Seminal vesicles are well developed and, in some species, their ducts join with the ductus deferens to form ejaculatory ducts. No ampullae are present. A small cranial and large caudal lobe of the prostate may be distinguished macroscopically. Bulbo-urethral glands are either lacking or very small.

The tests are suspended in a scrotum which varies from a shallow pouch to a pendulous structure. The epididymis is large in proportion to the size of the testis and, in Saimiri, the caput epididymis is approximately one-third the size of the testis.

Cercopithecoiden

In these monkeys most of the penis lies in the anterior wall of the scrotum. a bulblike glans lies at the end of the neck; the latter is surrounded by the prepuce. A well-developed baculum is present. Ampullac are lacking or poorly developed. Seminal vesicles are large in the rhesus monkey; they join the ductus deferens to form ejaculatory ducts. The ducts and lower seminal vesicles are surrounded by the lobulated cranial lobe of the prostate which is comparable in function to the coagulating glands of rodents. A smooth, dark caudal lobe also is present. Small bulbo-urethral glands are located just below the caudal lobes of the prostate.

Testes of the rhesus monkey lie within a well developed scrotum at birth, but ascend to near the inguinal canal shortly thereafter. They descend again and remain permanently in the scrotum after sexual maturity is attained. The caput epididymis is well developed, as it is in New World monkeys.

Mustelidae

Ferrets *(Mustela faro)* and mink *(M vison)* have a large baculum which external from the bulb of the penis to its distal end. In both species, the distal end of the baculum curves dorsally and ends in a hook, and a groove is present on the ventral surface of the distal portion.

The penis lies just below the ventral wall. The glans constitutes the distal one-third of the organ; it is divided into a proximal *pars bulbus glandis* and a distal pars *longa glandis*. During sexual stimulation, enlargement of the glans is pronounced and relatively uniform. In mink, the distal one third of the penis lies in a preputial cavity.

Prostate and ampullary glands are the only necessary sex glands which are present in mustelids. The prostate has been described as vestigial in ferrets, but is well developed in mink. In the latter species it completely surrounds the urethra. Several collecting ducts open into the urethra on the poorly developed colliculus seminalis.

Testes are permanently serotal in both ferrets and mink. they undergo seasonal atrophy in ferrets; redevelopment begins in late fall and active sperm are present in early spring. As the testes atrophy, the penis decreases in size and the ductus deferens decreases in diameter.

Canidae

Dogs (Canis *familiaris)* and foxes *(Vulpes* and *Urocyon)* have similar reproductive structures. The penis lies in a fold of skin beneath the ventral body wall. A well-developed baculum lies in the distal two thirds of the organ; in dogs, this bone curves ventrally at its distal end. The canine penis may be divided into (1) the root, which consists of the crura; (2) the body, which extends from the crura to the glans; and (3) the *glans,* which extends along the entire length of the baculum. The glans is divided into a proximal *pars bulbus glandis* and a distal *pars longa glandis;* erectile tissue of these two subdivisions are separated from each other by a fibrous sheath. During erection, a distinct *urethral process* with the external urethral orifice at its apex is present at the free extremity of the pars long glandis. *A corona glandis* is present on the distal end of the pars longa.

The prepuce is reflected onto the glans about midway of the bulbus. A retractor penis muscle, composed mostly of smooth muscle, extends from near the preputia fornix to the first and second coccygeal vertebrae. Canidae have no necessary sex glands except the prostate and the poorly developed ampullary glands. The prostate is a w~ll-developed gland which completely surrounds the urethra: Numerous collecting ducts open on the entire urethral circumference The testes lie within the pendulous scrotum at all times; they undergo no seasonal

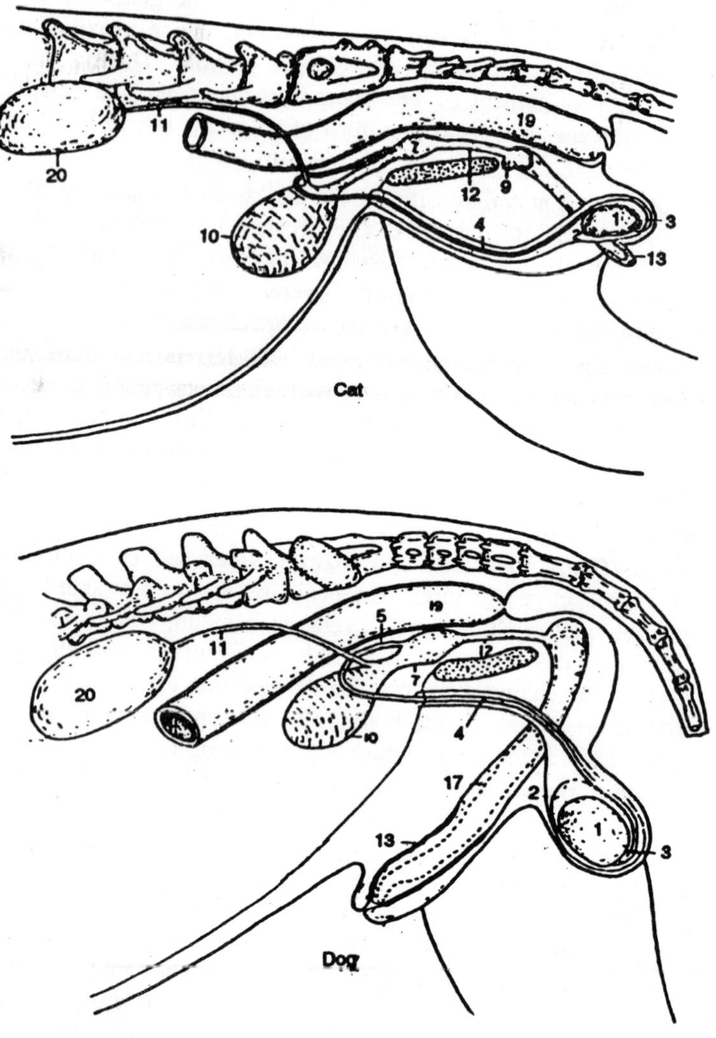

Fig. 1.3 A & B. Reproductive structures, in situ, of the cat and dog. (1) Testis. (2) Caput epididymis. (3) Cauda epididymis. (4) Ductus deferens. (5) Ampullary gland. (7) Prostate gland. (10) 'Bladder. (11) Ureter. (12) Urethra. (13) Penis. (17) Baculum. (18) Fat body. (19) Rectum. (20) Kidney.

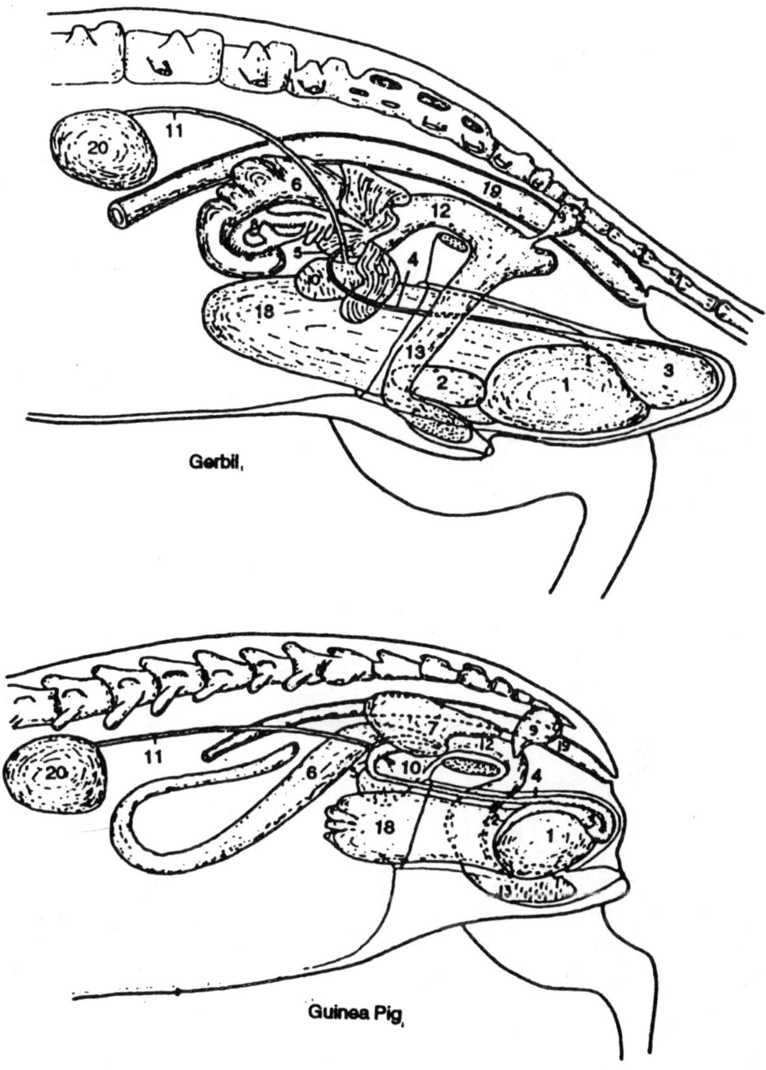

Fig. 1.3 C & D. Reproductive structure in situ, of the gerbil and guinea pig. (1) Testis. (2) Caput epididymis. (3) Cauda epididymis. (4) Ductus deferens. (5) Ampullary gland. (6) Vesicular gland. (7) Prostate gland. (8) Anterior lobe of prostate. (9) Bulbo-urethral gland. (10) Bladder. (11) Ureter. (12) Urethra. (13) Penis. (18) Fat body. (19) Rectum. (20) Kidney.

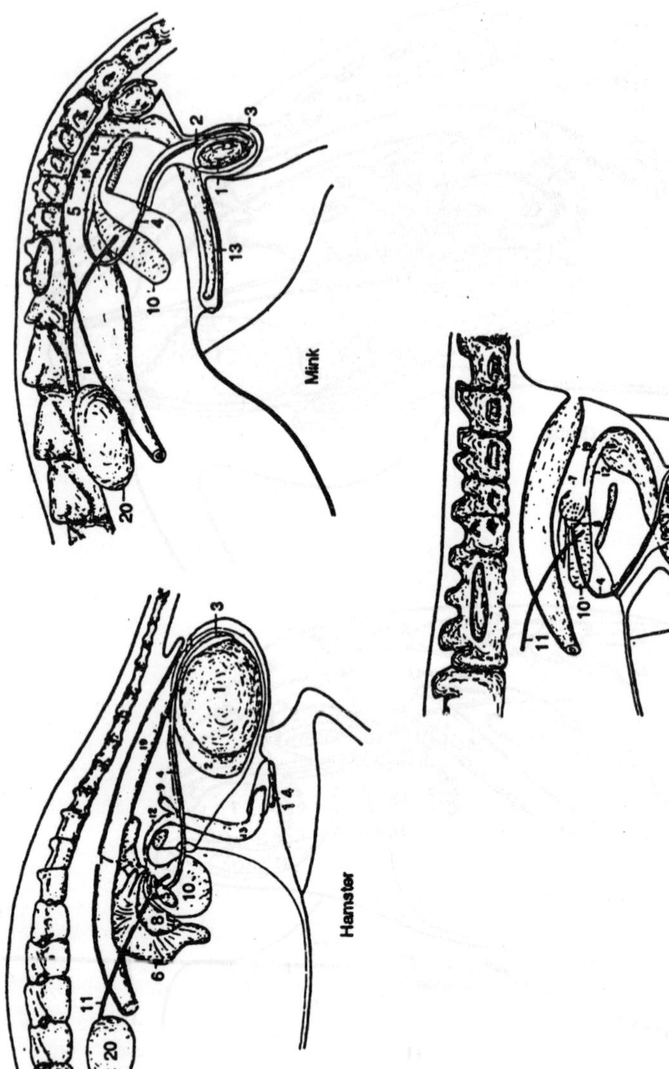

(Figure 1.3. contd)

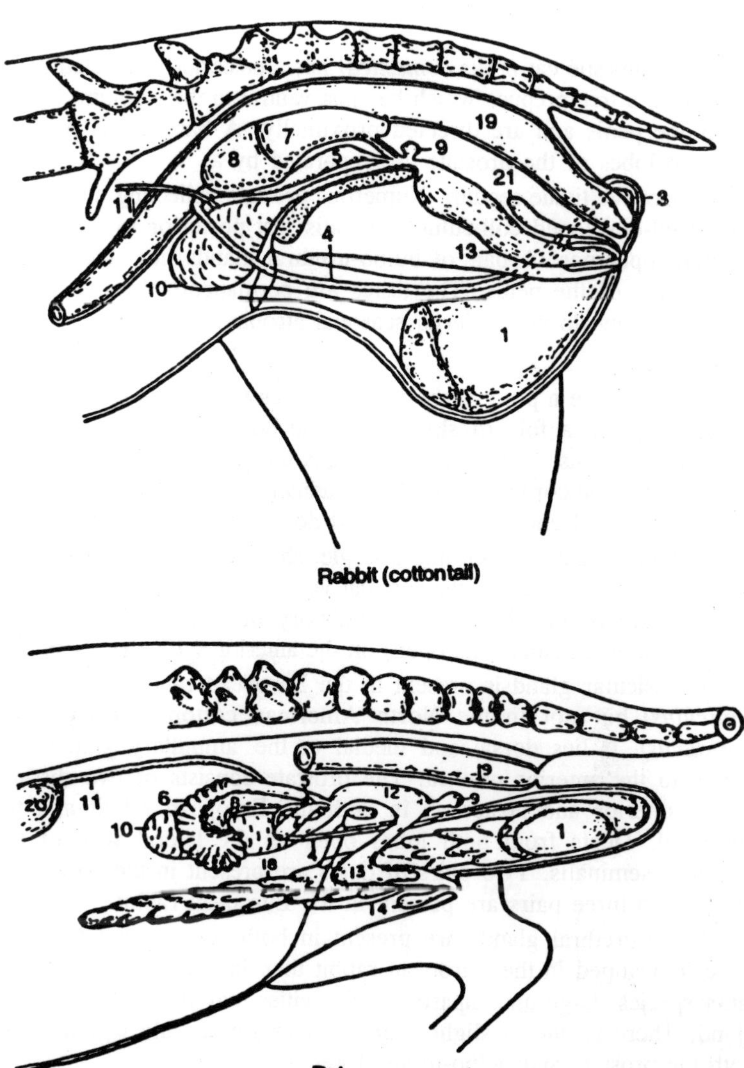

Fig. 1.4. Reproductive structures in situ, of the hamster, mink, monkey, cottontail rabbit, and rat. (1) Testis. (2) Caput epididymis. (3) eauda epididymis. (4) Ductus deferens. (5) Ampullary gland. (6) Seminal vesicle. (7) Prostate gland. (8) Anterior lobe of prostate. (9) Bulbo-urethral gland. (10) Bladder. (11) Ureter. (12) Urethra. (13) Penis. (14) Preputial gland. (19) Rectum. (20) Kidney.

atrophy. There may be some anterior-posterior displacement of the testes with respect to each other.

Felidae

The domestic cat *(Felis domestica)* has a posteriorly directed penis encased in a free prepuce which lies just ventral to the scrotum. Spines cover the penis and are directed proximally. A baculum is present. The two lobes of the prostate are separated by a

connective tissue septum. Numerous prostate collecting ducts open on a well-developed colliculus seminalis just posterior to the ductus deferens openings. A pair of bulbo-urethral glands lies anterolateral to the base of the penis. The testes are permanently located in the scrotum. They do not undergo seasonal atrophy.

Lagomorpha

Rabbits have a posteriorly directed penis which lies in a prepuce which hangs in a fold of skin below the body wall and opens just ventral to the anus. Paired inguinal glands lie lateral and slightly dorsal to the penis. The corpus spongiosum gradually diminishes in*a* diameter toward the distal end of the penis and does not expand into a glans.

Ampullary glands open into a single, short, ejaculatory duct, along with the excretory duct of the seminal vesicle. Longitudinal folds may incompletely divide the single ejaculatory duct into right and left halves. The ejaculatory duct opens on the anterior colliculus seminalis.

A vesicular gland is present in the European rabbit *(Orctolagus cuniculus)* but not in the North American cottontail *(Sylvilagus floridanus)*. It lies dorsal and medial to the ampullary glands and dorsal to the anterior urethra. The prostate consists of two distinct lobes, anterior and posterior, in both the European rabbit and the cottontail. Ducts from both lobes open on the lateral wall of the coliculus seminalis. Two pairs of ducts are present in the cottontail, and two to three pairs are present in the European rabbit.

Bulbo-urethral glands are present in both species, but they are better developed in the European rabbit than in the cottontail. In the latter species, large uncompartmented cavities may develop within the gland. There is only a slight depression in the capsule which coves both the prostate and bulbo-urethral gland.

Testes are relatively large and flaccid in sexually active animals. They lie in inguinal pouches which have a large canal through which the testes can be withdrawn into the coelom even when they are enlarged. Under natural conditions, testes and accessory sex organs undergo seasonal atrophy in both species.

Sciuridae

The penis of squirrels is flexed posteriorly just proximal to the glans. The glans is enclosed in a semipendulous prepuce. A short stout baculum is present; in most tree squirrels (Sciurus) it is characterized by a dorsal circular disc and a ventral spur at the distal end, while in ground squirrels *(Citellus)* the distal end is expanded into a spoon-shaped structure with toothlike projections on its edge.

Seminal vesicles of *Sciurus* are small in relation to other reproductive organs in this genus and to seminal vesicles of other genera. They consist of tightly coiled tubules in both *Citellus* and *Sciurus*. The seminal vesicles, the prostate, and the ductus deferens have a common opening on each side of the colliculus seminalis in *Sciurus;* in *Citellus,* each of these three organs has its own separate pair of openings. In the latter genus, openings of the ductus deferens are caudal, those of the seminal vesicle are medial, and those of the prostate are cephalic.

The prostate gland is large in both tree and ground squirrels. Compound secretory tubules, which are white and opaque in sexually active animals, open into thin translucent reservoir tubules at the ventral cephalic end of the gland. The reservoir tubules fuse to form a pair of excretory ducts.

Bulbo-urethral glands are especially large in *Sciurus* and, relatively, only slightly smaller in *Citellus*. The duct makes a spiral around the gland and gives the entire gland a coiled appearance, as shown in gross view of *Sciurus carolinensis*. These ducts constrict to enter the sheath of the bulb of the penis; within the sheath they expand to form the lateral lobes of the bulbar gland. This gland is restricted, in fully developed form, to members of the Sciuridae and is especially well developed in *Citellus*. Both the gland and the penile duct, which opens from it into the distal urethra, are absent in *Tamiasciurus*.

In *Sciurus* the testes lie in a serotum after sexual maturity is attained, but they may be temporarily withdrawn into the coelom through a wide inguinal canal, even during the breeding season. A scrotum develops in *Citellus* during the breeding season, but at other times the testes are abdominal. During hibernation the testes are covered with a heavy layer of fat.

Testes and accessory sex structures undergo seasonal enlargement and regression. Sciurus may produce two litters of young per year, so that the reproductive organs remain functional throughout spring and early summer. In *Citellus,* reproductive organs undergo an abrupt regression immediately after the spring breeding season.

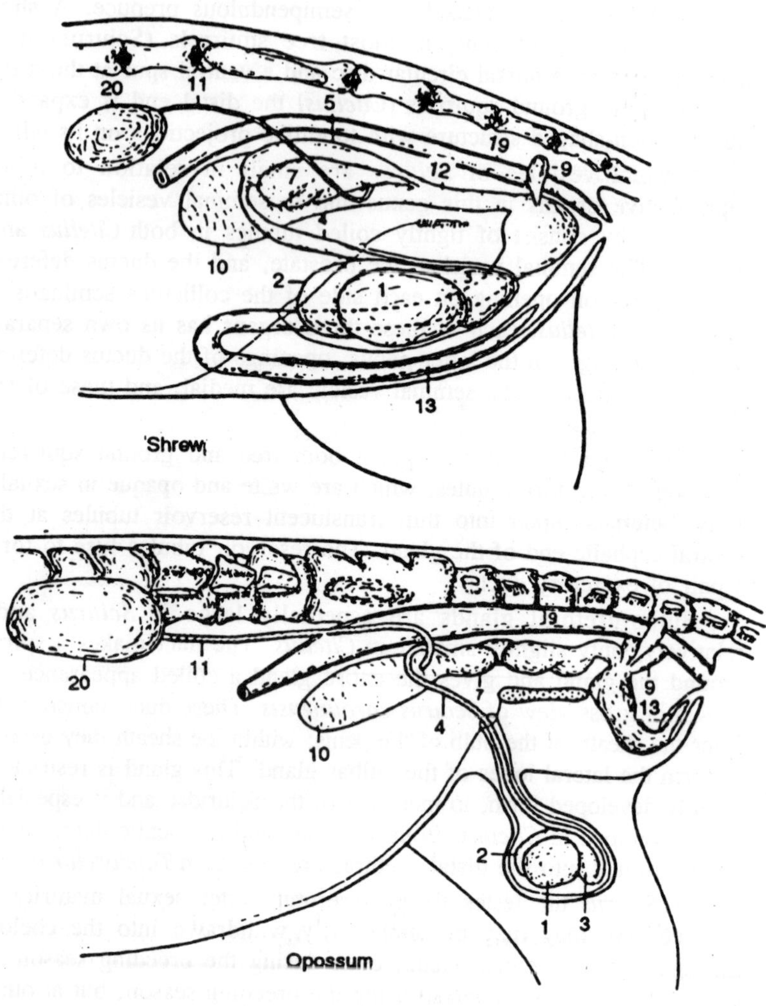

Fig. 1.5 A&B. Reproductive structures, in situ, *of the shrew and opossum. (1) Testis. (2) Caput epididymis. (3) Cauda epididymis. (4) Ductus deferens. (5) Ampullary gland. (6) Seminal vesicle. (7) Prostate gland. (9) Bulbo-urethral gland. (10) Bladder. (11) Ureter. (12) Urethra. (13) Penis. (15) Bulbar gland. (19) Rectum. (20) Kidney.*

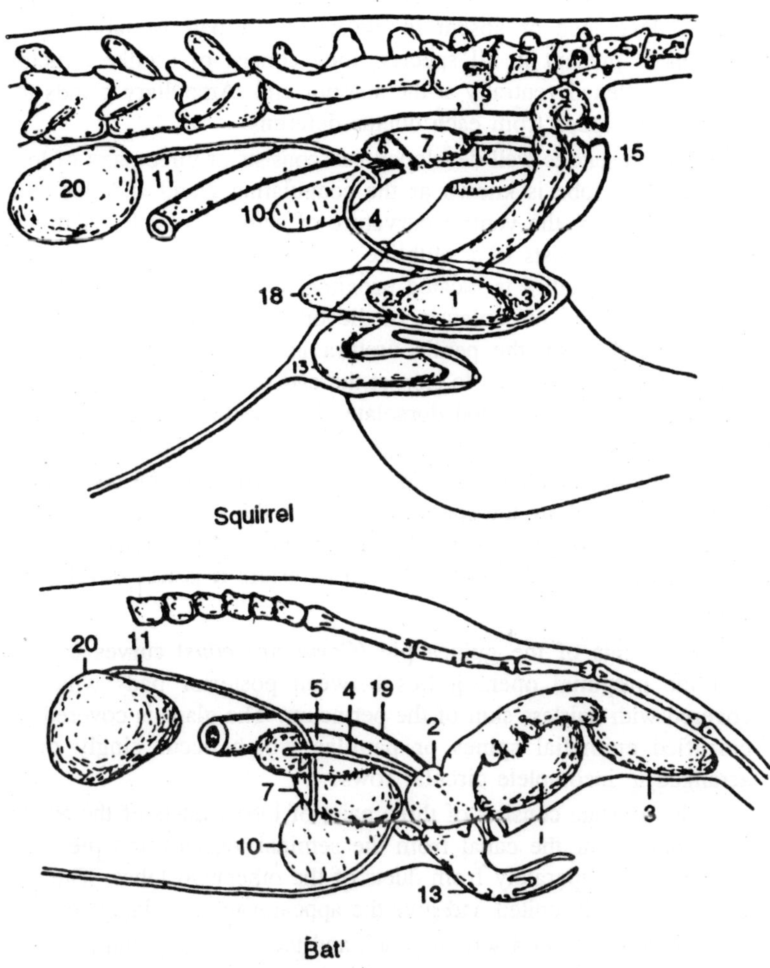

Fig. 1.5 C&D. Reproductive structures, in situ, *of the tree squirrel and bat. (1) Testis. (2) Caput epididymis. (3) Cauda epididymis. (4) ductus deferens. (5) Ampullary gland. (6) Seminal vesicle. (7) Prostate gland. (9) Bulbo-urethral gland. (10) Bladder. (11) Ureter. (12) Urethra. (13) Penis. (15) Bulbar gland. (19) Rectum. (20) Kidney.*

The penis is flexed posteriorly and the glans lies within a nonprotruding prepuce. Low epidermal papillae are present on the glans. A pair of well-developed preputial glands lies between the skin and ventral body wall and lateral to the penis in most species, but is poorly developed or absent in the gerbil. A pair of large seminal vesicles is present in all species; they consist of saclike structures which are flexed ventrally at the anterior end. Ampullary glands form two distinct lobes from each ductus deferens.

The prostate is well developed and consists of three pairs of lobes. The anterior lobe is known as the coagulating gland and lies along, and attached to, the ventral curvature of seminal vesicle. A urethral sinus which consists of a bulblike expansion or diverticulum of the membranous urethra is located proximal to the bulb of the penis. It is surrounded by musculature of the urethra. Glands in the wall of sinus extend down the penile urethra in the hamster, but in other species they are reported to stop at the end of the sinus. Paired bulbourethral glands are located dorsolateral to the bulb of the penis.

The testes lie in a scrotal sac, the posterior end of which may be partially or completely devoid of hair. A prominent fat body extends from the testis along the spermatic cord; in the rat, mouse, and gerbil it is greatly elongated and its anterior end is free of the cord and extends well into the coelom, but in hamsters it is less developed.

Caviidae

The penis of the guinea pig *(Cavia procellus)* curves caudally and the preputial opening lies between posterior pads which are covered with hairless skin of the perineum. The glans is covered with cornified epithelial spines or papillae which occur singly or are arranged in incomplete circular rows.

The prostate consists of three pairs of lobes; ducts of the anterior lobes open near the canal from the seminal vesicles and the ductus deferens and separately from ducts of the other two lobes. The three lobes are closely united and give the appearance of a single structure.

The testes lie in a scrotal pouch and their posterior end and cauda epididymis produce a slight bulge in the perineum. A large fat body covers the anterior end of each testis; it lies along the spermatic cord and projects through a large inguinal canal into the coelom. The testes may be withdrawn into the coelom through this canal at any time.

2

Formation of Male Sex Cells

Spermatogenesis

During the sexually inactive season in most seasonally reproducing vertebrates, the testes regress to a small fraction of their active mass and spermatogenesis and steroidogenesis are greatly reduced. This seasonal rhythmicity is under hypothalamic control, induced either directly or indirectly by environmental cues. The change in testicular mass reflects seasonal fluctuations in size and development of the seminiferous tubules, which comprise the bulk of the contents of the testis. There is also a reduction in size (but not in number) of Sertoli cells and Leydig cells. In extreme testicular reduction, which is characteristic of many species of small vertebrates in mid- and high latitudes, spermatogenesis is, in effect, almost at a standstill and rarely proceeds beyond meiosis I. This mature spermatozoa are absent during the nonbreeding season. In fully regressed testes of many kinds of bats, mice squirrels, and other small vertebrates, the cauda epididymides are shrunken and devoid of sperm.

In contrast to the embryonic ovary, gametogenesis does not occur in the embryonic testis. Some species of surfperch (Embiotocidae), however, appear to be an exception. The embryonic testes of *Amphigonopeterus aurora* and *Micrometrus minimus* develops prior to birth and contains various stages of developing germ cells, with abundant transforming spermatids and spermatozoa at birth.

Production of spermatozoa is best known for mammals, to which the following introductory comments refer:

The seminiferous, tubules and spermatogenesis are supported by testosterone. This has been shown by hypophysectomy and androgen replacement in rats. Hypophysectomy is normally followed by a regression of the seminiferous tubules, but testosterone may preserve the activity of the tubules in the absence of secretions from the anterior pituitary. The close proximity of the natural source of testosterone (the Leydig cells) probably allows continuous infiltration to testosterone. FSH may be needed for uptake of testosterone by Sertoli cells.

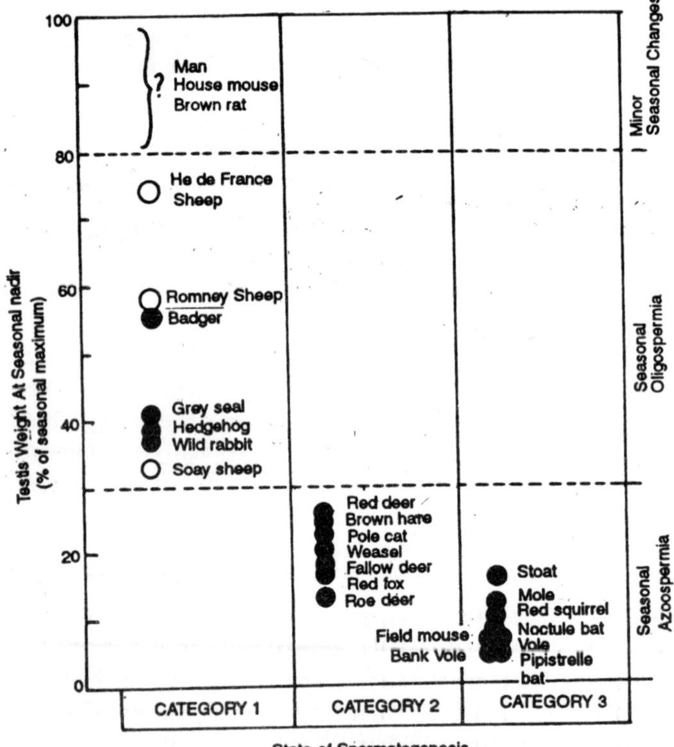

Fig. 2.1. The relationship between testicular mass (percent of seasonal maximum) and state of spermatogenesis at the time of maximal seasonal regression. Category 1, with some complete spermatogenesis; Category 2, with some meiosis but no complete spermatogenesis; Category 3, with no meiosis or spermatogenesis.

Lining the seminiferous tubules are germ cells, sometimes called gonocytes. In the early stages of spermatogenesis, germ cells, or gonocytes, produce spermatogonia. Initially stimulated by testosterone, the spermatogonia undergo several mitotic divisions. This commences in the embryonic testis, and spermatogonia are always in close association with one or more Sertoli cells. As in the mitotic divisions in oogenesis, these cells may remain connected by intercellular, bridges. The final mitotic division produces primary spermatocytes. Secondary spermatocytes, still diploid, result from the first meiotic division. The second meiotic division (the reduction division) results in spermatids, still connected by intercellular bridges.

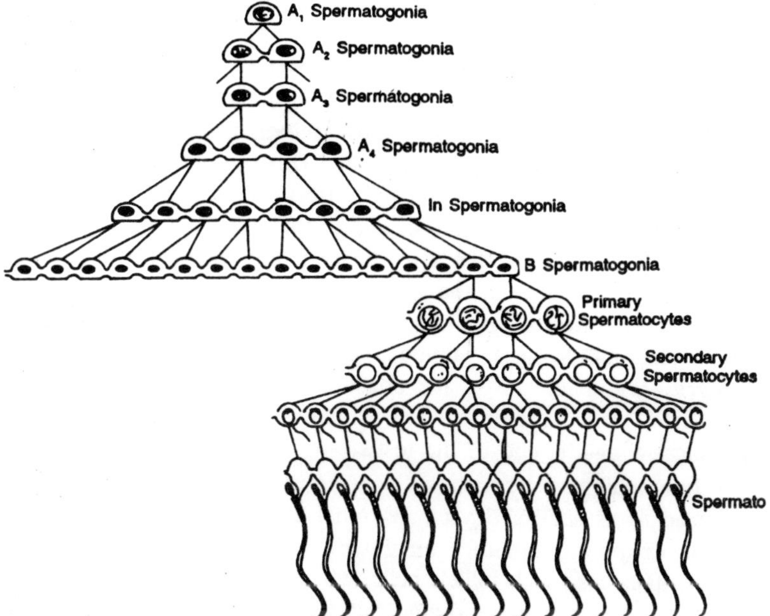

Fig. 2.2. The retention of intercellular bridges in spermatogenesis in several generations of cell division.

In contrast to the maturation of germ cells in the fetal ovary, meiosis in the testis is delayed until just prior to the onset of sexual maturity. Androgens from the human fetal testis apparently suppress the release of gonadotropins, which are at levels much lower than in the female fetus.

In spermatogenesis of elasmobranchs mitotic divisions begin at the anterior end of the testis and proceed caudad, following a migration of the ampullae. Epithelial cells surround the ampulla as spermatogonia divide, and these epithelial cells (also called nurse cells) are comparable, if not homologous to, Sertoli cells. A Sertoli cell surrounds a spermatogonium and seems to promote further development of the spermatogonium. Spermatocysts form as the ampulla moves toward the testicular margin. Eventually an ampulla will release spermatozoa, and the remaining ampullar elements are resorbed.

In fish and amphibians there are clusters of spermatogonia, among which spermatogenesis is synchronized. These clusters, or nests, are enclosed in seminiferous tubules, which are sometimes called lobes, seminiferous follicles, or spermatocysts. Within these spermatocysts, or follicles, are follicle cells, or nurse cells, which are similar in function (and probably homologous) to Sertoli cells. Frequently these nurse cells are called Sertoli cells, but usage varies among authors.

In the Indian teleost *Horaichthys setnai,* mature germ cells are encased within a barbed spermatophore. This spermatophore is secreted about the mature spermatocysts by Sertoli cells. As the germinal cyst moves from the bulbular anterior end of the testis to a narrowed region of the efferent ducts, the bard-bearing end becomes slender and pointed. After release of the spermatophore, the short efferent ducts, which were formed from Sertoli cells, seem to separate from the underlying tubule basal lamina. The basal lamina preserves tubule integrity within the testis and constitutes the foundation that guides the Sertoli cells in their movement and maturation as they approach the narrow caudal end of the testis.

In amphibians spermatozoa develop in discrete sections, variously referred to as spermatocysts, germinal cysts, capsules, and lobules, which occupy the seminiferous tubules. Developing spermatogonia are closely associated with follicle cells, which are the precursors of Sertoli cells. The spermatogonia divide mitotically several times, and unlike the Sertoli cells of mammals, the follicle cells also divide. With the onset of meiosis, spermatogonia become spermatocytes, and the follicle cells are referred to as Sertoli cells.

Spermatogenesis is seasonal in most midlatitude amphibians. After mating, which usually takes place in the spring, spermatogenesis produces gametes for the following year. In frogs and toads (Anura) spermatogenesis occupies the entire testis, but in salamanders (Caudata) it proceeds from one region, or lobule, to another in a wavelike sequence, from the caudal tip of the testis forward. In the red-backed salamander (*Plethodon cinereus*), for example, spermatogenesis commences in March (in Maryland) after mating, and the swollen, active region gradually advances until it occupies the anterior part of the testis in autumn.

In many reptiles spermatogenesis and steroidogenesis may not be concurrent, and spermatogenesis may take place either immediately prior to or shortly following mating.

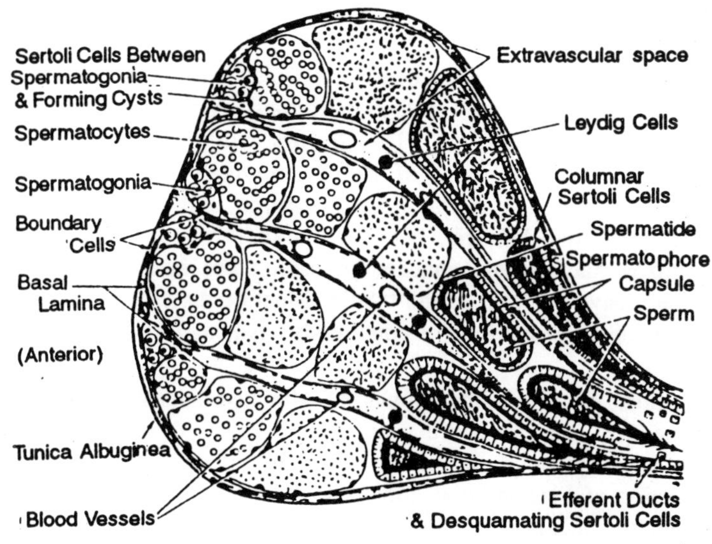

Fig. 2.3 A diagrammatic sectional view of the testis of Horaichthys setnai.

In postnuptial spermatogenesis, which characterizes turtles and some snakes, spermatozoa develop in late summer and are stored in the epididymides; Leydig cell activity and steroidogenesis occur in the spring. In prenuptial spermatogenesis, as in lizards and some snakes, Leydig cell activity and steroidogenesis are greatest during spermiogenesis.

Two annual peaks of testicular androgens have been reported for some lizards. One occurs at the time of maximal testicular mass, and a second postnuptial peak has been detected during testicular regression.

Avian spermatogenesis is similar to that in mammals. Germ cells reside in convoluted seminiferous tubules. Several generations of spermatogonia divide mitotically, greatly increasing their populations. Spermatocytes divide twice, meiotically, producing spermatids, which subsequently mature into spermatozoa. From the avian testis spermatozoa are released into an epididymis, which leads to a vas deferens, where the gametes may be stored. Sperm storage in the epididymis of birds is usually of short duration, and sperm may not survive there for extended periods. In the Japanese quail (*Coturnix coturnix*), spermatozoa contained by ligatures in the ductus deferens survive for only three days.

Spermiogenesis

Spermiogenesis is the process by which profound cytological changes in spermatids result in their becoming spermatozoa, following the second meiotic division. This occurs while the germ cell is embedded in the cytoplasm of the Sertoli cells. The spermatids develops a terminal tail and an apical acrosome, and the cell contents, especially the mitochondria, become markedly altered. Clusters of spermatozoa may remain attached to each other and they separate when they leave the wall of the tubule. Most of the cytoplasm of the spermatids is shed, and this "residual body" is phagocytized by Sertoli cells.

In most mammals the clones of attached spermatids mature simultaneously, and an entire generation is released as a unit. Thus there is a conspicuous uniformity of germ cell development in any given section of a seminiferous tubule. Replenishment of spermatogonia in vertebrates occurs continuously, by meitotic division of gonocytes or spermatogonia (in mammals). Unlike oogenesis, which in birds, mammals, and elasmobranchs is completed in the embryonic gonad, the meiotic divisions leading to primary and secondary spermatocytes continue throughout the reproductively active life of the male. Functional maturation of spermatozoa occurs mostly in the body, or corpus, of the epididymis, and the cauda epididymis is the main site of storage. Although testosterone and FSH are both needed for spermatogenesis, FSH is also required for spermiogenesis.

In seasonally reproducing vertebrates that store sperm, spermiogenesis occurs as spermatids move into the lumen of the tubules and away from the Sertoli cells. As the seminiferous tubules regress and shrink in diameter, the spermatozoa pass into the epididymis, where they remain until mating. In many mammals some sperm remains in the epididymides after the mating period; the sperm may be removed by luminal macrophages or by macrophages in the epididymal membrane.

In mammals spermatogenesis is continuous throughout the year, even in seasonally reproducing species in which the testes regress in the nonreproductive season. FSH is required for efficient sperm production, for in the presence of FSH, atresia declines. Variations in serum FSH determine the rate of germ cell degeneration and, ultimately the seasonal changes in fertility. In many midlatitude reptiles, there is a lapse of spermatogenesis in the nonreproductive season, which probably occurs in many other ectotherms of temperate regions.

The Testicular Environment

In ectotherms the testes are internal and have the same temperature as the core. In birds, also, the testes are internal and lie attached to the dorsal wall of the coelom. Passage of air through the air sac system may possibly reduce slightly the testicular temperature of birds. In anesthetized Japanese quail the testicular temperature is 0.6°C cooler than adjacent visceral tissues. This variation is attributed to endothermic reactions of the tissues and not to cooling by air sacs.

The body temperature of most birds lies well above 40°C. A mean temperature of passerine birds is 40.6°C, and more temperatures up to 46°C are not uncommon. Apparently heat does not inhibit testicular activity in birds. The rate of avian spermiogenesis is reported to be about 10 times greater than the rate for mammals.

In mammals, the testes of many species migrate to a position at least partly outside of the abdominal cavity, but in a few taxa (the testicondae or testiconda) the testes remain permanently and entirely within the body. Testiconid mammals include the elephants, hyraxes, cetaceans, and some others. In species with a discrete reproductive season, the testes enlarge and descend into a scrotum during the period of sexual activity, and regress and withdraw within the body cavity during the season of sexual inactivity. During mammalian prenatal and early postnatal development, the testes migrate to the region of the future scrotal development. The precise path seems to vary among different orders but may be assisted by pressure brought about from growth of the liver and viscera.

In several species of hyrax (Procaviidae) and the two species of elephants, for example, there is no scrotum. These mammals experience core and testicular temperatures of nearly 39°C. In the African elephant, core temperatures range from 36.2 to 38.9°C, and the hyrax (*Procavia capensis*) has core temperatures from 34.4 to 38.9°C. In both these families high temperatures clearly do not impair testicular function. Mammalian core temperatures vary between 33 and 39°C in most normally active individuals. Higher levels of temperature are similar among species with abdominal testes and scrotal testes, but lower core temperatures occur among species in which the testes are abdominal.

In those mammalian groups in which the testes descend into a well-developed scrotum, it is clear that scrotal temperatures are lower than core temperatures. In species with pendulous scrotal testes (many ungulates, primates, and most marsupials), both the size of the scrotum and the distance it descends from the body decrease in response to a decline in ambient temperature. This response is achieved by a contraction of the dartos muscle (tunica dartos), which lies beneath the scrotal skin, causing a folding and wrinkling of scrota wall. Contrariwise, in warm ambient temperatures, the scrotum becomes slightly larger and drops to a lower position. These adjustments tend to maintain a fairly constant testicular temperature of 3 to 7°C below the individual's core temperature. In those groups with a well-developed scrotum, the testicular artery and testicular vein lie appressed in the spermatic cord between the abdomen and testes. Presumably this results in a countercurrent exchange, with a reduction of heat entering the testes from the body.

There seems to be no compelling reason to suppose that testicular temperature was originally especially critical within the Mammalia. The need for a low testicular temperature is clearly a characteristic of only those mammalian taxa in which the testes are suspended in a scrotum. On the other hand, circumstantial evidence suggests that the movement of the testes to a cooler site has been an evolutionary tendency to provide a lower temperature for the epididymides.

Experimental evidence indicates that the epididymides require a body temperature lower than that of the core. The redirection of the epididymis to an abdominal position while the ipsalateral testis remained in its original scrotal position revealed that storage of sperm (retained by ligatures) resulted in survival for only 3 to 4 days in rats and 8 to 10 days in rabbits while sperm remained viable in the contralateral and scrotal epididymis.

Indeed, in those species in which the testes lie in a superficial cremaster sac (many insectivores and rodents), the epididymis forms a conspicuous swelling at the caudal part of the testis, exposing it to ambient temperatures. In hystricomorph rodents the testes lie within the abdomen, and the cauda epididymides may lie in postanal or cremaster sacs. Some of these species have been called facultative cryptorchid. An extreme example is the natural cryptorchid *Proechimys semispinosus,* a hystricomorph rodent of the mountains of western

South America, in which only the epididymides extend into the cremaster sac. The distal site and relatively avascular condition of the epididymis, in addition to its insulation by fat, may account for its temperature being significantly below that of the testes. Also, in a number of mammals with scrotal testes, the scrotum is furred except for the skin covering the epididymides.

An examination of the relative positions of the testis and epididymis also suggests that it is the epididymis that requires a temperature below that of the core. The epididymis is the site of storage of spermatozoa, and experimental evidence indicates that a lower temperature is needed for prolonged survival of spermatozoa. If a lower testicular temperature had been the main cause for the development of the scrotum, the most simple arrangement would be for the testis to occupy the scrotum with the epididymis remaining internal, a condition that does not occur.

Spermatophore

Spermatozoa are released in small packets called spermatophore in several groups of fish, including both elasmobranchs and teleosts, as well as in salamanders (Caudata). The spermatophore is a means of ensuring the efficiency of internal fertilization in an aquatic milieu.

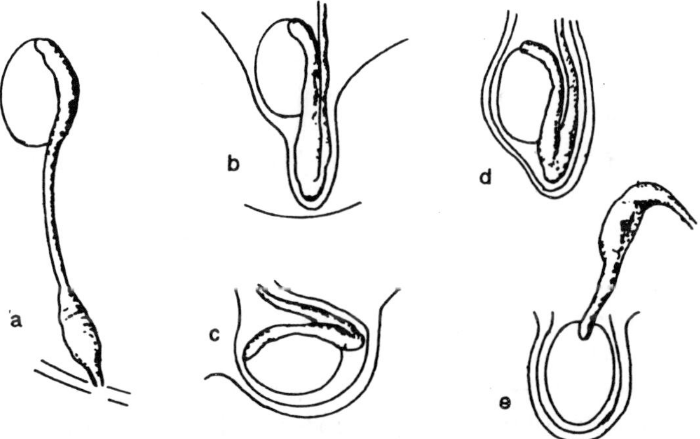

Fig. 2.4. Various arrangements of the mammalian testis and the epididymis. The typical testicondid condition as seen (a) in elephants and the hyrax; (b) the natural cryptorchid condition, in which the cauda epididymis extends into the cremaster sac, as in Glaucomys, Proechimys, Suncus, and Solenodon; (c) the scrotal epididymis and testis of the horse and the board; (d) the most frequent arrangement of scrotal testis and epdidymis; (e) and a nonexistent hypothetical condition that would be expected if the scrotum had evolved solely to lower testicular temperature.

In the rabbitfish, *Callorhycnhus antarcticus,* a holocephalan, the epididymides and seminal vesicles secrete a membranous noncellular covering in which the sperm are packaged. In elasmobranchs, all of which have claspers (modified pelvic fins) that serve as intromittent organs, sperm may also be concentrated in spermatophores. This condition has been described for the basking shark (*Cetorhinus maximus*). The seminal vesicles provide several jellylike envelopes about clusters of sperm, and this spermatophore is literally flushed into the uterus together with a large amount of fluid from the seminal vesicles.

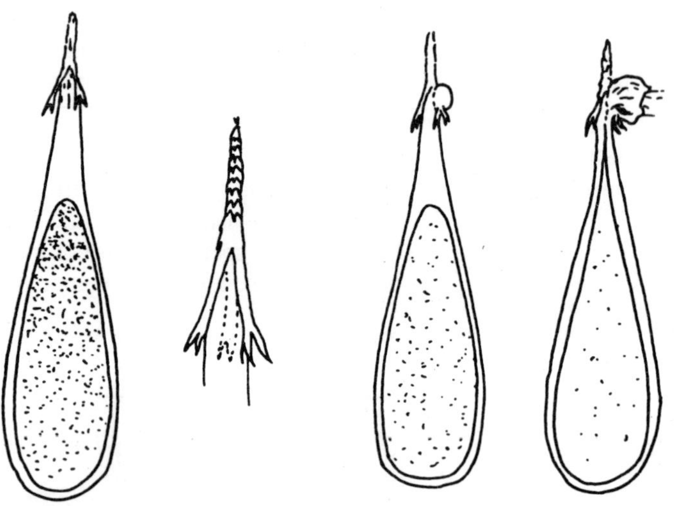

Fig. 2.5. Spermatophores of Horaichthys setnai. Left: in freshly extruded condition, with details of barbed spine. Right: the basal swelling of the spermatophore and escape of sperm upon exposure to water.

The spermatophores of poeciliid fish (guppies, mollies, and swordtails and their relatives) are weakly encapsulated clusters of sperm. They are placed into the uterus of the female by a modified anal fin. Spermatophores also occur in live-bearing brotulid and embiotocid fish. In the surfperch (*Cymatogaster aggregata*), an embiotocid of the eastern Pacific, sperm are densely packed as they leave the testicular cysts. Spermatophore capsule proteins are synthesized but the cells of the efferent ducts; the spermatophore membranes remain intact.while within the seminal fluid but dissolve when they enter the increased pH of the ovarian fluid. In *Horaichthys setnai* (Adrianichthyidae) of India the spermatophores are barbed and do not actually enter the reproductive tract of the female. Instead, the barb implants near the genital orifice of the female, and when in seawater, the spermatophore ruptures and slowly releases spermatozoa. Presumably the slow and directed release of sperm allows some to enter the genital tract of the female.

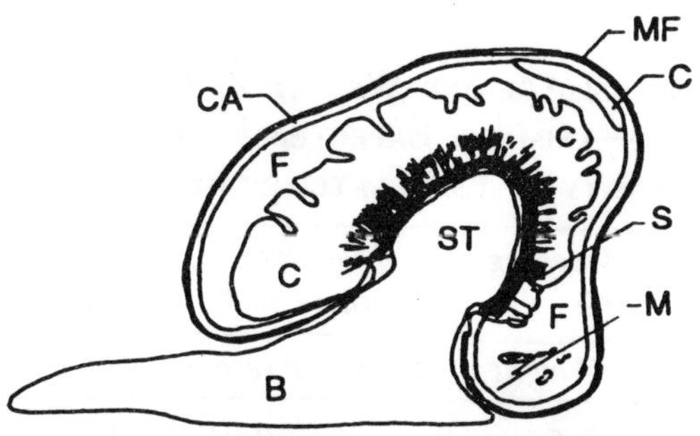

Fig. 2.6. Spermatophore of the salamander, Plethodon jordoni, *through the midsagittal plane: MF, mucous film; CA, capsule; F, fine granular layer; C, coarse ganular layer; S, spermatozoa; M, clusters of melanin granules; ST, stalk; B, base.*

Internal fertilization is the pattern among most salamanders. There is no intromittent organ, but sperm are contained in a spermatophore, which the male deposits on a substrate, such as a rock or submerged piece of vegetation. The spermatophore is subsequently picked up by the cloacal lips of the female. The spermatophore of salamanders consists of a basal stalk, which becomes attached to the substrate, and an apical cap, which contains the spermatozoa. In the plethodontid salamanders *Eurycea luçifuga* and *E. longicauda,* Kingsbury's and pelvic glands produce the spermatophore cap and enlarge prior to the release of spermatozoa. The female breaks off the cap, or part of the cap, from the stalk, allowing spermatozoa to escape into her genital tract.

THE SEMEN

Semen is the complete discharge of the male during normal ejaculation. It has two major components, the spermatozoa or cellular elements and the seminal plasma or liquid portion. Some laboratory animals such as the rabbit also ejaculate an amorphous, jelly copulation-plug which assures retention of sperm in the vagina after coitus. Semen is milky or creamy in appearance and yellowish to gray in color. The consistency of semen following ejaculation varies from a relatively low viscosity in the dog and rabbit to a high viscosity in cats to actual gel formation in most rodents and primates.

Sperm are produced in the seminiferous tubules of the testis which are controlled by hormones from the anterior pituitary gland. Luteinizing hormone (LH) stimulates growth of the interstitial or Leydig cells to secrete testosterone. Testosterone in turn is responsible for stimulating the seminiferous tubules and for normal growth, development, and function of the accessory glands which produce the seminal plasma.

TABLE 2.1. MINIMUM AGE AND WEIGHT TO BEGIN BREEDING MALE LABORATORY ANIMALS. EXPECTED VOLUME AND SPERM DENSITY OF EJACULATED SEMEN

	Begin Breeding Life		*Ejaculate Volume (ml)*		*Density (sperm/ml × 10)*	
Species	*Age*	*Weight*	*Range*	*Average*	*Range*	*Average*
Cat	9 mos	3.5 kg	0.01-0.3	0.04	1.5-28	14
Dog	10-12 mos	—	2-25	9.0	0.6-5.4	1.3
Guinea pig	3-5 mos	450 gm	0.4-0.8	0.6	0.05-0.2	0.1
Hamster	2 mos	90 gm	—	—	—	—
Monkey (*M. mulatta*)	6 yrs	9 kg	1.0-4.5	1.8	0.9-8.1	4.0
Mouse	45 days	25 gm	—	—	—	—
Rabbit	4-12 mos		0.4-6	1.0	0.5-3.5	1.5
Rat	45-50 days	225 gm	—	—	—	—

Follicle-stimulating hormone (FSH) appears to have a function in spermatogenesis but its specific role is not yet defined.

The number of sperm and the volume of seminal plasma ejaculated depend on the species. Variations in the volume of semen ejaculated are due largely to the amount of secretion from the accessory glands; however, many factors such as age, frequency of ejaculation, season of the year, environment, nutritional state, and general health of the animal play important roles in semen production.

Information concerning sperm and seminal plasma of many laboratory animals is not abudant because of the difficulty in obtaining experimental material. Also, the economic incentive which causes rapid advances in knowledge about the semen of domestic animals due to artificial insemination programs has not been present.

SPERMATOZOA

Development of Sperm

The total sperm producing capacity of the male is determined genetically but there are many factors which determine what portion of the germ cells are actually delivered for reproductive purposes. The important external or environmental factors affecting sperm production and development include temperature, photoperiod, humidity, nutrition, stress, and toxic substances.

Mammals with scrotal testes are more sensitive to high temperature than other animals. The scrotal environment which provides a temperature a few degrees below that of the abdomen is essential for normal sperm production. High environmental temperature with either very low or high humidity has an adverse effect on spermatogenesis. Low environmental temperatures do not seem to affect semen production. Photoperiod plays a major role because it mediates its effect through the gonadotropic activity of the anterior pituitary. Therefore the change in day length signals the beginning and ending of the breeding season in many wild species.

Production of sperm does not add greatly to the nutritional requirements of the body as a whole but spermatogenesis can be seriously altered by deficiency of trace minerals, fat soluble vitamins, and essential fatty acids. Stress, whether psychological (due to moving males to a new environment) or pathological (due to trauma or disease) can cause temporary cessation of sperm production.

Age is one of the dominant factors to influence sperm production. The age at which maturity is reached, i.e., *puberty,* when mature, sperm are produced and when the male can begin breeding, is controlled by factors such as toe general state of health, plane of nutrition, hormonal secretion, and balance. These factors also influence the total breeding life span of the male. The earliest breeding age and breeding life span of the male varies greatly from one species to another. The male usually matures later than the female in a given species, but because there is considerable variation in the time of maturity between individuals within a species, the minimum weight required for a male before breeding serves as a useful guide to breeding capacity.

Spermatogenesis

Spermatogenesis is the development and production of the germ cell in the mature male which involves cell division, differentiation, and reorganization, with the nucleus being reduced from the diploid to the haploid state.

Spermatozoa arise from the germinal epithelium lining the basement membrane of the testis tubules. The germinal epithelium contains the spermatogonia, the spermatocytes the spermatids, and Sertoli's cells. The youngest spermatogenic cells are on the basement mambrane and the successively older cells are in layers toward the lumen of the seminiferous tubules with the spermatids situated nearest the lumen. Sertoli's cells act as nutrient or nurse cells for the developing spermatids.

Estimation of the duration of spermatogenesis can be accomplished by injecting animals with radioactive isotopes that are specifically incorporated into deoxyribonucleic acid (DNA) in cells that are about to divide. Tritium-labelled thymidine (^{3}H) and radioactive phosphours (^{32}P) have been used for labelling DNA. The duration of spermatogenesis in the rat is 48 days.

The rat will be used as an example of the various developmental steps of the sperm because this species has been carefully studied and the stages of development precisely defined. The spermatogonium is the mitotic stage of spermatogenesis. This stage is important because large cell populations are formed and the spermatogonia are producing spermatocytes, which undergo meiosis. During proliferation of spermatogonia there are three types formed: type A, intermediate-type, and type B. Primary spermatocytes form from type B spermatogonia and undergo a long meiotic prophase stage. During this evolution they pass through leptotene, zygotene, pachytene and diakinesis stages. Then the first maturation division produces secondary spermatocyt and the second maturation division gives rise to spermatids. The maturing spermatids undergo nineteen cellular stages before they are released from Sertoli's cells. The male germ cell that is freed when the spermatid is released from Sertoli's cell of the seminiferous tubule is the *spermatozoon*.

There is a high degree of correlation between adjacent cells. The development of any one generation of cells is synchronized with the development of the other generations present in the seminiferous epithelium. The various cell associations succeed each other in a regular, ordered manner and the sequence repeats itself cyclically.

The sequence of events by which a complete series of cellular associations follows one another in time in any given area of the seminiferous epithelium is known as the *cycle of the seminiferous epithelium.* The cycle in the rat is subdivided into 14 stages. The duration of the cycle of the seminiferous epithelium is the time between two successive appearances of the same cellular association in one given area of the tubule. This duration is the same throughout the rat testis. The duration of the whole spermatogenesis may be assessed in relation to the durations of the cycle. Although it is difficult to define a precise time for the beginning of spermatogenesis, four successive cycles are requited for the complete spermatogenic evolution from the dormant type A spermatogonium to the free spermatozoon stage.

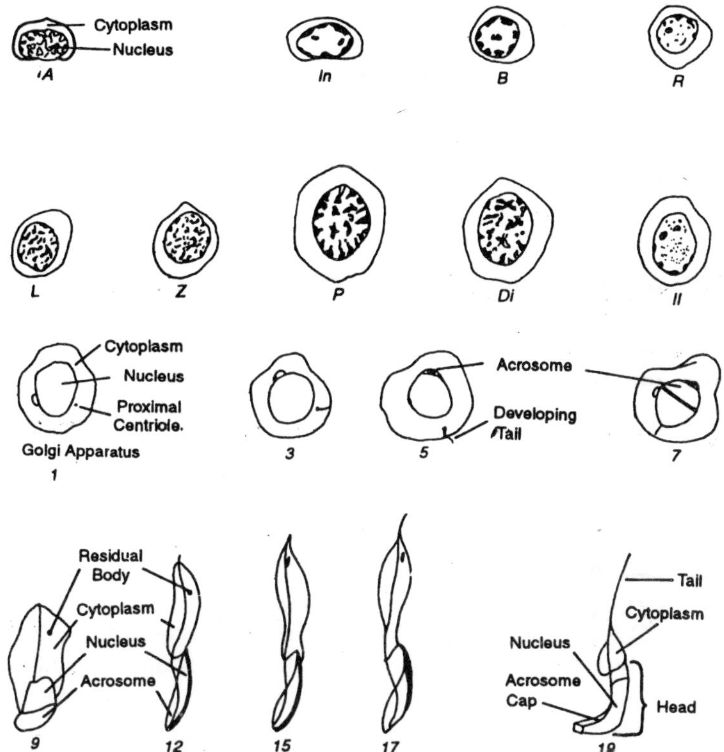

Fig. 2.7. Drawings showing the various steps of development of germ cells in the rat. Reading from left to right starting with the top row, type A spermatogonia (A) are shown first. Type A spermatogonia undergo three meitotic divisions to form intermediate type spermatogonia (In). The intermediate type undergoes a meitotic division to give rise to type B spermatogonia (B) which in turn divides to yield resting primary spermatocytes (R). These cells undergo the meiotic prophase through the following steps: leptotene (L, second row), zygotene (Z), pachytene (P) and diakinesis (Di), Then, the first maturation division produces secondary spermatocytes (II). These in turn undergo the s second maturation division and yield young spermatids (1, third row). The spermatids proceed through 10 stages of maturation before they are released from he seminiferous epithelium to become spermatozoa. (1, 3, 5, 7, 9, 12, 15, 17, and 19 are representative stages of spermatid development showing acrosome and tail formation with cytoplasm last off.)

Roosen-Runge has developed a chart or "clock" to depict the cyclic phenomena in mammalian spermatogenesis. The chart can be read in various ways. If one begins reading the outer circle at 12 o'clock, then following the arrows clockwise, one may run through the development of the germ cell. The diagrammatic nature of the figure should be kept in mind when drawing conclusions. The design simulates the seminiferous tubule in that the generations are arranged according to age from the periphery to the centers. However, a cross-section of a tubule of most mammals presents only one combination of germ cells, while the chart shows a multitude of combinations, one for each radius. In this way, not only the development of the individual cell is represented, but also the process of spermatogenesis as the generations differentiate in rigid correlation with each other.

In mammals, the male determines the sex of the offspring. The result of meiosis during spermatogenesis is the separation of the X and Y chromosomes into separate spermatids. An equal number of X chromosome and Y chromosome-bearing spermatids are formed. Therefore, an equal number of female-determining (X) and male-determining (Y) spermatozoa are produced. Since either type of sperm has the same probability of reaching and fertilizing the egg, an even number of male and female offspring can be predicted. A sex ration very close to unity does indeed occur in nature. Man's attempt to control the sex ratio of progeny remains one of the most interesting unsolved problems in biology.

Biochemical changes that accompany the germ cells during spermatogenesis have been studied mainly by histochemical methods are not well understood. There is a loss of cytoplasm containing residual bodies from the spermatid which is east off the spermatid tail. These residual bodies contain the Golgi membranes, vesicles, mitochondrial remnants, liquid, and RNA particles. The ejaculated sperm has only minute traces of RNA. Phosphatase activity in the nuclei progressively declines and a simultaneous disappearance of glycogen occurs during spermatocytic development. It is thought that lipids in Sertoli's cells serve as a nutritional source for sperm and act as precursors of certain steroids.

Transport of Sperm through the Epididymis

The sperm pass from the seminiferous tubules to the epididymis by means of the rete testis and the vasa efferentia. They require residence in the epididymis to become functionally competent. Spermatozoa removed from successive levels of the male reproductive tract show an increasing capacity for motility, for survival in *vitro,* and for fertility. The time required for sperm to travel from the testis to the distal epididymis varies with the species. Transport time varies from very rapid (1 day) in the rabbit to 6 to 8 days in the rat and mouse, 9 to 10 days in the hamster, and 14 to 18 days in the guinea pig. The accuracy of these estimates is affected by the method used and the sexual activity of the male.

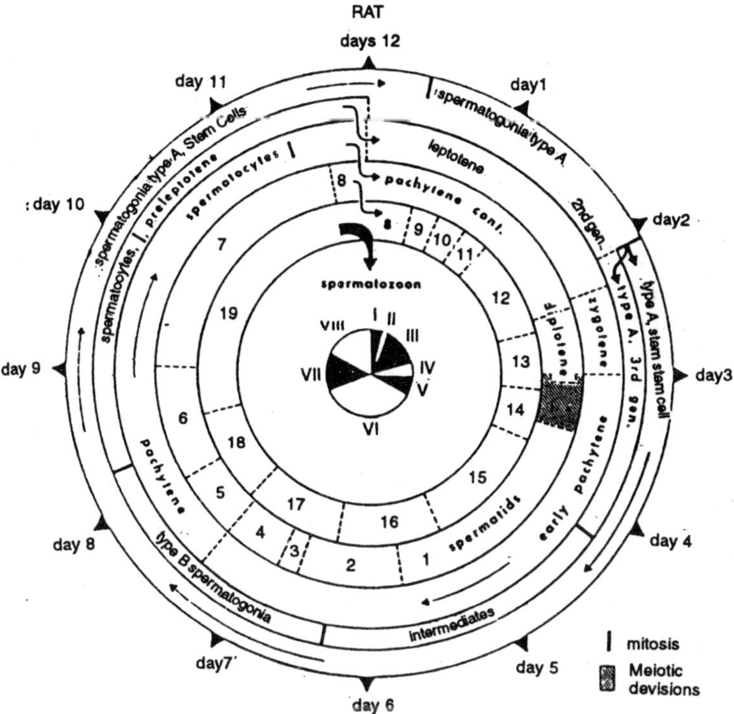

Fig. 2.8. "Clock" of spermatogenesis in the rat. Cell types are arranged in circles with the more primitive cells in the outer circle and succeedingly more mature cells arranged clockwise (arrows) and in circles toward the centre of the diagram. Different cell stages are separated from each other by broken lines. Thick black lines indicate mitosis and slanted lines indicate meiotic division. The circle in the center indicates the stages of spermatogenesis. Alternating shaded and light areas depict which part of total cell population is represented by each phase.

As sperm transcend the epididymis their cytoplasmic droplet migrates from the neck to the distal end of the midpiece and finally disappears altogether. There is a gradual shrinkage and dehydration of the sperm until the mature cell has a scanty cytoplasm. Most living animal cells have a 10 to 20 percent concentration of solids but spermatozoa have a content of 35 to 45 percent.

Sperm are immotile and their metabolic activity is low while within the epididymis. Their quiescenee is due principally to the low partial pressure of oxygen, but also in part to a high level of bicarbonate, mechanical overcrowding, a deficiency of glycolysible sugar, a high ratio of potassium to sodium, a metabolic inhibitor, and several other factors. Rabbit sperm receive a polysaccharide coating (decapacitation factor) from the epididymal secretion, one of the factors which must be altered by the female reproductive tract before the ovum can be fertilized.

The physiological conditions within the epididymis are dependent on the endocrine activity of the testes. Under normal conditions sperm are able to survive for relatively long periods of time. In most mammals they retain their capacity for motility for 50 to 70 days and, in bats, up to several months. Spermatozoa retain their fertilizing ability for 20 to 35 days in most laboratory species but they lose their ability to produce viable embryos well ahead of losing their ability to penetrate the egg. The incidence of non-viable embryos in the guinea pig is increased from 4 percent to 20 percent by retaining spermatozoa in the epididymis for 20 to 25 days before mating.

The mature sperm are stored in the tail of the epididymis and in the distal end of the vasa deferentia during the period prior to ejaculation. When there are long periods between ejaculations, the vasa deferentia are attributed with the function of dissolution and absorption of senescent sperm but the mechanism by which this is accomplished is not completely understood.

During ejaculation the sperm and epididymal secretions are passed out through the visa deferentia into the urethra with the secretions of the accessory glands. The whole semen is emitted from the penile urethra. In most rodents and the eat the ejaculate contains a small aggregate of sperm surrounded by a gelatinous seminal plasma. The dog ejaculates its semen in three fractions with the middle fraction among sperm-rich whereas during ejaculation in the rabbit, complete mixing of sperm and seminal plasma occurs.

Structure of Sperm

The basic physiological and biochemical functions of spermatozoa are fertilizatior of ova and motility. The sperm is designed to carry out these functions with two majo parts, the head and tail. The detailed structure of spermatozoa is shown ii electronmicrograps provided by

Bedford. The head has a nucleus which acts as transmitte of genetic material in the form of deoxyribonucleoprotein and an acrosome with lyti factors to aid in egg penetration. The tail is a long flagellum consisting of four regions the neck, the middle piece, the principal piece, and the end piece, which contains all th cellular components and enzymes needed for metabolic activity and motility.

The total length of mammalian sperm ranges from 41 to 250 μ, depending on th species. The sperm of man, rabbit, dog, and domestic animals are of similar size an range from 55 to 65 μ long. Mouse, rat and hamster sperm are several times longer.

The Head

There is great species variation in the shape of sperm head. Fowl sperm have elongated, cylindricalshaped heads whereas rat and hamster sperm heads are elongated but quite hooked. The head is flattened in near all mammals. The sperm of rabbits, cats, dogs, and domestic animals have ovoid heads. The sperm of the guinea pig has a flattered head with a large wrap-around acrosome and that of the mouse has a relatively fat head with a spicule-like hook at the anterior end. Human sperm are almond shaped.

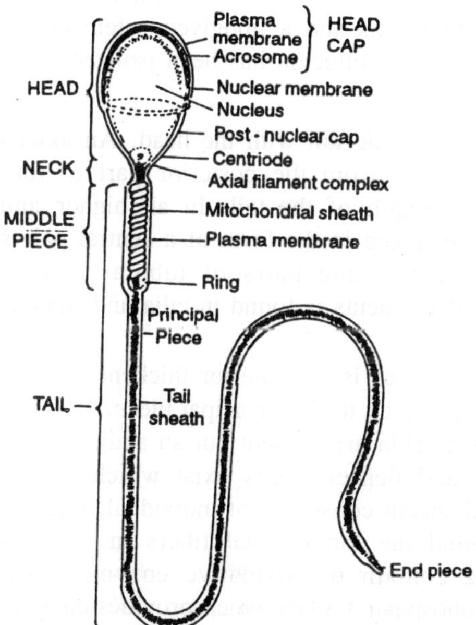

Fig. 2.9. Diagrammatic representation of a mammalian spermatozoa.

The two major components of the head are the nucleus and the acrosome. The nucleus is enclosed in a thick membrane. Anteriorly it is covered by the caplike acrosome and posteriorly by a cytosplasmic sheath, the postacrosomal region (postnuclear cap). The chemical composition of the nucleus is primarily densely packed chromatin consisting of DNA conjugated with basic nuclear protein of a histone- or protamine-like character. The nuclei of mammalian spem each contains about 3×10^2 gm of DNA, which is 40 percent of the dry weight of the nucleus and approximately half the DNA content of the nuclei of normal mammalian somatic cells. The nucleus stains intensely with basic nucleus dyes and gives a positive Feulgen reaction with Schiff's fuchsin-sulfurous acid reagent.

The acrosome is a saclike structure which covers the anterior two-thirds of the nucleus and combines with the plasma membrane to form the head cap. It arises from the Golgi apparatus of the early spermatid. The acrosome has become very important in reproductive physiology because of its association with penetration of the egg. Several lytic factors have now been described. Hyaluronidase is released from the acrosome to pave the way for the spermatozoon through the cumulus cell mass. An enzyme is present which disperses the coron radiata cells and a lipoglycoprotein enzyme (trypsin-like) to dissolve the zona pellucida has been isolated.

The Tail

The neck joins the tail with the head. An axial core of discrete filaments originates from the posterior part of the neck and runs throughout the length of the tail. In all higher animal species the filaments are arranged in the form of a central pair surrounded by a concentric ring of rune pairs of tubular filaments each. This arrangement of filaments is found in cilia and flagella throughout the animal kingdom.

The middle piece is the anterior thickened region of the tail that extends from the neck to the principal piece. In this section the usual two plus nine fibrilla are present but an additional outer row of nine much larger and denser fibers exist which are surrounded by a mitochondrial sheath consisting of individual, elongated mitochondria wrapped around the longitudinal fibers in a helical manner. The mitochondria contain the oxidative enzyme systems to produce adenosine triphosphate (ATP) which provides energy for motility and initiation of glycolysis. Thus the major portion of the metabolic activity of sperm takes place in the middle piece.

The principal piece is the longest part of the tail. There are no mitochondria present and the axial filaments are surrounded by a protein fibrous sheath which has characteristic circumferentially oriented dense fibers. The principal piece terminates abruptly a little distance before the end of the tail. The tail terminates with the distal end piece in which the nine outer filaments are absent and the inner axial filaments are bounded by a plasma membrane that invests the entire sperm.

There is a notable absence of glycogen and reducing sugar in mammalian spermatozoa. Plasmalogen located in the middle piece contains a fatty acid and which can be hydrolyzed and then oxidized via the tricarboxylic acid cycle, giving an endogenous source of energy when exogenous sources are not available.

Motility of Sperm

A male of normal fertility will ejaculate semen with 70 to 90 percent of the sperm motile and 5 to 25 per cent of the sperm abnormally formed. The tail is the propulsive unit of the sperm pushing the head along by the propagation of waves which pass distal along its length and exert pressure on the surrounding medium. The impulses arise from the inner fibers of the axial filaments at the level of the basal body of the neck and seem to coordinate the localized contractions in the outer fibers. The average frequency of the bending cycle of bull sperm in physiological solutions at 37° C is 9.1 /sec and the average forward movement with each contractile cycle is 8.3 μ. The mechanisms responsible for the motility of sperm are a complex series of biochemical events involving contractile protein elements and energy production and transfer that have been intensively investigated but are not clearly understood. Motility is probably important for sperm egg encounters in the oviduct and propulsion of the sperm through the outer layers of the egg. Motility is positively correlated with the fertilizing capacity of sperm.

Metabolism of Sperm

Mammalian sperm are highly active metabolic cells processing the enzymes necessary to carry out the biochemical reactions of the Embden-Meyerhof pathway, tricarboxylic acid cycle, fatty acid oxidation, electron transport system, and perhaps the hexose-monophosphate shunt. Sperm, from lower animal forms which reproduce by external fertilization appear to be devoid of glycolytic ability and depend chiefly on an aerobic type of metabolism. The metabolic enzymes appear to be contained within the spermatozoan tail. The respiratory enzymes are probably confined to the mitochondria, but the glycolytic enzymes are more widely distributed throughout the tail.

Sperm can metabolize a variety of exogenous and some endogenous substrates. During catabolism the sperm covert a large part of the liberated energy high energy phosphate bonds in the form of ATP and phosphocreatine. The synthesis of these compounds gives the cell an effective means to couple the production of energy with its utilization. The major portion of the high energy trapped is utilized in motility but an important contribution of some of the energy is to maintain the integrity of the cell against losses caused by diffusion and other physical processes.

Various tests on spermatozoa such as fructolysis, methylene blue reducing activity, and oxygen uptake correlate well with fertility of sperm but they do not have enough statistical advantage over simpler microscopic examination of sperm density, motility, incidence of dead sperm, abnormal forms, and storage survival to warrant their routine field use in semen evaluation. Bio-chemical investigations, however, have added greatly to our knowledge of semen and have made tremendous contributions toward our ability to store and handle semen for artificial insemination.

Glycolysis

The metabolic degradation of hexoses by mammalian spermatozoa is carried out through the Embden-Meyerhof pathway in the same manner as that known to occur in other animal cells. Conversion of hexoses to lactate is slower under aerobic conditions than under anaerobic conditions but the difference is not great. The major hexose in the seminal plasma of most animals is fructose; therefore, under natural conditions glycolytic activity of sperm is termed *fructolysis*. Sperm can convert fructose, glucose, and mannose to lactic acid. Galactose is not utilized by rabbit or bull sperm, probably because of the absence of the enzyme phosphogalactose uridyltransferase. Some mammalian sperm can use maltose and glycogen but not lactose or sucrose. The spermatozoan ability to utilize di- and poly-saccharides is limited due to the absence of enzymes that hydrolyze α and α-glucosidic.

Glycolysis is the important to sperm because it allows for their survival and for the production of utjlizable energy under anaerobic conditions such as are encountered during storage for artificial insemination. ATP along with the appropriate enzymes and cofactors plays an all important role in glycolysis. During the phosphorylation of

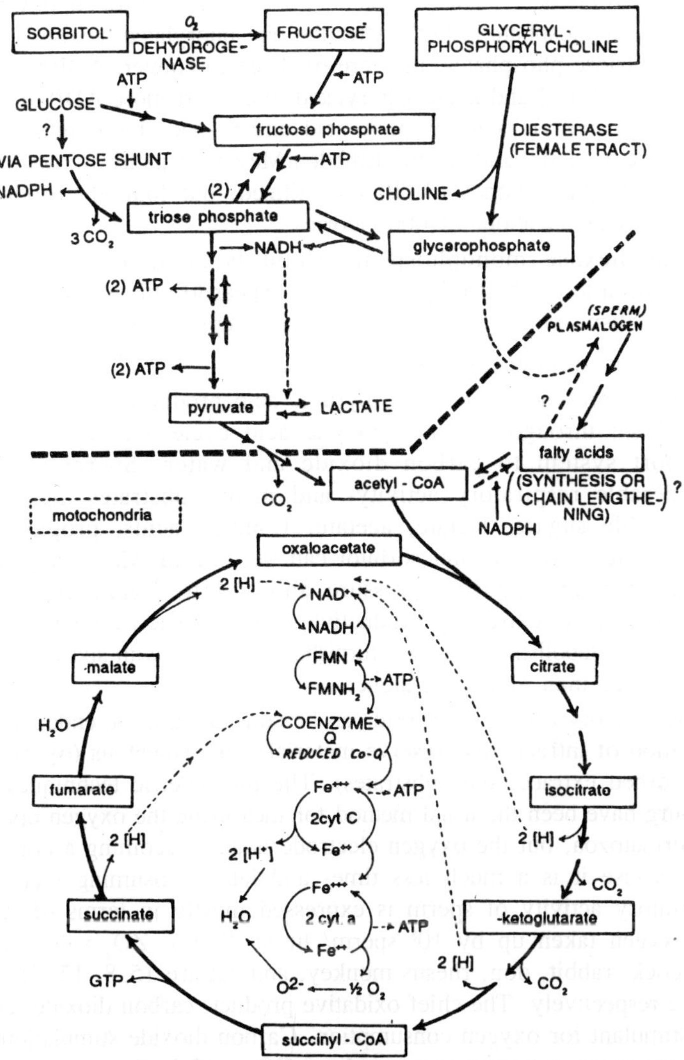

Fig. 2.10. A summary of the major metabolic pathways of spermatozoa. This metabolic pathw begins with the substrates found in seminal plasma. Intermediates which do not accumulate enclosed in elongated boxes throughout the pathway: An interrupted arrow indicates an intermediat product that has not been included. A thick broken line separates the glycolytic pathway frc oxidative pathways found in the mitochondria. The electron transport system, cofactors, and cert, enzymes are shown by slanted lattering. A question mark indicates that evidence for the existence a pathway is not well documented. The end products are lactate, carbon dioxide and water.

hexoses, ATP acts as a phosphate donor and is broken down to adenosine diphosphate (ADP). After the phosphorylated hexose is split into two triose phosphates, they are oxidized to convert ADP to ATP and then hydrated and dephosphorylated to convert more ADP to ATP to produce pyravic acid. Pyruvic acid under anaerobic conditions is converted to lactic acid. In the Embden-Meyerhof pathway two high-energy phosphate bonds (ATP) are utilized, but four are produced for a net gain of about 21,000 calories.

The hexose monophosphate shunt is another method for spermatozoa to catabolize hexoses. They appear to utilize this pathway in metabolism while residing in the female reproductive tract.

Respiration: Endogenous and Exogenous

In the presence of oxygen, pyruvic acid produced by glycolysis is oxidized through the tricarboxylic acid cycle and the electron transport system to carbon dioxide and water. Sperm exhibit considerable respiratory activity- and many substrates including glycolysible sugars, lactate, acetate, L-amino acids, propionate, oxaloacetate, glycerol, and sorbitol can be utilized when oxygen is available at an O_2 partial pressure above 4 to 5 mm mercury. Respiration is an extremely productive source of energy for the cell. Oxidative metabolism of hexoses furnishes the sperm with sixteen times more energy than glycolysis alone.

Respiratory activity of sperm can be considered to be endogenous (oxidation of intracellular reserve material), or exogenous (oxidation of absorbed extracellular substrates). The manometric techniques of Warburg have been the usual method for measuring the oxygen uptake of spermatozoa, but the oxygen electrode is also becoming a popular tool because it is a much less time- and labor-consuming method. Respiratory activity of sperm is expressed mostly in terms of ZO_2 (μl. oxygen taken up by 10^8 sperm/ hr at 37^0 C). ZO_2 values for bull, cock, rabbit, dog, rhesus monkey, and cat are 15, 8, 12, 16,16 and 12 respectively. The chief oxidative product, carbon dioxide, acts as a stimulant for oxygen consumption. Carbon dioxide stimulation is very important to human sperm, whose ZO_2 *is* 13 in the presence of 2 percent CO_2 but very low (ZO_2 = 1.4) when bicarbonate is absent. Similar changes in respiratory rates occur with the sperm of the cock, bull, rabbit, boar, and cat at appropriate CO_2 concentrations. Carbon dioxide is similar to potassium and phosphate in that small amounts will stimulate metabolism but high concentrations will inhibit it.

Endogenous respiration is supported mainly through intracellular plasmalogen depletion in mammalian sperm. A fatty acid residue is hydrolyzed from plasmalogen and oxidized through the tricarboxylic acid cycle. Plasmalogen acts as a reserve source of energy that is utilized when exogenous material are exhausted. The degradation of plasmalogen produces a metabolic end product, lysoplasmalogen, which may cause auto-intoxication and thus depress the viability of sperm. Sperm can utilize carbohydrates to replenish their lipid reserves through synthesis of phospholipids and diglycerides. Sperm of lower animals such as sea urchin and starfish are less exacting in their requirements for oxidizable lipids than are mammalian sperm. The sperm of sea urc are more dependent on phospholipid metabolism because they do not have glycolysi material at their disposal and they process enzymes that can hydrolyze both lecithin cephalin.

There are at least two major types of enzymes involved in amino acid metabol by sperm. L-amino acid oxidase is responsible for oxidative deamination of L-tyros L-phenylalanine, and L-tryptophane, and several transaminase enzymes such as glutar oxaloacetic (GOT) and glutamic-pyruvic transaminases also influence the metaboli During oxidative deamination, hydrogen peroxide, which is spermicidal beca spermatozoa do not process the enzyme catalyze present in other body cells to destro is formed.

The discovery that bull sperm can incorporate ^{14}C amino acids into the protei: the acrosome is interesting because of the virtual absence of ribonucleic acid in spew provide messenger RNA for protein synthesis.

Survival of Sperm *in vitro*

The three principal ways to assess survival of sperm *in vitro* are retention of moti metabolic activity, and fertilizing *capacity*. *Motility* and certain metabolic tests (determination of the rates of respiration, methylene blue and resazurin reduction times, and fructolysis) correlate well with conception rates. However, the capacity of spermatozoa to effect normal fertilization and give rise to a normal offspring is unequivocal evidence of functional survival. Sperm are quite responsive to environmental change but are able to survive over a wide range of conditions. Conditions that stimulate metabolism usually also stimulate motility and decrease survival time. Many factors influence the survival of sperm but the most important ones appear to be variations in ionic strength, temperature, light, and sperm density.

Effect of Media Composition: pH, Electrolytes, Osmotic Pressure

Sperm metabolism and motility have an extremely wide range of tolerance to hydrogen ion concentrations. Rabbit sperm remain motile over a pH range of 5 to 10. Optimum survival of sperm is seen at just over a pH of 7, with progressive decline in motility and metabolism below the optimum but better compatibility in an alkaline pH of up to 8.5. Phosphate biffers are most commonly used in studies to regulate the hydrogen ion concentration but an appropriate buffer is difficult to select. Phosphate tends to depress respiration and motility citrate buffers are objectionable because of their chelating properties unless traces of heavy metals are present; bicarbonate buffers depress respiration at concentrations above 5×10^{-3} M and this buffers depress respiration and motility above 0.1 M concentration.

Sperm are tolerant to changes in ionic strength. Rabbit sperm remain fertile when suspended in media corresponding to as little as one-tenth or as much as four times the ionic strength of Ringer's solution. The effect of variation in osmotic pressure depends upon the nature of the dissolved substances. Usually electrolytes penetrate cell membranes much more slowly than do nonelectrolytes; consequently they are much more damaging on an equi-osmotic basis. Bull sperm are quite tolerant to high concentrations of glycine and glycerol in semen diluents. Maximal oxygen consumption and motility of the sperm of the bull, dog, ram, and fowl occur longest at the osmotic pressure of blood plasma (freezing point, -0.55 °*C*). *A* certain amount of electrolytes is necessary for normal sperm irritability but the precise action of any electrolyte is not well understood. Magnesium stimulates both motility and glycolysis and potassium improves motility of washed spermatozoa in 0.15 M of sodium chloride solution. Phosphate is necessary for glycolysis but high concentrations (above 0.1 M) depress respiration and motility.

Effect of Temperature and Photo period

Optimum metabolic activity and motility of sperm occur at body temperature (37 to 39° C). The life span of spermatozoa is shortest at 37° C and higher, and they will not survive at temperature above 45° *C*. Metabolism decreases as the temperature is below body temperature and movement of sperm ceases at 5° to 10° C. If spermatozoa are cooled too fast they suffer irreversible immobilization called *cold shock,* with increased cell permeability, leakage of cytochrome c, and inhibition of *ATP* synthesis. However, the longevity of sperm can be greatly increased by slowly cooling (over a 5 hour period) them to 4° C. Lipids and lipoproteins of egg yolk protect sperm from cold shock above 0° C; this is the basis for using egg

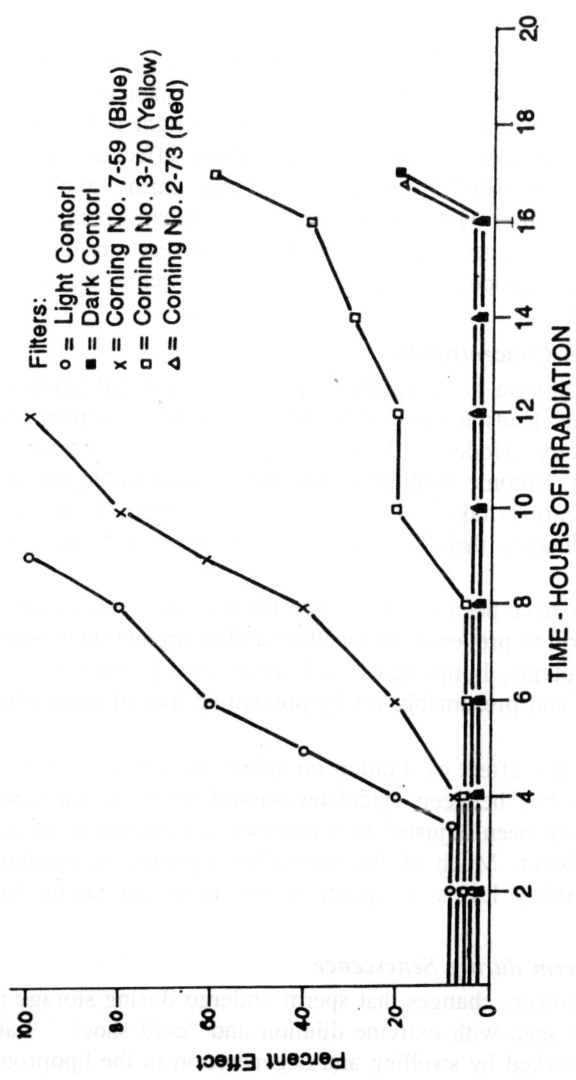

Fig. 2.11. The effect of various wavelength bands, with approximately, equal quantities of radiant energy, on the rate of photo-immobilization of bovino sperm. One hundred percent represents complete immobilization.

yolk or milk diluent for routine *grtifiC1d11nSeminafion and* storage for several days. Glycerol, 7.5 percent, is most commonly used to protect sperm below freezing. But sperm have been stored in a functional state for several years at 79° C and 190° C.

In recent years it has become apparent that ordinary room light and sun light are deleterious to sperm motility and fertility. The respiration of the sperm of the rabbit, cock, and man is stimulated by visible light. The most harmful wavelength of light is 440 μ with red light being the least detrimental. The harmful effect is enhanced by oxygen and retarded by catalase, certain amino acids, and 0-mereaptoethylamine. The spermicidal effect appears to be due to the formation of hydrogen peroxide and a series of reactions damaging to the cytoplasmic components of the sperm cell as well as a reduction in DNA content.

Effect of Sperm Concentration

Excessive dilution of mammalian sperm with seminal plasma or artificial diluents leads to loss of motility, metabolic activity, and fertilizing capacity. Moderate dilution of sperm, on the other hand, with a buffered, isotonic medium containing a glycolysible substrate is harmful. If care is taken to protect the sperm from light during collection and dilution, their life span can be increased without cooling them to 4° C.

Sulfate ions have been recommended for inclusion into media for suspending sperm to prevent their swelling and to protect their plasma membranes. Proteins, lipoproteins, and starch give protective action against dilution and presumably act by preventing loss of intracellular constituents.

Because of the effect of dilution on sperm all measurements for comparative studies between ejaculates should be made on semen samples that have been adjusted to a common concentration of cells in the same diluent. Much of the variability reported in metabolic activity and fertility levels of sperm results from not taking such precautions.

Changes in Sperm during Senescence

Although slower, changes that sperm undergo during storage are similar to those seen with extreme dilution and "cold shock." Early senescence is marked by swelling and degeneration in the lipoprotein complex which coats sperm, causing chemical and physical changes. There is oxidation of intracellular sulfydryl groups needed for normal motility, leakage of vital enzymes and coenzymes, and disturbance in ionic exchange reactions. After two days' storage of bull semen in egg yolk and citratemilk diluent at 4°C, there is a consistent decrease in the fertilizing capacity of the sperm and an associated increase in prenatal deaths of the developing embryos. It is theorized that changes in the DNA of the sperm are responsible for the increase in prenatal deaths of the developing embryos.

SEMINAL PLASMA

Function of Seminal Plasma

Its volume and composition, are quite variable. Birds ejaculate scant amounts of seminal plasma, and rodents and eats produce an aggregrate of sperm surrounded by only a small volumc of viscous plasma compared to the amount produced by dog or man, in which seminal fluid represents a considerable volume.

Epididymal sperm are capable of fertilizing eggs after artificial insemination. Therefore, the presence of seminal plasma is not essential to the process of reproduction; however, its role as a vehicle during natural mating certainly has physiological significance. Seminal plasma provides a physiological dilution which stimulates both the motility and the metabolism of epididymal sperm. Also, its buffering capacity combats the acidic condition of the vagina, and the presence of pharmacodynamically active substances such as *prostaglandin may* elicit contraction of the smooth muscle of the female genital tract to aid in sperm transport.

Chemical Composition of Seminal Plasma

Extensive studies on the chemical composition of seminal plasma of most laboratory animals have not been conducted because of the difficulty in obtaining experimental materials. The usual method of collection from domestic animals with an artificial vagina is suitable to dogs, rabbits, and most cats, but other species are difficult to train. Forced collection with an electro-ejaculator often yields ejaculates that are rather different from those obtained by artificial vagina. Mann, White and MacLeod, and White have reviewed the literature on the composition of seminal plasma of man and farm animals. There is considerable variation in composition and volume of seminal plasma between species because it is contributed by the accessory glands, which vary from one species to another.

Fructose and lactic acid are the principal metabolic substrates but sorbitol, phospholipids, amino acids and fatty acids may be catabolized to a limited degree. The hydrogen ion concentration of seminal plasma is buffered at about a pH of 7.0 by bicarbonate, citric acid, proteins, and amino acids. Sodium, potassium, calcium, magnesium, and chloride are the major electrolytes of seminal plasma, which is iso-osmotic with blood plasma. However, much of the osmotic activity of seminal plasma is created by organic constituents of low molecular weight, resulting in a low ratio of electrolytes to nonelectrolytes compared to that of blood plasma.

TABLE 2.2. CHEMICAL COMPOSITION OF DOG SEMINAL PLASMA. AVERAGE VALUES GIVEN FOR UNFRACTIONATED EJACULATE AND SEMINAL FRACTIONS IN THE ORDER OF APPEARANCE AT EJACULATION

	Unfractionated Ejaculate	*First Fraction*	*Second Fraction*	*Third Fraction*
Dry weight (percent)	2.5	2.1	3.1	2.5
pH	6.4	6.2	6.3	6.5
Sodium(mEq/1)	114		192.0	172.0
Potassium(mEq/1)	8.1	5.8	12.4	7.5
Calcium(mEq/1)	0.7	1.4	0.4	0.5
Magnesium(mEq/1)	0.7	1.5	0.8	0.3
Chloride(mEq/1)	152.3	—	206.3	160.1
Lactic acid(mg/100 ml)	17.5	9.0	27.2	16.3

There are several unusual and miscellaneous substances present in seminal plasma that are difficult to explain from a functional standpoint. Various lipids, polypeptides, and proteins that are present may help to protect the spermatozoan membrane from the effect of dilution. An "*antiagglutinin*" is present and maintained in the an active reduced state by ascorbic acid and ergothioneine to prevent agglutination of spermatozoa during dilution. A polysaccharide decapacitation factor (D. F.) coats the sperm and prevents them for penetrating the egg unit it is removed by enzymes in, the female reproductive tract. The enzymes of the seminal plasma include proteolytic enzymes, various *phosphates, glycosidases, choline esterase, diamine oxidase,* and *lactic dehydrogenase.* Hormones in semen include epinephrine, norepinephrine, androgens and estrogens. Ascorbic acid, inositol, and riboflavin are among the vitamins present in seminal plasma. A most interesting compound, glycerylphosphorylcholine (GPC), occurs in high concentrations in the seminal plasma of many animals. Sperm cannot use GPC directly from seminal plasma, but a diesterase in the female reproductive tract can break it down and provide glycerol phosphate as an energy source.

Seminal plasma from laboratory species such as the dog, rabbit, guinea pig, and poultry has been investigated in some detail.

Dog

The ejaculate consists of three fractions. The first is a clear watery fluid, devoid of sperm, and probably derived from the urethral mucosa. Its volume is 0.25 to 2.0 ml. The second fraction is "sperm rich," viscous, and whitish in appearance and amounts to 0.5 to 3.5 ml. The third fraction from the prostate gland is watery and varies in volume from 3 to 20 ml. The pH of whole semen ranges from 6.1 to 7.0 with the third fraction having the highest pH values. Dog semen is characteristically low in fructose content by the sperm readily metabolize added fructose and glucose. Sodium and chloride are the principal cation and anion present in dog seminal plasma. There is 5 times more copper and 20 times more zinc in canine seminal plasma than whole blood.

Rabbit

An ejaculate from the rabbit varies from 1 to 6 ml, depending on the volume of the gel plug. The fluid portion usually ranges from 0.5 to 1.5 ml. Fructose, 40 to 400 mg/100 ml, and occasionally glucose are found in the fluid portion along with considerable glycerylphosphorylcholine, 215 to 370 mg/100 ml. Several enzymes have been identified and rabbit sperm resistance to hydrogen peroxide is due to a higher level of catalase in rabbit seminal plasma than in other animals.

Guinea Pig

Collection by electro-ejaculation produces 0.4 to 0.8 ml of semen containing an average fructose concentration of 101 mg/100 ml.

Poultry

The anatomy of the male reproductive tract of birds is quite different from that of mammals and the chemical composition of the semen also differs considerably. The interpretation of information about the semen of fowl is complicated by the possibility that transparent fluid generated by the internal vascular bodies escapes through their surface epithelium to be mixed with seminal plasma during semen collection.

Lake, being careful to exclude transparent fluid, collected seminal plasma having a freezing point depression of 0.593° C. When transparent fluid was present, the freezing point depression was quite large (0.630° C). Cock semen is low in fructose (4 mg/100 ml) and contains 7.7 to 81 mg/100 ml of glucose. The glucose is thought to originate from the cloacal glands rather than the ejaculatory ducts. There is an absence of citric acid and only scant amounts of the ergoth-ioncinc, inositol, phosphorylcholine, and glycerylphosphorylcholine that are found in semen of mammals. Cock seminal plasma has a high nonprotein nitrogen due to free amino acids and creatine. Glutamic acid represents 90 percent of the 15 different free amino acids present. The amino acids probably are very important to maintaining proper osmotic pressure for the spermatozoa.

The pH of cock seminal plasma is 7.0 to 7.2 and the bicarbonate content is 119.6 mg/100 ml. Calcium, chloride, copper, iron, magnesium, potassium, sodium, and zinc are also present. Potassium and magnesium content is several times higher than that in blood plasma.

INFLUENCE OF THE FEMALE REPRODUCTIVE TRACT ON SPERM

The location, in the female reproductive tract, of the deposition site of semen varies between species. Uterine insemination of copious amounts of semen and retention of the penis occur in the dog and pig. The guinea pig, rat, and mouse ejaculate small amounts of gelled semen into the uterus. Vaginal insemination with a gel-plug or slight coagulation of the semen is characteristic of the eat, the rabbit, and primates.

Sperm Transport

Migration of sperm through the female reproductive tract is accomplished mainly by contractions of the uterus and oviduct and partially by motility of the sperm. Passive transport of spermatozoa is much affected by the stage of the estrous cycle. The uterus is most active and sensitive to neuroendocrine stimulus at the time natural mating occurs. It generally takes less than 15 minutes for sperm to reach the site of fertilization in the ampulla of the oviduct in mammals. The release of oxytocin induced by sexual stimulation at mating causes increased tone. and contraction of the uterus. Transport of sperm is greatly reduced during anestrus and diestrus and nil during pseudopr-egnancy or under the influence of progesterone. Tremendous reduction in sperm number occurs as they are transported. Millions of sperm are deposited at ejaculation but only a few hundred reach the ampulla of the oviduct where fertilization occurs. The major barriers are the cervix, the uterotubal junction, and the isthmus of the oviduct, the areas where a significant decrease in lumen size occurs.

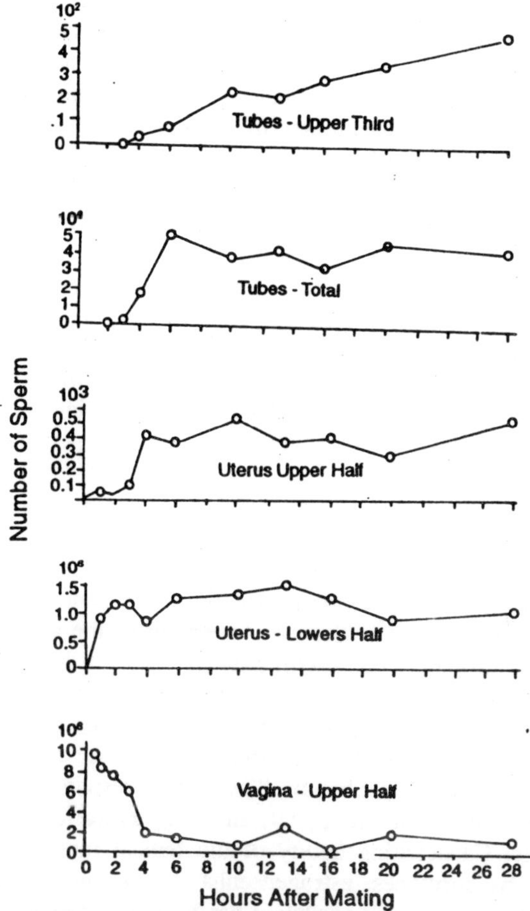

Fig. 2.12. The number of sperm in different segments of the rabbit female genital tract after coitus. Each graph indicates changes in numbers of sperm (note power of 10) with time after mating for various segments of rabbit reproductive tract.

Several other factors appear to be important is sperm transport. Seminal plasma contains prostaglandins which may stimulate uterine motility. Cervical mucus becomes very viscous and impenetrable to spermatozoa under the influence of progesterone. Certain strains of mice have very low fertility due to a genetic problem that develops with certain combinations of alleles at the T-locus. The infertility is caused by the virtual inability of sperm to pass through the uterotubal junction.

Prefertilization Changes of Sperm

In most mammals natural mating occurs during early estrus, several hours before spontaneous ovulation. In the rabbit, cat and ferret, however, ovulation is induced by copulation. In either case, under natural conditions the sperm are deposited in the female and transported to the site of fertilization well ahead of the arrival of the ovum.

Sperm must undergo certain changes while residing in the female reproductive tract in order to obtain the capacity to fertilize the egg, i.e., *capacitation*. Capacitation is known to be necessary in the rat, rabbit, hamster, ferret, and sheep. The time required for capacitation ranges from 1½^{1}h hours in sheep to 6 hours in rabbits but the necessary requirements for capacitation are unknown. The end result of capacitation is to improve the change of establishing contact between the sperm and egg and to enable the sperm to penetrate the zona pellucida.

Many of the physiological requirements for capacitation have recently been defined. There are at least two specific changes in sperm which potentiate the capacitation state. First, removal of the polysaccharide (*decapacitation factor*, D. F., in seminal plasma) from the surface of the sperm. Second, loosening of the aerosome, which releases hyaluronidase for sperm passage through the cumulus and a lipoglycoprotein, which is a lytic agent active on the zona pellucida. There is an increase in respiration and glycolysis of sperm and an activation of the hexose monophosphate shunt and tricarboxylic acid cycle during *in utero* incubation. The factors responsible for capacitation are similar in the rabbit, rat, and dog, indicating universality of the process. Capacitating ability of the female reproductive tract is influenced by hormones: estrogen enhances the process and progesterone inhibits it. Partial capacitation has been achieved in uterine fluid, β-amylase solutions, leukocyte suspensions, and perhaps the bladder and colon. However, the complete complement of factors needed are restricted to the female reproductive tract. They may be species-specific and appear to be found to the membranes of the epithelium of the uterus and oviduct. Because of the need for capacitation in laboratory animals, artificial insemination should be instituted prior to the expected time of ovulation in order to achieve high fertility rates.

Viability of Sperm in Female Reproductive Tract

Duration of fertilizing ability in most laboratory animals is 1 to 2 days but may be as short as 6 to 12 hours in the mouse and rat or as long as 7 to 10 days in the chicken and 135 days in the bat. The factors that influence the survival of mammalian sperm include the anatomy, physiology, pathology, and the immunological response of the female reproductive tract in a given species, the sperm concentration and motility, the endocrine state of the female, and the dilution of seprm by the female tract secretions. The sperm stay motile for a considerably longer period than the one during which they are capable of fertilization. Once they gain the state of capacitation their survival time is shortened. Sperm begin to degenerate and are phagocytized by polymorphonuclear leukocytes in the lumen of the tract within a few days.

Birds are able to retain sperm in glandular regions of the uterovaginal junction and in fundibulum in the "sperm nest" or crypts of the epithelium. The fact that sperm are slowly released for fertilization purposes explains their ability to maintain fertilizing sperm for long periods.

Little is known about the effect of luminal secretions on sperm. A detailed biochemical analysis of reproductive tract secretions has been confined to rabbits and sheep. Bicarbonate in the secretions stimulates respiration and metabolism of spermatozoa. Sperm are stimulated more by secretions from estrous animals. Survival of sperm in *vitro* in the female reproductive tract secrilion in limited to a few hours due to agglutination, which can be delayed by the addition of heated blood serum and reducing agents.arranged in incomplete circular rows.

The prostate consists of three pairs of lobes; ducts of the anterior lobes open near the canal from the seminal vesicles and the ductus deferens and separately from ducts of the other two lobes. The three lobes are closely united and give the appearance of a single structure.

The testes lie in a scrotal pouch and their posterior end and cauda epididymis produce a slight bulge in the perineum. A large fat body covers the anterior end of each testis; it lies along the spermatic cord and projects through a large inguinal canal into the coelom. The testes may be withdrawn into the coelom through this canal at any time.

3

FEMALE SEXUAL ORGANS

The female reproductive organs are the ovaries, oviducts, uterus, vagina, and external genitalia. The internal organs are supported by the broad ligament, including a mesovarium for the ovary, a mesosalpinx for the oviduct, and a mesometrium for the uterus. The development of the reproductive organs is greatly enhanced by estrogens. Ovariectomy, for example, retards their normal growth, whereas estrogens induce rapid growth of the oviduct, uterus, and vagina in immature or ovariectomized animals. Such growth involves increases in cell division and protein synthesis.

The following discussion deals with the embryology, comparative anatomy, histology, physiology, and biochemistry of the female reproductive tract in laboratory mammals.

EMBRYOLOGY

The rudimentary reproductive system of the mammal consists of 2 sexually undifferentiated gonads, 2 pairs of ducts, a urogenital sinus, a genital tuberele, and vestibular folds. It arises primarily from 2 germinal ridges on the dorsal side of the abdominal cavity and can potentially differentiate into a male or female system (this is referred to as *embryonic bisexuality*).

The sex of an animal depends on 3 distinct but related things:

(a) inherited genes, (b) gonadogenesis, and (c) the formation and maturation of accessory reproductive organs. The sex of an embryo is basically determined by its genes, but the expression of the genetic sex is a developmental process depending on the function of the fetal gonads, and occasionally, the adrenal cortex.

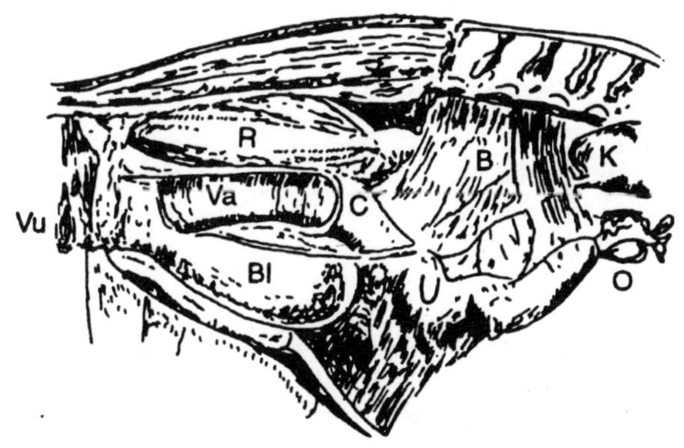

Fig 3.1. The arrangement of the reproductive organs of female mammals within the pelvic cavity: B = broad ligament; Bl = bladder; K = kidney; 0 = ovary; R = rectum; U = uterus; Va = vagina; Vu vulva.

Estrogen and androgen cause sex reversal in male and female embryos, respectively, during a brief period early in sexual differentiation. In contrast, the accessory reproductively organs remain sexually labile for a much longer time and hormone treatment late in development can induce considerable reversal. The age at which this libosual potential is completely lost various with the species.

Gonads

The gonads form from a group of large granulated yolk sac cells which invade the germinal ridges. Two invasions occur in the female. The initial one is abortive, but the second results in the formation of sex cords which later break up into primordial germ cells (oogonia). The sex cords of the female are called *medullary cords;* those of the male are the *seminiferous tubules.*

The testis develops predominantly from the medulla of the sexually undifferentiated gonad, whereas the ovary arises primarily from its cortex. The primordial germ cells congregate in the developing gonad and proliferate the oogonia of the female. They and the secondary sex cords which are forming concurrently move into the cortex while the primary sex cords and the medulla regress in size.

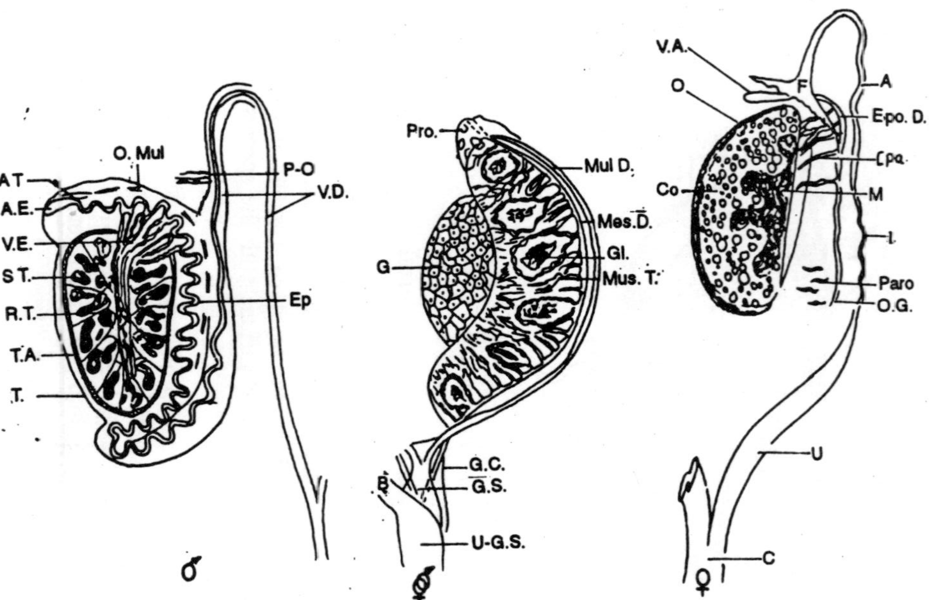

Fig. 3.2. Diagram representing embryonic differentiation of male and female systems. Center: *the undifferentiated system with its large mesonephros, mesonephric duct, Millerianc duct, and undifferentiated gonad. Note that the Mullerian and mesonephric ducts cross before they enter the genital cord.* Right: *the female system, in which the ovary and Mullerian ducts differentiate while the remnants of the mesonephros and mesonephric ducts atrophy into the epoophoron, paroophoron, and Gartner's duct.* Left: *the male system in which the testes and mesonephric (Wolffian) ducts .differentiate; the sole remnants of the Mullerian ducts are the testicular appendix and the prostatic utricle (vagina masculinus).*

Table 3.1. Summary of Female Reproductive Anatomy in Laboratory Mammals

Organ	*Main Anatomical Types*	*Species*
Ovarian bursa	Infundibulum funnel-shaped and lies close to ovary forming an open ovarian bursa	Rabbit, primates
	Infundibulum and ovary enclosed by a fold of mesosalpinx which forms a periovarial sac	Rat, mouse
Fimbriae	Extensively developed fimbriae enclose the ovarian surface	Rabbit, cat
	Fimbriae moderately developed	Primates
	Poorly developed fimbriae make very limited contact with ovarian surface	Rat, mouse
Uterotubal junction	Very complex; glandular mucosal lip; projecting papilla	Guinea pig
	Rosetter type projections; no intramural portion	Rabbit
	Single papilla; short intramural portion of oviduct	Rat
	Singe mound; short intramural portion of oviduct	Dog
	Simple fold which projects into a pocket in uterine	Mink wall; no mound
	No projections; extended intramural portion	Primates
Uterus, cervix and vagina	Two uteri; two cervices; two vaginas	Opossum, kangaroo
	Two uteri; two cervices; one vagina	Rabbit, rat (Norwegian), chinchilla
	Two well developed horns, small uterine body; one cervix; one vagina	Cat, dog
	One uterine body without compartments; one cervix; one vagina	Primates

Reproductive Ducts

Wolffian and Mullerian ducts are both present in the sexually undifferentiated embryo. In the female, the Mullerian ducts develop into a gonaduct system and the Wolffian ducts atrophy. The opposite is true for the male. The female Mullerian ducts fuse caudally to form a uterus a cervix and the anterior part of a vagina. The oviduct becomes coiled and acquires differentiated epithelia and fimbriae just before birth. Signs of epithelial differentiation include increased mucosal height, pseudostratification, the presence of peg cens, and evidence of secretory activity. The onset of these developmental events varies with the species.

In the male fetus, testicular androgen plays a role in the persistence and development of the Wolffian ducts and the atrophy of the Mullerian ducts. However, the growth of the female Mullerian ducts beyond the ambisexual stage is apparently hormonally independent and the duct is capable of considerable autonomous growth, coiling, and epithelial differentiation. Adrenal hormones are thought to stimulate oviductal growth in the guinea pig.

Urogenital Sinus

The urogenital sinus gives rise to the vestibule. The folds of skin which border the sinus form the lips of the vulva. The female phallus or clitoris, homologous to the male penis, grows little in size.

TABLE 3.2. SOME ANATOMICAL CHARACTERISTICS OF THE FEMALE REPRODUCTIVE ORGANS IN LABORATORY MAMMALS

Species	*Some Analomical Characteristics*	*Number of Mammary Glands*
1	2	3
Cat	Ovary is ovoid and lies with a peritoneal fold Cervix is remarkably short; lacks true internal os, and is directly continuous with dorsal wall of vagina; external os is V-shaped	8 (all or some may function at one time)
Chinchilla	Mesosalpinx tends to enclose ovary Accessory corpora lutea during pregnancyVaginal closure membrane	6 (2 inguinal and 4 lateral thoracic)
Dog	Ovary is flattened and completely enclosed in a roomy peritoneal pouch Slender uterine horns are long and straight	10 (arranged in two ventrolateral

Species	*Some Analomical Characteristics*	*Number of Mammary Glands*
1	2	3
	Cervix is a short thick-walled segment Vagina is wider above (cranially) than below	series)
Guinea pig	Two internal cervical openings, but only one common external os Intestinal and urinary tracts open into a groove (the *"fossa anovaginoure-thralis")* Lower end of the vagina is closed by an epithelial membrane, but opens periodically at estrus and during parturition	2 (inguinal)
Hamster	Ovary is compact and encapsulated; oviducts and uterus similar to those of the mouse Two cervical canals remain separate for about two-thirds of the length of the cervix, but then fuse Vagina has a mucified type of epithelium; its wall contains urethral glands similar to those in the female prostate	12 or 14 (thoracic and abdonimal)
Mink	Ovary has abundant interstitial tissue; fimbriae onlyslightly developedUterine glands are sparseExternal os of the cervix is a transverse uterine slit. Vagina is long and has a transverse fold across itsdorsal wall	6 or 8 (thoracic and abdonimal)
Monkey	Uterus is divided into an upper segment, consisting of the body and fundus, and a lower segment formed by the thick-walled cervix; the fundus is irregularly pear-shaped and has a shallow depression Sexual skin does not usually swell, but undergoes variations in color which are not always clearly related to the menstrual cycle	2 (poorly developed) unless pregnant; supernumerary nipples sometimes present below normal nipples)
Mouse	Ovaries lie just below (ventral) the kidneys within transparent ovarian capsules A narrow, tunnel-like passage connects the periovarial space with the peritoneal cavity	10 (6 thoracic and 4 abdomino-ingenial)
Rabbit	Complete duplication of the uterine segment; two	8

Species	*Some Analomical Characteristics*	*Number of Mammary Glands*
1	2	3
	long uterine horns and two entirely separate cervical canals, each of which has an internal and external os; endometrium arranged in numerous transverse and longitudinal folds which are particularly prominent along the mesometrial borders; cervical canals have a narrower lumen and a more extensively folded mucous membrane than the uterine horns Vaginal portions of the cervical segments are surrounded by a complete ring of fornices	(arranged in ventrolateral series)
Rat	Ovary lies within ovarian bursa Periovarial space opens into the peritoneal cavity through a slit on the antimesometrial side of the bursa at the tip of each uterine horn	12 (two ventrolateral) series along thoracic and inguinal regions)

TABLE 3.3. DEVELOPMENTAL FATE OF THE SEXUAL RUDIMENTS IN THE MALE AND FEMALE MAMMALIAN FETUS

Sexual Rudiment	*Male*	*Female*
Gonad		
cortex	Regresses	Ovary
Medulla	Testis	Regresses
Mullerian ducts	Vestiges parts of vagina	Uterus, oviducts
Wolffian ducts	Epididymis, vas deferens	Vestiges
Urogenital sinus	Urethra, prostate	Part of vagina, urethra
	Bulbourethral glands	
Genital tubercle (phallus)	Penis	Clitoris
Vestibular folds	Scrotum	Labia

OVARY

The ovaries are paired organs suspended from the body wall by *a mesovarium.* Unlike the testes, they remain in the abdominal cavity.

They are both endocrine (estrogenprogesterone, and androgen-secreting) and exocrine (egg-producing) glands.

The rabbit ovary is located in an open ovarian bursa, whereas that of the rat, mouse, and gerbil lies in a closed capsule called the *periovarial sac*. If the latter ruptures, at least in the rat, the reproductive capability is reduced because the eggs can then escape into the body cavity at ovulation.

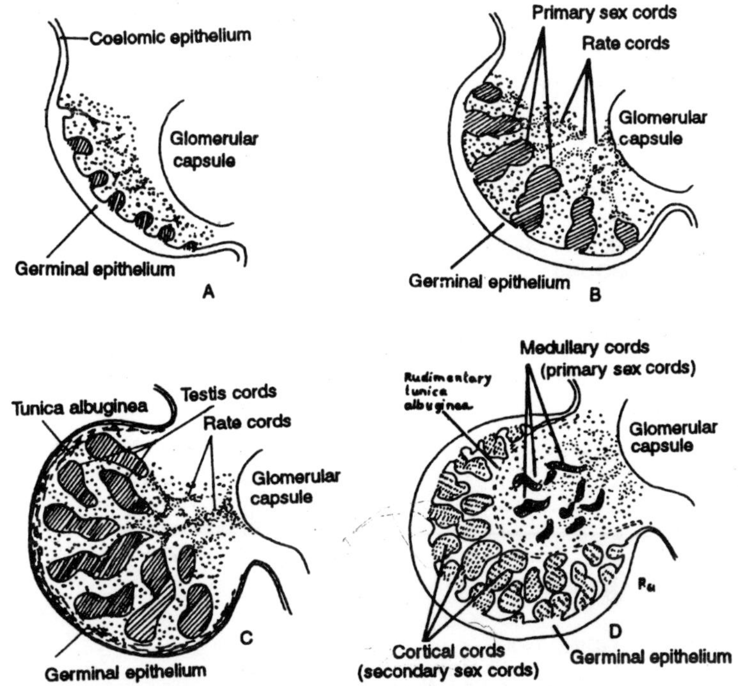

Fig. 3.3. Differentiation of the undifferentiated gonad of higher vertebrates into testis and ovary. A, The primary sex cords arise from the g terminal epithelium. B, Primary sex cords have developed, but the gonad is still undifferentiated. C, Differentiation of the testis is taking place: the primary sex cords continue to proliferate, while the germinal epithelium diminishes in size; the tunica albuginea also develops. D, Differentiation into an ovary involves development of secondary sex cords from the cortex and reduction of the primary sex cords and tunica albuginea.

The ovary is enveloped in *a germinal epithelium,* usually a single layer of cuboidal or low columnar cells. It contains *a medulla* and *cortex*. The medulla consists of fibroelastic connective tissue and an extensive network of- nerves and spiral blood vessels which enter the ovary at the *hilus*. It also houses large polyhedral interstital cells which are more prominent in the ovaries of rodents and carnivores than in those of primates and ungulates. The cortex contains immature, developing, and graafian follicles, atretic follicles and corpora lutea. It is the site of both egg and hormone production. It also contain fibroblasts, collagen, and reticular fibers, blood vessels, lymphatics, nerves, and smootl muscle cells. The connective tissue cells and fibers which form the tunica *albuginea nea* the surface of the ovary (just below the germinal epithelium) are arranged somewhi more compactly and regularly than those in the interior.

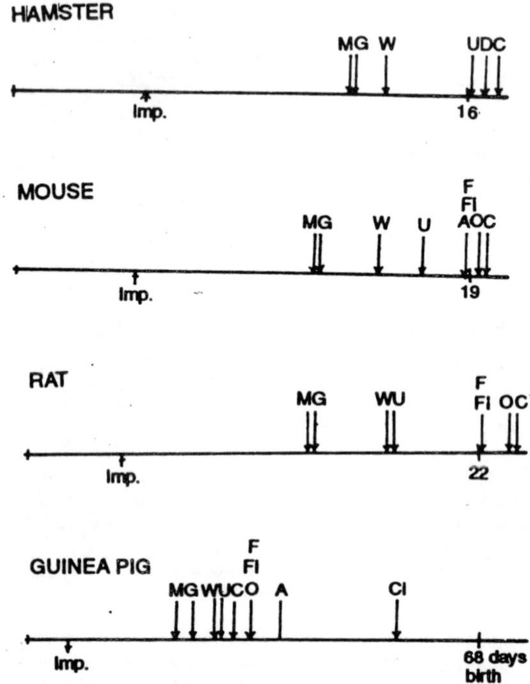

Fig. 3.4. Comparative sequence of developmental stages in the female reproductive tract of different laboratory mammals. Arrows mark the beginning of such important events as implantation (imp.), Mullerian duct development (M), gonadal sex differentiation (G), formation of the uterovaginal canal (U), and Wolffian duct degeneration (W), as well as the beginning of the following events in oviductal differentiation: demarcation from uterus (0), coiling (C), the formation of epithelial folds (F), and fimbriae (Fi), ampulla differentiation (A), and ciliogenesis (Ci).

Development of Ovarian Follicles

The germinal epithelium of the female lies on the surface of the ovary. Its stage development at birth is still a matter of controversy:

the consensus is that all oogon become primary follicles during late fetal and early neonatal life.

To reach maturity, these follicles then pass through successive developmental stages: from primary to secondary, to growing (tertiary), and finally to mature (graafian) follicles. The primary follicle consists of a "potential egg" or *oogonium* encompassed by a single layer of small follicular cells. Large "nests" of these follicles aggregate under the tunica albuginea.

In secondary follicles, near the center of the cortex, proliferating follicular cells have formed a multicellular layer around the vitellus and a membrane, the *zona pellucida,* has developed between the oogonium and the follicular cells.

The growing or tertiary follicle arises when the cells of the follicular layer separate to form clefts and an *antrum* (cavity) into which the oogonium will eventually protrude. The antrum is lined by many layer of follicular cells, collectively forming the *membrana granulosa,* and filled with the *liquor folliculi,* a protein and estrogen rich fluid.

Because of its size, the mature or graafian follicle protrudes from the ovarian surface like a "blister." Two layers of stromal cells condense around the membrane granulosa in the cortex to form an additional coat, the *theca folliculi,* which can be subdivided into an inner vascular *theca interna* and a peripheral fibrous *theca externa.* Estrogens are probably secreted by cells of the theca interna directly into the antrum through a basement membrane, the *membrana propria,* which separates the theca interna from. the membrana granulosa.

The egg-containing follicle reaches its maximal size just before ovulation. A watery follicular fluid is released at this time and the thecal blood vessels which enclose the follicle collapse.

The number of graafian follicles which develop per estrous cycle depends on hereditary and environmental factors. In most primates, 1 or 2 eggs are released at each ovulation. In rodents, 4 to 14 egg are released at ovulation. Polyovular follicles occur in a number of species, however. They are especially frequent in the opossum *(Didelphis virginiana)* and the striped skunk *(Mephitis mephitis)*. If 1 ovary is removed, the remaining one undergoes compensatory hypertrophy.

Hormonal Control of Follicular Development

Pituitar gonadotropins regulate both the rate at which ovarian follicles develop and the number which mature per estrous cycle. If

Table 3.4. Comparison of Prepubertal Ovarian Development in Some Laboratory Mammals

	Guinea Pig	*Hamster*	*Mouse*	*Rabbit*	*Rat*
Early postnatal neogenesis	No 23	Yes 86	No 25	Yes	No
Initiation of interstital development (age in days)	Secondary: 21	Primary: 18 Secondary: 28 +	Primary: 11 Secondary: 23	Primary: 60 Secondary: 86	Primary: 11 Secondary: 25
First appearance of antral follicels (age in days)	21-60	26	14	64-70	12
Earliest induced ovulation or follicular stimulation (age in days)	65-105	27	14	65-105	18
Earliest spontaneous ovulation (age in days)	139	30	35	139	38-71

hemicastrated mice are treated with small doses of PMSG, they produce nearly twice as many mature ova as control animals. One would expect this ovulatory compensation because the single ovary is exposed to twice the normal amounts of FSH. However, the dose-response line is steeper for normal females than for hemicastrated ones and at high PMSH doses, the single ovary sheds no more eggs than does each ovary of the control female.

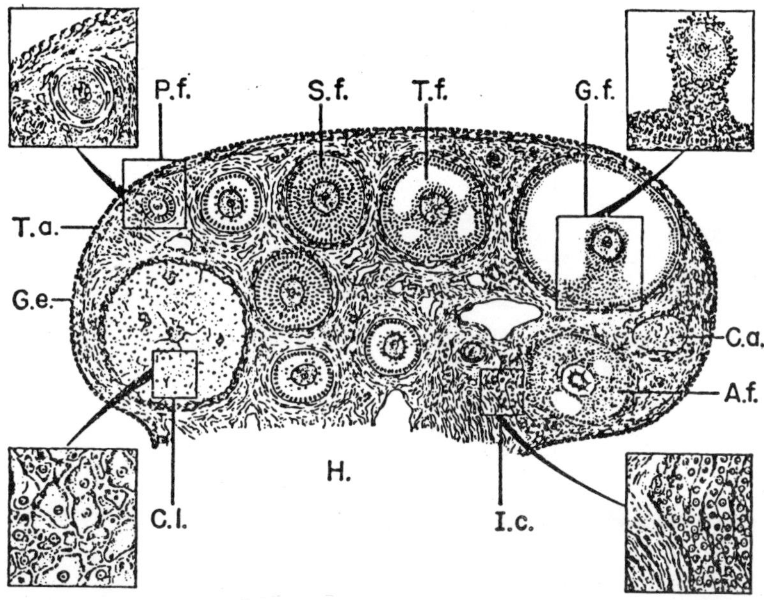

Fig. 3.5. A composite diagram of the mammalian ovary. Progressive stages in the differentiation of a graafian follicle are indicated (upper left to upper right). The mature follicle may become atretic (lower right) or develop into a corpus luteum after ovulation (lower left). A.f. = atretic follicle; C.a. = corpus albicans; C.I. = corpus luteum; G.e = germinal epithelium; G.f. = graafian follicle; H = hilus; I.c. = interstitial cells; P.f. = primary follicle; S.f. = secondary follicle. T.a. = tunica albuginea; T.f. _ tertiary follicle.

Many follicles grow during the first stages of the estrous cycle, but few mature completely. Perhaps less FSH is required to initiate the growth of small follicles than to maintain larger follicles and bring them to ovulatory size, since the number of follicles which mature can be greatly increased (superovulation) by injecting animals with large doses of gonadotropins. Why then do *so* many follicles begin to grow? They may supply substances, like estrogen, which are essential for the ovulation of other larger follicles.

Formation of Eggs

The consecutive stages of egg development are (1) the proliferation of the oogoruum; (2) the growth and maturation of the oocyte; (3) the formation of the ovarian follicle containing the mature egg; and (4) the release of the egg (ovulation). These processes occur cyclically in nonpregnant animals during the sexual season.

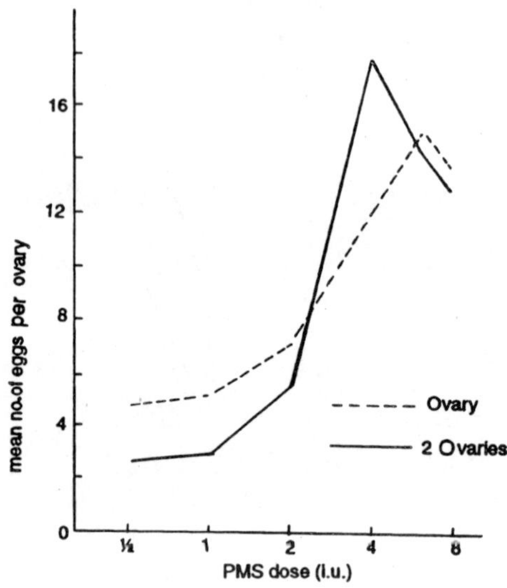

Fig. 3.6. Induced ovulation in unilaterally ovariectomized and normal female mice, 26 days old when injected with HCG. Note the compensatory effect in the ovariectomized animals.

Proliferation of the Oogonium

The precursor cells of female gametes, called gonocytes, probably originate outside the gonad from extra-embryonic endoderm and then migrate into the embryonic ovary to differentiate into oogonia. Oogonia proliferate before or shortly after birth. In the rabbit and hamster, oogenesis continues into the postnatal period, whereas the oogonial divisions of the rat and mouse are completed several days before birth. In the guinea pig, neo-oogenesis ends when the animal is about 50 days of age. Hence, most, if not all, definitive ova are formed by birth, and de novo oocytogenesis does not generally occur in postnatal life.

Growth of the Oocyte

The growth of the oocyte is characterized by (a) the accumulation of yolk in the cytoplasm, (b) the development of a zona pellucida, and (c) the mitotic proliferation of the fgllicular epithelium and adjacent tissue. Initially, the ovum and ovarian follicle grow explosively. Later, when the antrum forms, the oocyte does not enlarge further, but the ovarian follicle, responding to pituitary hormones, continues to do so very rapidly.

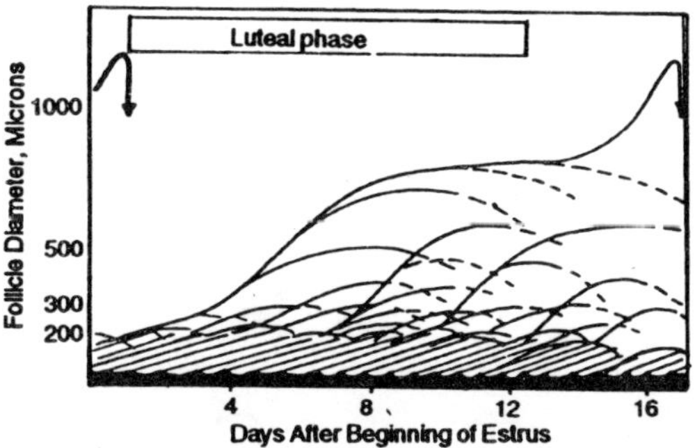

Fig. 3.7. A schematic representation of the follicular cycle in the guinea pig. The heavy solid line indicates the average diameter of the largest follicles. Ovulation occurs at the arrow. The other solid and broken lines represent the concomitant growth and atresia, respectively, of other groups of follicles that do not normally ovulate.

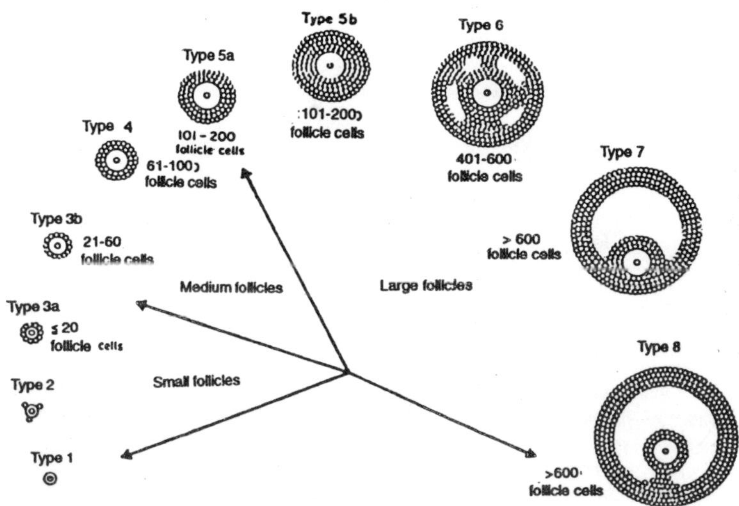

Fig. 3.8. Proposed classification of oocytes and follicles in the mouse ovary: the small oocyte has a diameter of less than 20 p; the growing oocyte has a diameter of 20-70 p; the large mature oocyte (follicle) has a diameter of 70 p.

Maturation of the Oocyte

The oocyte matures during the second phase of follicular growth. The nucleus, which entered the prophase of the first meiotic division during the first phase of growth, now undergoes a meiotic or reduction division. Nucleoli and nuclear membranes disappear and the chromosomes condense. The *centrosome* divides into *2 centrioles* which move to the opposite poles of the cell. *Spindle fibers* appear joining the centrioles with the chromosomes. Diploid pairs of the latter move to the center of the cell and arrange themselves in one plane, the *equatorial plate* of the spindle (metaphase 1). They then separate, one member of each pair going to each pole of the cell. A membrane forms at the equatorial plate and divides the original cell into 2 daughter cells.

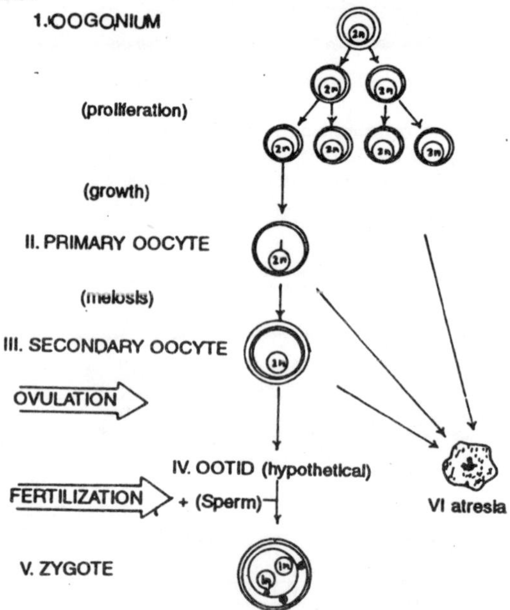

Fig. 3.9. Nuclear changes during oogenesis. Somatic cells contain the diploid (2n) number of chromosomes, whereas gametes contain the diploid or haploid (en) number, depending upon the stage of oogenesis. I. Proliferation of oogonia during prenatal life. II. Transformation of oogonia into primary oocytes; only a few oogonia grow at a time; (t = tetrad formation.) III. The first maturation division gives rise to the secondary oocyte and the first polar body. IV. The formation of an ootid and extrusion of the second polar body without fertilization is a hypothetical stage. V. The completion of the second maturation division with extrusion of a second polar body occurs after fertilization. The pronucleus of the female and the male form in the zygote. VI. Atresia of the oocyte may occur at any stage of oogenesis.

The primary oocyte undergoes 2 such meiotic divisions. The 2 daughter cells which arise from the first division contain one half (n) of the chromosome complement (2n) of the parent cell. Unlike the meiotic division process which occurs in spermatogenesis, 1 of the daughter oocytes acquires almost all of the cytoplasm and is called the *secondary oocyte;* the other, much smaller cell becomes the *first polar body*. During the second maturation division, the secondary oocyte divides into an *ootid* (with n number of chromosomes) and *a second polar body* (also with n number of chromosomes). The polar bodies are extruded into the perivitelline space and degenerate.

The time at which the 2 reduction divisions occur is not necessarily coincident with ovulation. The oocyte is usually in the pachytene or diplotene stage of prophase I during diestrus. It may undergo the first meiotic division shortly before ovulation, but does not complete the second one until or unless fertilization takes place. In the dog and fox, the first polar body is not extruded from the ovum until several days after the egg has been shed. The tenrees of Madagascar (insectivorous mammals) are exceptional in that sperm apparently enter the ovarian follicles and penetrate the eggs, which are consequently ovulated in the pronuclear stage of development.

Ovulation

Within the graafian follicle, the eggs is embedded in a mass of follicular cells, the cumulus *oophorus,* which protrudes into the fluid-filled antrum. The cumulus oophorus is usually situated on the side of the follicle opposite that which will rupture during ovulation. When the theca externa ruptures at ovulation the inner layers of the follicle protrude through the gap to form the *stigma* (papilla).

Many views have been advanced to explain how the follicle ruptures, but the precise mechanism is still unknown. It may be facilitated by the contraction of the smooth muscle fibers which enclose the follicle, but apparently does not depend on the follicle size or the internal pressure of the liquor folliculi.

Atresia and Degeneration

There are 60,000 to 100,000 oocytes in both ovaries at birth, depending on the species are breed. Few will mature into graafian follicles; many begin to develop, but then degenerate. Consequently, every normal ovary contains some degenerating oocytes in follicles that fail to rupture (atretic follicles). Atresia is not abnormal unless an ovary contains large numbers of degenerating follicles. It is especially marked during pregnancy and lactation. The degenerating oocyte characteristically hyalinizes and fragments; its zona pellucida thickens. It is phagocytized by ovarian fibrocytes and replaced by connective or scar tissue.

Corpus Luteum Formation

Immediately after ovulation, the follicular cavity fills with blood and lymph and is aptly called the *corpus hemorrhagicum.* Its membrana granulosa plicates and proliferates cords of hypertrophic granulosa cells which bridge the cavity. Cells and blood vessels of the theca interna then invade this mass, forming *a corpus luteum* with columns of lutein cells interlaced with blood vessels and connective tissue. Its shape and color vary with the species and the reproductive cycle. It grows very rapidly for slightly longer than half of the estrons cycle. If fertilization does not occur, it then regresses and is replaced by connective tissue an is consequently called the *corpus albicans.* After 2 or 3 estrous cycles, a barely visible scar is all that remains of it.

The mammalian corpus luteum is a short-lived endocrine gland which synthesizes and releases progesterone. No one has yet determined how the luteal phase of ovarian activity, i.e., the endocrine activity of the corpora lutea is regulated. The nongravid uterus is apparently involved, since hysterectomy prolongs the life of the corpus luteum in rodents such as guinea pigs or pregnant or pseudopregnant rats, and in ungulates. It does not, however, affect the corpora lutea of the unmated rat. In the rabbit, a reflex ovulator, the effect of hysterectomy upon the corpora lutea depends upon the time when it is done. There is some evidence that LH and the uterus dually control the luteal phase of the estrous cycle.

If pregnancy occurs, the corpus luteum remains functional and is known as the *corpus luteum verum;* it may be larger than the *corpus luteum spurium* (false yellow body) of the estrous cycle. In the chinchilla, corpora lute persist throughout gestation and many accessory ones are also present. The latter probably arise from follicular luteinization at about 50 and 90 days of gestation and are indistinguishable histologically from the corpora lutea of ovulation.

THE OVIDUCT

The oviduct holds a strategic position in the reproductive process. Its luminal fluids provide the environment in which capacitation of sperm, fertilization, and early embryonic development occur. Its ciliary activity and coordinated muscular contractions regulate the rate at which sperm move to the fertilization site and eggs to the uterus.

The oviduct can be subdivided into the infundibulum with its fimbriae, the ampulla, the isthmus, and the uterotubal junction. Its length, degree of coiling, and anatomical relationships with the ovary and adjacent ligaments vary among mammals. In the mouse, for example, the oviduct is coiled into some 10 loops, whereas in the rabbit it has fewer coils and a visibly distinct border zone between the ampulla and isthmus.

Ligaments

One side of the oviduct is bound to the *mesosalpinx,* a peritoneal fold derived from the lateral layer of the broad ligament. The other is attached to the *mesotubariuni superius,* a thin muscular membrane tying it to the medial edge of the fimbriae. At ovulation, the mesotubarium contracts vigorously and rhythmically so that the fimbriae slide over the surface of the ovary. Independent and intermittent contractions of the mesosalpinx are less vigorous, but also change the contour and position of the oviduct. The mesovarium also contracts, causing longitudinal rotations of the ovary and changing its position with respect to the fimbriae.

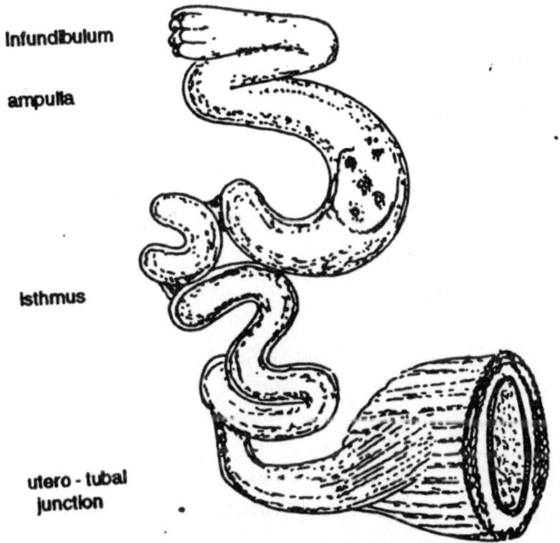

Fig. 3.10. Oviduct of the mouse. Note that the undeveloped fimbriae are usually located in the periovarial sac.

Considerable specific variation exists in the anatomical and histological characteristics of the supporting ligaments. In some species at least, the ligaments are particularly well developed and seem to have major physiological significance in moving, flexing, and closing the uterotubal junction.

Ovarian Bursa

The ovary and oviduct are closely associated with each other anatomically. In Lagomorpha, for example, the ovary lies in an open pouchlike *ovarian bursa* consisting of a think peritoneal fold of the mesosalpinx which is attached to the upper oviduct. In Mustelidae and Muridae, the ovary lies in a closed fluid-filled *periovarial sac* into which the eggs are shed. Large numbers of sperm reach the ovarian bursa of the rat, ferret, and bat.

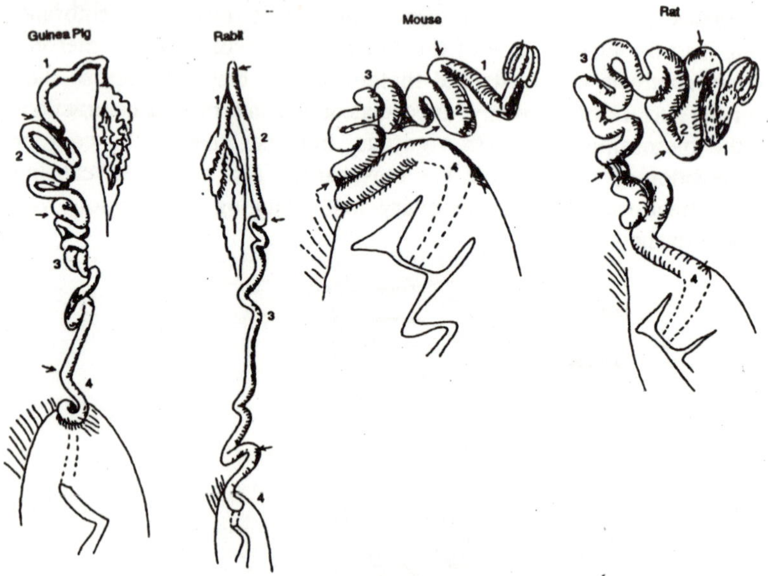

Fig. 3.11. Comparative anatomy of the oviduct in several mammalian species. 1 = preampulla; 2 ampulla; 3 = isthmus; 4 = uterotubal junction.

Fimbriae and Infundibulum

The end of the oviduct adjacent to the ovary is expanded into a funnel-like structure called the *infundibulum,* whose size varies with species and age. The opening of the infundibulum *(ostium abdominal) is* in the center of a fringe of irregular processes, the *fimbriae.* Animals with a well developed ovarian bursa (mink, mice, rats, and dogs) have poorly developed fimbriae, whereas animals with only slightly developed ovarian bursae (rabbits, primates, and ungulates) have well developed fimbriae. These anatomical arrangements assure close association of the oviduct with the ovarian surface.

Specific variation also occurs in the anatomy of the fimbriae and infundibulum and their relationship with the ovary. In the rat and mouse, for example, the infundibulum occupies only a small area of the periovarial sac. Its fimbriae make very limited contact with the surface of the ovary. On the other hand, the expansive fimbriae of the guinea pig and rabbit almost completely enclose the ovary during ovulation. The anatomical association of fimbriae and ovary in primates is intermediate to these 2 extremes.

The appearance and contractability of the fimbriae also vary with the stage of sexual cycle. In the rabbit, for example, the fimbriae appear shrunken and cover only part of the ovarian surface until ovulation, when they expand into a bursa which enclose the entire ovary. The fimbriae of the rat are narrow during diestrus, but more expansive and vigorously active during estrus.

The fimbriae contain erectile tissue, a network of smooth muscle fibers and several large blood vessels, especially veins, which become engorged with blood at ovulation The fimbrial surfaces are also covered by innumerable cilia which beat actively in the direction of the oviductal ostium. The vigorous peristaltic activity of the oviduct nol only assumes that the ciliated fimbriae contact all surfaces of the ovary, but also create, a negative pressure which, together with the directional beat of the fimbrial cilia, vacuum the egg into the ostium.

Ampulla and Isthmus

The *ampulla,* which accounts for about half of the length of the oviduct, merges with a constricted segment of the oviduct called the *isthmus*. The significance of the ampullary-isthmic junction is not fully understood. The isthmus has a narrower lumen, fewer mucosal folds and ciliated cells, and a thicker muscularis than the ampulla. It is adrenergically innervated and apparently acts as a sphincter in several species (rabbit, cat, dog, rat, and man).

Mucosa and Submucosa

The tunica mucosa lines large primary and small secondary folds of the oviductal wall. The latter are particularly complex in the ampulla. The mucosa consists of epithelial cells. The underlying submucosa of smooth muscle fibers and connective tissue are permeated by fine blood and lymph vessels. The epithelium contains ciliated and nonciliated cells, together with "peg cells" (Stiftzellen or intercalary cells) which are presumably depleted secretory cells. At the ovarian end of the oviduct, the wall is lined mostly with ciliated columnar cells; such cells are less common at the uterine end of the oviduct.

Epithelial folding is almost nonexistent in the mouse and rat, but extensive in the rabbit and primates. The number of ciliated cells in the mucosa also varies: they are rare in the oviducts of the mouse and rat, found in small numbers in the guinea pig, and relatively numerous in the rabbit and primates.

Ciliated Cells. The ciliated cells of the oviductal mucosa have slender motile cilia *(kinocilia)* that extend into the lumen. In the rhesus monkey, cilia are 5 to 6 in length and 0.2 to 0.3in diameter. Those of the rabbit beat some 1200 times each minute. The frequency of the beat increases by 25 percent after ovulation and facilitates the movement of the egg toward the uterus. Their primary function is probably to keep the canal free of choking debris, as is true of cilia in the respiratory tract. Their activity, coupled with oviductal contractions, keeps oviductal eggs in the constant motion which is essential for bringing egg and sperm together (fertilization) and preventing oviductal implantation.

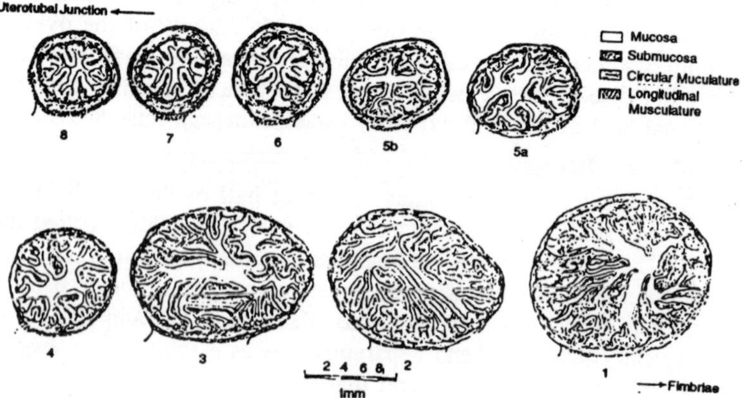

Fig. 3.12. Representative sections of the oviduct of the rabbit. Note differences in diameter, wall thickness, lumen size, and mucosal folding. These differences are particularly striking at segment 5, where the ampulla anmd isthmus meet. 5a and 5b represent the cranial and caudal ends of segment 5, respectively. Teh ampullary isthmic junction lies somewhere between segments 5 and 6. Its narrow lumen retains eggs for 2 days after ovulation.

Ciliation of the oviduct is hormonally controlled in primates. Cilia disappear almost completely after hypophysectomy and develop in response to exogenous estrogens. Progesterone, on the other hand, antagonizes the estrogen-driven growth of cilia.

Secretory Cells and Fluid

The secretory cells of the oviductal mucosa are nonciliated and characteristically contain secretory granules whose size and number very widely among species and during different phases of the estrous cycle. They are, for example, large and numerous in the rabbit, but small and sparse in primates. In general, they become increasingly abundant as one moves from the infundibulum toward the isthmus; this is also true of the nonciliated cells which produce them. Like cilia, the presence and number of secretory granules depend on ovarian activity. Ovariectomy causes them to disappear in all regions of the oviduct except the isthmus. They reappear if the animal is subsequently treated with estrogen.

The metabolic activity of the epithelium of the oviduct appears to be most pronounced in the vicnity of the egg. In the rabbit, for example, the uptake the radioactive sulfate is always highest in the segment which contains the egg as it passes along toward the uterus.

By means of extra- and intra-abdominal devices which are used to cannulate the oviduct and collect its fluids, it has been possible to show that ovarian hormones also regulate the secretory activity of the epithelium of the oviduct. The latter exhibit predictable variation during the estrous cycle: secretory fluid volume is low during the luteal phase, increases at the onsets of estrus, reaches a maximum 1 day later, and then declines again. The secretions are composed predominantly of mucoproteins and mucopolysaccharides.

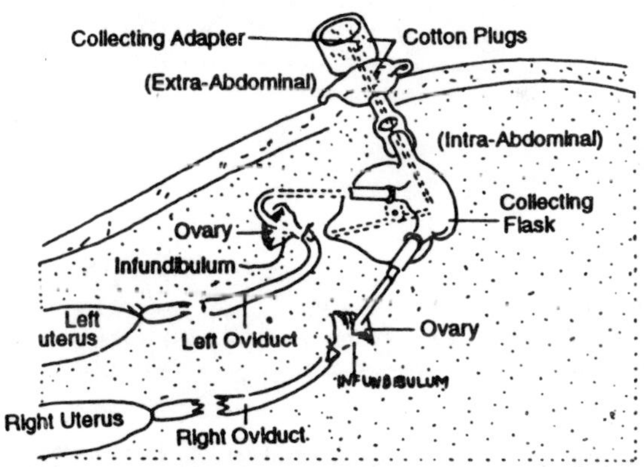

Fig. 3.13. Diagram of an installed intra-abdominal flask for collecting oviductal fluid.

Cyclical Changes

During the sexual cycle, there are cyclical changes in the size of the epithelial cells, the activity of secretory cells, the number and activity of cilia, and the size of subepithelial capillaries. The width of the oviductal lumen also varies and is related to contractions of the wall muscle and the fluid content of the wall and the lumen. In the mouse and rat, for example, oviductal loops which contain eggs are distended with fluid, whereas neighboring empty loops are smaller and have occluded lumina.

Muscularis and Serosa

The tunica muscularis consists of an inner circular layer and an outer longitudinal layer of smooth (unstriated) muscle. Muscle also extends from these layers into the connective tissue of the mucosal folds, permitting coordinated contractions of the entire wall. The thickness of the musculature increases as one advances from the

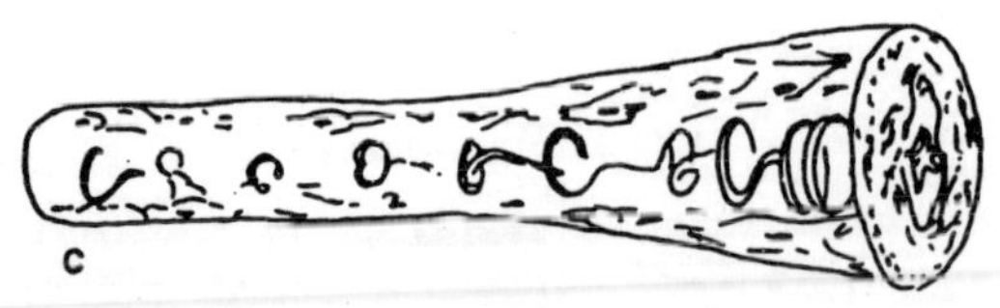

Fig. 3.14. The musculature in the oviduct of ungulates. A, Ampulla; the musculature consists of spiralling circular fibers. B, Isthmus: note differences in the morphology of muscle fibers. C, Uterotubal junction: note the longitudinal muscle coat of uterine origin, as well as the peritoneal fibers.

ovarian to the uterine end of the oviduct. In the mouse and rat, the isthmus contains the typical outer longitudinal and inner circular layers of muscle; however, in the guinea pig the outer layer is circular and the inner one longitudinal. The serosa consists of connective tissue and is enveloped externally by the same mesothelial coat which lines other visceral organs and the peritoneal cavity.

Contractions of the Oviduct

The contractile activities of the oviduct are independent of those which occur in the uterus. They appear to occur in specific peristaltic and antiperistaltic patterns which propel the egg at a definite rate and in a defined rotational manner. The latter is reflected in the remarkably uniform mucinous coats of rabbit ova.

In part, these patterns of contraction arise because of the architecture of the oviduct. The ampulla, for example, has a wide lumen surrounded by a wall with a think layer of circular muscle and a mucous membrane with highly branched folds. The folds are laced with numerous capillaries and muscle fibers (erectile tissue). The circular muscle occurs in spiral sheets of different shapes and sizes which contract in a segmented sequential fashion. In areas where the muscle has relaxed, the wall becomes engorged with blood and may expand to twice its normal size. Transport of an ovum through the ampulla depends mainly on the rate and amplitude of these segmenting contractions, which originate in the infundibulum and pass progressively toward the isthmus.

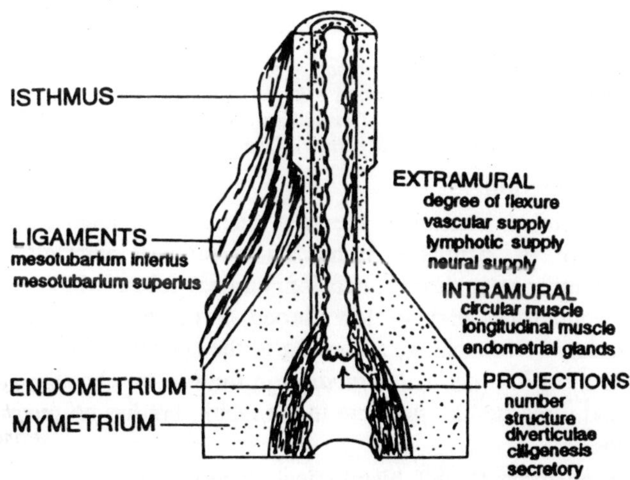

Fig. 3.15. Species differences in the uterotubal junction of laboratory mammals. Anatomical differences are encountered in extramural and intramural portions of the oviduct as well as in the nature of oviductal projections into the uterine lumen.

Norepinephrine and acetylcholine may also initiate oviductal contractions. The oviduct and the uterine horns have opposite sensitivities to these 2 compounds; the ampulla is more sensitive to acetylcholine and less sensitive to norepinephrine than the uterus.

The contractile activities of the fimbriae, oviduct, and oviductal ligaments are also partly coordinated by the ratio of estrogen to progesterone in the blood. The oviduct is most efficient at engulfing ovulated eggs during estrus, less efficient during other periods of the sexual cycle. In some species, neurohormonal mechanisms also increase the muscular activity of the fimbriae at copulation, but in ways which are not yet well understood.

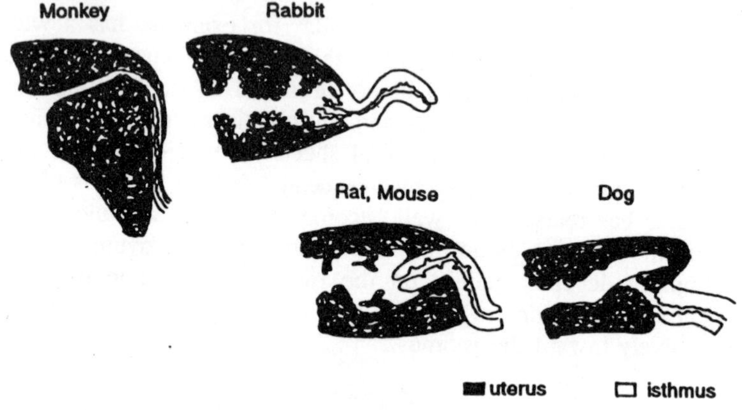

Fig. 3.16. Species differences in the morphology of the uterotubal junction (not drawn to scale). Various anatomical relationships exist between the isthmus and the uterus: the conspicuous folds of the rabbit, the moundlike papilla of the dog, the archiform junction of the rat, and the intramural portion of the oviduct in primates.

Uterotubal Junction

The uterotubal junction is the area where the oviduct meets the uterine cornu. In. primates, it has an extramural and intramural portion. Its mucosa is thrown into longitudinal folds, which may be sparse or numerous, high or low, broad or narrow, and may also show a variety of branching, according to the species. The uterotubal junction is a papilla *(colliculus tubaris)* in the rat, an elevated site in the.dog, and a rosette-like structure in the rabbit, but has no projections in primates.

Other anatomical and histological differences have also been observed in the uterotubal junctions of different species. These include differences in (a) the degree of flexure and the angle at which the oviduct and the uterine cornu meet; (b) the narrowing of the lumen in the caudal isthmus; (c) blood and lymph supplies; (d) the number and morphology of ciliated cells; (e) the cytology of mucosal secretory cells and uterine glands; (f) ciliary activity during stages of the reproductive cycle; (g) the relative thickness of the circular and longitudinal bands which make up the tunica muscularis; and (h) the blending of the oviductal musculature with the myometrium.

OVIDUCTAL EGGS

An egg *(ovum)* is a highly differentiated cell capable of being fertilized and of undergoing embryonic development. Since most laboratory mammals have efficient nutrient-exchange systems (e.g., placentae) for the *in utero* development of their offspring, their eggs are much smaller than avian eggs and lack the large supply of nutrients (yolk) of the latter. Mammalian eggs were first identified by de Graaf and somewhat later described by Cruickshank and von Baer.

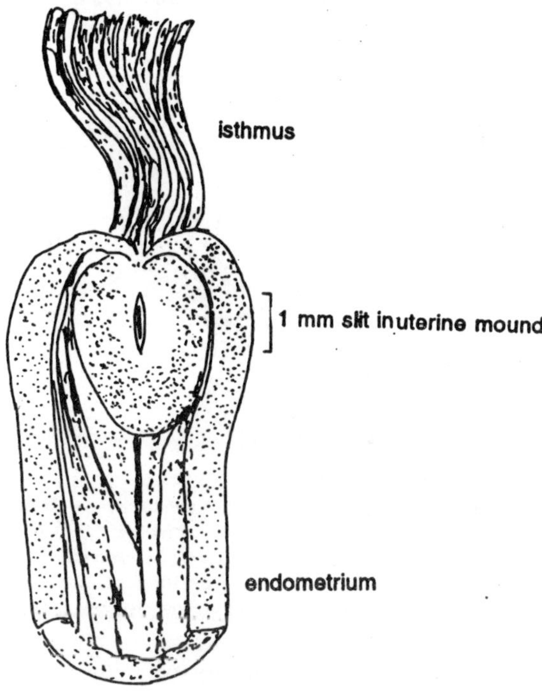

Fig. 3.17. The uterotubal junction of the dog is a slit in an expansion of the uterus.

Structure and Ultrastructure

Structural differences exist in the mammalian egg, both between and within families.

Corona Radiata

Recently ovulated eggs are usually surrounded by a variable number of granulosa cell layers, collectively called the *corona radiata,* in a matrix of follicular fluid, both of which come from the cumulus oophorus. The adherences of the egg to the granulosa cells of the

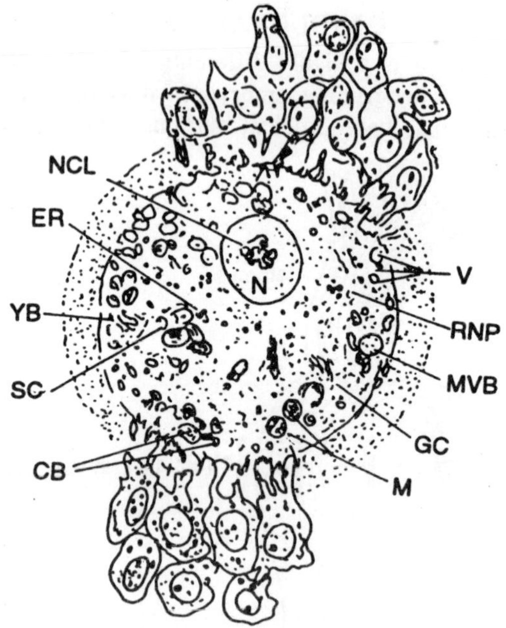

*Fig. 3.18. The structure of the mammalian egg before ovulation. MVB = multivesicular body; nucleus; NCL = nucleolus; endoplasmic reticulum *(ER) is scant; unattached particle ribonucleoprotien (RNP) are also present; mitochondria (M) are the size of the light and cytoplasmic bodies (CB) which are present. The Golgi complex (GC) resembles the "yolk body Balbiani (YB) which may give rise to secretory canaliculi (SC) and cytoplasmic vesicles (V).*

cumulus oophorus is reduced prior to ovulation by the development of liquid-filled, intercellular spaces in the latter. The corona persists for only a few hotus after ovulation. Protoplasmic extensions of its cell penetrate the zona pellucida, and interdigitate with think projections (microvilli) of the oocyte itself. These oocytic projections are withdrawn from the zona pellucida soon after ovulation. *In vitro* exposure of recently ovulated eggs to oviductal fluids (which contain fibrinolytic enzymes) causes these projections to retract and degenerate; the cell bodies of the corona radiata then undergo necrosis and the egg is thereby denuded.

Egg Membranes

The egg has 2 membranes, a *vitelline membrane* and *a zona pellucida*. The vitelline membrane has essentially the same structure and properties as the plasma membrane of somatic cells. The zona pellucida, on the other hand, is an apparently semipermeable membrane composed of conjugated protein and is broken down by such proteolytic enzymes as trypsin and chymotrypsin.

In some species, still another "membrane" is present which develops as the egg passes through the oviduct. Fish and amphibian eggs, for example, are sealed in gelatinous envelopes. In monotremes and marsupials, many albuminous layers are deposited around the zona pellucida; a similar coat occurs on the eggs of lagomorphs and is composed of complex mucopolysaccharides. A thinner but chemically identical layer also envelopes the eggs of dogs and horses.

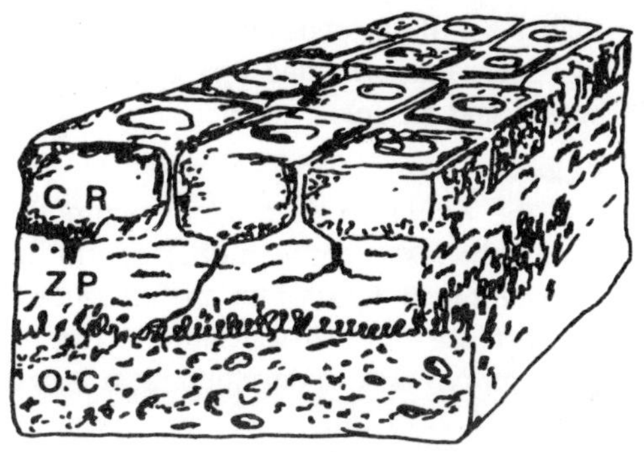

Fig. 3.19. The structural relationship between the follicular cells and the oocyte in the ovary of the as revealed by electron microscopy. Extensions of the cells in the corona radiata (CR) pass thro the zona pellucida (ZP) and end blindly at the surface of the ovum (OC). They do not connect i microvilli which extend from the surface of the ovum into the zona pellucida.

The egg membranes probably have absorptive properties which are adapted to accommodate the physiochemical changes which occur in the egg and its environment during fertilization, cleavage, and the expansion of the blastocyst.

Vitellus

The vitellus is the cytoplasm and fluid enclosed by the zona pellucida. The part between the vitelline membrane and the zona pellucida shrinks after fertilization, forming *a perivitelline space* into which the polar bodies are extruded. Specific differences in the morphology of the vitellus are related to its content of yolk and fat droplets. In rabbit eggs, for example, the yolk granules are finely divided and uniformly distributed.

The ultrastructure of the vitellus has been more extensively studied among invertebrates and lower vertebrates than among mammals. Its mitochondria are granular or rod-shaped and cluster around the Golgi apparatus. Spherical cortical granules within it range between 150 and 350 $_{p}$ in diameter and frequently aggregate near the vitelline membrane.

Structural Abnormalities

Structurally abnormal ova include those which are minute or monstrous, oval or flattened; and those with a ruptured zona pellucida, large polar bodies, or a vacuolated vitellus. Such abnormalities may result from faulty or incomplete maturation of the oocyte, genetic factors, or environmental stress. During incomplete maturation, for example, polar body extrusion may not occur, so that the ovum contains more than 1 set of chromosomes (polyploidy). The incidence of abnormal eggs increases with the age of the female parent and varies among breeds and strains.

Transport of Eggs

The fact that the oviduct can conduct nonmotile eggs in one direction and simultaneously move motile sperm in the opposite direction has evoked much interest in the mechanisms of gamete transport. The importance of such transport in fertility can be seen by the fact that the embryo fails to develop unless it reaches the uterus within a prescribed period of time.

Movement of the cumulus through the ampulla is quite rapid but discontinuous and involves a series of short rushes. Anti-peristaltic contractions may, in fact, temporarily reverse the movement of the egg.

Once within the oviduct, the egg passes rapidly to the ampullary-isthmic junction where it is retained for 40 to 50 hours. Fertilization occurs at this junction in most mammals.

Transport appears to depend largely on the activity of kinocilia, smooth muscle in the oviductal wall, and the patency of the ampullary-isthmic and uterotubal junctions. Ovarian hormones integrate the activities of these parts and it is not surprising then that ovariectomy or the administration of steroid hormones can markedly upset them. In general, estrogen promotes the contractility of the oviduct and causes partial occlusion of the isthmus. The latter effect probably accounts for the "temporary oviduct blocking" which occurs at the ampullary-isthmic junction. Progestin, on the other hand, depresses the muscular activity of the ampulla and thereby reduces the rate of ovum transport in some species.

Fertilized or unfertilized ova reach the uterus within 2 to 3'/2 days after ovulation. Transport time is approximately that required for the corpus luteum to become active. Thus, the embryo arrives in the utrus when the activity of the ovary, reflected by the condition of the uterus, is optimal for its survival.

Fertilizable Life and Aging of Eggs

The fertilizable life of the egg is the period during which it can fuse with a sperm and then undergo normal development. In most species this period is 12 to 24 hours. The egg rapidly loses its fertilizability when it reaches the isthmus. It can not be fertilized after it reaches the uterus.

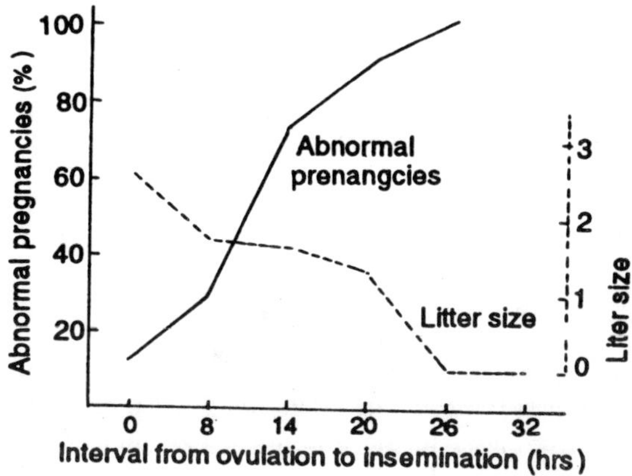

Fig. 3.20. Aging the ova causes abnormal pregnancies and smaller litters in guinea pigs. Although the ova were fertilized and implanted when the animals were inseminated 26 hours after ovulation, the embryos did not continue to develop.

By delaying breeding, it is possible to obtain eggs which have been fertilized near the end of the period during which they are capable of fusion. Such eggs may or may not implant, and those which do produce mostly nonviable embryos. In guinea pigs, for example, the incidence of abnormal pregnancies and small litters rises with the age of the egg prior to fertilization. Fertilization of aged eggs in swine is associated with polyspermy and the abnormal embryonic development to which it leads. In single-bearing animals, aging of the egg may also cause abortion or embryonic resorption. Similar abnormalities result when eggs are fertilized by aged sperm. It is also possible that some of the congenital abnormalities found in postnatal life are no more than the consequence of fertilizing senile gametes. If an egg is not fertilized, it disintegrates into fragments which are phagocytized in the uterus or expelled through the vagina.

TABLE 3.5 SPECIES DIFFERENCES IN THE FERTILIZABLE LIFE AND STAGES OF DEVELOPMENT OF EGGS.

Animal	*Fertilizable* Life of Egg (hrs)	*Length of Development Stages of Fertilized Eggs (hrs)* 2-cell	5-8 cell	morula	blastocyst	*Time after* Ovulation (hrs) and Stage at Which Egg *Reaches Uterus*
Dog	24					
Gerbil		48				72
Guinea pig	20	30-35	80	100-115	115-150	80-85 (8-cells)
Hamster	5					(8-cells)
Monkey (rhesus)	23	0-24	36-48	72-96		96 (16-cells)
Mouse	15	24-38	50-64	68-80	74-82	72 (morula)
Rabbit	6-8	22-26	32-40	47-68	68-76	70 (blastocyst)
Rat	12	45	79		107	

THE UTERUS

Several types of uteri occur among the different mammalian orders. In general however, they fall into 4 anatomical categories based largely on differences in the prominence of their 2 parts, the body and the 2 horns.

Rats, mice, rabbits, and guinea pigs have a duplex uterus. There are 2 separate uterine horns and 2 cervices. The pig has a *bicornuate uterus:* the horns have fused caudally into a small uterine body, but are still mostly separate; there is only one cervix. Carnivores and certain ungulates possess *a bipartite* organ with one cervix, a prominent uterine body, and 2 horns in various degrees of anastomosis with each other. In cats, dogs, and ruminants, a septum partially bisects the uterine body. In the horse, a septum is absent and the body is larger. The uterus of primates is *simplex* in type. Its body is very large and horns have disappeared entirely; there is again 1 cervix.

The simplex uterus of the rhesus monkey can be roughly divided into an upper segment, consisting of the body and pear shaped fundus, and a lower segment formed by the thick walled cervix. The uterine lumen in the fundus is distinctly bicornuate. In the marmoset *(Ha pale jacchus),* it has 2 lateral projections and a midventral groove which indicate its bicornuate origin.

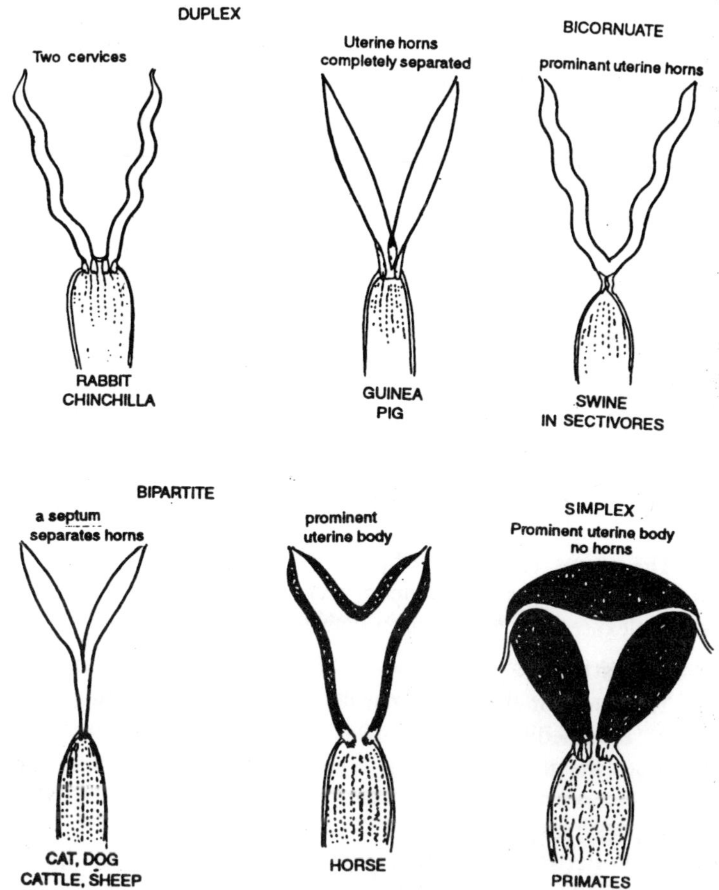

Fig. 3.21. The relative length of the uterine horns and the uterine body varies among laboratory mammals. In litter bearing species the uterine horns are elongated and the uterine body is small or absent. In ruminants, a septum separates the uterine horns and is especially prominent in the uterine body.

In mammals which have a well-defined reproductive season (e.g., mink), the size of the uterus changes dramatically during the year. As the sexual season approaches, it elongates and its wall thickens in conjunction with ovarian growth (ovariectomy depresses uterine growth, whereas estrogens stimulate it).

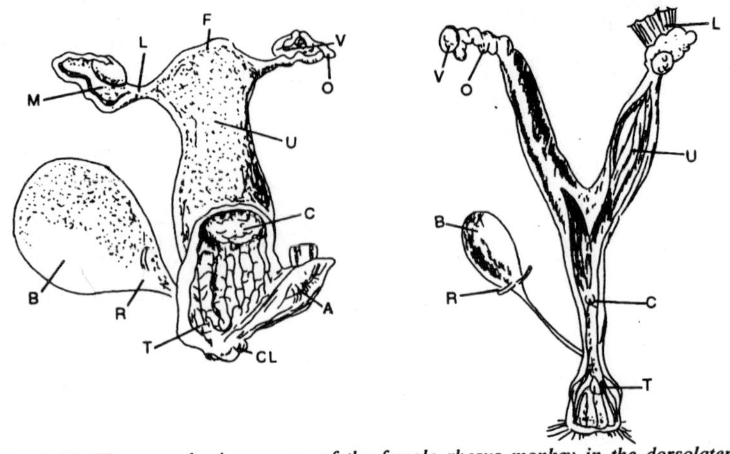

Fig. 3.22. The reproductive organs of the female rhesus monkey in the dorsolateral view (left) and the female cat in the dorsal view (right).

A = anus | *M = mesosalpinx*
B = bladder | *O = oviduct*
C = cervix | *R = ureter*
Cl = clitoris | *T = urethral orifice*
F = fundus of uterus | *U = uterus*
L = ligament | *V = ovary*

The uterus receives its blood and nerve supply by way of the broad ligament. Its sympathetic nerves originate in the uterine and pelvic plexuses and terminate in both the muscle coats and submucosa.

Uterine Structure

The walls of the uterus consist of a luminal mucous membrane lining, intermediate smooth muscle layer, and an external serous envelope, the peritonea From a physiological standpoint, however, only 2 layers are recognized: the *endometrium* and the *myometrium.*

The Endometrium

The endometrium is comprised of the epithelial lining of the uterine lumen and glandular subsurface layer with its supported connective tissue. Its thickness vascularity are influenced by hormones from the ovary (e.g., during the estrous cy and from the placenta (during pregnancy). In primates, it contains 2 types of arteries: long coiled arteries which stretch from 1 side of the endometrium to the other and h an abundance of elastic fibers in their walls; and (b) smaller arteries whose walls 1 elastic fibers. The former undergo pronounced periodic changes in growth during menstrual (estrous) cycle and degenerate after ovarictomy, whereas the smaller arte: do not.

Uterine Glands

The endometrial glands are branched and tubular in type and characteristically coiled, especially near their alveoli. Their number varies with spec breed, parity, and phase of the estrous cycle.

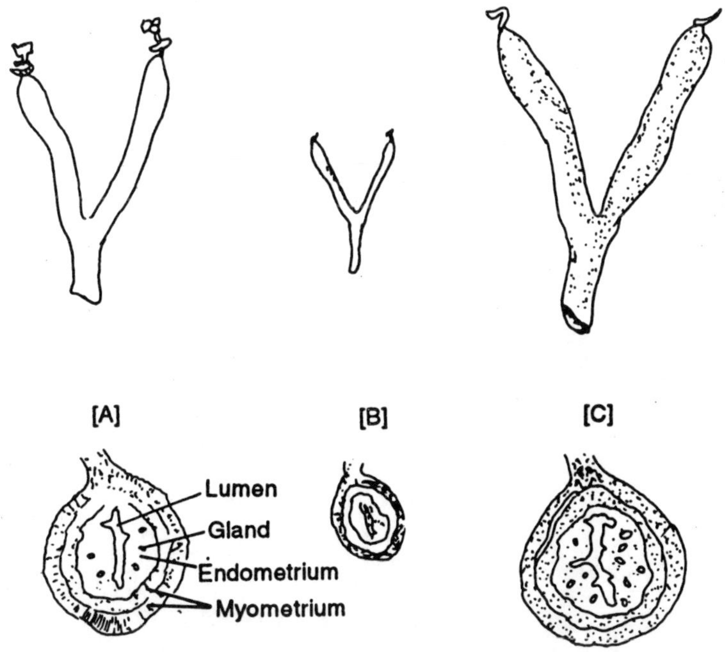

Fig. 3.23. Effects of estrogen on the growth of the uterus and vagina of the rat. A = normal female rat. B = rat which has been castrated for 4 weeks. C = rat which has been castrated for 4 week and given estrogen during the last 10 days. *The lower drawings are cross-sections of the corresponding uteri.*

Cyclical Changes in Endometrium

During proestrus, the endometrium is conditio] by estrogens from the ovarian follicles *(follicular phase);* its vascularity consequei increases, the surface epithelium becomes low columnar in height, and·the endomel glands undergo some growth although they remain straight and only slightly brancl During *estrus* and *early diestrus (luteal phase),* the structure of the endometrium is contro by progesterone from the corpus luteum: the endometrium thickens, its surface epithel becomes high columnar in type, and the uterine glands grow to their maximal (larger, more coiled, and more highly branched than at other phases of the cycle); glands are now actively secretory. In *late diestrus,* the endometrium shrinks anc glands lose size and cease to secrete. These cyclical changes occur whether fertiliza takes place or not.

The periodic sloughing of the endometrial surface during the estrous cycle not cause the extensive bleeding which occurs during the menstruation of primate the latter case, a substantial portion of the endometrium is shed.

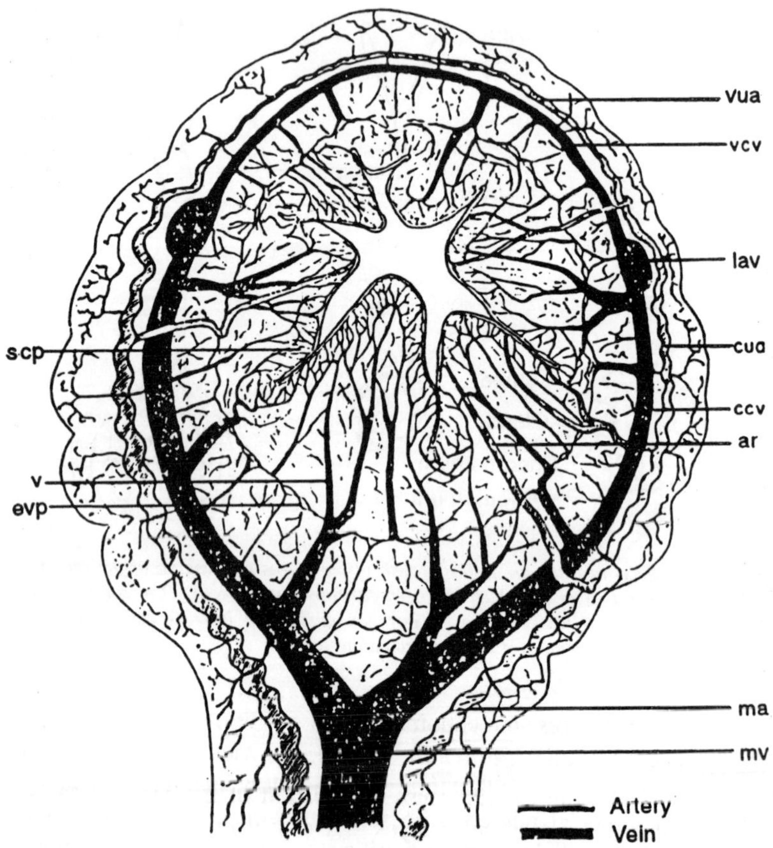

Fig. 3.24. A diagrammatic illustration of the rabbit uterus in cross-section. Note the complex architecture of arteries and veins. Ar = arteriole; ccv = circumferential collecting vein; cua = circumferential utrine artery; evp = endometrial vascular plexus; lav = lateral arcuate vein; ma = mesometrial artery; my = mesometrial vein; scp = subepithelial capillary plexus; v = venule; vev = ventral collecting vein; vua = ventral uterine artery.

TABLE 3.6. CHARACTERISTICS OF FEMALE REPRODUCTIVE ORGANS DURING THE FOLLICULAR AND LUTEAL PHASES OF THE ESTROUS CYCLE

Organ	Follicular Phase	Luteal Phase
1	2	3
Ovary	Primary follicle; secondary follicles; graafian follicles; ovulation; corpus hemorrhagicum; atresia of follicles	Corpus luteum (C.L.); C.L. albicans (nonpr-egnancy); C.L. verum (pregnancy); atresia of corpora lutea
Oviduct	Columnar epithelium is higher; secretionby nonciliated cells more marked,muscle fibers and cilia longer than atluteal phase	
Endometrium	Vascularity increases; surface epithelium is simple columnar	*Early diestrus:* endometriumincreases in thickness;endometrial glands elon-gate, coil, and secreteactivity; epithelium ishigh columnar *Late diestrus:* endome-triumshrinks; secreti-onsdiminish
Cervix	Height of the secretory activity of mucus-secreting cells; blood vesselscongested	Mucosal edema and congestion disappear; osuteri blanched, dry, andconstricted
Vagina	Changes in the vaginal epithelium laga few days behind ovarian changes	

The Myometrium

The myometrium is the muscular portion of the uterine wall. It consists of a 1 inner circular layer and a thinner outer longitudinal layer of smooth muscle, bets which is sandwiched a connective tissue sheet containing blood and lymph vessels nerves. The amount of muscle tissue in the uterine wall increases noticeably di pregnancy, both by cell enlargement and increases in cell number.

Uterine Functions

The uterus has several important functions. At copulation, its contractile action facilities the transport of sperm into the oviduct. Prior to implantation, it produces fluids which sustain the blastocyst. After implantation, it participates in formation of placenta and is the site of fetal development. At parturition, it plays the major role in delivery (fetal expulsion). The uterus undergoes tremendous changes in size, structure, and position in order to accommodate the growing conceptus. Nonetheless, it returns to nearly its former size and condition after part union, by a process called *involution.*

The Relationship between Uterus and Ovarian Activity

The uterus has a demonstrable effect on ovarian activity. If an animals, for example, is hysterectomized during estrus, the corpus luteum remains viable and active for a protracted period thereafter; furthermore, the more uterus is removed, the longer the functional life of the corpus luteum is extended. The changes in luteal activity which follow hysterectomy probably involve the hypophysis, since hormones of the latter directly control ovarian activity. The existence of a luteolytic hypophysial hormone, secreted in response to stimuli from the nongravid uterus, could, for example, explain the prolonged life of the corpus luteum after hysterectomy.

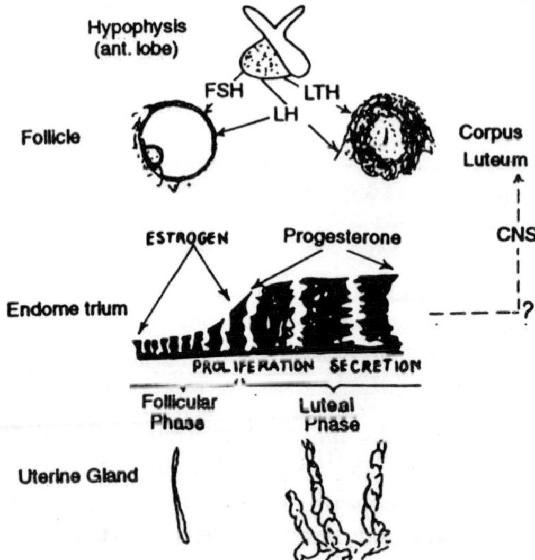

Fig. 3.25. The relationship between pituitary gonadotropins, ovarian hormones, and cyclic changes in the uterus during the follicular and luteal phase of the estrous cycle. During the progeostational stage, the endometrium thickens and the uterine glands become more coiled and secrete actively. The effect of the uterus on the maintenance of the corpus luteum, by means of neural pathways, is not well understood.

Stimulation of the uterus (e.g., by placing a small *foreign body in* its lumen) during the early stages *of* the estrous cycle hastens regression of the corpus luteum and causes precocious estrus. A subsequent estrous cycle may be either shortened or prolonged, depending on when the foreign body is inserted into the uterine lumen and on the nature and size of the introduced material. In this case, the nervous system appears to be involved since the estrous cycle is normal if the uterine segment containing the foreign body is denervated.

Uterinc Secretions

The fluid in the lumen of the uterus is belicved to be a combination of blood plasma and the secretory products of uterine glands. Differences in the composition of uterine fluid and blood indicate that secretion, as well as transudation, is involved in its formation. For example, the potassium concentration of the uterine fluid of the rat is 10 times that of its blood; yet, the sodium levels of the two are nearly identical. Furthermore, at least 2 proteins which occur in uterine fluid are not present in blood. One of these is uteroglobin (or blastokinin), which is also found in the blastococlic fluid of the rabbit.

The volume and biochemical composition of uterine fluid change during the sexual cycle. Uterine fluid has 2 important functions to which these variations are related: it provides a favorable environment for sperm capacitation and nutrition for the preimplantation blastocyst.

Uterine Motility

The motility of the uterus also changes during the estrous cycle. The diestrous uterus exhibits slow, feeble, and uncoordinated contractions which may arise in any part of it and extend in any direction. At estrus, however, the contractions become rhythmic and move in waves which begin at its oviductal end. After ovulation, the uterine muscles become quiescent long before the egg reaches the uterus. Muscular contractions are also minimal during pregnancy. Similar patterns of myometrial activity can be induced experimentally by treating an animal with estrogen and progesterone.

Biochemical Aspects of Uterus

Like many other tissues, the endometrium metabolizes carbohydrates, fats, and proteins during periods of growth and glandular activity. However, particularly conspicuous metabolic variations occur in its nucleic acid, glucose, and glycogen content during the estrous cycle.

Glucose is probably the most important single endometrial metabolite. In phos-phorylated form, it produces ATP energy (by means of aerobic and anaerobi glycolysis), pentose for nucleic acid synthesis, and reducing agents ($NADPH_2$) for biosynthetic reactions (by means of the hexose mono phosphate shunt). It is also converted to glycogen and stored as such in the endometrial glands.

Ovarian hormones regulate uterine metabolism. Estrogen promotes uterine growth (protein synthesis and cell division) in several ways: it causes hyperemia and increases amino acid incorporation, nucleic acid synthesis, and nitrogen retention in the endometrium. It also stimulates phosphorylation, aerobic and anaerobic glycolysis, and glycogen deposition. The progestational (progesterone-induced) changes ire. the endometrium include marked growth, striking increases in DNA and RNA, and water loss. The glycogen content of the myometrium increases during the luteal phase of the estrous cycle coincident with the period when uterine muscle is least active.

The Cervix

The cervix is a muscular sphincter which projects caudally into the vagina from the posterior end of the uterus. It has a small lumen and a thick well which frequently bears transverse interlocking ridges *(annular rings)*. The prominence of the latter varies according to the species.

The wall of the cervix consists of a mucosa-submucosa, muscularis, and serosa. The prominent primary and smaller secondary folds of its wall produce its typical "fern-leaf" appearance in sections. The transition from the squamous epithelium of the vagina to the columnar one of the uterus occurs in the cervix and may be gradual, abrupt, or irregular, according to the species. The cervix has no multicellular glands, but is equipped with myriads of mucosal goblet cells which produce cervical mucus. Its myomerium is rich in dense fibrous tissue and smooth muscle. The inner circular layer of muscle is particularly well developed and forms most of the annular rings.

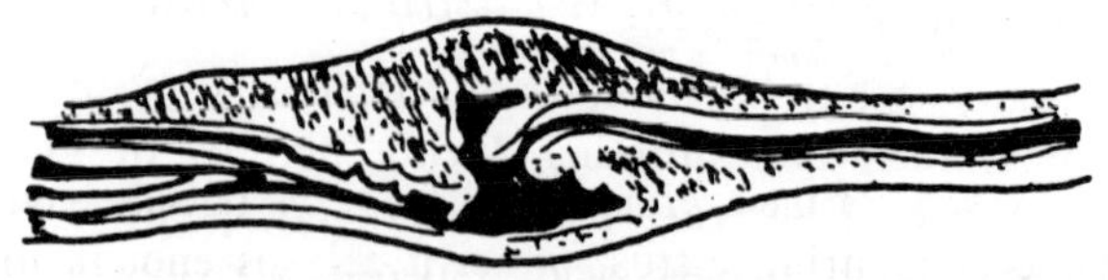

Fig. 3.26. Longitudinal section through the cervix and vagina of the mink.

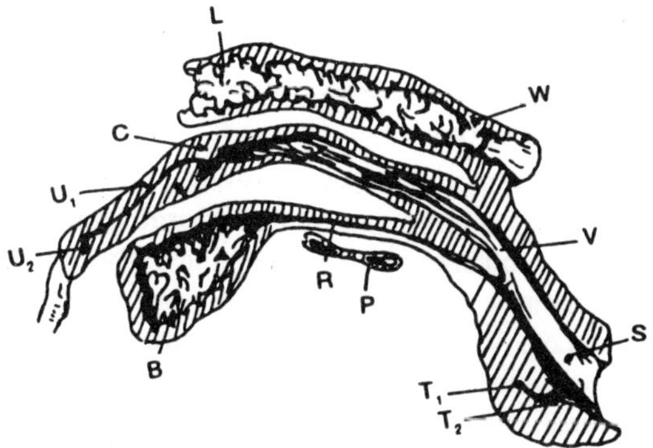

Fig. 3.27. Midsagittal section of the vagina and cervix of the bitch. Note the constricted lumen leading to the uterus. B = bladder; C = cervix; L = colon; P = pelvic symphysis; R = urethra; S vestibule; T, = clitoris; T_2 = fossa for clitoris; U, = body of uterus; U_2 = fundus of uterus; V = vagina; W = rectum.

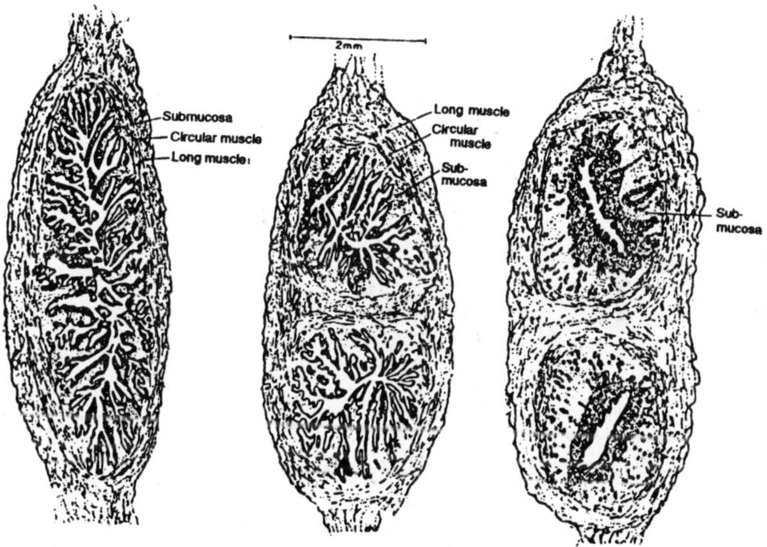

Fig. 3.28. Cervix of the guinea pig near the external os (left), in the middle of the cervical canal (centre), and near the internal os (right). Note the conspicuous mucosal folds and the endocervical glands in the submucosa.

Functions of Cervix

The cervix seals of the uterine lumen from the outside environment at all times except during estrus, when it relaxes enough to permit sperm to pass into the uterus. During pregnancy, its mucus occludes the cervical canal and prevents infectious agents from entering. Prior to parturition, this cervical plug liquefies and the cervix dilates so that the fetus and its membranes can pass out. The role of cervical mucus in sperm migration is of special physiological significance and will be discussed separately.

Cervical Mucus and Cyclical Changes

Cervical mucus is a complex chemical substance containing sialoglycoproteins (combinations of sialic acid and glycoproteins), free sugars, glycogen, cholesterol, lipids in-organic salts, free amino acids, proteins and enzymes. The glycoproteins of the mucus has a high carbohydrate content and is consequently classified as a mucoid. The properties of cervical mucus and the amount of it which is produced are under endocrine control.

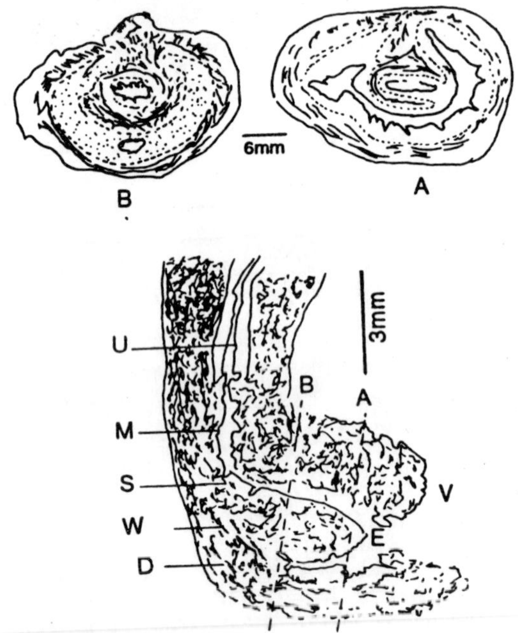

Fig. 3.29. Sections through the cervix of the squirrel monkey. Top: Cross-sections positions A and B to show the fornix of the vagina surrounding the cervical lumen. Bottom: Longitudinal section which shows the cervical canal between the uterus (U) and the vagina (V). D = diverticulum, M = muscular layer, S = submucosa, W = connective tissue in cervical wall.

This is reflected by cyclical changes in the secretory activity of the cervix and the physiochemical composition of its mucus during the estrous cycle. Cervical mucus, for example, is most copious during the estrogenic (follicular) phase of the cycle. Its viscosity and cellular content decrease markedly at ovulation. It also contains less sialic acid at estrus than during gestation.

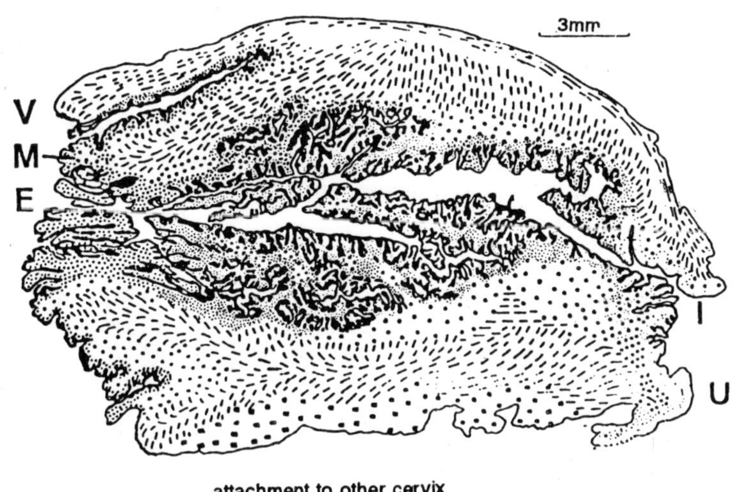

Fig. 3.30. Longitudinal section in the uterine cervix of the rabbit. Note the complexity of the mucosa folds. E = external os; I = internal os; M = mucosa; U =uterus; V = vagina.

Cervical tissues, particularly the musculature, grow actively during pregnancy. The cervical canal dilates and acquires the muscular force necessary for parturition. At this time, cervical goblet cells also produce large amounts of mucus which occlude the canal and prevent uterine infection.

Several attempts have been made to correlate the cyclical changes in the cervix with endocrine events. Large doses of estrogen increase cervical growth and cause desquamation of the mucosa; smaller ones induce slower increases in growth, but no mucosal sloughing.

Attempts have also been made to duplicate gestational changes in the cervix by treating ovariectomized females with various combinations of estrogen and progesterone. Experiments of this kind have been only partially successful. Estrogen produces a solid thick-walled cervix that tends to be larger than normal. Progesterone by itself does not promote cervical growth and development of goblet cells unless very large doses are used, and even then, it stimulates little, if any, secretion. Best results have been obtained with combinations of estrogen, progesterone, and relaxin.

Cervical Mucus and Spermigration

Massive numbers of sperm adhere to cervical mucus following copulation. Fertilization and pregnancy consequently depend on the biophysical and biochemical complexion of this secretion and the manner in which it accumulates around the internal and external os at the time of insemination. If semen is deposited in the vagina or cervix (as it is in primates, ruminants, and rabbits), the uterine cervix acts as a sperm reservoir and sperm periodically escape from its mucus into the uterine lumen. However, if semen is deposited directly in the uterus (as it is in the rat, mouse, and horse), the uterotubal junction is the sperm reservoir.

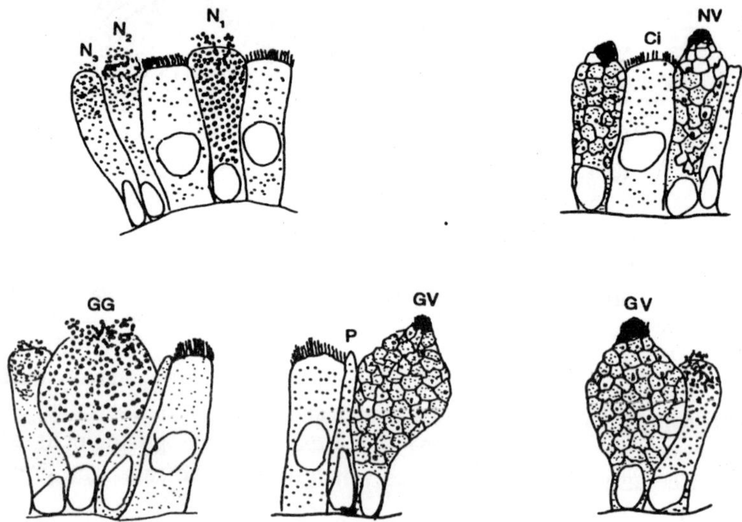

Fig. 3.31. Diagrammatic illustration of types of epithelial cells found in the cervix of rabbits. Classification is based on cytological characteristics and histochemical properties of secretory materials.

The pH of cervical mucus is particularly critical to the motility and survival of sperm in the cervix. Sperm are motile for longer periods in the alkaline secretions of the cervix than in the acid environment of the vagina. There is also evidence that cervical mucus functions in sperm capacitation.

THE VAGINA

The vagina is the female reproductive organ in which semen is generally deposited. It is also the expandable passageway through which the fetus and placenta pass during delivery. In the guinea pig and chinchilla, it is sealed off by a membrane, which ruptures spontaneously during estrus. In rates, the vaginal opening occurs near the time of the first ovulation and is used as in index of puberty. It coincides with an increase in the weight of the pituitary and a decrease in the gonadotropic content of that gland.

The wall of the vagina consists of mucosa-submucosa, muscularis, and scrosa. The mucous membrane is a stratified squamous epithelium. Epithelial growth and desquamation of cornified cells occur at all stages of the estrous cycle, but at different rates. In primates, the epithelium is thinnest at menstruation, gradually builds up during the follicular phase, and is highest at ovulation.

The vaginal epithelium of rodents undergoes characteristic changes during the estrous cycle. It is markedly cornified and devoid of leukocytes at estrus. The cornified layer is shed at the end of estrus and the wall is invaded by leukocytes. The vaginal smear is, therefore, an excellent indicator of the stage of the estrous cycle.

The muscular coat of the vagina is less well developed than its counterpart in the uterus. It consists of a thick inner circular layer and a thin outer longitudinal one. It is well supplied with blood'vessels, nerve bundles, and connective tissue. As indicated in figure 3.40, the junction of the uterus and vagina is quite complex in some species.

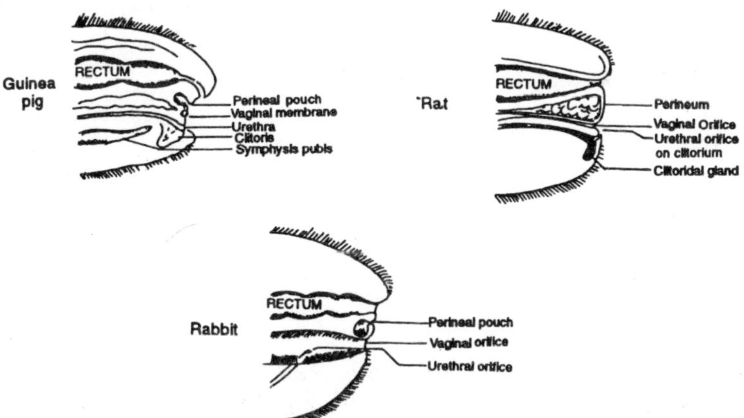

Fig. 3.32. Location of the urethral and vaginal orifices in the abdomen of the guinea pig (anestrous condition; vagina closed by an epithelial membrane), rat, and rabbit.

Prostate

In several species, well-developed prostate glands occur in the female. Examples include the rat and Eastern cottontail rabbit

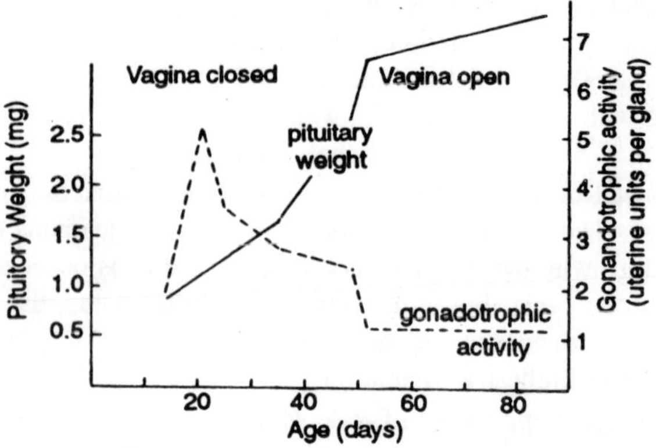

Fig. 3.33. The time at which the vagina of the female rat opens is related to changes in the weight and the gonadotropic content of the hypophysis before and after puberty.

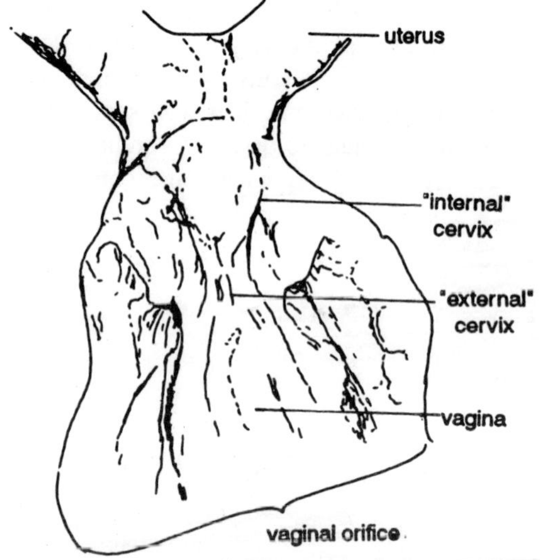

Fig. 3.34. Diagram showing the complexity of the hamster's uterovaginal area.

(Sylvilagus floridanus). The incidence of prostate glands in female rats has been increased by selective breeding.

THE EXTERNAL GENITALIA

The external genitalia are the vaginal vestibule, the labia majors and minors, and the clitoris. Their size and morphology vary considerably among mammalian species. True labia occur only in the human female.

The vagina opens into the vestibule at the urethral orifice, which is frequently demarcated by a ridge (the vestigial hymen). Gartner's tubes (remnants of the Wolffian ducts) enter the vestibule posterolaterally to the urethra.

The integument of the labia majors is richly supplied with sebaceous and tubular glands. It also contains fat deposits, elastic tissue and a thin layer of smooth muscle, and has the same surface structure (dermis-epidermis) as external skin. The labia minors are smaller and have a core of spongy connective tissue. They too house many.large sebaceous glands.

The ventral commissure of the vestibule conceals a clitoris which is composed of erectile tissue and covered by stratified squamous epithelium. It contains numerous sensory nerve endings.

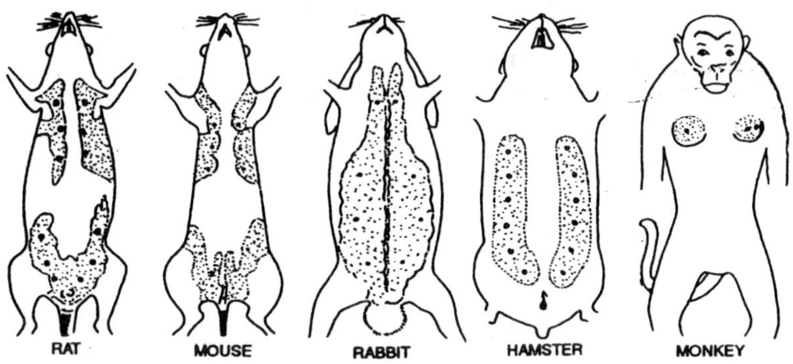

Fig. 3.35. Location of the nipples and size of the mammary glands in common laboratory mammals during lactation.

Sexual Skin

Some primates have specialized areas of skin contiguous with the external genitalia, which are called the sexual skin. Sexual skin is well developed in the baboon, chimpanzee, mangabey, mandrill, and the Celebes black apes. It is characterized by a thick dermis with conspicuous edema and an immense vascular supply. It frequently undergoes cyclical changes in color and general conformation (i.e., swells and becomes tumescent) during the menstrual cycle. However, these changes vary among species, individuals, and even in the same individual during different cycles. They are pronounced, for example, in *the* pig-tailed monkey and baboon, but are absent in the rhesus monkey. The tumescence of the sexual skin can sometimes be used as in indicator of ovulation.

MAMMARY GLANDS

The mammary glands are distributed within loose fatty tissue along the lateral aspects of the thoracic and inguinal regions. Their number and position vary with the species. In the rat, for example, the first thoracic gland is anterior to the forelimb; the second and third are thoracic and extend into the axillae; the abdominal and the first and second inguinal glands are separated from the thoracic glands and generally lie between the iliac crest and the ischial tuberosity. The abdominal glands are usually the largest and produce the most milk.

Each mammary gland is a modified skin gland connected with a teat by a streak canal. The latter is lined by stratified squamous epithelium. The mammary tissue itself is divisible into lobules, each of which is composed of many alveoli. The *alveolus is* the secretory unit of the gland. It is lined by a single layer of cuboidal to columnar epithelial cells and surrounded by branched *myoepithelial cells.* The myoepithelial cells contract under the influence of oxytocin and cause the discharge of accumulated milk within the alveolus.

Formation of Female Sex Cells

OOGENESIS

The growth and proliferation of oogonia and their development to the occyte stage constitute oogenesis. A narrower considers oogenesis to be the growth of oogonia to the onset of the first meiotic division, the point at which oogonia become primary oocytes. Within this period both mitotic division and degeneration (atresia) of oogonia take place. These changes occur early in ovarian development in lampreys, elasmobranchs, birds, and mammals but are seasonal events in other vertebrates. They constitute the prefollicular development of ova. Although oogenesis and folliculogenesis are sequential aspects of a single extended process-the development of ova-it is convenient to separate them in discussion.

Oogonia and Oocytes

In the embryonic ovary, germ cells divide mitotically, and mitosis in the ovaries of the elasmobranchs, birds, and most mammals ceases at birth. Intercellular bridges characterize these cells, and such bridges are almost always absent in PGCs. Some oogonia continue to divide mitotically after others have initiated the first meiotic division and produced primary oocytes. The two processes are thus not entirely mutually exclusive, and oogonia may persist in the postnatal ovary of a few mammals.

In almost all mammals the primary occyte remains arrested in meiotic prophase I for a prolonged period, and it does not resume growth and division until shortly before ovulation.. It has been postulated that meiosis is suppressed by secretion of an oocyte maturation inhibitor from granulosa cells.

In some mammals, such as voles, hamsters, rabbits, weasels, and lemurs, oocyte formation takes place in the first few days or weeks of postnatal life. In marsupials, which are born in a state comparable to a eutherian fetus, oogenesis proceeds postpartum. In the tammar wallaby *(Macro pus eugenii)*, for example oogonia form after birth, and the first meiotic division forming primary oocytes occurs at 24 to 30 days of age.

Fish

Oogonia divide actively in the larval stage of cyclostomes. In the early embryonic ovary of bony fish, extensive oogonial mitosis occurs. Proliferation is followed by the formation of clusters, or *nests*, of oogonia. The ovary of adult teleosts usually has a supply of oocytes. In seasonally breeding bony fish, oogonia usually divide -after spawning, so that these oocytes mature as a synchronized population of germ cells. Oogenesis is irregular and more or less continuous in tropical species, which have a prolonged breeding season. In any case a new generation of oogonia may occur annually.

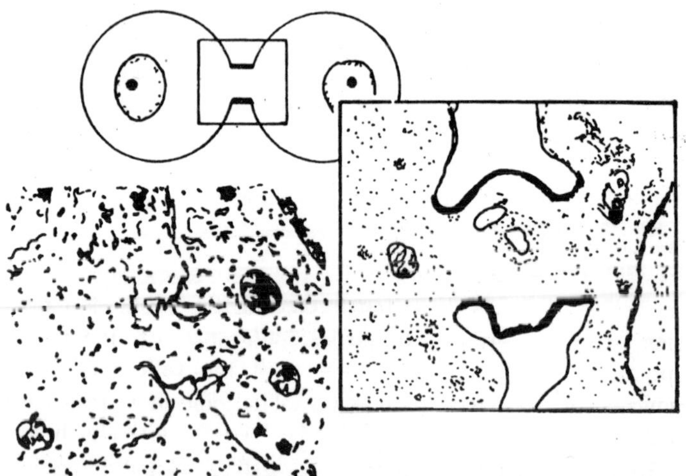

Fig. 4.1. Intercellular bridges connecting adjacent oogonia and oocytes. These bridges allow cytoplasmic exchange between cells and are known to occur in a broad spectrum of vertebrates, including many mammals.

Oocyte maturation is stimulated by a gonadotropin (or gonadotropins), apparently together with one or more steroids from the ovary and the adrenal cortex. Progestogens and 11-deoxycorticosteroids induce final maturation of the teleost oocyte in *vivo*.

Amphibians

In urodeles and anurans oogonia form in the larval ovary. After each seasonal ovulation in the adult, waves of oogonia move near the surface. Mitotically dividing oogonia occur in clusters, and such synchrony is perhaps assisted by intercellular bridges. Similarly, the annual formation of oocytes is synchronized, a necessary pattern in species releasing large numbers of eggs within a brief period. Synchronous maturation of oocytes in the toad *(Bufo bufo)* may be achieved by the suppressive action of growing oocytes on those that have not yet begun growth, resulting in a large number of ova of rather uniform size. In tropical amphibians several generations of oocytes may exist at any given time, and ovulation may occur two or several times a year. Development is usually arrested at prophase I, as in most vertebrates, to resume shortly before ovulation.

In mitosis of anuran oogenesis the cytoplasmic divisions may not occur at all, so that instead of the cells being held together by cytoplasmic bridges there are multinucleate oocytes. In the bell toad *(Ascaphus truei),* after the final three oogonial mitoses, each oocyte his eight nuclei; in late oogenesis, maturation eliminates all but one. In some species of marsupial hylid frogs of the Neotropics, apparently the same process produces oocytes that may have up to 2000 nuclei.

Reptiles

In reptiles, in contrast to fish and amphibians, there are fewer oogonia of uniform size at any given time. Mitosis begins in the embryonic ovary and oogonia persist in the adult in groups called germinal beds. Mitotic division within a single bed is synchronized. Meiosis to prophase I occurs in the adult. Oogenesis in reptiles occurs at a distinct point in the annual reproductive cycle, but this point varies with each group. In turtles maturation of oocytes follows oviposition but is not completed until the following spring. In freshwater species oogenesis may be annual, and there may be several sets of follicles in those species that lay two or more clutches a year.

Birds. Most studies concern the domestic fowl and domestic strains of the Japanese, or migratory quail *(Coturnix coturnix)*. Mitotic divisions of oogonia occur in the embryonic ovary of birds and cease at hatching. There are relatively few intercellular bridges, perhaps accounting for only limited synchrony in avian oogenesis. Clusters of developing oogonia occupy only a small part of the ovary at any one time, and these groups tend to be in different stages of development. At the time of hatching, avian oocytes are mostly in meiotic prophase 1. Follicles are continuously lost to atresia.

In teleost fish, amphibians and reptiles, meiosis II is completed after fertilization. In the event no sperm are present to stimulate the completion of the second meiotic division, as in some parthenogenetic species, the chromosomes of the nucleus of the secondary oocyte together with those of the polar body contain the full (diploid) complement, and fatherless offspring may develop. In birds and most mammals meiosis is completed by the time of ovulation.

Folliculogenesis

Folliculogenesis has been most carefully followedd in mammals and is reviewed by Midgely and Sadler, Peters, Williams and Hodgen, and others. The following initial comments refer to mammalian folliculogenesis, and some differences in nonmammalian vertebrates will be noted.

At birth each oocyte is surrounded by a single layer of undifferentiated spindle shaped cells, which lie in cell nests closely associated with the cords and rete ovarii. These cells constitute a population of nonproliferating follicles. Initial growth is shown by an increase in the size of the oocyte and in the number of surrounding granulosa cells. Continuation of the development of primary follicles occurs throughout the active life of the individual, but may be seasonal and seems to be independent of gonadotropins or sexual steroids.

The gradually enlarging oocyte moves toward the surface of the ovary. The adjacent granulosa cells are characterized by concentrations of Golgi, mitochondria, rough endoplasmic reticulum, and lipids. Granulosa cells originate in the vicinity of the cords and may be products of the invaginated epithelial covering. Granulosa cells produce steroids. They also secrete a fluid, which at least partly surrounds the oocyte; this fluid-filled region is the antrum. An acellular membrane, the zona pellucida, develops around the oocyte.

One or more follicles mature before ovulation. In most mammals folliculogenesis includes the formation of the antrum and the synthesis and release of estrogen, progesterone, and androgen; it includes an infusion of yolk in most nonmammals. The antrum is absent in the oocyte of the platypus, this space being filled with yolk. The antrum is very small is some, if not most, shrews (Soricidae).

In the developing follicle an outer layer or theca cells surrounds the inner layer of granulosa cells. These layers are targets of luteinzing hormone (LH), follicle-stimulating hormone (FSH), and prolactin. FSH and estradiol increase LH receptors on granulosa cells, and estradiol may induce growth in the number of granulosa cells in some mammals. During follicular development the granulosa cells proliferate, and some form a clump, the cumulus oophorus, which surrounds the oocyte and connects it to the wall of the follicle. With continued enlargement, the cumulus separates from the follicle wall, which then becomes thin in the region adjacent to the surface of the ovary.

Theca cells encircle the oocyte in its initial growth. Theca cells differentiate into two layers, the theca interna and theca externa. Both of these layers are provided with capillaries, which fail to extend to the granulosa cells. Theca cells are sensitive to LH, and granulosa cells respond to FSH. Theca cells produce androgens, which stimulate the formation of LH receptors in the granulosa cells; additionally, the androgens may provide for the synthesis of estradiol by the granulosa cells. Thecal androgens also induce the formation of prolactin receptors in the granulosa cells, providing for the synthesis of progestin by the mature follicle. Luteinization of the granulosa cells commences prior to ovulation.

The primary occyte now resumes meiosis, and the nucleus, still diploid, begins to assume a position near the edge of the cell. The completion of meiosis I generally occurs only hours before ovulation. In this condition the secondary oocyte leaves the ovary and enters the upper oviduct. The second meiotic division proceeds to metaphase, where the oocyte remains until the sperm enters the egg. Penetration of the zona pellucida and plasma membrane of the ovum stimulates the completion of the second meiotic division, releasing a second polar body. The pronuclei of sperm and egg then unite to form the zygote, restoring the diploid complement of chromosomes.

In many mammals one or more oocytes are released at ovulation, but in some species it is primary oocyte. In some insectivores sperm may enter the ovary and penetrate the unovulated oocyte; this has been observed in the short-tailed shrew *(Blarina brevicauda)*.

Maturation (resumption of meiosis) of oocytes of fish has been reviewed by Goetz. From a large number of in vitro studies on a variety of teleosts, 11-deoxycorticosteroids and progestogens appear to bc the most powerful steroids in effecting final oocyte maturation. The direct effect of estrogens in this, process appears to be much less important. In seasonal ovarian recrudescence of the rainbow trout *(Salmo gairdneri)*, there are initial (preovulatory) high pulses of gonadotropin hormone (GtH) release, which seem to regulate estradiol synthesis and oogenesis. In amphibians and reptiles stimulation of the ovary, for both oogenesis and steroidogenesis, is induced by pituitary gonadotropins, similar to the hormonal stimulation described for mammals. Oogonia proliferate mitotically, in a synchronous fashion, so that a large number initiate meiosis and reach prophase I simultaneously at about the time of ovulation.

Teleosts that spawn several times a year have oocytes at various stages of development. The ovaries of semelparous fish (those that spawn only once and die) have oocytes all in the same stage of development, in contrast to iteroparous species (those that seasonally spawn once in successive years); which have two distinct generations of oocytes.

In nonmammals, as in mammals, there is a zona pellucida composed of mucopolysaccharides. Exchange of nutrients and other materials occurs through the zona pellucida, but it forms a barrier to the entrance of sperm. A zona pellucida surrounds the developing follicle of elasmobranchs; as the follicle matures, this membrane is called the zona radiata. The teleost follicle is similarly surrounded by a zona pellucida, which forms adjacent to the granulosa cells and may be a product of them. Surrounding the maturing anuran oocyte are layers of cells apparently homologous to theca and granulosa cells of other vertebrates. During the infusion of vitellogenin, a vitelline membrane develops about the oocyte and within the cellular layers. This membrane is called the vitelline envelope (or zona radiata) and is probably homologous to the zona pellucida of otter vertebrates.

Vitellogenesis

In most nonmammalian vertebrates the egg is characterized by a substantial amount of nutrient known as *yolk*, which is composed mostly of lipids and proteins. Yolk volume is reduced in many viviparous nonmammalian vertebrates and is virtually absent in a few. Physically, the addition of yolk is the most conspicuous aspect of folliculogenesis in nonmammalian vertebrates. Yolk is most abundant in those species in which (1) the condition of young at birth is advanced and (2) the young receive little

or no parental care. Yolk is least abundant in those species in which (1) young are born or hatched in a relatively undeveloped or larval condition and (2) the young receive parental care from the mother either before or after birth, including in utero parental nourishment. The sudden growth seen in the developing ova of birds and most ectotherms comes from an infusion of the yolk precursor, vitellogenin. In all vertebrates vitellogenin comes from the liver, and its release into the circulatory system and acquisition by the follicle(s) are both under hormonal control.

Vitellogenesis in lampreys includes the release of vitellogenin, as in other oviparous vertebrates. In the Pacific hagfish *(Eptatretus stouti),* estrogen induces vitellogenesis. In the lamprey *(Lampetra fluviatilis),* implantation of estradiol (0.5 mg/animal/month) was followed by an increase of serum calcium and ovarian mass, apparently as a result of an induction of yolking. Normally, vitellogenesis begins before lampreys ascend rivers on their anadr4mous migrations. In the spotted dogfish *(Scyliorhinus canicula)* there is an annual cyclicity of the thyroid gland, and the changes are more pronounced in the female. Thyroidectomy causes a failure of vitellogenesis in this species.

Initial vitellogenesis of amphibians includes a great increase of cytoplasm. In temperate latitude species this event typically follows the laying of the previous generation *of eggs* and precedes hibernation.

In amphibians yolking is induced by estrogens, which cause the release of fat from fat bodies, and this fat is carried in the blood to the liver. Gonadotropin administration induces the release of yolk proteins from the liver, but not in ovariectomized females. After the release of vitellogenin from the liver, the incorporation of these yolk proteins from plasma into oocytes is mediated by gonadotropins. The appearance of vitellogenin in the blood is concurrent with an increase in serum calcium, and when released from the liver, vitellogenin binds free calcium ion. This situation exists in the clawed frog *(Xenopus laevis),* in which circulating vitellogenin was found following treatment with human chorionic gonadotropin and estrogen. This response also occurs in vitellogenic females and estrogen-treated males. Vitellogenins have been identified in a broad spectrum of oviparous vertebrates.

In amphibians yolk consists mostly of protein, with lesser amounts of lipids and glycogen. The protein is mostly incorporated into yolk platelets, which have a delicate crystalline structure. The release of yolk precursors from the liver is induced by estrogen, and the uptake of vitellogenin by oocytes is stimulated by FSH in many diverse kinds of oviparous vertebrates. Growth hormone may promote or assist the estrogen-induced release of vitellogenin from the liver in some iguanid lizards.

In both hypophysectomized and intact tiger salamanders *(Ambystorna tigrinuin), in vitro* and *in vivo* administration of prolactin enhances maturation and ovulation prior to the normal reproductive season, and thyroxine blocks the effect of prolactin. Ovulation in the toad (Bufo bufo) is stimulated by immersion in water and not by amplexus.

In an in *vivo* experiment with ovariectomized lizards *(Lacerta vivipara),* only estradiol stimulated vitellogenin synthesis, and there was no response from progesterone or androgens.

The anamniotic egg of amphibians contains a large yolk sac over which small blood vessels not only carry food and oxygen to the developing embryo but remove metabolic wastes. It is essential that the surface be in contact with water or moist air so that gas exchange can be rapid. In the amniotic egg of birds and egg-laying reptiles, oviposition is on land. Birds always have rigid-shelled eggs, and oviparous reptiles have eggs with either rigid or leathery shells. In both reptiles and birds these shells contain pores and allow the passage of gases and some fluids. The rather coriaceous shell of many reptilian eggs allows for a substantial increase in egg dimensions and mass from absorption of water. Hard-shelled eggs are characteristic of many species of turtles, crocodilians, and geckos. The adaptive significance of eggshell texture and thickness is equivocal.

The avian egg contains adaptations that allow for its survival on land. In addition to the yolk, there is an abundance of albumen, which is entirely in an egg membrane and eggshell. Both the yolk and albumen consist of proteins and lipids. Enveloping the yolk and extending the long axis of the egg are fibrous strands of albumen, the chalazae. In both birds and reptiles the shell, which contains calcium carbonate, is deposited by the shell, gland the homologue of the mammalian uterus. Calcium is extracted from the circulation, which draws on calcium intake from the intestine; on a calcium-free diet, calcium can be mobilized from bone. Calcium moves across the shell gland by active transport under hormonal stimulus, possibly as a result of estrogen secreted after ovulation.

Atresia

Of the multitude of oogonia present in the neonatal ovary of all vertebrates, very few reach the secondary oocyte stage. Throughout the various stages of follicle formation, atresia accounts for a mass disappearance of potential ova. Although Atresia is a continuous process, it is appreciably greater prior to sexual maturity of the female than it is subsequently. Atresia frequently involves pairs of follicles, perhaps as a consequence of intercellular bridges. In more sexually mature birds and mammals, atresia attacks larger, more nearly mature follicles. In the older' follicles, atresia is accompanied by a loss in blood supply. In mammals necrosis attacks the older oocytes: while the theca cells hypertrophy and become surrounded by lipid droplets, the occyte is last. Following atresia, phagocytic leucocytes and granulosa cells fill the cavity of the follicle.

If not ruptured in ovulation, mature follicles normally become atretic, but they may survive in the ovary of hibernating bats. In the autumn several antral follicles develop in the right ovary of the greater horseshoe bat *(Rhinolophus ferrum-equinum)*, and all but one are atretic by spring. The surviving oocyte seems to be maintained by an abundant supply of lipids and carbohydrates from the cumulus cells. In the southern elephant seal *(Mirounga leonina)* the blastocyst lies free in the uterus for several months, during which time folliculogenesis results in a series of immature follicles wherein the theca interna become luteinized and then atretic. Later, after implantation, a second wave of follicular activity occurs, and these follicles also degenerate.

Atresia occurs in teleosts as in high vertebrates. Oogonia and oocytes are phagocytized by granulosa cells, which then become corpora atretica, or "corpora lutea." A steroidogenic role has sometimes *been* attributed to them, but there is little evidence for this. In most oviparous teleosts a postovulatory corpus luteum-like structure does not develop. In amphibians and reptiles atresia occurs both before and after folliculogenesis.

Although there may seem to be a great waste of oocytes, the larger atretic follicles produce (or contain) appreciable amounts of steroids. In a mature mammalian ovary the large atretic follicle, now without an oocyte, will sometimes become luteinized and produce substantial amounts of progesterone, comparable, to that produced by the corpus luteum.

Ovulation in Mammals

The process by which one or more primary oocytes mature and are released from the ovary constitutes the ovulatory cycle. As part of this recurring event, there is a cyclical ebb and flow of circulating hormones from the hypothalamus, pituitary, gonads, and some other structures. These hormones not only induce follicular and uterine growth and development but also produce behavioral changes that announce the female's pending fertility to nearby, and sometimes distant, males of the same species. Most mammals have one or several cycles annually, but a few have a single annual cycle and some have only one in a lifetime.

The period of folliculogenesis leading up to ovulation is called the follicular phase, and the period from ovulation to the demise of the corpus luteum is termed the luteal phase. The length of the luteal phase varies considerably among various taxa, generally being longer in live-bearing forms. In marsupials the luteal phase is of the same duration as pregnancy, which is greatly abbreviated.

The physical changes that effect the development of an ovum are accompanied by rather pronounced hormonal changes, which are well known for some mammals. These hormonal changes include the role of the hypothalamus in controlling the activity of the anterior pituitary as well as the feedback mechanisms from ovarian steroids. Additionally exogenous signals affect the ovulatory cycle, including photoperiod, temperature, food, and courtship, and they are discussed in subsequent chapters. Here we shall review the major hormonal changes along with their endogenous cyclical causes and effects.

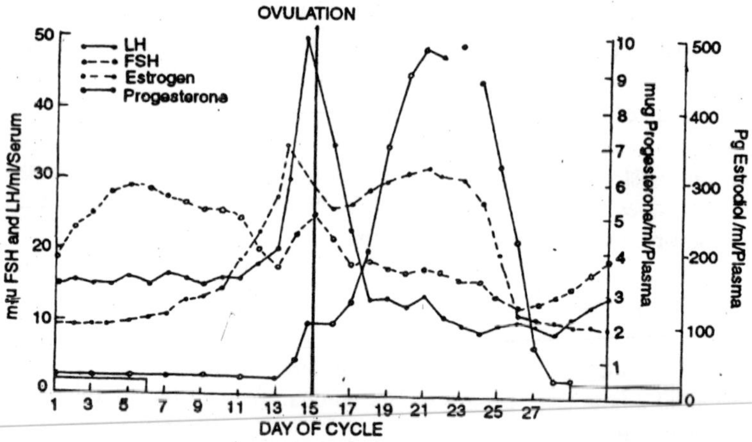

Fig. 4.2 Levels of ovarian steroids and gonadotropins throughout the human menstrual cycle.

As already noted the initial endogenous stimulus of the cycle is the gonadotropin-releasing hormone (GnRH) from the hypothalamus. During the period of follicular growth, there is a low and rather constant (tonic) release of GnRH, which induces a steady, low-level release of both LH and FSH. Initially estrogen, through its negative feedback effects, suppresses the release of both GnRH and FSH; but as estrogen secretion increases, there is a continued, but low-level, synthesis and release of LH. In the preovulatory ovary the level of FSH rises, probably because of an increase in GnRH. This rise is followed by an increase in follicular size (due to an increase in follicular fluid) and an increase in estrogen secretion. This production of estrogen is apparently a synergistic response to both FSH and LH.

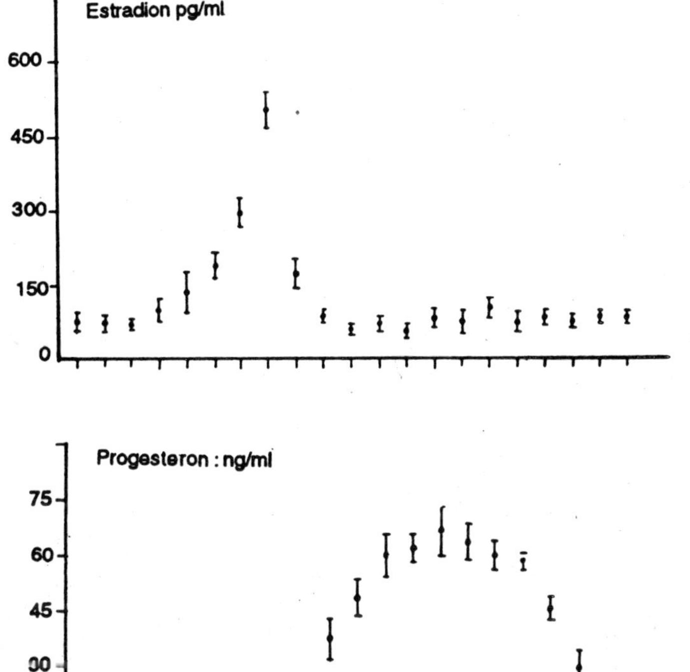

Fig. 4.3. The mean (±SEM) levels of serum estradiol (top) and progesterone (bottom) from nine capuchin monkeys (Cebus apella) *through an entire menstrual cycle.*

Estrogen finally reaches a stimulatory level, and there is then a sudden and substantial rise in the release of LH. This is followed by the discharge of one or more ova from one or more follicles on the ovary. This well-documented pattern is seen in the human female and is rather typical for most vertebrates. In most primates the level of serum estradiol appears to remain steady through the menstrual cycle, with a brief rise just before ovulation.

Prior to ovulation serum progesterone increases in placental mammals, birds, and many other vertebrates. This steroid emanates from the preovulatory follicle and/or the adrenal cortex, most of it probably coming from the follicle. However, serum progesterone rises before there is an increase from the ovarian vein, and the adrenal cortex may be a source. The action of progesterone is enhanced when the target tissue has been previously sensitized by estrogen; such synergistic response requires that many of the target organs of the two hormones be the same. Although estrogen and progesterone usually have distinct and separate peaks-estrogen being preovulatory and progesterone being postovulatory-their occurrences broadly overlap in the ovulatory cycles of many species.

In many, perhaps, most, mammals lactation delays or prevents ovulation, apparently through elevated levels of prolactin. Physiological levels of prolactin inhibit FSH-induced synthesis of estrogen in cultured granulosa cells.

Gonadotropins that appear in one cycle affect the timing and growth of follicles in the subsequent cycle. FSH release during proestrus and estrus of rats and hamsters stimulates the development of follicles for the following cycle. Experimentally inhibited FSH release in the hamster results in a reduced number of follicles at the next estrus. Additionally, in the hamster the LH surge prior to ovulation not only stimulates preantral follicles that will mature at the next proestrus but may be the synchronizing signal for the theca cells to synthesize progesterone. After the LH surge, the prenatal follicles, synthesize androstenedione and estradiol.

Prostaglandins have at least two roles in the regulation of the ovarian cycle. Following gonadotropin release, prostaglandin F_{2a} (PGF_{2a}) increases in the mature mammalian follicle, probably from granulosa cells and perhaps from stimulation by LH. Prostaglandin stimulate the synthesis of both cAMP and steroids. They also cause contraction of both intestinal and uterine tissue during menses and may promote the extrusion of the ovum from the follicle.

In the theca of several groups of vertebrates are elements resembling smooth muscle, and presumably their contraction is followed by ovulation. There are microfilaments in theca cells resembling smooth muscle cells, and they presumably account for the follicular contraction at the time of ovulation. Levels of PGF_{2a} drop immediately after ovulation. The role of prostaglandins in ovulation is suggested by a failure of ovulation following administration of prostaglandin inhibitors (aspirin or indomethacin) and by a reversal of this effect by injections of prostaglandins.

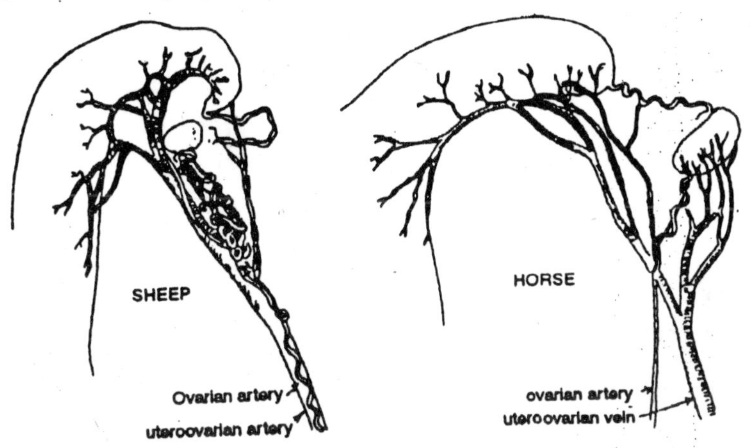

Fig. 4.4 The uterine and ovarian vascular systems of a sheep and a horse. In the sheep, which has an ipsilateral communication from the uterus to the ovary, the ovarian artery is closely applied to the uteroovarian vein. There is little or no uteroovarian communication in the horse.

Experimentally PGEs and PGFs induce labour and terminate pregnancy in several laboratory mammals. Also, both PGEs and PGFs have a luteolytic effect on the corpus luteum and seem to bring about its demise at the close of the luteal phase of the cycle. Prostaglandins are release from the uterus of the ewe and carried directly through the uterine vein, which lies appressed to the ovarian artery. This arrangement may allow a countercurrent exchange of PGF_{2a} to the ipsilateral ovary. Prostaglandins uncouple LH from adenylcyclase, resulting in cAMP production and thus preventing LH from acting on the corpus luteum. Prostaglandins from the uterus cause diminished regression of the corpus luteum in several well-studied mammals, including the guinea pig, ewe, cow, and mare.

Ovulation in Nonmammalian Vertebrates

Ovulation in fish is associated with a rise in GtH. Among several salmonid fish, increased release of GtH occurs with gonadal recrudencence, and a conspicuous rise is seen at the time of ovulation and spermiation, GtH secretions in at least some salmonid fish rise with an increase in day length. In the carp *(Cyprinus carpio)*, GtH increases in the summer, the season of ovarian growth, but is low in the spring, at the time of spawning. In some bony fish, mammalian LH induces ovulation. In some teleosts ovulation occurs together with a rise in corticosteroids from both ovarian and extraovarian sources, perhaps the interrenal tissue.

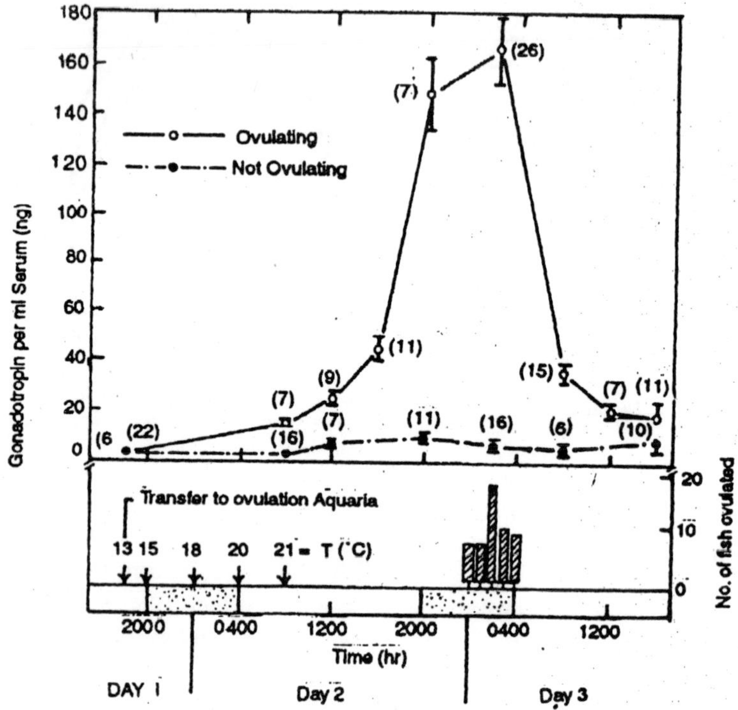

Fig. 4.5 Times of ovulation and serum gonadotropin (GtH) (mean ±SE) of sexually mature goldfish kept under 16L-8D photocycle and warmed from 13° to 21°C. Number of fish ovulating per each hour is shown in the lower graph. GtH measured in serum from ovulatory fish sampled at time of ovulation (0000-0400 on day 3) were pooled and expressed as a mean at 0200 on day 3.

In vivo administration of prostaglandins E_1, E_2 and $F_{2\alpha}$ were all followed by ovulation in female goldfish in which natural synthesis of prostaglandins had been blocked by indomethacin. $PGF_{2\alpha}$ is generally the most effective inducer of ovulation and may account for the follicular constriction in at least some teleosts. PGF is known to increase about the time of ovulation in a number of fish species. Prostaglandins also account for spawning behaviour.

The presence of eggs in the oviduct of a female goldfish has been shown to be the stimulus for spawning behavior. Removal of eggs by stripping will stop the spawning behavior, but spawning behavior resumes when the eggs are injected back into the ovarian lumen. This behavior is under the control of prostaglandin; nonovulated females will continue spawning behavior following prostaglandin injection. Prostaglandins have been implicated in spawning behavior of several unrelated species of fish. Experimentally, spawning behavior can be suppressed by indomethacin, prostaglandin inhibitor, and restored subsequently by prostaglandin injection.

Therc is some variation in the pathway mature ova follow when released from the ovary. In cyclostomes gametes are released directly into the coelomic cavity. In elasmobranchs the eggs are shed into slender oviducts; the lower oviducts are expanded and secrete a shell or, in live-bearing forms, house embryos. In teleost fish, ovulation varies: eggs may be released directly into the coelomic cavity (gymnovarian, as in salmonid fish) or into the ovarian lumen (cystovarian), in which case an oviduct is connected to the ovarian capsule. Unless fertilization is internal, as in some cystovarian species, oviposition soon follows ovulation (in several hours or days). The daily photocycle determines the time of day of both ovulation and oviposition of many species.

In teleosts a large number of eggs are ovulated within a short period, and they have a short life span if not soon laid and fertilized. It is essential, therefore, that ovulation is cued not only by endogenous factors but also by the presence of a male and, in oviparous species, an appropriate site for oviposition.

Ovulation in terrestrial ectotherms (amphibians and reptiles) seems to be controlled by gonadotropins. Experimentally, anurans with mature ova will ovulate following the administration of LH. Maturation of anuran ova normally follows a rise in gonadotropins. Gonadal steroids appear to constitute the direct cause of ovulation, for ovulation occurs as a result of the administration of steroids, especially progesterone the release of which is normally induced by a rise in gonadotropins. Amphibian ovaries are gymnovarian, as in most teleosts. Ova leave the ovaries and enter the coelomic cavity; they enter the oviducts at the ciliated funnel-like ostia.

Ovulation in *Bufo* may be the result of gonadotropin release. Progesterone induce the final meiotic division *in vitro. As* the eggs passes through the amphibian *oviduct, a* series of capsules enclose the ovum. It is enclosed by a vitelline membrane, which at this time becomes free of follicle cells. These capsules provide physical support for the developing embryo and probably control passage of materials to and from the embryo. The exterior capsule is usually not sufficiently hard to provide adequate physical protection against small predators, but the contents of the capsules of some salamanders (Salamandridae) and anurans *(Bufo* spp.) are sufficiently toxic to deter predators.

Ovulation has been carefully studied in several kinds of domestic fowl and the canary, which seem to exhibit a general pattern. Ovulation follows a peak in LH release. *A* series of follicles mature until a clutch is completed. Ovulation occurs during specified periods in the female's daily activity cycle. The space during which the LH surge may occur is called the *open period* and lasts about eight hours in the domestic fowl. It begins at the end of the daylight period and is apparently part of an entrained circadian rhythm. In the turkey hen there is a distinct surge of both LH and FSH prior to ovulation. Both gonadotropins seem to be essential to ovulation, but the separate role of each is not clear.

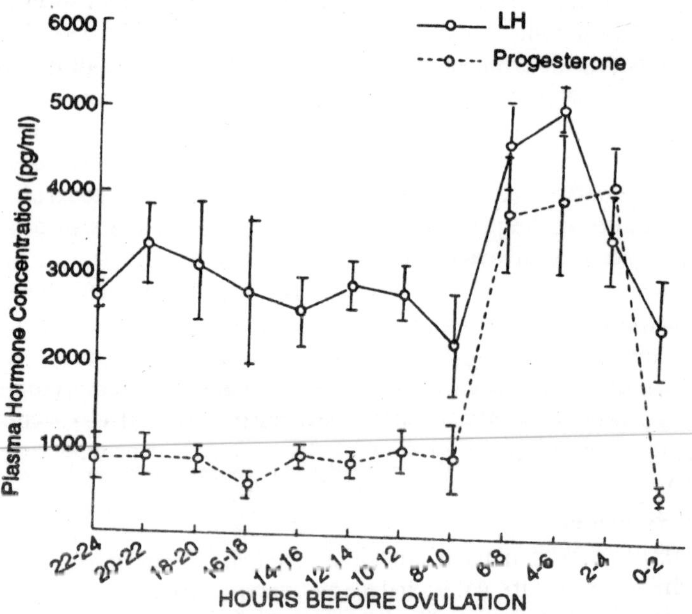

Fig. 4.6 Progesterone and LH levels in the plasma of turkey hens during the ovulatory cycle.

There are high levels of LH in the immature fowl, but they drop conspicuously as follicles develop in the mature hen. High levels of LH induce synthesis of estrogens and serum estrogens, which in turn depress the release of LH. The preovulatory surge of LH results primarily from secretions of progesterone; but experimentally the effect of progesterone requires priming by previous levels of estrogen. Through positive feedback the preovulatory release of progesterone induces the LH surge in birds. During follicular maturation and with the approach of ovulation in the domestic (white Leghorn) hen, steroidogenesis by the granulosa cells increases while activity of the theca cells declines.

The posterior lobe of the avian pituitary contains arginine vasotocin, a hormone to which the avian uterus is very sensitive. Circulating arginine vasotocin increases immediately prior to ovulation, and this hormone may constitute a stimulus for oviposition.

The avian ovulatory cycle differs from that of mammals in (1) the serial ovulation of single ova, until a clutch is formed, and (2) the large amount of yolk laid down with the ova during vitellogenesis. Following ovulation, the egg remains in the oviduct for some hours, during which time the egg is fertilized and provided with a shell and increases in mass. In many birds one egg is laid every day until the clutch is complete, and until the last egg is laid, oviposition is shortly followed by ovulation. The presence of an egg in the oviduct postpones the next ovulation.

Prostaglandins appear to have a role in regulating oviposition in birds. PGF increases fourfold in the preovulatory follicle of the domestic fowl 4 to 6 hours before the estimated time of ovulation, and this level increases about a hundredfold 24 hours later. Although indomethacin, which depresses levels of prostaglandins, does not prevent ovulation, it does delay laying up to 48 hours. Prostaglandins cause an increase in electrical activity of uterine muscle, the intensity varying with the dosage. This suggests the mechanism of their role in oviposition.

Induced Ovulation

Some vertebrates ovulate only after, and as a consequence of, cotton: these species are called induced ovulators. Induced ovulation is characteristic of the domestic rabbit, the ferret, the domestic cat, the vole, and many others. The short-tailed shrew *(Blarina brevicauda)*, an abundant insectivore of eastern North America, is an induced ovulator, as are probably many other soricid shrews. Ovulation is also induced in the house, or musk, shrew *(Suncus murinus)*. Although this phenomenon has been reported mostly for mammals, it may be widespread in other vertebrates with internal fertilization. It has been noted in the dogfish *(Mustelus can is)* and may well occur in other elasmobranchs. Although distinct in concept from spontaneous ovulation, the differences become somewhat blurred in reality.

The human female, for example, usually ovulates at midcycle, but there is evidence for ovulation induced by coition. Ova and corpora lutea may be present during any phase of the cycle, and conception may occur at any time, including during menstruation. Evidence for induced ovulation is derived from instances of conception following rape in women with definite knowledge of the last menstruation, and induced ovulation could reasonably result from the intensity of intercourse during rape. Also, the occasional failure of the rhythm method for birth control might be a manifestation of induced ovulation at a time other than the point at which ovulation would be expected to be spontaneous.

In induced ovulators stimulation of the cervix is followed by an increased release of LH, as a consequence of GnRH release from the hypothalamus. The hypothalamus apparently receives a neural communication from impulses initiated during cervical stimulation. Coition not only stimulates the pelvic nerve, thereby initiating the release of GnRH, but also induces a release of prolactin from the anterior pituitary. This prolactin is responsible for full development of the corpus luteum Copulation in the vole *(Microtus (grestis)* causes a large release of GnRH, which in turn stimulates a surge in LH. In the domestic cat, coitus is promptly followed by a rise in LH, and ovulation occurs about one day later.

Among species of voles (Arvicolidae) known to be induced ovulators, the ovulatory cycle is irregular. In *Microtus townsendii*, for example, estrous cycles begin at intervals of from two to eight days, and most vaginal scars indicate estrus or diestrus. Prolonged estrus in a species with induced ovulation enhances the likelihood of a fertile mating; this is one mechanism for promoting a rapid population increase.

Species with short life spans, high reproductive potential, and early sexual maturity tend to have induced ovulation. Although ovulation is usually induced by coition, olfactory signals sometimes have the same effect. A substantial body of evidence shows that odors of males may stimulate ovulation in females of the same species.

Unilateral Ovulation

In mammals ovarian activity and implantation are commonly random, with more or less equal activity on the left and right sides, but in some groups asymmetry exists. A departure from the norm is seen in (1) the release of an ovum always from the same side and (2) implantation always on one side only, which may not be ipsilateral to the active ovary.

In most bats ovulation and implantation appear to be random, but in some well-studied species there is a clear unilateral pattern. In at least two species of horseshoe bats *(Rhinolophus ferrumequinum* and *R. hipposiderous)*, only the right ovary releases ova, and implantation is always in the right uterine horn. A similar pattern is seen in the free-tailed bat *(Tadarida brasilliensis)* of the New World. Follicles do not develop in the left ovary, but the development of interstitial tissue suggests that steroidogenesis occurs in this "inactive" ovary. Among vesper bats *(Myotis sp.* and *Eptesicus spp.)* ovulation is random, but implantation is always in the right uterine horn. In the Indian vampire bat *(Megaderma lyra)* both ovulation and implantation are confined to the left side. A unique situation is seen in the bent-winged bats *(Miniopterus)* of the Old World. In at least three species *(M. schreibersii, M. austrails,* and *M. natalensis)* only the left ovary ovulates, but the zygote invariably implants in the right uterine horn. Although the California leaf-nosed bat *(Macrotus californicus)* ovulates from the right ovary, removal of the right ovary is followed by activation of the left ovary.

In the mountain viscacha *(Lagidium peruanum)*, a South American chinchillid rodent, ovulation is invariably from the right ovary and implantation always follows in the right horn. However, removal of the right ovary is followed by ovulation from the left ovary and implantation in either horn. In the rat such compensatory growth is follicular, so that the enlarged ovary releases a greater number of ova. Presumably the elimination of one ovary reduces inhibin and estrogen, allowing an increase in FSH, which causes the increased growth of the remaining ovary.

This asymmetry of the reproductive tract almost always appear to be associated with litters of one. Perhaps suppression of one half of the uterus allows greater development of the opposite half. Such asymmetry, however, is clearly lacking in those primates that usually have single births.

In some groups of mammals that characteristically have a single young, ovaries are alternatively ovulatory. This pattern is seen in seals, sea lions, porcupines, and many primates, but it is not asymmetrical. Alternating ovarian activity is also seen in some reptiles. The gecko *(Lepidodactylus lugubris)* on Oahu, Hawaiian Islands, lays a clutch of two eggs, and each ovary functions alternately.

Estrus or Heat

Cyclical changes in hormonal levels not only prepare the female for the production of a mature ovum and its release into the oviduct but also induce important behavioral changes. In all vertebrates the female becomes receptive to the sexual advances of a male, a condition known in mammals as estrus or *heat.* In almost all vertebrates certain behavioral signals, and frequently scents, announce the receptivity of the female. Estrus occurs shortly before ovulation and mating times so that the introduction of sperm is synchronized with ovulation. Notable exceptions are those species in which sperm is stored in the reproductive tract of the female. In these groups (some bats, many reptiles, some amphibians, and some fish), ovulation may follow mating by days, months, or even years.

In addition to olfactory advertising by a female mammal in estrus, some species may tend to move about more, and thereby increase the likelihood of an encounter with a male. In captives of two species of kangaroo rats *(Dipodomys microps* and D. *nterriami),* which are spontaneous ovulators, there is intense locomotor activity from just before to just after estrus.

Although most nonprimates mate only at estrus, the Asiatic house shrew *(Suncus)nurinus)* appears not to experience estrus, and mating seemingly occurs only at the will of an aggressive male. In this shrew the uterus and vagina seem not to depend upon estrogens. There is no uterine and vaginal atrophy after ovariectomy, and sexually inexperienced shrews will mate after ovariectomy.

Behavioral aspects of estrus precede physiological aspects and enhance the likelihood of sperm meeting a recently ovulated ovum, or coition may induce ovulation. Behavioral estrus may be somewhat prolonged: in the domestic dog, heat may persist for more than a week after ovulation, while estrogen levels remain high. In many mammals tactile stimulation of the genital region of the female at a point in proestrus may induce lordosis, an arching of the back indicating receptivity to the male. Postures vary among different groups of vertebrates, but the message is the same.

In several mammals the estrous cycle may be interrupted by a period of relative inactivity, or anestrus, at which time the ovary regresses to a small portion of its active mass. If fertilization occurs, estrous cycles cease. If there is a sterile mating or no mating, however, another follicular phase and ovulation may follow immediately or with only a brief delay. There may also be a postpartum estrus, at which time fertile mating may occur. A succession of estrous cycles is called a polyestrous pattern. This is characteristic of many species of small mammals. The polyestrous pattern and postpartum ovulation both enhance reproductive capacity. The occurrence of a single annual ovulatory cycle is called monestrous.

Silent heat is a phenomenon observed in sheep and some other mammals prior to the reproductive season. In silent heat there may be one or more ovulatory cycles in which ovulation occurs without overt behavioral signs. This presumably results from a lower threshold for ovulation than for the external manifestations of heat in response to gonadotropins. Some wild mice may have one or more ovulatory cycles, with the formation of corpora lutea, at the beginning of the reproductive season while the vagina remains closed. Normally the vagina opens prior to ovulation and closes after ovulation.

Menstruation and Menopause

The ovulatory cycle in primates is not profoundly unlike that of other vertebrates. However, in Old World primates, including humans, and a few other mammals, there is an appreciable buildup of the endometrium, the uterine lining. This is seen also in the elephant shrew (Elephantulus spp.) of Africa. With 'the decline of serum progesterone toward the end of the cycle, the endometrium loses its hormonal support. The thickened endometrium then becomes loosened and sloughs off, with a concomitant loss of blood, the menstrual flow.

In the human female, menarche, the onset of menstruation, usually starts at about 12 years of age and continues, with interruptions for pregnancies, until sometime between the ages of 48 to 55. Menarche occurs earlier in cultured societies today than in the nineteenth century, presumably as a result of improved nutrition. Following the release of progesterone from the corpus luteum, body temperature rises above the normal 37°C for some two to three days, which may be taken as evidence that ovulation has occurred.

Adolescent sterility is well established for humans. Among aboriginal tribes in many parts of the world, sexual intercourse commences at menarche, or sometimes before, but pregnancy is usually rare until four to six years later. This phenomenon has been observed by numerous anthropologists and is clearly not attributable to either abortions or any sort of birth control. Although estrogen fluctuations can produce secondary sexual characteristics as well as menstruation, ovulation does not occur without the midcycle surge of LH together with estrogen stimulation. Adolescent sterility is the occurrence of estrogen cycles (and menses) in the absence of adequate progesterone and without LH; it has been found to occur in most mammals in which it has been explored. Anovular cycles occur with the greatest frequency in the early years and gradually become minimal between 26 and 40 years, after which they increase somewhat.

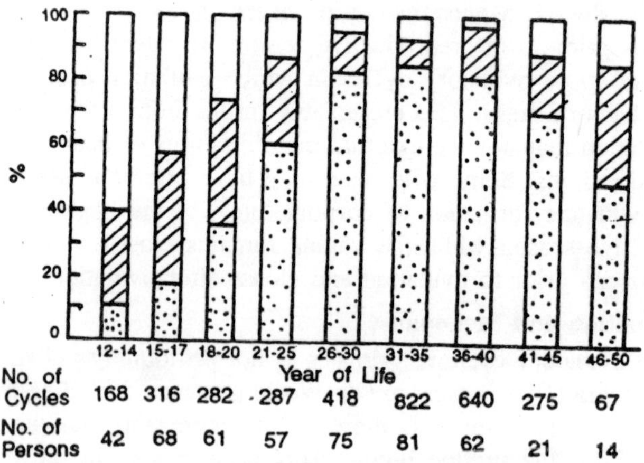

Fig. 4.7. Secular changes in ovulation in the human female. Black areas indicate incidence of normal ovulation; shaded areas show shortened (luteal) phase, and white areas show anovular menstrual cycles.

Menarche in the rhesus monkey *(Macaca mulatta) is* seen at about three years of age and, as in the human, it may not be accompanied by ovulation. In initial menstrual cycles there is only a brief luteal phase with little progesterone secretion. The hypothalamus appears not to respond to injections of estradiol, and this failure may account for the prepubertal, premenarchial condition. Maturity in the rhesus monkey is eliminated by destruction of the median basal hypothalamus, abolishing gonadotropin secretion by the anterior pituitary; but menstrual cycles are restored by treatment with GnRH in both adult and immature females. This indicates that in immature females sexual maturity is not dependent upon performance by either ovaries or the anterior pituitary. Current thought is that final maturation of hypothalamic control over gonadotropin release does not occur in the female until puberty, unlike the male, where the hypothalamic-pituitary-gonadal axis matures within a short period after birth.

Toward the end of fertility in the human female, menstrual cycles usually becomes less frequent than the "normal" 28 days, with the final menstrual flow being called menopause. The gradual decline in ovarian function is called the climacteric. Menopause is sometimes also considered to be the gradual decline in ovarian activity, resulting from a decrease in sensitivity to gonadotropins. The onset of this transition from an active to an inactive ovary most commonly occurs in the late forties, but in some individuals ovarian activity continues until age 55 and occasionally until the late sixties.

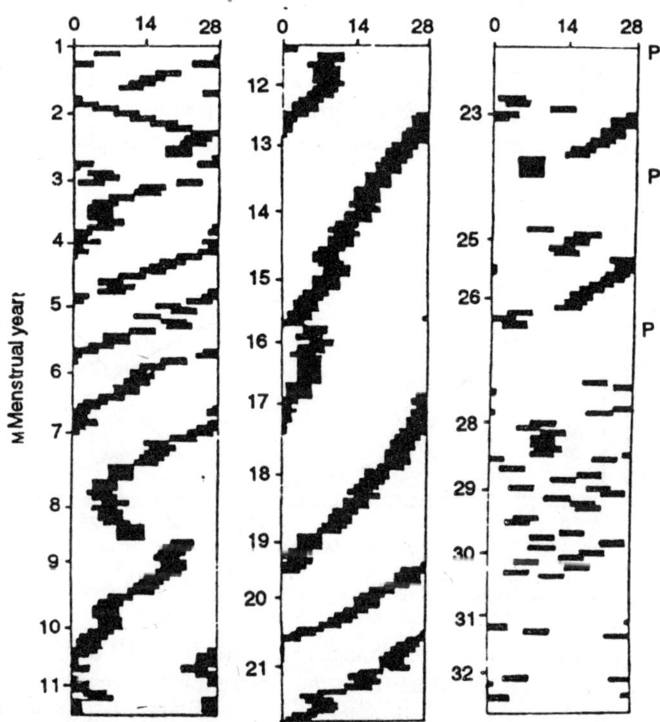

Fig. 4.8. A history of menstrual activity of one human female from the time of menarche (year 1) until menopause. In the right column, P indicates pregnancies.

Conception and healthy fetal development rarely occur beyond the age of 55. Conception after menopause in the human is very unusual, but there are examples of ovulation and conception after cessation of menstruation.

After menopause the ovary is shrunken and reduced in mass in contrast to an active premenopausal ovary. There may be many normal primordial follicles after the cessation of regular menstrual flows, but they lack the capacity to be stimulated by high levels of gonadotropins. Estrogen synthesis declines gradually to very low levels, during which time androgen production remains constant; and the conversion of some of this androgen accounts for the presence of low levels of serum estrogen.

Menopause is a known, definite phenomenon in the human female and at least some other Old World primates. In the macaque *(Macaca mulatta)*, menopause occurs after 25 years of age, and at 30 years of age females are considered postmenopausal. After the cessation of menstrual bleeding in the rhesus monkey, there are persistent high serum levels of gonadotropins and low levels of ovarian steroids. Also, the African elephant *(Loxodonta africana)* experiences a decline in reproductive activity with age and a cessation of reproduction after about 50 years.

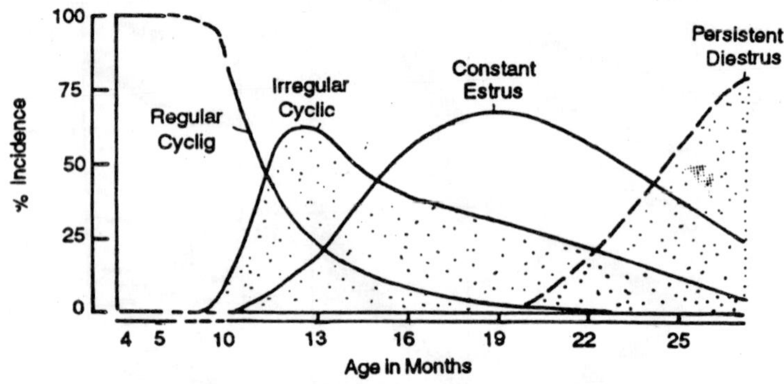

Fig. 4.9. Secular changes in the regularity of the ovulatory cycle of laboratory rats, between 9 and 26 months of age.

Age-related reproductive changes increase from 10 to 12 months in the laboratory rat, at which time the frequency of irregular cycling increases. As female rats grow older, uterine concentration of estrogen receptors steadily decreases. Subsequently, there is a gradual increase in frequency of anovulatory female rats, with reduced production of ovarian steroids and also diminishing cyclical releases of gonadotropins and prolactin.

Senescence and a decline in ovarian activity have been noted in such fish as the guppy *(Poecilia reticulata)*, the molly *(P. formosa)*, and the fighting fish *(Betta splendens),* as well as some marine fish. There is a reduction in vitellogenesis and an increase in atresia.

THE CORPUS LUTEUM

The earliest phylogenetic appearance of the corpus luteum is that of a corpus luteum-like structure in an ascidian *(Ciona intestinalis).* In this urochordate the expended follicles regress, but the unruptured (atretic) follicles become luteinized and have been called "preovulatory corpora lutea." They are not known to be secretory.

In many vertebrates ovulation is followed by luteinization of the remnant tissue in the collapsed follicle, and this constitutes the corpus luteum. The occurrence is highly variable among nonmammalian vertebrates. It is usually absent or short-lived in oviparous forms. Prior to ovulation both FSH and estrogens seem to increase the number and sensitivity of LH binding sites. Following ovulation, with the concurrent surge of LH, a blood supply reaches the granulosa cells in the ruptured follicle, and luteinization of this tissue induces the development of the corpus luteum (or corpora lutea). The granulosa cells are receptive to a host of steroids, peptides (LH and prolactin), and prostaglandins, which are assumed to induce steroidogenic enzymes.

Luteinization actually begins prior to ovulation in most species. In the event of pregnancy, prolactin levels are high and help maintain the corpus luteum in certain mammals. In a sterile cycle, prolactin remains low and the corpus luteum degenerates rather quickly. Prolactin prolongs the functional life span of the corpus luteum by increasing LH binding sites on granulosa cells. In some mammals, such as the guinea pig, the corpus luteum survives without prolactin.

The corpus luteum appears as a conspicuous yellow protrusion on the surface of the ovary in most viviparous vertebrates. It produces progesterone, and its development among various taxa may perhaps vary with their need for this steroid. Corpora atretica and postovulatory corpora lutea develop in both oviparous and viviparous elasmobranchs, but their function is not clear. The development of secretory corpora lutea in.sharks has been suggested, and corpora lutea of the viviparous torpedo *(Torpedo marmorata)* are reported to be steroidogenic.

Several teleost fish produce luteinized corpora atretica from unovulated follicles. They occur in the long-jawed goby *(Gillichthys mirabilis),* but they are not known to be secretory. The postovulatory follicles in this teleost are quickly resorbed and do not form corpora lutea.

Among oviparous amphibians the ruptured follicle contains granulosa cells and some lipids, but there is little evidence of secretory activity. In several live-bearing species (both ovoviviparous and viviparous), functional corpora lutea form and secrete progesterone until the birth of young. In the viviparous toad *(Nectrophrynoides occidentalis)* of Africa, for example, the corpora lute remain throughout pregnancy and secrete progesterone. Corpora lutea persist in both egg-laying and live-bearing caecilians. The function of the corpus luteum in oviparious species is equivocal, but there could be some intrauterine development prior to oviposition.

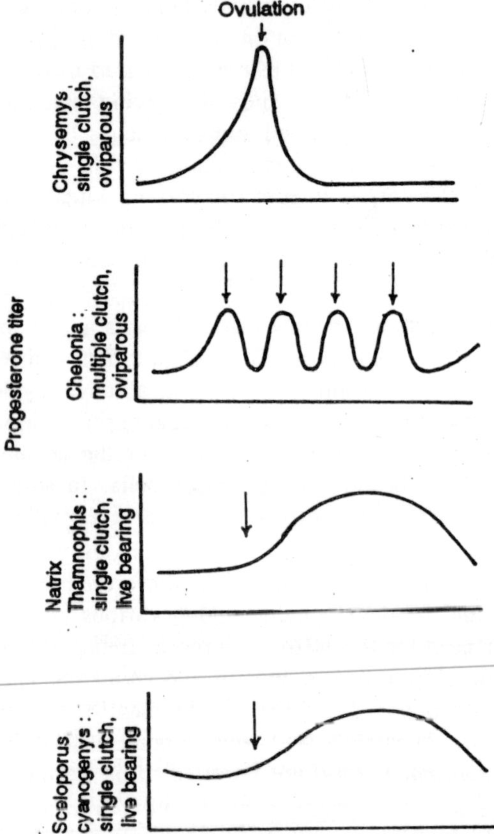

Fig. 4.10. Plasma progesterone titers during the annual reproductive cycle of several reptiles. The two upper patterns represent turtles, showing an ovulatory peak of progesterone, and the lower two patterns show the postovulatory peak of progesterone in some live-bearing snakes and lizards.

The role of the corpus luteum in reptiles is not clearly understood. Corpora lutea invariably follow ovulation in reptiles, but the duration is brief in egg-laying species. In two oviparous lizards *(Crotophytus collaris* and *Eumeces obsoletus)* progesterone synthesis is greatest during luteogenesis and is positively correlated with atresia. Luteal regression occurs approximately at the time of oviposition in many lizards, and the decline in gonadal steroids may cause oviductal contractions associated with oviposition. In viviparous species it persists and presumably accounts for a high level of progesterone, whereas there is an ovulatory peak in oviparous reptiles. In the New World natracine snakes, all of which are viviparous, the corpus luteum may persist throughout pregnancy and produce progesterone. In the garter snake *(Thamnophis elegans)*, luteectomy performed in the first trimester does not terminate pregnancy, although parturition is delayed and about half the young have placentae with yolk still in the yolk sac. In the DeKay's snake ovulation *(Storeria dekayi)*, a small natracine of eastern North America, the corpus luteum contains 2-1 hydrolase, an enzyme implicated in the synthesis and secretion of progesterone.

Unlike the corpus luteum of eutherian mammals, that of the tammar wallaby *(Macro pus eugenii)* continues to grow after hypophysectomy and stimulates uterine growth in the absence of the hypophysis. Removal of the corpus luteum in the pregnant tammar wallaby before day 17 interferes with successful parturition. Presumably both progesterone and relaxin from the corpus luteum are essential for a healthy birth in this marsupial.

Large corpora lutea develop in monotremes *(Ornithorhynchus anatinus* and *Tachyglossus aculeatus)* and persist until the eggs are laid. In an individual with near-term eggs in the oviduct, very high levels of progesterone were noted.

Preservation of the Corpus Luteum

The corpus luteum attains its maximal role only if the ovum is fertilized, and if fertilization does not occur, progesterone secretion is less than maximal. The life of the corpus luteum following fertilization varies among different taxa, but the corpus luteum of pregnancy is essentially similar to that of a sterile cycle, except that it persists longer and may become larger in a fertile cycle. In the guinea pig the corpus luteum forms in sterile cycles and may persist much longer than in the rat. This may account for the long ovulatory cycle (16-18 days) of the guinea pig. Also, in the domestic dog the corpora lutea remain functional in the absence of mating, and progesterone release is substantial up to 80 days after estrus. In a number of laboratory rodents, however, there is a small amount of postovulatory progesterone for about one day, and such mammals are called *incomplete cyclers*. In these mammals the corpus luteum becomes a major source of progesterone only after an ovum is fertilized.

The corpus luteum can be maintained by several substances: (1) prolactin, from the anterior pituitary, secreted as a result of coition; (2) LH from the anterior pituitary, also secreted as a result of stimulation of the cervix; *(3)* estrogen from the blastocyst; and (4) a placental gonadotropin, such as pregnant mare serum gonadotropin (or PMSG), from the fetal cells of the placenta. In the ferret *(Mustelus putorius)*, prolactin is necessary to maintain the corpus luteum and its production of progesterone during the first half of pregnancy. Subsequent progesterone levels decline until parturition, but mammary development suggests continued secretion of prolactin. Seemingly the corpus luteum of the ferret becomes decreasingly responsive to prolactin.

Among its several effects, progesterone in some domestic and laboratory mammals stimulates the uterus to secrete PGF_{2a} in the absence of fertilization. This material is luteolytic, leading to the decline of the corpus luteum. Oxytocin from the corpus luteum of the ewe may stimulate release of PGF_{2a}, which, in turn, by a positive feedback may induce release of luteal oxytocin. This cycle would amplify the luteolytic effect, causing the demise of the corpus luteum. In contrast to this relationship of uterine prostaglandins and the corpus luteum in some domestic mammals,' uterine prostaglandins do not cause a regression of the corpus luteum in primates, including the human. In primates ovarian

PGF_2 blocks LH binding by the corpus luteum, and although PGF_{2a} does depress serum levels of progesterone, it does not induce regression of the corpus luteum. Functions of the corpus luteum vary among different taxa of mammals. In many mustelid carnivores and in some kangaroos, for example, the corpus luteum seems to regulate the embryonic diapause of the blastocyst, probably via photoperiodic cues (in the mustelids) or via nervous cues from the nipples or photographic cues (in the kangaroos). In either case, resumption of luteal activity seems to be related to implantation of the blastocyst.

Accessory Corpora Lutea

Some species of mammals have more, sometimes many more,

corpora lutea than fertilized ova. These corpora lutea are usually postovulatory structures, but some may result from unovulated follicles (corpora atretica). Some may be secretory, but for the most part their role is unknown.

In the early pregnancy of the horse, there is a single corpus luteum. This corpus luteum secretes progesterone until implantation, after which PMSG is secreted by the placenta. PMSG stimulates the ovary to further ovulation, producing a series of ovulations, and the subsequently formed corpora lutea continue to secrete progesterone throughout pregnancy.

Accessory corpora lutea have been noticed in carefully observed laboratory populations of the Australian hopping mouse *(Notomys alexis)*. These structures are typical corpora lutea that result from postfertilization ovulations and occur in both pregnant and lactating females. Similarly, the Canadian porcupine *(Erithizon dorsatum)* usually has a single young. A single follicle ruptures and becomes luteinized, and the remaining structures become atretic and luteinized. The African elephant *(Loxodonta africana)* ovulates after conception, and there may be several very long-lived corpora lutea in each ovary. In three species of elephant shrews *(Elephantulus myurus, E. capensis,* and *Macroscelides proboscideus),* each ovary releases about 60 eggs at one time, with the subsequent development of 60 corpora lutea in each ovary. The total lutein tissue in these species, however, seems no greater than in *Elephantulus intufi,* which releases one or two ova and forms one or two very large corpora lutea.

5

COPULATORY ORGANS

To ensure the placement of the sperm within the oviduct, various hold-fast mechanisms, as well as organs of copulation, have been evolved in different animals.

Holdfast Mechanisms

The amphibians, which are halfway land animals, have been so occupied with adapting themselves to a dual existence that apparently they have not been able to accomplish much in an evolutionary way for their accessory reproductive apparatus. The result is that for the most part they return to the water during the breeding season, where fluid for the locomotion of the sperm cells is freely provided; and there is no necessity for elaborating organs to accomplish internal fertilization.

Amphibians do, however, improve upon the improvident and wasteful ways of most fishes, with their countless eggs and unthinkable numbers of sperm. For example, frogs practice *amplexation* during the breeding season, that is the male frog saddles himself on to the back of the female, whose body, unfettered by hooplike ribs, becomes more and more swollen by the increasing mass of eggs within. The male retains his grasp upon the slippery back of the female by means of temporarily roughened glandular swollen thumbs, which are inserted under the armpits of the female and act as holdfasts. He remains in amplexation until the female extrudes the eggs, when he immediately sheds the sperm over them. In this way the hazards and uncertainties

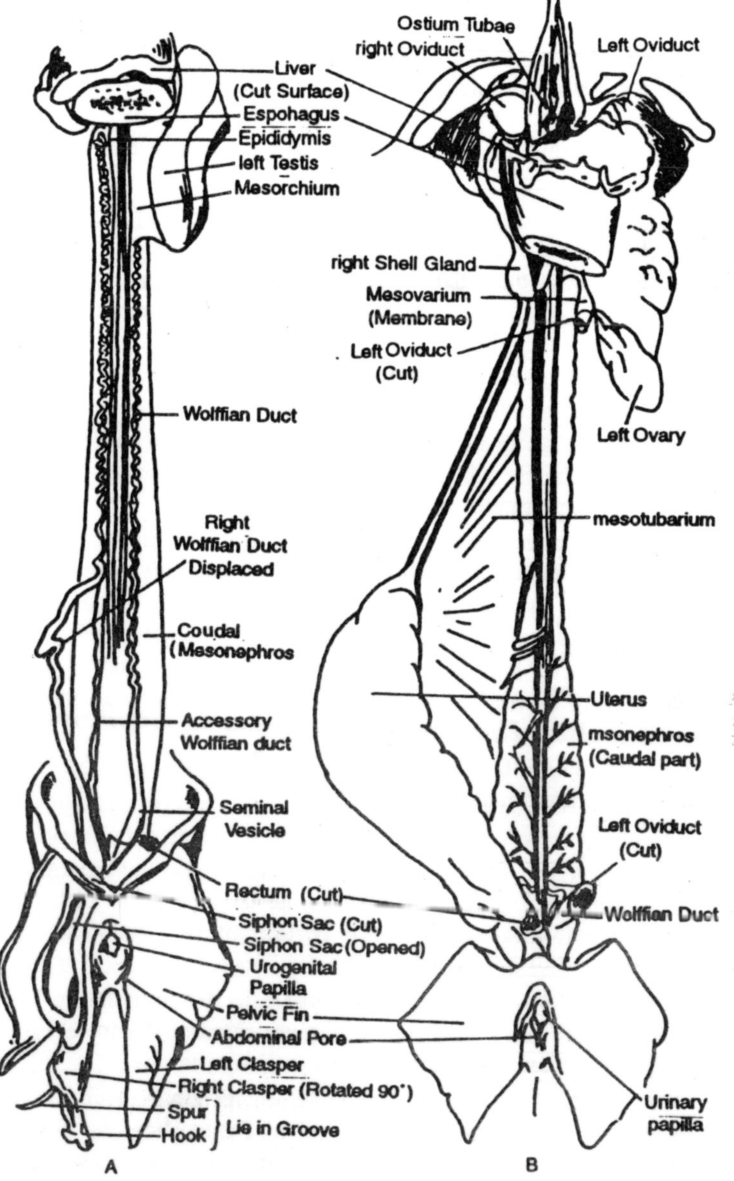

Fig. 5.1. Urogenital organs of the spiny dogfish, Squalus acanthias. A, *male; B1 female. In both cases the gonad of the right side was removed to show more dorsal structures. (From Sayles,* Vie Spiny Dogsh, Squalus acanthias).

of distance between the germ cells of the two sexes are greatly lessened.

The hylas, or tree frogs, and the "obstetric frog" *Alytes,* of Europe, do not ordinarily resort to the water to breed, but Kammerer reports that when *Alytes is* compelled to breed in water, amplexation occurs and the thumbs of the male become swollen and roughened as in other frogs.

Many male lizards possess a row of peculiar porthole-like "glands" down the inner surface of the hind legs. These femoral structures are not true glands, producing a liquid secretion. Instead they extrude a dry scaly substance that roughens the surface of the legs so that when the male lizard in mating grasps the female between his hind legs, the security of his grip is insured.

Snakes coil around each other in the mating embrace. The male boa-constrictor, according to Boas, is supplied with *and hooks* that aid in holding together the cloacas of the two sexes during the transfer of sperm to the female.

Among higher vertebrates, organs already present but not especially evolved to accomplish the holdfast function in reproduction are utilized for this purpose. Thus, the cock when treading a hen employs his beak and claws. In animals like ruminants, where holdfast organs would be difficult to imagine, the sexual act is usually accomplished very quickly, as in the case of the tumultuous and almost instantaneous leap of the stag. Camels solve their copulation difficulties by assuming a sitting-down posture.

Male Copulatory Organs

Copulation consists of the introduction of a male copulatory organ, the *penis,* in which the sperm duct terminates, into the enlarged end of the eviduct, or *vagina.* The discharge of the sperm cells under these circumstances makes more certain their placement in the immediate vicinity of the eggs to be fertilized.

It is to be expected that the apparatus for copulation in the aggressive male with sperm cells to deliver should be more elaborated than that of the receptive female, and such is the case.

Not all the organs for copulation among vertebrates are homologous. Thus, male elasmobranchs of many species possess a pair of "claspers," one on each side of the cloaca, which are modifications of the medial parts of the pelvic fins. In these animals, whose young are "born alive" in an advanced stage of development, copulation and internal fertilization are effected by the aid of these claspers, equipped with hooks, which are inserted into the cloaca of the female and serve to direct the sperm along their grooved inner margins into the oviducts.

Rarely a similar contrivance is found among teleosts, that serves as an intromittent organ. This is formed sometimes out of the ventral or anal fin, as in the strange Brazilian bony fish, *Girardinus,* and sometimes from the metamorphosed haemal spine of a caudal vertebra.

It is with land life, however, that the evolution of internal fertilization and attendant copulatory mechanisms really begins, although none of the amphibians have a penis, with the possible exception of the footless caecilians. In these tropic amphibians, which have taken to land life in damp situations, the walls of the male cloaca during copulation are everted into the cloaca of the female, thus serving as an intromittent device.

Fig. 5.2. Dogfish in copulation.

Internal fertilization without the assistance of copulatory organs is accomplished among certain urodeles, *Triturus, Amblystoma, Triton,* and the viviparous *Salamandra atra* of Alpine streams, by a very different method. The males during the breeding season deposit their sperm in small compact packets or *spermatophores,* surrounded by a protective gelatinous mass, while the females follow after the males as the spermatophores are produced, and use their cloacal lips to pick up the spermatophores, even when the latter are deposited on land as sometimes occurs.

Among modern reptiles two types of penes have been evolved. First, among lizards and snakes, *double cloacal organs* are found, which may be everted somewhat after the manner employed by caecilians. Each *hemipenis* has a spiral groove along its medial surface for the conveyance of the sperm. Second, turtles and crocodiles have a single penis, lying along the ventral wall of the cloaca, slightly protrusible and supplied with erectile tissue, dorsally grooved along its length. During copulation this groove is made into a temporary canal by its contact with the upper dorsal wall of the cloaca.

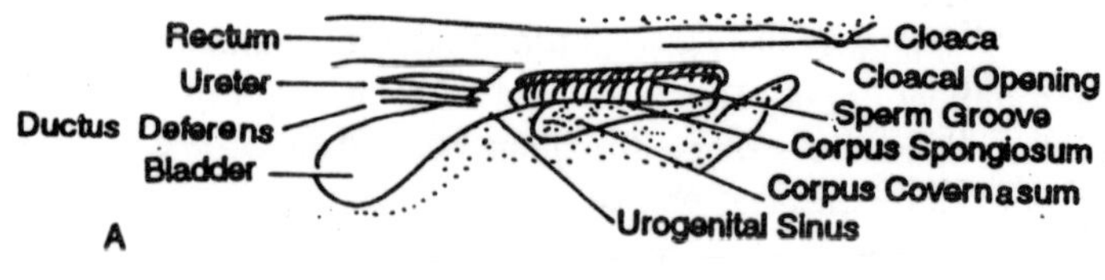

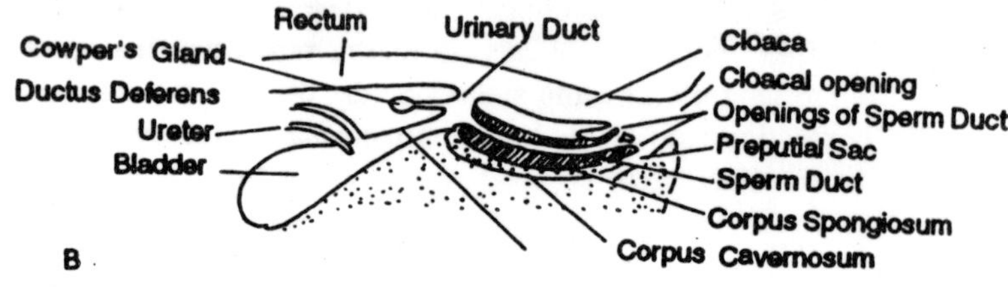

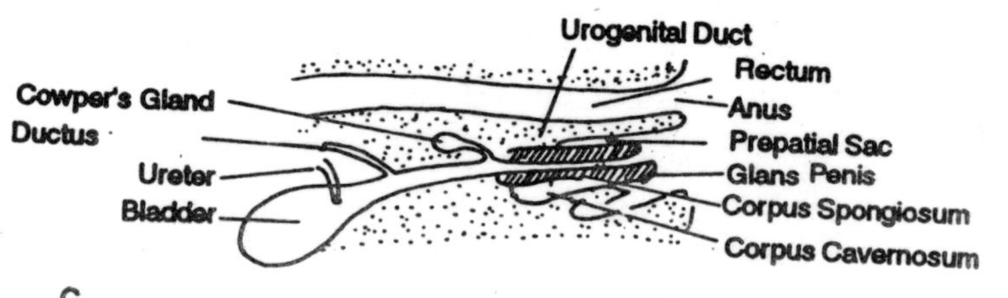

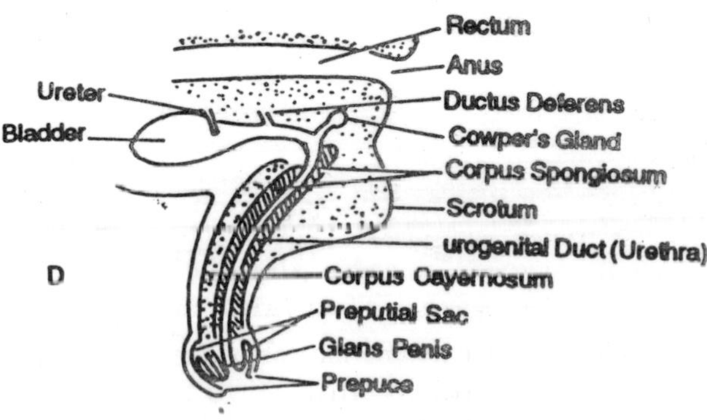

Fig. 5.3. Stages in the evolution of the penis. A, tortoise; B, spiny anteater; C, kangaroo; D, man.

The single penis of the crocodiles is formed by two component parts suggesting a double origin. In turtles the size of the penis bears a distinct relation to the difficulties encountered in copulation because of the awkward shell. It is smaller in marine turtles having a flattened or incomplete plastron, than in fresh-water or land forms with a more complete and over-arching shell.

Among birds there is no true copulation, but impregnation by the method of the cloacal kiss is the general rule. There are, however, a few birds, notably ostriches and other ratitates, certain ducks, and the South American "tinamou," which have well-developed penes, resembling those of crocodiles.

The penis in all mammals, with the exception of monotremes, is a closed tube and not a grooved structure as in reptiles. Intermediate forms between reptiles and mammals are not known. It is typically a turgescent organ under the control of vaso-dilator nerves which arise as autonomic fibers in the sacral region of the spinal cord, and is composed of two masses of erectile tissue side by side, the *corpora cavernosa,* with a third similar mass, the *corpus spongiosum* beneath them, held together by fibrous tissue and enveloped by a layer of loose skin.

The corpus spongiosum is perforated for its entire length by the urethra. Consequently the urethra is considerably longer in the male than in the corresponding female. It terminates in an enlargement of the corpus spongiosum called the glans, which is split in marsupials where the female has a double vagina.

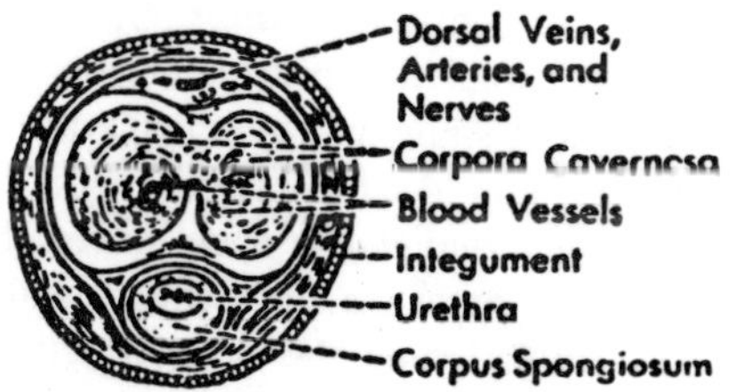

Fig. 5.4. Transverse section through middle of human penis.

In some animals, for example the cat, guinea pig, and wombat, the glans is beset with horny recurrent spines or corneal scales that stimulate the female during copulation, although in most cases the skin extending over the surface of the glans is extremely sensitive and delicate without any hard corneal layer. Ruminants, cetaceans, and some rodents are exceptional in that there is no glans present, while sheep, goats and many antelopes possess a peculiar threadlike elongation of the sperm duct beyond the end of the penis itself, called the *processus urethrails*.

Among higher animals the glans is enveloped in a double fold of retractile skin, the *preputium*. This is present only in forms with a pendent penis and is homologous with the sheath in which the penis is withdrawn in many animals such as ungulates.

In several kinds of mammals, namely, marsupials, cetaceans, moles, carnivores, rodents, bats, seals, lemurs, monkeys, and some apes, there is present in various degrees of development, lying in the connective tissue between the two corpora cavernosa and above the urethra, a penis bone, *os priapi*, which increases the rigidity of the organ which in most cases is attained by temporary turgidity caused by an influx of blood.

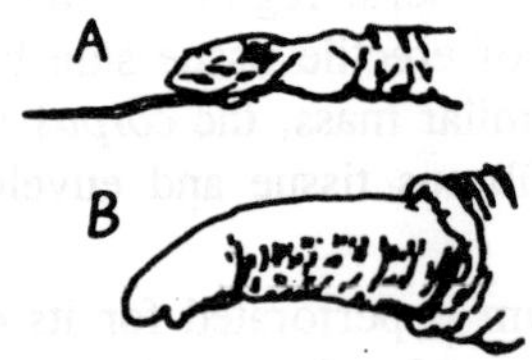

Fig. 5.5. A, distal end of ram's penis, showing glans and processus urethralis, *or filiform appendage. B, distal end of bull's penis, showing glans and urethral papilla, representing vestigial filiform appendage. In both cases the prepuce is folded back.*

Among mammals the obliteration of the cloaca goes hand in hand with the evolution of the penis, or *phallus*. In monotremes a cloaca is still present, and the small non-protrusible penis is enclosed in a sac between the urogenital sinus and the cloaca itself. It is a fibrous, slightly erectile structure of double origin, with a groove between the two parts that is converted into a canal except posteriorly where the urogenital and cloacal passages still connect with each other. The ureters, instead of terminating in the bladder with a urethral outlet for the urine, empty through a urogenital sinus into the cloaca, the penis being utilized solely for the conduction of the sperm.

The marsupial penis, with the reduction of the cloaca, becomes an external erectile structure directed backward, through which both urine and sperm have common passage-*way*, as in *all higher* mammals. *The scrotum containing* the *testes is located anterior to* the *penis. The distance* between the penis and the anus *is so* slight in these animals that both penis and anus are enclosed together within a common muscular sphincter. The opossum *Didelphys,* the bandicoot *Perameles,* and some other species, have a bifurcate glans that is probably correlated with the double vagina in the females of these forms.

Among placental mammals the penis is in front of the scrotal sac and usually withdrawn within a protective sheath, except during sexual activity.. In most cases it is directed forward and, when no sheath is present, is pendulous, as in bats and man. In monkeys and apes it is partly pendulous and partly ensheathed. In cats and rodents it is directed backward, except during copulation, so that these animals micturate posteriorly. Armadillos, handicapped by their awkward armor, have a relatively enormous penis which may extend as much as one-third of the length of the body during copulation.

Female Genitalia

The female genitalia concerned in copulation, aside from certain glands and the rudimentary *clitoris,* are the vagina, vestibule, hymen, and the labia minora and majora. All of these structures are differentiated to a point comparable with the degree of evolution attained by the copulatory organs of the corresponding males, reaching their maximum in the primates.

The *vagina* is that part of the oviduct adapted to receive the penis. It is absent in the monotremes where the cloaca serves the same purpose. In the opossum, *Didelphys,* and other marsupials, there are two distinct vaginas which barely coalesce into one at the outer entrance, while in some other marsupials there-is a coalescence at the inner ends from which a median diverticulum, or third vagina, extends posteriorly as a blind alley between the two lateral vaginas. Whenever a fetus becomes deposited in this closed middle vagina instead of in one of the two lateral open passage-ways, there must be a rupture at birth at the blind end of the middle vagina to allow for the expulsion of the young.

In placental mammals the outer ends of the two oviducts open into a single vagina, located between the rectum dorsally and the urethra ventrally. It is lined with mucous membrane, frequently crossed by transverse rugae, particularly in young individuals. The vaginal mucosa is without glands, the mucus that is present there coming from the walls of the *uterus,* especially the *cervix,* which is continuous with the vagina. The walls of the vagina are muscular and collapsible, and the muscular fibers near the external orifice form a sphincter.

The outer part of the vagina constitutes the *vestibule,* which is separated from the vagina proper by a temporary fold of mucous membrane, more or less complete, called the *hymen.* This is the real end of the embryonic Mi llerian duct, and it partially occludes the passage-way, particularly before copulation has taken place. Originally in all mammals, the hymen persists in bears, seals, hyaenas, and most apes, but is present only in the young of the horse, pig and mole.

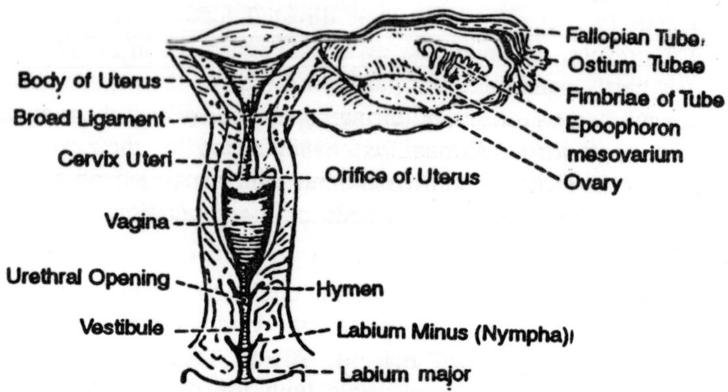

Fig. 5.6. Dorsal view diagram of human female reproductive organs.

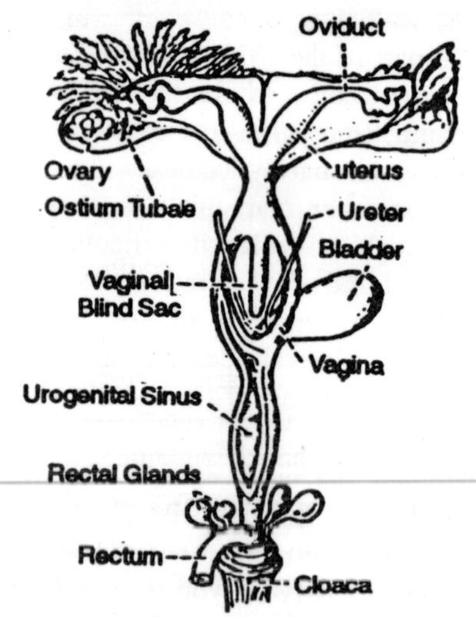

Fig. 5.7. Female urogenital organs of the wombat, Phascolomys, *a marsupial.*

The walls of the vestibule are supplied with erectile tissue which at times becomes surcharged with blood. In primates generally around the vestibule on either side are two folds of skin, the *labia minora,* while in the higher primates there are in addition two external folds, the *labia majora,* covered outwardly with pubic hair and supplied with a certain amount of fatty tissue. There ig also a pad of adipose tissue anterior to the vestibular orifice at the edge of the public bones. Likewise covered with hair, it is called the *mons Veneris*. It is better developed in the human females of civilized races than in those of more primitive types. The female bushman is remarkable for the hypertrophy of the labia minora, as well as for the enlarged posterior gluteal muscles, resulting in enormously prominent buttocks, or the condition described as *steatopygy*.

The *clitoris* in the female is homologous with the penis in the male. It is situated just anterior to the vestibular opening between the folds of the labia minora and consists of two corpora cavernosa that are erectile, but there is no corpus spongiosum present, and the clitoris is not traversed by the urethra like the male penis, except in a few rodents, insectivores, and lemurs. In this latter case the urethra is not a urogenital canal, as in the penis, but is exclusively for the transmission of urine, as in other mammals. An imperforate clitoris is present in turtles, crocodiles, and a few exceptional birds whose males possess a penis. There is even a clitoris bone in certain mammalian species that corresponds to the os priapi of the male. The clitoris, which is relatively large in monkeys, being six or seven centimeters long in the young spider monkey, *Ateles, is* comparatively small and degenerate in the human female.

ACCESSORY GLANDS

Associated with the reproductive apparatus are various glands which (1) provide a fluid medium for the locomotion of the sperm cells; (2) facilitate copulation by reducing friction; (3) produce odors that are alluring to the opposite sex; and (4) furnish nutriment for the developing young. These glands may be grouped according to their place of origin into those (1) in the sperm duct or oviduct; (2) in the urogenital canal; or (3) in the integument.

Originating in the Sperm Duct or Oviduct

In many cases, for example in ruminants, most rodents, dogs, bears, martens, and shrews, the outer end of the sperm duct, near its entrance into the urethra, enlarges into an *ampulla,* which serves as a temporary reservoir for the sperm. This is lined with *ampullar glands* that secrete mucus. Such glands are absent in the cat, mole, European hedgehog *Erinaceus,* and the pig. In most mammals a saclike *seminal vesicle,* lined with mucous glands, empties into each ductus deferens just beyond the ampulla. Between the seminal vesicle and the urethra the sperm duct is known as the ejaculatory duct. In general these vesicles have a glandular rather than a storage function, although sperm cells are frequently found therein. In the case of bats and some mice, the seminal vesicles enable these animals to exercise a sort of "births control," in that after copulation the mucus that they produce forms a gummy plug which fills the entrance to the uterus, the cervical orifice, and prevents for a considerable time subsequent impregnation. There are no seminal vesicles in monotremes, marsupials, cetaceans, or carnivores. In man they appear first about the end of the third month of fetal life.

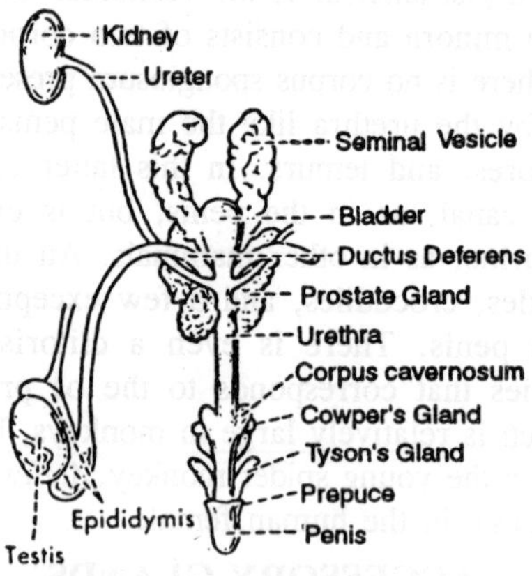

Fig. 5.8. Urogenital apparatus of a hamster, Cricetus.

In the human female there are present at least three sorts of glands, namely, uterine, cervical, and vestibular, associated with corresponding regions of the oviduct.

The *uterine glands* are tubular structures lining the uterus. They have to do with the epithelial regeneration of the uterine walls during menstruation, rather than with glandular secretion.

The much branched *cervical glands,* found in the cervix of the uterus, produce mucus which moistens the inner surface of the glandless vagina, while the scattered *vestibular glands,* located in the vestibule near the clitoris and around the outlet of the urethra, perform a similar function.

Originating from the Urogenital Canal

The glands of the urogenital canal are the prostate, in the male, and the urethral glands, which appear in both sexes.

The *prostate gland,* in man at least, is the most important of all the accessory reproductive glands. It *is* a compound tubulo-alveolar gland about the size of a horse-chestnut, made up of thirty to fifty lobules and opening into the urethra by means of two large and fifteen to thirty lesser ducts. It is embedded in a tough capsule of connective tissue and abundantly supplied with blood, nerves, lymph, and more smooth muscle cells than any other accessory reproductive gland. It surrounds the beginning of the urethra at the point where the ducti deferentes, or sperm ducts, enter.

The secretion produced by the prostate gland, forming a large part of the *semen,* or spermatic fluid, is a thin milky emulsion, faintly alkaline with a characteristic odor. The prostate gland is well developed in rodents, bats, perissodactyls, primates, and most carnivores. It is less well developed in ruminants, and is absent in monotremes, marsupials, edentates, and among carnivores, in the marten, otter, and badger. In man the prostate gland frequently becomes hypertrophied in old age and may deposit concretions of calcium phosphate, causing trouble by pressure upon the urethra which it envelops.

The urethral glands are of two sorts. First, mucous glands, called *glands of Littre,* in the male, that are most numerous in the dorsal region of the urethral wall along the penile part of its course; and second, paired *oulbourehtral glands,* called *Cowper's glands* in the male and *Bartholin's glands* in the female.

Cowper's glands are two small structures about the size of peas in the human male, with ducts an inch long opening into the urethra at the base of the penis. They produce a clear glairy mucus during sexual excitement which protects the sperm against traces of acid that may be present. Bears, dogs, and aquatic mammals lack Cowper's glands, but in other mammals they are quite generally present, being especially large and active in rodents, elephants, pigs, camels, and horses. They are the only accessory reproductive glands in the male *Echidna.*

Corresponding to Cowper's glands of the male, are the glands of Bartholin in the female, that open into the vestibule in the groove on either side between the hymen and and labia minora. They produce mucus which functions largely as a lubricant during copulation.

In the formation of the semen it has been shown that the first contributions come from Cowper's glands and the glands of Littre, followed by the secretion of the prostate gland before the sperm from the ductus deferens are added, while the final glandular contribution is from the seminal vesicles.

Originating in the Integument

Various odoriferous glands of integumentary origin, named in different cases *anal, inguinal, perinaeal,* and *cloacal glands,* occur among vertebrates. These are usually located around the anus or genital aperture and serve to stimulate the opposite sex. The famous scent glands of skunks belong to this category, as do also the anal glands of dogs, which are well known to be of paramount important in the social life of these animals.

Tyson's glands are small sebaceous glands that are situated around the base of the glans on the penis in the depths of the preputial fold of skin. They also produce an odorous substance called *smegma.*

The male alligator has *submaxillary glands* at the edge of the lower jaw on either side, which enlarge and emit a musky odor during sexual excitement.

Finally, under integumentary glands there should be mentioned the *mammary glands,* already described in a previous chapter, that have a place in the general scheme of reproduction in the mammals, since they provide sustenance for the newly born young.

Marsupials, which have no true placenta, nourish the fetus before birth with "uterine milk" produced by uterine glands.

Devices for the Care of Eggs and Young

Uterus

With most animals that practice internal fertilization, a part of the oviduct becomes modified into a brood organ, the *uterus,* for the protection of the developing embryo. This structure is located midway between the upper portion of the oviduct, called in human anatomy the *Fallopian tube,* which receives the egg from the ovary, and the vagina below. The virgin uterus is completely within the pelvis but during pregnancy it is shifted to a position higher up in the abdomen. Its thick muscular walls are capable of great distension, enlarging over 200 times when accommodating a growing fetus. When unoccupied by young the cavity within the uterus is relatively small and the shrunken inner walls are more or less in contact with each other. The rounded mouth of the uterine cervix, where it meets the vagina, frequently projects somewhat into the vaginal cavity.

Even in frogs the oviduct during the breeding season enlarges but its cloacal end into a "uterus" for the temporary lodgment of the eggs. Viviparous teleosts, as also some elasmobranchs, have a well-developed highly vascularized uterus. Mammals, however, show the greatest differentiation of this organ.

A uterine modification of the oviduct, when found among lower vertebrates, is usually a double structure, one for each oviduct, but with increasing coalescence of the oviducts in mammals to form a single vagina, there is a tendency for this fusion to involve either a part or the entire uterine region. All the theoretical intermediary evolutionary stages from a double uterus to a single one have their actual counterparts stages from a double uterus to a single one have their actual counterparts in nature among mammals.

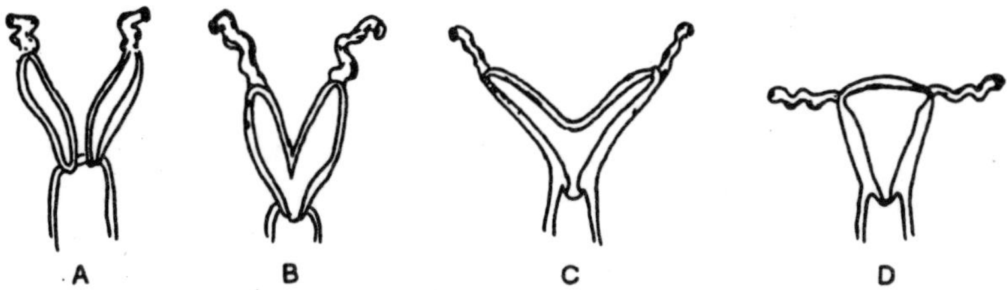

Fig. 5.9. Types of uteri. A, uterus duplex; B, uterus bipartius; C, uterus bicornis; D, uterus simplex.

Thus, there are two distinct nuteri *(uterus duplex)* without vaginas in monotremes, and each with a separate vagina in marsupials. Among placental mammals, some rodents, for example the mouse, hare, marmot, and beaver, as well as elephants, certain bats, and the "aard-vark" *Orycteropus* of South Africa, have a duplex uterus which opens into a single vagina. A beginning of coalescence between the two uteri *(uterus bipartitus) is* apparent in pigs, cattle, certain rodents, some bats, and carnivores. A two-horned uterus *(uterus bicornis) is* characteristic of ungulates, cetaceans, insectivores, and some carnivores, while a single uterus *(uterus simplex)* with two slender Fallopian tubes projecting from it, is the type found in apes and man.

Various pathological anomalies that suggest doubling are encountered in the human uterus, which find a ready explanation in the story of the comparative anatomy of this organ.

The curious South American teleost *Girardinus,* already mentioned as having a metamorphosed haemal spine of a caudal vertebra for a copulatory organ, has a hollow ovary that serves as a uterus or brood sac for the young. The eggs, which dehisce into the cavity of the ovary after the teleostean tradition, are fertilized in place by sperm that penetrate all the way into the ovarian cavity, where the early stages of embryonic development occur.

Brood Sacs

Among vertebrates there are various instances, more or less exceptional, of brood sacs for eggs or young, aside from the uterus of the female. For example, among fishes there is a modification of the pelvic fins into a brood sac on the ventral side of the male pipefish, *Syngnathus,* into which the eggs are deposited by the female. In the sea-horse, *Hippocampus,* a relative of the pipefish, there is a similar arrangement whereby the male becomes responsible for the care of the eggs.

Among amphibians a dorsal pouch is located on the back of the female frog, *Nototreina pygmaeum,* of Venezulea, for carrying eggs, while the male *Rhinoderma darzvini* of Java contributes his vocal sacs temporarily to serve as brood pouches.

The transient brood sac of monotremes and the permanent "marsupium" of the marsupials among mammals are further examples of structures belonging to the reproductive apparatus, since they obviously have been developed in the interests of the race rather than of the individual.

Nidamental Glands

Eggs destined to leave the body of the female before development are provided with some sort of a protective envelope or capsule. In water this does not need to be a very complicated structure, but exposure to dry air demands a shell of some kind.

It is apparent that fertilization must occur before the shell is put on to the egg, otherwise, the sperm would encounter an insuperable barrier. Consequently *nidamental glands,* which produce the shell, are located in the walls of the oviduct some distance from the *ostium abdominale,* in order to allow opportunity for the egg and sperm to meet before the shell is added. Incidentally, putting a workman like shell around a soft egg is an accomplishment which would be baffling to a human inventor.

Albumen glands, that furnish the "white of the egg," are also located in the walls of the oviduct between the ostium abdominale and the nidamental glands, since this extra store of nutriment must be added after fertilization, but before the egg is encased in a calcareous shell. The familiar cackling of a hen that has just succeeded in laying an egg is a true song of triumph, stimulating to a comparative anatomist who appreciates something of the intricacies of its elaboration.

Not only does the calcareous shell protect the exposed egg from injury, but, in the case of many birds, blending colors or blotches which help to camouflage it from searching enemies are deposited in the substance of the shell.

The aquatic eggs of the internally fertilized elasmobranchs are enclosed in purselike horny capsules, supplied at each corner with curling tendrils, which entangle them among seaweeds, so that the embryo fishes sway and rock within their curious cradles in comparative security until ready to emerge.

Placenta in Mammals

True mammals provide a placenta for the developing young. This is an elaborate compound vascular organ, made up of interdigitating villi from the walls of the uterus and from the allantois of the embryo, which brings the capillaries of the mother into intimate contact with the capillaries of the fetus, thus establishing a nutritive and respiratory bridge between mother and offspring.

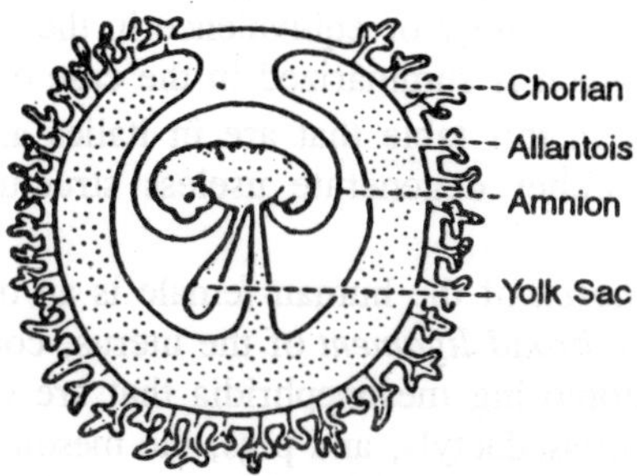

Fig. 5.10. Diagram of the embryonic envelopes of a mammal

There are other embryonic devices in mammals, such as the aranion and other fetal envelopes, which provide for the welfare of young reptiles, birds, and mammals. These should not be overlooked in reckoning up the anatomical contrivances that aid in the preservation of the species.

Degenerate and Rudimentary Organs

With the supplanting of the pronephros and mesonephros by the metanephros among amniote vertebrates, there are left behind several structures in the developing animal that are deprived of their original usefulness. Some of these structures, like the mesonephric tubules which become transformed into the epididymal tubules of the male, are rescued and made over to serve a new function. Many other structures, however, degenerate, finding their way to the anatomical rubbish pile where they remain as useless parts of the animal mechanism, even becoming a source of pathological ills.

There are various *rudimentary organs* also that are useless because they never attain functional efficiency. Unlike degenerate structures which have had their day, these are incipient organs that have never completely developed.

It is quite important for the pathologist to be thoroughly grounded in comparative anatomy, since it is just these degenerate anatomical relief and rudimentary structures that are most likely to prove the focal points for the formation of cysts, tumors, and other bodily abnormalities.

The young embryo presents a condition with respect to the reproductive apparatus, for example, that suggests a hermaphrodite with the rudiments of both sexes present. As development. proceeds one sex becomes dominant, and the structures which characterize the other sex into the background as degenerate or rudimentary remains. There results a homology or equivalence in the anatomical details of the two sexes which is summarized in the case of man in Table 5.1.

The organs in this table that are in italics are functional, while the others are either degenerate useless structures or of doubtful function.

The *epoophoron* of the human female is an organ lying between the layers of the *broad ligament* of the uterus, composed of eighteen or twenty anastomosing mesonephridia that are closed at both ends. In ruminants, perissodactyls, and pigs, the mesonephridia forming the epoophoron are connected with a fragment of *Gaertner's duct,* which corresponds to the Wolffian duct in the male.

The *paradidymis* and the *paroophoron* in the two sexes respectively are all that remain of the posterior mesonephridia. The paradidymis lies within the spermatic cord near the globus major of the epididymis. Both the paradidymis and its homologue in the female are found only in older embryos and young children.

The *ductuli aberrantes* are also tubules, originally nephridia, blind at one end and opening into the duct of the epididymis. There may be one, two, or several of them, although the number is usually two. They lie between the testis and the epididymis. The "inferior ductule," which is the more constant of the two, may attain the length of two inches in man.

The *appendix epididymidis,* which is a degenerate tip of the mesonephros lies upon the globus major of the epididymis. Toldt found it persisting in 29 out of 105 human autopsies. A similar structure is sometimes found in the female.

TABLE 5.1. TABLE OF HOMOLOGIES OF STRUCTURES DERIVED FROM THE MESONEPHROS AND ITS ASSOCIATED DUCTS

		Male	*Female*
Mesonephros	Sexualpart	Appendix epididymidis *Rete testis* (in part)	*Epididymis* (in part) Epoophoron
	Urinarypart	ParadidymisDuctuli aberrantes	Paroophoron
Wolffian duct	Proximalpart	*Epididymis* (in part) *Ductus epididymidis*	Epoophoron (in part)
	Distalpart	*Ductus deferens*	Gaertner's duct
Mulleriaduct	Proximalpart	Appendix testis	*Fallopian tubeUterus*
	Distalpart	Vagina masculina Colliculus seminalis	*VaginaHymen*

The *appendix testis,* a small spherical sac attached to the testis, represents the tip of the Miillerian duct. It has been reported as present in 90 per cent of the cases examined.

The other end of the embryonic Miillerian duct remains in the male in the form of the *vagina masculina,* a small sac homologous with the vagina. It is embedded in the prostate gland along with the base of the urethra and is usually distally bifid, which is additional evidence that it represents the remains of coalescing oviducts.

Around the opening of the vagina masculina is a small fold of tissue, the *colliculus seminalis,* that marks the ends of the Miillerian ducts, and is homologous with the hymen of the female, which partially separates the vagina from the vestibule, and likewise locates the true termination of the Miillerian ducts.

The anterior fusion of the outer labio-scrotal folds, which make the labia majora in the female, becomes the *mons Veneris.*

So-called human "hermaphrodites" usually present intermediate embryonic features with respect to the external genitalia, as for instance, a small undeveloped penis with an unclosed urogenital slit (hypospadia), resembling the grooved cloacal penis of the turtle.

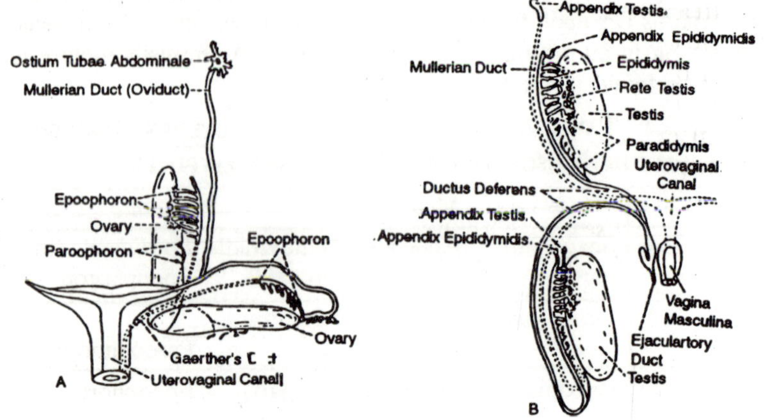

Fig. 5.11. The urogenital organs of man before and after descent. A, female; B male. (After Felix in Keibel and Mall.)

The general relations of the genitalia, both external and internal, of the two sexes in man.

PEPRIODICITY IN REPRODUCTION

After reaching sexual maturity, a stage which is usually less marked in the male than in the female, most animals exhibit a periodical recurrence of reproductive activity. This, as applied to the species, may be called the *breeding season*. During the breeding season, the individual animal may react to a single sexual crisis, or it may undergo several rhythmical waves of sexual activity, while between breeding seasons the pairing instincts and behavior are in abeyance.

The onset of the breeding season is probably due to a variety of causes, both external and internal, differing largely in various groups of animals. There is some underlying, common ground, however, for it is apparent that the reproductive cycle of most plants and animals is timed more or less to accord with the changing seasons, and to occur at a time that is favorable for the development of the forthcoming young. This is usually the spring or early summer, particularly among insects, annual plants, and cold-blooded animals.

A host of aquatic forms, for example, respond sexually to the rising temperature of the water in the spring of the year. Ocean fishes shift in schools into warmer shallow or surface waters to spawn, while amphibians and reptiles, arousing from their winter lethargy, proceed at once to increase the census returns in their cold-blooded world.

Birds stream northward in their annual "Canterbury Pilgrimage" as soon as the cold of winter in our northern latitudes has given way to the breath of spring At this season they show considerably more purpose than in the more leisurely fall migration. The factor of changing temperature, however, does not wholly account for the remarkable nuptial flight of birds' in their spring migration.

Mammals also generally exhibit enhanced vitality and courtship behavior at the spring season. According to Bissonnette it is the gradual increase in the daily light ration which brings about this increased sexual activity of birds and mammals. Even man, whose breeding season has been extended to include the entire year, feels the spell of spring, so that Tennyson stated a biological fact when he sang:

"In the spring a livelier iris changes on the burnished dove;

In the spring a young man's fancy lightly turns to thoughts of love".

The breeding season of fishes in the valley of the Nile is during the annual period of inundation. Lungfishes, which pass the dry season burrowed inactively in the mud, breed at once when the rainy season begins, being at that time restored to activity. It is rather remarkable that hibernating animals, as well as aestivating lungfishes, when they awake starved and hungry after their dormant sleep, proceed immediately to the business of propagating the species before they attend to their own individual needs. This is a good illustration of the imperative law of reproduction, which places the preservation of the species above the welfare of the individual.

In the same self-effacing way the salmon of the Pacific Coast, when they leave the ocean for the long perilous run up rapids, waterfalls, and past countless dangers for many hundred miles to their breeding grounds in the upper reaches of the Columbia and Yukon rivers, ascetically forego feeding and devote themselves entirely to the great adventure of reproduction. It is quite probable that some internal factor, perhaps a physiological urge set in motion as a consequence of rhythmical metabolic processes, must account for the astonishing behavior of the salmon. It is certainly not entirely due to the fact that their gonads have swollen to a degree demanding immediate action, because in the "Silver Horde" of the salmon run fishes of all stages of sexual development are found. Moreover, it has been pointed out by Jacobi that the gonads of the eel, *Anguilla,* which migrates in the opposite direction, from fresh to salt water for its one breeding season in a lifetime, do not become enlarged until it reaches salt water.

The breeding rhythm of some animals is even gauged to a certain time of day. Thus amphioxus in the Mediterranean region always spawns at sun-down,, and the famous "pololo worm" of the South Pacific, *Eunice viridis,* produces its myriads of eggs and sperm in quantities sufficient to color the water for miles about, at daybreak of a particular day falling in the last quarter of the moon in September and October.

Many invertebrates breed once for all, the act frequently marking the end of their life cycle. Animals like most marsupials and seals breed annually, the walrus once in three years; and elephants at considerably longer intervals.

There is a curious correlation between the breeding season of bats and a favorable time of year for the appearance of the future offspring. Pairing is effected in the fall, a mucous plug sealing the uterus after copulation so that the sperm can winter over in the vagina. After copulation has occurred the sexes go their separate ways to hibernation quarters, the males in one place, the females in another, where they literally "hang up" for the winter. Since the period of gestation in the bat is only two months, the young would normally be born during the somnolent hibernation period-an impossible state of affairs with no available insect food on the wing - were it not for the fact that fertilization is not consummated for several months after copulation, the sperm remaining viable in the vagina of the female throughout all that time.

Among mammals, the female during the breeding season passes through an *oestrous cycle,* or "heat," in which preparation is made for the fertilization of the egg. If only one oestrus occurs during the breeding season, as in the case of the bear, the animal is said to 'be *monoestrous. Polyoestrous,* on the other hand, are those which, like rodents, have recurrent oestrous periods following each other throughout the breeding season.

Domestication frequently works changes in the periodicity of reproduction. Many wild animals refuse to breed at all in captivity, while domestic animals, such as cattle, have been changed from a monoestrous to a polyoestrous condition. The breeding season has been greatly extended in poultry, for example, to include practically the entire year.

In the human female the breeding season is not dependent upon external factors, but continues uninterrupted from the time of puberty until the *menopause* at the age of 45 or 50 years, throughout which

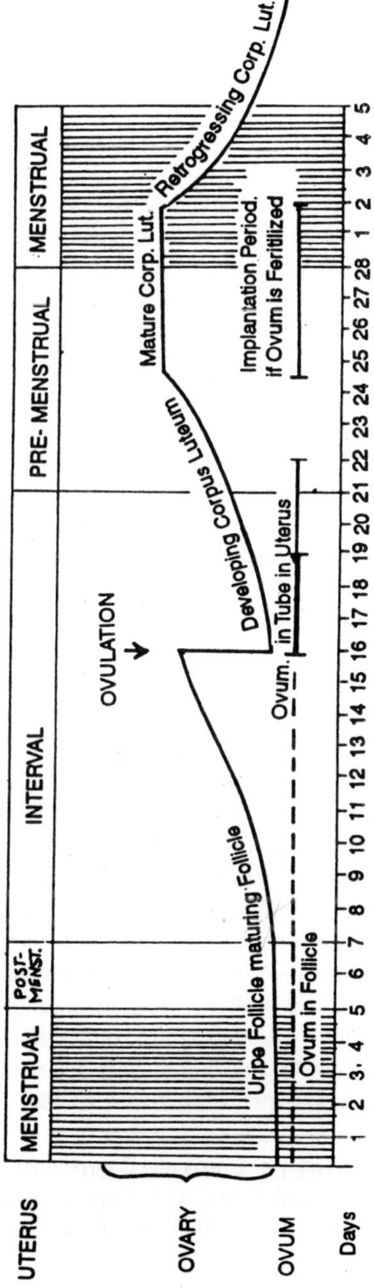

Fig. 5.12. The course of events in the human menstrual cycle.

time the oestrus, unless interrupted by pregnancy or some abnormal condition, recurs rhythmically approximately every four weeks.

Associated with the oestrus in humankind the walls of the uterus undergo marked periodic modification, throughout the sexual life, in preparation for the possible implantation of an ovum. These changes include enlargement of the uterine glands and accumulation of fluid in the mucosa which becomes distended to several times its ordinary thickness, a state which can be maintained for only a few days. If no fertilized egg is implanted, the mucosa undergoes further changes, leading to a gradual breakdown of the superficial layers which are discharged to the outside together with secretions and 40 to 60 cc of blood, as the *menstrual flow*. Menstruation, which lasts four or five days, is followed by repair of the mucosa and the next period of preparation. Counting the first day of menstruation as the first day of the oestrous cycle, the egg is usually discharged from the Graafian follicle on the twelfth to sixteenth day. If the descending mammalian egg meets an ascending sperm in a Fallopian tube, it may become implanted in the wall of the uterus that has been prepared for- it and there undergo development. Under these conditions destructive changes in the uterine mucosa do not occur, menstruation being in abeyance during pregnancy and lactation. This monthly recurrence of the reorganization of the uterine mucosa begins and ends earlier in life in the tropics than among inhabitants of colder countries. The human menstrual cycle has been diagrammed by Corner.

Ethnologists find indications of a former primitive breeding season in man coupled with the annual feasts and orgies of savages and in the yearly festival of the Saturnalia of classical times, when great sexual license was known to prevail.

Many instincts and dawning intelligence seem to center around the care of the young. Distinctive secondary modifications in the female have to do largely with this function. It has its beginnings in the unconscious equipment of eggs with nutritive materials and in the provision by the female of a sheltering uterus or brood sac of some kind. Later in evolution parental care may take the form of building nests in which to incubate eggs after they have been laid, and of behavior that supplements the helplessness of the newly hatched or born.

In higher animals there is a prolonged period of dependence upon the parents, after hatching or birth, which makes "schooling" possible through association with the parents. The relation is a reciprocal one, for the child or offspring is an educator as well as the parent. Cooperation, no competition, is the key to family life exhibited by man and the higher animals. In this way the traditions and acquired wisdom are handed on among animals as soon as an adequate vehicle by way of brain equipment is elaborated for it.

The lower animals, on the other hand, never have any schooling. They are supplied once for all with a single "box of tricks," " or instincts, and as soon as they come into the world they know as much as their parents or as much as they need to know to fill their niche in nature. They never can experience the joy of learning from their parents or others of their kind and in the majority of instances they never even encounter their parents.

A prolonged dependence upon parental care is a mark of superiority, since it furnishes the soil in which budding intelligence may grow and flourish.

PREGNANCY FAILURE

Sterility is a term which can be correctly applied only to an individual who has some absolute factor preventing *procreation. Infertility,* however is the inability to achieve pregnancy within a stipulated period of time, usually stated as 1 year. This view is adequately based on statistics. For example, Whitelaw found that 56.5% of fertile couples achieve pregnancy within 1 month and 78.9% within the first 6 months. *Primary infertility* is the term used to designate those patients who have never conceived, whereas *secondary infertility* indicates that the patient has had a pregnancy. This may be further qualified as secondary to term pregnancy, miscarriage, etc.

Occurrence

In the United States 12% of all marriages are estimated to be involuntarily barren. Thus the problem is one of some magnitude.

Medical Considerations

Medically, infertility is a rather unique condition in that one must consider two individuals. As the husband or wife, or both, may have factors contributing to the condition, both must cooperate in the investigation. Although the woman is usually the most interested and aggressive in her desire for medical help, it is not satisfactory to initiate an infertility inestigation without the cooperation of the husband. It is psychologically desirable to begin the evaluation of the husband and wife at the same time as this emphasizes for the couple the dual responsibility which they share in the condition.

Evaluation of the Problem

It has been adequately demonstrated that in formulating a prognosis the age of the wife and the duration of the marriage are major factors which must he taken into consideration along with the medical findings. Fertility in woman declines after the age of 35 years. Guttmacher has shown that marriages of women between the ages of 16 and 20 years have only a 4.5 % infertility rate: the incidence has risen to 31.3 % for women married between the ages of 35 and 40 years, and after the age of 40 the infertility rate approaches 70 %. This is further substantiated by the relative infrequency of pregnancy after the age of 45 years. This so-called "aging factor" is, however, a difficult one to assess. A routine infertility investigation in older women may fail to reveal any abnormality. In a preliminary study of ovaries removed in the over 50-year-old woman we have found evidence of recent ovulation in 15% despite almost uniform absence of pregnancy beyond the age of 48. Indeed we have found histological proof (corpus luteum) of ovulation in a few women past the age of 55.

It may therefore be assumed that the infertility is caused by a defect in the ovum itself, making it unfertilizable. The increased incidence of congenital anomalies and miscarriages in pregnancy among older women might seem to substantiate this theory. The duration of the infertility, which has long been recognized as a reliable yardstick for prognosis, obviously serves as an indication of the seriousness of the condition.

According to statistics from various clinics, 20 to 50% of patients investigated for infertility can be helped. It is estimated that with our present investigative techniques between 10 and 30% of the patients will he found to have no discernible etiological factors responsible for the infertility.

There is no evidence for fertility differentials of racial origin. Guttmacher estimates the average number of children per couple married before the age of 20 years, without the use of contraception, to be approximately 9.5, and this figure is the same for five different nationality groups.

INVESTIGATION

Although it was once thought unjustifiable to initiate an infertility investigation short of 3 years of barren marriage, it now appears that no couple who seeks medical aid for infertility should be turned away without some consideration of their problem, be it real or fancied.

This is scientifically justifiable on the basis of the statistics just cited and psychologically desirable as often the fears of the overanxious couple can be allayed by a few explanations and suggestions from a sympathetic and well informed physician. Such a discussion may. perhaps. prevent the development of major psychological problems which aggravate or cause infertility.

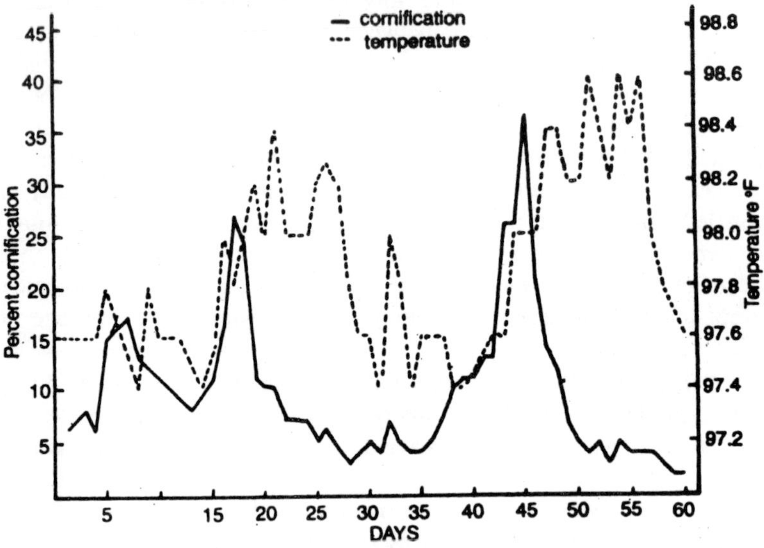

Fig. 6.1. Ovulation determined by cornification pattern of urinary sediment smears. The veginal smear pattern parellels that of the urinary cells. Ovulation can be seen coincide with the cornifieation peak.

The Initial Interview

The investigation of the infertile couple begins with a careful history and physical examination which will exclude major medical or gynecological conditions. A proper history must include the age of the patient and her husband, the duration of the marriage, previous marital histories of both partics. and other efforts to obtain medical aid as well as a medical and social history. Physical examination includes a vaginal smear with maturation index and an examination of the cervical mucus in addition to the usual general examinations of urine for sugar and protein. a hematocrit, and white count. It is generally impossible to make an etiological diagnosis at the first visit. However, it is well to make a tentative diagnosis if there are suggestive factors in the history or physical examination. as these observations are valuable signposts in focusing our attention on important details during the subsequent examinations and tests.

At the first visit it is wise to discuss with the patient and her husband, if possible. the need for a complete investigation, as well as the time and expense involved. the statistical probabilities of help, and the value of the investigation from a prognostic point of view. The couple should be advised that if treatment seems indicated it is usually necessary to allow at least 1 year before evaluation of therapy is possible. At this time it is well to set up a subsequent appointment with both the husband and wife to discuss the in estigational findings and recommendations.

Fundamental Tests

Pertinent investigations must include tests of the five major factors concerned with fertilization and implantation of an ovum: (1) the occurrence of ovulation, (2) the production of normal sperm, (3) the presence of adequate cervical mucus which can act as a transport medium for sperm and as a sperm repository, (4) the patency of tubes for transport of sperm up and ovum down, and (5) the development of the endometrial implantation site which depends upon both ovarian endocrine function and end organ response.

If no abnormalities are found in the above studies. certain ancillary factors must be checked. A protein-bound iodine, a basal metabolic rate, a glucose tolerance test, and a 17-ketosteroid assay will detect metabolic disease processes which are associated with infertility problems. However, it is our experience that when there is no evidence of ovarian insufficiency. these diseases are usually not the cause of the infertility. A psychiatric evaluation or a psychological test may be advisable. The blood grouping of husband and wife may also have some significance, as there is statistical evidence to indicate that blood incompatibilities may occasionally be the cause of infertility.

If at the end of the complete examination, no cause is found for the infertility, and after 1 year no pregnancy has occurred, a culdoscopic examination should be performed. This may reveal unsuspected endometriosis or peritubal or periovarian adhesions. If no cause for infertility is found no treatment should be given. It is likewise inadvisable to repeat tests after one has satisfactorily established a diagnosis, as such unnecessary procedures or therapy can prove harmful. interfering with the process of fertility rather than improving it. The one possible exception to this rule for patients with no discernible infertility factors is the use of synthetic progestational compounds. As suggested by Garcia. Pincus. and Rock. progestational drugs may be used in an effort to put the ovary at rest. with the hope that at the end of the treatment period a rebound phenomenon will occur allowing for improved ovarian function and pregnancy.

OVULATION

Of the many methods advocated for the detection of ovulation, four are currently outstanding as clinically proved and applicable: (1) the cornification of the daily vaginal smear pattern or urinary sediment followed by a progestational smear; (2) increased amount and fluidity of the cervical mucus followed by a decreased amount of mucus and absence of the fern formation; (3) the biphasic basal body temperature graph; (4) secretory changes observed in the endometrium.

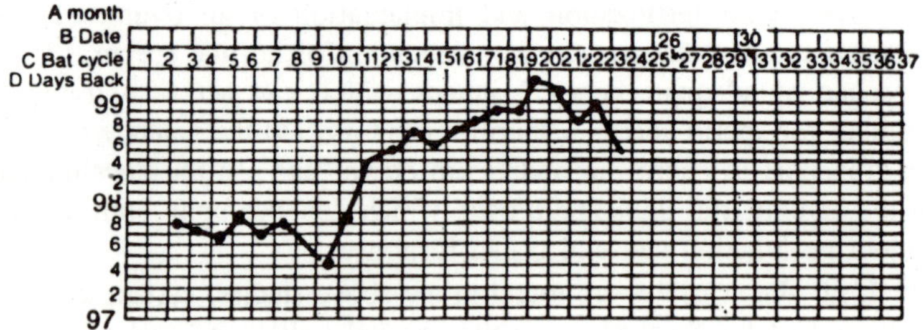

Fig. 6.2. Typical ovulatory basal temperature record in a 24 day cycle. Ovulation probably occurs at the low point prior to the contineous rise. In this case it would be on 10 days.

Of these the first two are most useful in predicting the probable occurrence of ovulation, as the changes take place within the 24-hour period preceding ovulation. However. such findings can be associated with follicular maturation without ovulation and therefore must be interpreted absolutely in the light of knowledge of the entire cycle. The latter two tests are not useful in prediction of ovulation but are perhaps more reliable in the retrospective evaluation of the cycle, as they are a function of progesterone and therefore imply ovulation by determination of an active corpus luteum.

As far back as 1904 van de Velde reported that the normal basal body temperature throughout the menstrual cycle is biphasic. The temperature is taken orally as soon as the patient awakens each morning, and before she moves about. eats. drinks. or smokes. This low point occurs at or about the time of ovulation. although there is still some uncertainty as to the precise chronological relationships involved the Stein-Leventhal ovary must be wedge-resected or treated with clomiphene. Unfortunately there is no treatment for ovarian failure at this writing, since attempted application of the newer grafting techniques has been unsatisfactory.

Other clinical tests are currently available but as yet are either unsatisfactorily tested or perfected. The presence of glucose in the cervical secretions as measured by glucose oxidase was reported almost simultaneously by Birnberg *et al.* and by Doyle and has been further assayed by Cohen; the detection of urinary gonadotrophins by the Farris test depends upon the evaluation of an ovarian hyperemia reaction in the mouse ovary and, although readily reproducible by thc originator, is either too subjective or too dependent upon specific animal strains to be practical.

Methods which depend upon complicated hormons analyses are too expensive and too time-consuming to be clinically applicable; these are the detection of urinary estrogenich peaks which occur about 24 hours before ovulation; measurement of total urinary gonadotrophins which exhibit a peak just prior to ovulation: and urinary pregnanediol excretion, which is a retrospective test for ovulation in that it measures progesterone production by the corpus luteum.

For a summary of recent attempts at timing ovulation, the reader is referred to a review by Speck.

Ovulation Defects

The etiology of ovulation defects has been discussed in detail "Amenorrhea," and will be simply itemized here. Generalized major factors are: (1) nutrition; (2) metabolic disease, e.g., pituitary insufficiency, hyper- or hypothyroidism, diabetes, the adrenogenital syndrome and related diseases, and Cushing's disease; (3) chronic illness; (4) psychogenic disturbance; (5) neurogenic disturbances; and (6) specific ovarian factors. These latter comprise ovarian tumors, polycystic ovaries of Stein, and congenitally defective ovaries. such as those in Turner's syndrome which lead to ovarian failure.

The treatment of anovulation depends upon the etiology, and any specific factor found must be specifically treated as indicated, by diet. thyroid. or adrenal hormone. Pituitary insufficiencies or neurogenic disturbances leading to inadequate pituitary excitation and secondarily to inadequate ovarian stimulation should theoretically be best treated by substitution therapy with pituitary hormones. Gemzell and others have demonstrated that this therapy is satisfacton. The use of cyclic steroid hormones. estrogens followed by progestogens in an effort to stimulate pituitary function, although less expensive and less complicated is usually unsuccessful. Cloiniphene is also useful in patients with an intact pituitary gland. These therapeutic agents will be discussed in detail under the treatment of Amenorrhea. Ovarian tumors must be surgically removed:

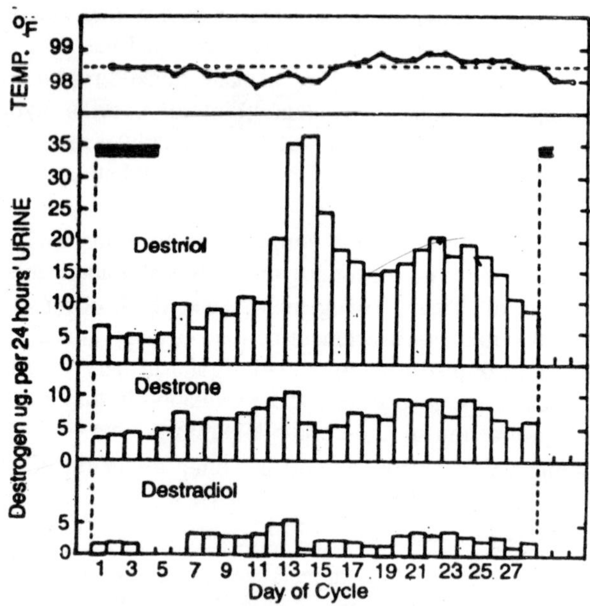

Fig. 6.3. Urinary estrogen excretion during a normal 28-day cycle correlated with the basal temperature record. The estrogen peak occurs just prior to ovulation.

SPERM

Evaluation

As least two semen analyses should he performed for, proper evaluation of the male factor. If these do not show a satisfactory agreement. samples should he taken until a reasonable assessment of fertility capacity has been reached. Samples should not be collected after a specific abstinence period but in accord with the usual intercourse habits of the couple. A clean, wide-mouthed container should be used for collecting the specimen, which may be procured either by induced ejaculation or by intercourse with withdrawal. A total ejaculate must be obtained, as any loss may seriously influence the sperm count. The sample should be collected and brought to the laboratory within 1 hour. if possible. marked with the hour of collection and the date of the previous intercourse. Liquefaction of seminal fluid may be expected to occur at room temperature within 20 minutes. Failure of liquefaction indicates a lack of proteolytic enzyme and makes the evaluation of the sample difficult. The quality of the semen is judged by the motility of the sperm, the numbers per milliliter. and the presence of abnormal forms. The total volume is also recorded and is of some importance as the normality of the sample frequently varies inversely, within limits, with the amount of the semen. Thus a large volume is often indicative that the sperm is of poor quality. The total sperm count is not of too great importance. The number of epithelial cells and leukocytes present is obviously significant.

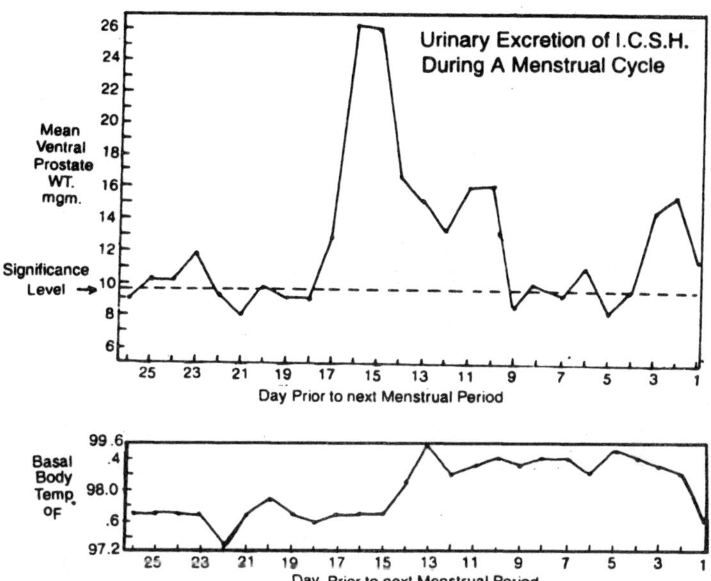

Fig. 11.4. Illustrating the pituitary gonadotrophin peak which occurs just prior to ovulation. Interstitial cell-stimulating hormone (I.C.S.H.) assay by the AlcArthur technique.

Although absolute criteria of male fertility cannot be obtained with the present rather crude methods of evaluation. the following standards may be considered as representative of the usual fertile male. *Count per milliliter:* normally fertile, above 60,00,000 per ml.; subfertile. betwecn 20,000,000 and 60,000,000 per ml.; sterile, less than 20,000,000 per ml. *Volume*: 2.5 ml. *Motility* : 60% (moltility within 4 hours). Differential less than 25% abnormal forms.

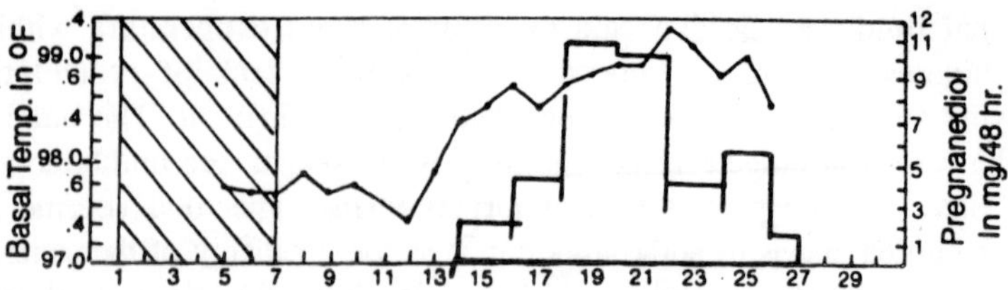

Fig. 6.5. The basal body temperature charted with the urinary pregnanediol excretion. (Astwood gravimetric method). The pregnanediol is plotted in black-blocks. indicating the amount in milligrams per 48-per hour periods. The base line represents the days of the menstrual cycle, counting day -1 as the first day of menstruation. Pregnanediol excretion begins as the 14th days.

The occurrence of an abnormal differential with an otherwise normal semen analysis is rare. The studies of Leuchtenberger *et a!.* have suggested the deoxyribonucleic acid (DNA) content of spermatozoa might be used as a fertility index. These authors' investigations indicated that the DNA value will detect deficiencies in otherwise apparently normall semen. From a theoretical point of view this would be attractive, as the DNA is a measure of chromosomal material and thus would be an accurate measure of genetic abnormalities. Studies by Knudsen in animal husbandry indicate that certain forms of nondysfunction of chromosomes which would give rise to increased or decreased DNA measurements, are incompatible with reproductive capacity.

The survival time of sperm in the human female genital tract is still debatable but, at the proper time in the cycle, motile sperm can normally be seen in the cervical mucus 48 hours after intercourse and it is not unusual to find adequate numbers of motile sperm after 76 hours. It is also apparent in certain types of experimental animals that sperm require a 24-hour period in the female genital tract in order to acquire fertilizing ability. This property has been called *capacitation* and has been extensively studied in the rabbit by Chang. This interesting phenomenon is reviewed by Noyes.

Seminal Insufficiency

Seminal insuffcienc% can be attributed to constitutional factors such as nutritional problems. acute or chronic illness. general metabolic disease specific poisonings or occupational hazards. central defects occurring in the pituitary or hypothalamic areas. specific diseases within the genital tract such as infections causing blockage to the vas and scarring of the tubular elements or congenital defects of testicular development such as the Klinefelter syndrome. Diagnosis can be facilitated by a 17-ketosteroid determination, a urinary gonadotrophin assay. and a testicular biopsy. Testicular failure is indicated by a low 17-ketosteroid and a high urinary gonadotrophin excretion and confirmed by the microscopic appearance of the testicles.

For detailed and specific treatment the reader is referred to urological texts. For the treatment of many constitutional factors general hygiene is important: limitation of smoking and elimination of excessive alcohol. attention to diet and adequate rest, relief of emotional tension states, treatment of any chronic illness or metabolic disease. Specific hormone therapy has been occasionally successful; this involves (lie administration of testosterone, first described by Heckel, until the sperm count is reduced to zero, at which time the drug is withdrawn and the pituitary, which has been suppressed, is allowed to resume its function. This pituitary rebound phenomenon sometimes produces a much improved sperm count which may or may not be permanent. Unfortunately, there is no method for detecting which group of patients will respond to the testosterone rebound phenomenon and it is estimated that approximately only 20 % of men showing low sperm counts, presumably due to inadequate pituitary stimulation, will show improvement on this form of therapy. Human pituitary gonadotrophin therapy has also been successful in restoring spermatogenesis and fertility (MacLeod).

For those men having blockage of the vas deferens. surgical therapy may help on occasion. For those having destruction of the testis or congenitally defective spermatogenic elements, no therapy is available. and adoption or donor insemination must be considered. In the unusual case in which hypospadias is present so that deposition of spermatozoa on the cervix is inadequate, or in which a neurological cord lesion occurs. semen may be obtained mechanically and artifical insemination attempted.

A more concentrated semen sample can be obtained by collection of a split ejaculate since the first portion of the ejaculate often contains the majority of sperm. In men whose counts are between 20,000,000 and 60,000,000 sperm per ml.. this method of concentration, followed by cervical insemination. may on occasion be justifiable. Other means of mechanical concentration are centrifugation of the ejaculate and the use of a millipore filter, as described b% Perloff.

Artificial Insemination

The procedure of artificial insemination or, as we prefer to call it. semiadoption is still a highly controversial one. It is a medical problem which also involves moral issues. These issues must be resolved by each physician according to his own conscience. The entire subject of artificial insemination in the human is very adequately treated in the book by Schellen.

Any physician who takes it upon himself to perform this service should remember that he accepts a grave responsibility. He is, in effect, placing an adopted child in a home and in so doing must be sure that this home is worthy and capable of contributing happiness and security to the child. It has been our practice to interview couples over a 3- to 6-month period before instituting therapy or to request a psychiatric interview in an effort to evaluate the stability of the individuals and their compatibility as a couple. A child, be it natural, adopted, or semiadopted, cannot be regarded as cementing material for a marriage. If there is dissension, the rearing of a baby offers one more matter for disagreement.

In addition to repeated interviews with the couple, there are several rubes of thumb which should be followed. First, the husband must have been aware of his inadequacy for at least a year prior to the first serious consideration of the planning of insemination. Second, the physician must be convinced that the husband is taking the initiative and not being pushed by an overaggressive and overanxious wife. Third. there must be no religious background in either partner which would suggest that either might harbor moral scruples about the procedure. Fourth, every possible medical investigation and aid must have been employed to diagnose and treat the cause of the male infertility. Fifth, a basal temperature chart, Rubin's test, and endometrial biopsy must indicate normal fertility in the female.

In the first interview it is explained to the couple that they must count on at least 3 months, with the possibility of 6 months, of insemination prior to anticipating success. The figures given by Belirman *et al.* for the occurrence of conception in 50% of the women within 3 months and in 90% within 6 months are strikingly similar to those quoted for normal fertile couples by Tietze, Guttmacher. and Rubin. again confirming the rationale for instituting infertility investigations after 1 year of barren marriage if the couple so desires.

The problem of mixing semen is complicated by the occurrence of sperm agglutination in some specimens. It is therefore practical to request that intercourse be practised prior to insemination: or. if the couple prefers the husband's semen is concentrated and used intercervically while the donor's is used in a cervical cap. Intrauterine insemination should probably never be performed. In women with regular menstrual cycles, our figures indicate that a single insemination is as satisfactory as repeated inseminations and this observation is substantiated by Kleegman.

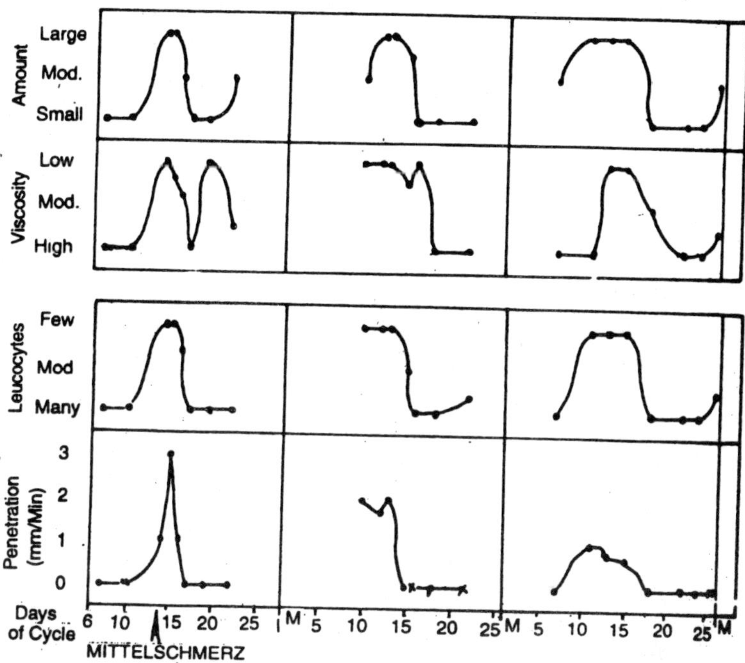

Fig. 6.6. Characteristics of cervical mucus throughout the menstrual cycle correlated with sperm penetrability. Curves are a composite from three cycles of a single individual.

The selection of a donor is of course of utmost importance. He should be physically fit, emotionally stable. intelligent, and free of any history of congenital hereditary defects. In addition his semen analysis must be in the normally fertile range. Every effort should be made to match his blood group and type with that of the patient to be inseminated.

CERVICAL MUCUS

The examination of the cen·ical mucus ww ith reference to the amount. quality. and presence or absence of infection should be made at the first office visit. The quality of mucus is judged by the viscosity and *spinbarkeit* (ability to spin a thread) as well as the number of epithelial cells and bacteria and the crystallization patterns. A good estrogenic mucus is watery and clear, has excellent *spinbarkeit* (5 *cm.* or longer) and few, if any cells. When the mucus is dry, fern patterns may be seen. These are characteristic of the mucus in the preovulatory and ovulatory phase. In the pre- and postmenstrual phase, when estrogen influence is either low or dominated by progesterone, the mucus is scanty, thick, cloudy, and contains numerous cellular elements, and the dried sample does not exhibit ferning. The changes in the mucus throughout the cycle have been described by LaMarr, Shettles, and Delfs and elaborated upon by Pommerenke and his associates.

A postcoital examination (the Sims- Huhner test) should be scheduled at approximately ovulation time. The patient is requested to have intercourse within 12 to 24 hours of her visit. It is often well not to make an issue of this as many husbands do not do well with command performances and the patient may be allowed to call for her appointment the day on which she is prepared. In order to make this test as uniform as possible, recordings should be standardized in certain broad aspects. The last menstrual period, the date of the previous intercourse, the hour of the last intercourse, and the hour of the examination must be recorded. The cervix should be wiped free of all vaginal contaminants and the mucus aspirated from the cervix by a pipette with a fine tip attached to a good suction ball. The removal of the mucus is further facilitated by clipping it off with a long clamp. The amount of mucus is estimated as poor, fair, or abundant. The quality and presence or absence of infection are recorded, and the number actively progressive sperm per high power field as well as those with poor or no activity. A successful test is one in which there are 5 or more actively motile sperm per high power field.

A successful Sims-Huhner test implies (1) satisfactory intercourse techniques. (2) normal mucus for the transport and preservation of sperm, and (3) adequate ovarian estrogenic function, as well as (4) at least the possibility of a normal male fertility. This test, however, does not substitute for a semen analysis but merely complements it. An unsuccessful Sims-Huhner test may result from a variety of causes. Faulty intercourse techniques. oligo- or azoospennia, or poor timing of the test are among the more usual causes since sperni consistently survive and penetrate mucus only in the preovulatory and ovulatory mucus. An inadequate ovarian estrogenic function, cervical infection, or in rare instances. a specific vaginitis due to *Candida krtvcei* are other causes. There remains a small residue of cases of unexplained etiology. These are the patients who show no evidence of infection, no evidence of ovarian insufficiency, and whose husbands have a normal semen analysis.

The treatment of the so-called "hostile mucus" depends upon the etiology of the condition. Those patients showing an inadequate estrogenic mucus at the ovulatory time of the cycle can be treated by the daily administration of 0.1 mg. of stilbestrol, or its equivalent, or 0.5 mg. of stilbestrol suppositories every night. If suppositories are used they should be discontinued at the 12th day of a 28-day cycle or approximately 2 days prior to the ovulation date. In the majority of Ratients the dosage of 0.1 mg. of stilbestrol daily is too small to interfere with the menstrual rhythm, and therefore can be administered continuously. If cervical infection is present, this may not always be amenable to cauterization. Chemotherapy should be tried; a broad spectrum antibiotic four times a day for 10 days, as advocated by Home and Rock, has proved successful in the majority of cases. However, as recurrences are frequent it is wise to give medication at the onset of the menstrual period in order to insure a normal mucus at the time of ovulation. If a vaginal infection of C. *krusei* exists, this can usually be eradicated by scrubbing the vagina with green soap and painting with a 2 % aqueous solution of gentian violet every other day for three times. No treatment is known for the normal type of estrogenie-appearing mucus with no evidence of infection which, nevertheless, fails to support sperm activity. Fortunately these cases are extremely rare.

TUBAL FUNCTION

Tubal tests serve not only as diagnostic procedures but also as therapeutic ones in that they tend to overcome minor obstructions. There are three accepted methods for establishing the patency of fallopian tubes. The first is gas insufflation described by Rubin in 1920 and known by his name, Rubin's test. This procedure is the least likely to be associated with any complication and is, therefore, preferable as a first test unless the history or pelvic findings suggest an abnormality which indicates some pelvic pathology. In this case another form of tubal test may be preferable. The Rubin's test is best performed by using a mercury manometer, and tubal patency is estimated to exist if gas is heard to pass through the tubes at pressures below 180 mm. of mercury. Partial occlusion is probably present if pressures above 180 and below 200 are obtained, and tubes are completely obstructed for practical purposes if pressures of 200 or over are unsuccessful. By using a mechanical system. Rubin found that tubes requiring 200 mm. of mercury for passage of gas were too small to transport a particle the size of an ovum.

The second method of tubal evaluation is by means of a hysterosalpingogram. This examination is indicated when the Rubin's test is unsuccessful and especially when operative procedures are contemplated. Because of the high amount of radiation to the ovaries which this procedure entails, it should be limited to carefully selected cases. A water-soluble, opaque medium is preferable to an oil-soluble medium which carries a greater potential for serious complications such as oil emboli and granulomata. Protagonists of oil-soluble media believe that there is a greater therapeutic value in these media but the facts substantiating these claims are tenuous, and such nebulous evidence does not seem to warrant the additional risks.

The third method of assessing tubal function is by means of culdoscopy. The Decker culdoscopic procedure, performed simultaneously with the insertion into the cervix of a No. 14 Foley catheter with a 5-cc. bulb (to be inflated to not over 2 ml.), allows the instillation of indigo carmine into the tubes and any blockage may be demonstrated under direct vision. This method is the treatment of choice if there is some question about the accuracy of the Rubin's test or discrepancy between two tests. It is also useful when extratubal or periovarian adhesions are suspected. Because of the preponderance of tubal factors responsible for infertility in the female, a culdoscopic examination should be offered when the infertility investigation has failed to demonstrate any etiological factor and no pregnancy has resulted within 1 year after completion of the total investigation.

As a word of warning it must be remembered that neither a Rubin's test nor hysterosalpingogram is infallible. Each can be technically unsatisfactory, giving false results of either a positive or a negative nature. Therefore three tests, preferably of different types. must be performed before a diagnosis of tubal occlusion can be made and certainly before considering a tubal plastic procedure. On the other hand, it is not justifiable to perform repeated tubal studies if a normal test has been obtained. As previously stated, if real doubt exists a culdoscopic examination should be made. No tubal procedures should be repeated before a 3-month interval, as any such intrauterine manipulation produces some tissue damage.

Tubal occlusion may be the result of adhesions from pelvic inflammatory disease due to gonorrhea, tuberculosis, er postabortal or postpartum infections. Adhesions may be due to endometriosis or other more unusual causes of blood in the peritoneal cavity, such as an unrecognized ectopic pregnancy. a ruptured corpus luteum cyst. or a bleeding follicle at ovulation. Extrapelvic inflammatory processes such as an appendiceal abscess may also occasionally cause tubal adhesions with occlusions.

The treatment of tubal occlusion must usually be surgical in the final analysis. However, as indicated, at least three tubal patency tests should be performed in an effort to rupture adhesions. Pelvic diathermy may be used, and recently corticosteroids have been advocated for pelvic inflammatory disease, as noted in the review by Kurland and Loughran.

All of these medical procedures should be given an adequate trial prior to the discussion of surgery. A tubal plastic procedure in our opinion should be undertaken only as a last resort since the chances of success are slight.

The data on 2285 operations collected by Siegler and Hellman from questionnaires to 734 gynecologists showed an over-all livebirth rate of 16.5%. The breakdown according to the tubal location indicated that tubal lysis, as might be expected, is most successful-29% pregnancies in 930 operations. For operations upon the tubal fimbriae, there was a 20 pregnancy rate among 891 operations. The worst results were with tubal implantation for obstruction at the cornua. Here the pregnancy rate was but 16 % and the livebirth rate was but 9 % of 272 operations. A report from the Mayo Clinic, in 1964, on results in 75 tubal plastic procedures, interestingly enough gives almost the same over-all statistics, e.g., 16% livebirths and 24% pregnancies. However, the intertubal implantation procedure was the most successful in this series, resulting in 10 livebirths out of 22 implantations. For a complete discussion of techniques the reader is referred to a monograph by Shirodkar.

The patient should wait until the last opportunity at which the operative procedure may be performed with any reasonable expectation of success. The age of 30 years is our arbitrary standard. She should then be adequately informed concerning the poor prognosis of the operation. A thorough investigation for other factors which might be contributing to the infertility is mandatory.

THE ENDUAIETRIUDI

A study of the premenstrual endo- metrium gives information about the implantation site for the fertilized ovum and the ovarian luteal function as well as presumptive evidence concerning ovulation. This, therefore, is an extremely important test.

An endometrial biopsy can be obtained by a Novak curette. The biopsy should be timed according to the basal temperature chart to be approximately 2 days prior to menstruation, as this time is the most satisfactory for accurate endometrial dating by criteria of Noyes, Hertig, and Rock.

If the presumptive diagnosis of a luteal phase defect is made, it is well to recheck the endometrial dating by using a thorough curettage. The diagnosis of a luteal phase defect is substantiated if the histological pattern is 2 days bet ind the expected date. An inadequate endometrium may reflect (1) an inability of the endometrium to respond to hormone stimulation which, in our experience, is unusual, or (2) an insufficiency of progesterone production by the ovary.

The cause of this condition may be due either to factors discussed under the sections on ovarian failure that is, nutritional insufficiencies, metabolic disease processes, chronic illnesses, or deficient pituitary stimulation (neurogenic)-or to specific inherent ovarian defects. The inadequate luteal phase is more apt to be associated with early repeated miscarriages but can occasionally be severe enough to cause primary infertility.

The treatment of the inadequate luteal phase is dependent upon the etiology. However, if the specific factors have been corrected as well as possible or if no specific factors are found, progesterone substitution therapy must be instituted. Usually the most satisfactory substitution therapy is the administration of 12.5 mg. of progesterone intramuscularly daily, given within 2 days after ovulation and continued until the menstrual period begins. This amount of progesterone is adequate for the repair of the average luteal defect but is not enough to override a normal menstrual period. A repeat biopsy while the patient is on therapy will tell whether or not the defect has been repaired. If this amount of progesterone is inadequate, 25 mg. of progesterone can be given daily until approximately 2 or 3 days before the period is expected, at which time the dosage may be reduced to 12.5 mg. or its equivalent. In this fashion one can prevent a pseudopregnancy reaction.

Synthetic progestogens are not advised since the effect upon the endometrium is often not equivalent to that of progesterone. Chorionic gonadotrophin from human pregnancy urine can also be used as a luteotrophic agent. A daily dose of 2500 IU given 2 days after ovulation has occurred will produce an adequate stimulation of corpus luteum function and is usually insufficient to cause pseudopregnancy. If in addition to the luteal phase defect, there is an estrogenic deficiency as judged be an inadequate cervical mucus. 0.1 tmg. of stilbestrol daily throughout the menstrual cycle will as eported by Hughes and Van Ness sometimes be sufficient to produce a proper endometrial build-up for a progestational response.

If infection is present, proper antibiotic therapy must be instituted. If there is endometrial scarring, as in Asherman's disease, repeated gentle curettage may suffice.

7

Abnormal Vaginal Discharge

LEUKORRHEA

Laukorrhea is the term applied to any vaginal discharge other than blood. It is perhaps the most frequently encountered of gynecological symptoms, occurring in at least one-third of all gynecological patients. Certainly it has a greater nuisance value in its frequent recalcitrance to therapy. Rarely, however, is it of serious cause, and generally it is associated with simple infections of the cervix, vagina, or tube. Indeed the only justification for devoting a chapter to it is for the convenience of the medical student who is often asked the various causes of leukorrhea.

Leukorrhea, it need hardly be said, is a symptom and not a disease. Under normal conditions all parts of the genital mucous membrane are kept moistened, either by secretions of their own or by those having their source in a higher segment of the canal. Normally there is no escape of secretions to the outside, although there are comparatively few women who do not at some time or other in their lives have at least a slight external discharge. The discharge may consist of a mere excess of otherwise normal secretion, or it may consist partly or dominantly of abnormal exudates from pathological lesions at one point or another in the genital canal.

SOURCE AND CHARACTER OF GENITAL DISCHARGES

Vulva

Strictly speaking,,vulvar secre- tions do not come into the present discussion, as the vulva is an external structure. At times, however, v ilvar secretions contribute to the leukorrhea complained of by the patient, who herself cannot know the source of the discharge.

In addition to the numerous sebaceous and sudoriferous glands found in the vulva, the vulvovaginal gland is to all intents and purposes a part of the vulva, and this gland plays the most important role in the lubrication of the vaginal introitus and the vulvar mucous membrane. It secretes a thick viscid mucus. which is greatly increased during sexual excitement. Finally. in the periurethral region of the vestibule are situated Skene's ducts and a considerable number of mucous crypts which likewise contribute to the lubrication of the vulvar structures. In infections of Bartholin's gland, there is often a profuse purulent discharge either from the duct or from a ruptured abscess. Such discharges are apt to be interpreted by the patient as of vaginal nature. The same statement may be made concerning discharges from the periurethral structures above mentioned, and may be extended even to the purulent exudate of actual acute urethritis.

Vagina

While the vagina is itself devoid of glands, its surface is normally kept moist by the secretion of the cervical glands, and to a much less extent by transudation from its own surface. Normally the secretion found in the vagina is acid in reaction, with a pH averaging 5 %. This acidity is due to the acid-forming propensities of certain organisms normally found in the vagina, the chief being the large rod-shaped organism known as the bacillus of Doderlein.

The acid reaction is dependent upon the presence of the lactic acid produced by the action of these organisms upon the glycogen content of the vaginal epithelium. The latter undergoes constant desquamation, so that discharges of vaginal origin are characterized by the presence of many epithelial cells, giving the discharge a milky or curdy appearance. During pregnancy, vaginal desquamation is intensified, and a milky or curdy exudate is complained of by many women during the latter part of gestation. On the other hand, when actual inflammation and infection of the vagina ocurs, as in trichomonas or monilial vaginitis, an exudate develops which is usually cucopurulent or purulent in character, extremely profuse, and associated with marked pruitus. There may be little or no odor to the discharge, or it may be very offensive.

Lang, Fritz, and Menduke have emphasized the frequency of associated trichomonal and candidal forms of vaginitis; even though only one type is apparent on wet smear, the other organism may be present on culture. There would appear relatively little difference in the bacteriological findings in pregnant and nonpregnant women although it is also stated that the gravid female is particularly prone to harbor these fungus type of infections.

Flagvl (merronidazole) is the new wonder drug for Trichomonas, but it is quite specific for this organism. The usual treatment is 250 mg. three times a day for 10 days for one or both sexual partners with vaginal therapy for the female on occasion. Concomitant antifungal therapy as with Mycostatinseems appropriate for a mixed infection. British authors who have a much more extended experience indicated that pregnancy is in no way complicated by use of this medication, the availabilityy of which in this country was. Until recently, markedly curtailed by the thalidomide tragedies. A recent double-blind study by Forster, Ramincz. and Rapaport leaves little doubt as to the efficacy of the drug and the infrequency of complications.

Cervix

The mucous glands of the cervix are the chief source of the secretion normally found in the vagina, and it is not strange, therefore, that they are the chief source of leukorrheal discharge.. The normal secretion is a clear, viscid, alkaline mucus, which varies in its amount and viscidity at different phases of the menstrual cycle. Recent investigations have shown, for example, that its permeability to the spermatozoa is greatest at about the time of ovulation. The secretion may be merely increased in amount without alteration in character, as a result of hyperactivity of the glands produced by hyperemic or endocrine factors.

The histological structure of the cervix, with its numerous gland invaginations, makes it peculiarly prone to persistent infections, characterized by increase and pathological alterations of the secretion. Invariably minor childbirth lacerations become secondarily infected, with resultant mucoid hypersecretion. Neoplasms of the cervix characteristically produce a discharge, and this is usually offensive and bloody.

Uterine Body

While the endometrium contains innumerable glands, these are inactive until the postovulatory phases of the cycle, and even then the secretion seems to be designed chiefly for local nutritional purposes in the event of pregnancy. At any rate it seems to add little to the secretory content of the lower genital canal. Aside from this, however, a certain amount of serous transudation undoubtedly occurs, and this may at times be increased in amount as a result of vascular or endocrine factors.

Even actual endometritis is commonly believed to be of little importance as a cause of leukorrhea. An exception to this is the occasional case of acute septic endoinetritis in which a profuse purulent discharge may be given off from the uterine cavity. In cases associated with retention of placental tissue, this may be extremely odorous as a result of saprophytic invasion of the uterus. While not so easy to demonstrate, the histological appearance of chronic endometritis. sometimes showing considerable amounts of exudate in the gland luinina. makes it difficult to believe that this may not contribute to the vaginal discharge so often seen in such cases, and no doubt due chiefly to the associated cervical infection.

Finally, uterine polyps, submucous myomas: carcinomas, and other tumors are not infrequently the cause of uterine discharges. particularly when complicated by infection and necrotic changes.

Tubes

While certainly rare. Leukorrhea of tubal origin may occur, the usually cited example being that of the so-called profluent salpingitis, in which a hydrosalpinx may periodically expel its content through a partially patent inner orifice into the uterus and thus cause gushes of watery fluid from the vagina. In most cases of hydrosalpinx, however, the uterine end of the tubal lumen is completely closed, so that the above mentioned mechanism must be extremely uncommon.

CAUSES

The chief causes of leukorrhea may be briefly summarized as follows.

Constitutional

These include such conditions as anemia, tuberculosis, chronic nephritis, and other diseases associated with general debility. In the same category may be included conditions which bring about circulatory disturbance, such as the chronic passive congestion of heart disease and cirrhosis of the liver.

Endocrine Disorders

Certain types of endocrine disorders may bring about Leukorrhea, which is usually slight in amount and due to hypersecretion of the cervical glands. A good example of this is the moderate mucoid discharge not infrequently observed in patients suffering with functional uterine bleeding. In these the hypersecretion is due to the excessive estrogen effect upon the cervical glands. An even simpler example is the premenstrual mucoid discharge seen in many normal women. The frequent leukorrhea of pregnancy is due partly to endocrine factors and partly to the hyperemia associated with gestation.

Inflammations of Any Part of the Genital Canal

These include (1) vulvitis or vulvovaginitis. (2) vaginitis. (3) cervicitis, (4) endometritis, and (5) salpingitis.

(1) Vulvitis or Vulvovaginitis

Numerous organisms may be concerned in the etiology of vulvitis. such as the *.1licrococcu's* catarrhalis. Streptococcus. Staphylococcus.

Hemophilus vaginalis, tubercle bacillus. or the colon bacillus. .Protozoal infections, especially with the trichomonas vagina, may occur, but these are far less important on the vulva than in the vagina. Fungus infection with the yeast organisms. especially the thrush fungus or the monilia, may likewise be encountered, and in children one may occasionally see inflammations produced by parasitic worms, especially the pinworm, or *Oxyuris vermicularis*. Gonococcal infection is relatively uncommon in this era.

(2) Vaginitis

The adult vagina is far more resistant to gonorrheal infection than that of the immature child, but inflammatory disease is not uncommonly produced by such organisms as the bacillus of Daderlein, the *Micrococcus catarrhalis,* Streptococcus, and the colon bacillus. The same organisms may be concerned in the vulvovaginitis of children, but the chief clinical type in this group was formerly produced by Gonococcus.

At the opposite end of the age scale may be put the fairly numerous cases of senile vaginitis and endometritis. As a result of the frequent cessation of ovarian function at the menopause, the lining of both the vagina and uterus becomes thin, atrophic, and prone to secondary infection. Not infrequently tiny areas of ulceration are produced, so that not only leukorrhea but also slight vaginal bleeding may be noted. Estrogen (stilbesterol) suppositories or creams are usually curative. and rarely lead ·to bleeding where the uterus is present.

(3) Cervicilis

This extremely common cause of leukorrhea is etiologically divisible into two groups, the gonorrheal and pyogenic. The latter, in which puerperal lacerations often play an important causative role is the result of infection by various organisms. chiefly of Streptococcus and Staphylococcus groups.

(4) Endometritis

Here again various organisms may be concerned. the gonococcus much less frequently than the pyogenic group. which so frequently. with saprophytes. are the secondary invaders in cases of retained pregnancy products and ulcerative or necrotic neoplasms.

(5) Salpingilis

In this rare source of leukorrhea. the causative organisms are almost always the Gonococcus. Streptococcus or Staphylococcus. or tubercle bacillus.

Other Local Pathological Conditions. These include a variety of conditions in almost any part of the genital canal. Among the most important are benign or malignant tumors, especially when infection and necrosis have occurred; uterine displacements; puerperal lacerations of the cervix; fistulas of one sort or another, especially frequent being the vesicovaginal and rectovaginal varieties; the retention of gestation products within the uterus; and the presence of foreign bodies such as neglected pessaries in the vagina or cervix, or bougies and other abortifacient implements in the uterus.

Diagnosis of cause of Leukorrhea

The mere diagnosis of leukorrhea means nothing, being usually made by the patient herself. As already emphasized, leukorrhea is a symptom and not a disease, and the responsibility of the physician is to determine the cause if possible. This is simple in some cases, exceedingly difficult in others. The history of the case may be of great importance, as in the case of discharge developing after coitus with a partner in whom gonorrhea is known or suspected to exist. In all cases a complete appraisal of the patient's physical condition is indicated, with consideration of constitutional as well as local factors.

The routine of pelvic examination should be thorough, and this may readily reveal the source of the abnormal discharge, and often its probable nature. However, in a large proportion of cases, microscopic and bacteriological examinations are imperative. This is particularly true in the differentiation of cases in which a gonorrheal etiology is possible, and in the differentiation of vaginal leukorrhea, in which parasitic and fungus infections are so often concerned.

The character of the discharge is often suggestive, although never conclusive, of the source of the abnormal discharge. A thick, milky, or curdy discharge is suggestive of a vaginal source, a viscid mucopurulent one of a cervical source. The admixture ofblood in leukorrheal discharges of women of middle life and beyond should always lead to the suspicion of malignancy, although similar discharges may be seen as a result of senile endometritis or ulcerative benign tumors. Such considerations, however. are merely of suggestive value. and cannot take the place of careful examination.

The examination of various special conditions characterized by leukorrhea. together with a discussion of examination techniques is to be found in the appropriate chapters (on cervicitis and vagini(is).

TREATMENT

The treatment must obviously be based on removal of the cause, whatever this may be. Since the possible etiologic factors embrace such a large proportion of gynecological lesions, the reader is referred to the appropriate chapters for details of the treatment of the symptoms of leukorrhea.

8

VULVULAR DISEASES

Since the vulva is of ectodermal origin it is subject to all skin disorders seen elsewhere in the body. *Eczematoid* dermatitis is especially prevalent, since the vulvar area is exposed to a variety of irritants. Clothing, topical applications (medicinal and cosmetic), vaginal discharge, and systemic drugs, particularly certain antibiotics, are responsible for many of the allergic reactions. Antihistamines, local hydrocortisone, and elimination of irritants are of great therapeutic value in such instances.

As a result of the vaginal secretions as well as the excretions of the skin glands, the vulva is kept almost constantly moist. Consequently, *intertrigo* is frequently noted, not only in the labia, but also in the crural folds. In the later stages these linear, reddened excoriations become lichenified with thick, white edges, grossly resembling leukoplakia. Obviously, scrupulous cleanliness, careful drying, and use of drying powders are the most important therapeutic measures.

Seborrhea and *seborrheic dermatitis* are not infrequent offenders in the vulvar area, and *folliculitis* may occur with or without any of the above excitors. *Psoriasis* is rarely seen of the vulva, and is usually associated with lesions elsewhere on the body. *Herpes genitalis* is similar to herpetic lesions elsewhere, and is often painful, especially when secondarily infected. Obviously otherdermatological lesions such as lichen planus, vitiligo (leukoderma), seleroderma, etc., may affect the vulva. A recent report by Douglas in *The Journal of Obstetrics and Gynaecology of the British Commonwealth* is an excellent treatise on vulvar dermatology.

Fungus infections may be primary on the vulva or secondary to an associated, *aginitis*, in either case pruritis is the common symptom. Similarly yeast may present as a "*vulvitis*" with the development of thrushlike patches on the external genitalia. Either of these mycotic infections may be associated with diabetes and its characteristic "beefy-red" vulva. Again. as the vagina is frequently involved. there is an irritating discharge which adds to the patients's discomfort and pruritis. Both the diabetes and its associated infectious process must be treated simultaneously and persistently if good results are to be obtained. The recognition of the combined etiologies depends obviously on careful urinanalysis and blood sugar evaluations if necessary, and the demonstration of the offending organisms in vaginal smears and upon culture of the discharge on Nickerson's or Sabouraud's medium. The former common therapy with 1 aqueous solution of gentian violet has largely been superceded by the use of such fungicides as propion jelly or mycostatin because of the frequent irritation and staining which resulted from the gentian violet therapy.

Similarly trichomonas and postmenopausal vaginitis may produce a severe vulvar edema, erythema, and concomitant pruritis. Thorough inspection of the vaginal canal and the secretions generally reveals the correct diagnosis.

CIRCULATORY DISEASES

Among circulatory disturbances involving the vulva, *i'arices* are perhaps the most common. They affect especially the labia majors, and are usually seen in women who suffer also with varicose veins of the lower extremities. A common cause is intrapelvic pressure from pregnancy or large tumors. As with varicose veins elsewhere, they distend with blood when the patients stands and tend to empty and become smaller when she lies down. The varices may become extremely large andinay even rupture, with resultant bleeding. Most commonly, however, the dilated veins appear as multiple small purplish, elevations which simulate and are often mistaken for hemangiomata. *Edema* of the vulva may likewise be the result of intrapelvic pressure from large tumors, marked ascites, or lymph nodes, enlarged by metastatic tumor as in carcinoma of the cervix. More often it is due to inflammatory lesions of the vulva itself. Even a small lesion, such as a furuncle or a small chancroid, may cause enormous swelling of the vulva, because of its dependent position and the looseness of the subcutaneous tissue. Finally, inflammatory or parasitic blockage of the vulvar lymphatics may cause extreme edema, as in elephantiasis.

INFLAMMATIONS

Diseases of Bartholin's Gland

Since *Bartholin's gland* is commonly classed as one of the constituent structure of the vulva. a discussion of its diseases is properly included in this chapter. The lesions of this gland are either inflammatory or neoplastic. the former being extremely common. the latter very rare.

Inflammation (Bartholin Adenitis)

In the majority of cases the causative organism is the Gonococcus. There is no question, however, that other organisms may at times be concerned, such as the colon bacillus. the pyogenic group, or the *Alicrococcus catarrhalis*. Even the *Trichomonas vaginalis* may occasionally invade the glands, and produce an inflammatory reaction.

In the *acute* stage the gland becomes turgid, swollen, and painful, and a purulent exudate can be expressed from the duct by gentle pressure or may issue from it spontaneously. There is a strong tendency toward suppuration, the swelling *becoming* more pronounced and the overlying skin red and tender. *Abscess* is a common sequel, manifesting itself often by fluctuation over the mass, with surrounding edema which may be so marked as to cause enormous swelling of the entire labium of the affected side.

Treatment

The treatment should consist, first of rest in bed, and this is not difficult to enforce, as almost any activity causes considerable pain. Sulfonamides are usually adequate antibacterial medications. There is no indication for douches; however, Sitz baths usually *afford* great relief. An ice bag or hot water bag also gives local relief from pain, but the latter is preferable when suppuration and abscess formation is imminent, as is so commonly the case. Analgesics are important to relieve the discomfort.

When abscess formation is evident, early incision is advisable. This usually *afford* immediate relief, and healing takes place within a few days to a week. The infection, however, is not eradicated, the glands often remaining the seat of a chronic inflammation.

Chronic Bartholinitis

Chronic Bartholinitis (properly *Bartholin adenitis*) may persist for many years. A history of an initial acute attack may or may not be obtained. The only clinical evidence of the disease may be the presence of a small nodular swelling, palable deep beneath the posterior portion of the labium majus, where it can often be rolled between the thumb and finger of the examiner. The patient herself is frequently unaware of the existence of such a nodule. The course of chronic bartholinitis may be punctuated by acute exacerbations, with occasional recurrence of abscess.

In other chronic cases, as a result of occlusion of either the main duct or one of its subdivisions. *cysts* of Bartholin's duct commonly develop. They may be very small or they become as large as an egg. While often producing little or no discomfort. they frequently undergo suppuration with abscess formation, as described above.

The *pathological changes* in chronic *bartholinitis* or cyst formation are those of chronic inflammation. The main duct is lined by transitional epithelium while a single layer of flattened cells lines the smaller branches. Severe inflammation may destroy all epithelium, however, the mucous secreting acini are almost always demonstrable in the deeper tissues.

Treatment

The treatment of chronic *Bartholin adenitis* and of cysts of Bartholin's glands is complete excision of the gland. Simple marsupialization is quite efficacious in cases of simple, uncomplicated cysts; however, when recurrent infection has been the problem it is necessary to remove not only the cyst but the entire infected gland. This is important because the smaller cysts often involve only'one lobule of the gland, and incomplete removal of the latter may be followed by recurrences of syst or abscess.

Tumors

Carcinoma of Bartholin's gland may be *primary or secondary.* The former constitutes one type of vulvar carcinoma, although it is far less frequent than other than types (see "Carcinoma of vulva"). It appears as a carcinoma of the squamous, transitional or adenomatous types. Secondary carcinoma may occur as a result of metastases in cases of uterine, ovarian, or other genital cancers, and rarely with carcinoma of distant extragenital organs. The gland may also be involved by direct extension from a suchas sarcoma, hypernephroma, and chorionepithelioma are rare.

ULCERATIVE LESIONS

Simple Acute Ulcer (Lipschiitz)

This rather nebulous condition may affect either the vulva or the lower vagina, the latter being more frequently the case. The ulcers may be single or multiple. They appear as shallow, rounded, or oval lesions which produce only slight local soreness and discomfort and which are readily amenable to simple antiseptic treatment. The causative agent has been said to be the *Bacillus crassus,* a normal inhabitant of the vagina, however, it seems unlikely that this is true. It is more feasible to accept these lesions as aphthous, due possibly to Vincent's-type organisms or even more nonspecific varieties.

Chancroid (Soft Chancer, Ulcus Molle)

This lesion belongs to the group of venereal infections being transmitted by coitus. The *etiological agent* is the *Hemophilus ducrevii* which can be demostrated in scrapings made from'the base of the shallow ulcerations.The initial lesion presents as a small papule or pustule which appears within 2 or 3 days of exposure, with progressive ulceration but little induration. The lession may affect any part of the vulva. When the labia are involved, there is often a marked local edema and swelling of the entire labium. Charateristically this ulcerative lesion is painful at the onset, differing from the majority of the so-called "venereal diseases." Inguinal adenitis infrequent but the infected inguinal glands rarely show a tendency to suppurate.

Diagnosis

The diagnosis of chancroid is based on the history of exposure, the short latent period of usually 2 to 4 days, the clinical characteristics of the ulceras described above, the usual absence of induration, primary painful lesion,and the demonstrations of the *Ducrey bacillus* in smears or scrapings from the ulcer.

Treatment

The treatment of chancroid is, with few exceptions, eminetly satisfactory. Reliance is placed on meticulous cleanliness arid the use of local antiseptics and sulfonamides, together with Chloromycetin, Achromycin and other antibiotics, with as yet no complete unanimmity as to which is the most effective.

SYPHILIS

Chancer

This, the initial lesion of syphilis, is observed less commonly in women than in men. Chancre, however, is much more frequent on the vulva than in the vagina, probably because of the greater frequency in the former area of small abrasions offering portals of entry to the spirochete. The lesion does not appear until 3 or 4 weeks after exposure. In many cases of syphilis in women the initial lesion is overlooked, although it undoubtedly occurs, if not on the vulva, in the vagina or on le cervix.

The vulvar chancre is apt to be smaller than the lesion as it occurs in men, but otherwise its appearance is quite similar. It presents as a rounded or ovoid ulcer with raised, indurated edges and a depressed center. The surface is reddish or reddish brown. It appears usually on one or the other of the labia majora, in which case there may be considerable surrounding edema. There is marked associated inguinal lymphadenitis. This initial lesion usually regresses spontaneously in 4 to 6 weeks.

Diagnosis

The diagnosis of syphilis in this primary stage is dependent upon the demonstration of the spirochete in the lesion. The surface of the lesion is gently wiped with gauze moistened in normal saline solution, care being taken not to start bleeding. By firmly squeezing the lesion, droplets of lymph may be made to exude, and it is this exudate which should be examined by the darkfield technique for the characteristic spirochetes. If positive, the *T pallidum* may be recognized by the corkscrew-like activity. Various aerological tests may not be positive at this time.

Secondary Lesions-Condyloma Latum

The typical secondary lesion observed in the vulvar area is the condyloma latum, or moist patch, which corresponds to the cutaneous macules or papules characterizing the secondary stage.The typical syphilitic condylomas are slightly raised, plateau-like lesions which are round or oval, of various sizes, and often occur in clusters. The edges are slightly indurated, the surface is moist, and covered with a grayish necrotle exudate. The condylomas not only cover the vulva, but extend to the surrounding perineum, the inner side of the upper thighs, and the buttocks. Again there is marked lymphadenitis.

The *diagnosis* by microscopic examination is made *by* the same technique as described for the initial lesion. In this stage, corroborative evidence for the existence of syphilis can be obtained from blood tests, which by this time are routinely positive. *Treatment* is generally penicillin to a total of 7 to 8 million units over a period of 5 to 7 days. The longer therapy is wise in an effort to prevent the Herxheimer reaction. Terramycin or similar antibiotics may be used in the patient sensitive to penicillin. Only cleanliness is necessary locally. Unfortunately, due generally to poor reporting of initial lesions and consequent inadequate social service follow-up of contracts, there has been approximately a 75 % or more increase in primary syphilis in many areas during the past 5 years.

Tertiary Syphilis-Gumma and Syphilitic Ulcer

While the characteristic tertiary syphilitic lesion is the gumma, and while this may occur on the vulva, its tendency to necrosis and ulceration is so great that the most common tertiary lesion is the syphilitic ulcer. The latter appears as a large, sluggish, necrotic ulceration which may cause much surrounding induration and edema, and which may produce fistulas between the vagina and rectum. In some cases the hypertrophic changes are pseudoneoplastic, and must be distinguished from lymphogranuloma inguinale or carcinoma. Such lesions are rarely seen today.

Granuloma Inguinale

This "venereal disease", transmitted usually by coitus, presents primarily as single or multiple small ulcerations affecting the vulva and adjacent perineum. It is found especially in the tropics and the southern section of our country. It is most common among Negroes, although occasionally seen in whites. It is of interest that granuloma may at times affect various *extragenital sites*. particularly in the skin and bone.

The incubation period of this disease varies widely from a few days to several months. The disease usually begins as a small papular lesion of one of the labia minora or in the inguinal region, followed in a few weeks, by ulceration which tends to assume a characteristic serpiginous form. The surface is reddish and granular and there is a considerable amount of seropurulent exudate. By contrast with some of the other chronic ulcerative vulvar lesions, the lesions of granuloma tend to remain superficial, but in some cases they may become deep and destructive, probably as a result of secondary infection. Inguinal lymphadenopathy with suppuration rarely occurs.

The *microscopic picture* of the disease is characterized by an initial stage of subcutaneous infiltration with plasma cells, leukocytes, and large mononuclear cells, after which typical granulation tissue is formed. Especially characteristic are the so-called *granuloma cells*, which are large mononuclear cells with foamy, vacuolated cytoplasm. There is now general agreement that the *causative factor* of granuloma inguinale is the Donovan inclusion, variously felt to be viral, bacterial (the Donovan virus or bacillus), or protozoal. This can be demonstrated in smears from 60 to 80% of the lesions and can be stained in tissues by the methods of Wright and Giemsa in 100 % of the cases (von Haam), during the acute and subacute stages of the disease. Greenblatt, Baldwin. and Dienst have reported the experimental production of the disease by the injection of an exudate containing no other organisms except the Donovan inclusions. The latter are described as small encapsulated bodies resembling a "closed safety pin" as the result of the bipolar staining of the inclusions. Occasionally they are not encapsulated in various southern clinics, ***a proportion of cases of vulvas carcinoma have been found to have been preceded by granuloma or lvmphopathia***.

Diagnosis

The diagnosis is made from the characteristic picture of the superficial granular inguinal lesion, together with the microscopic demonstration of the Donovan bodies. The lesion is generally more superficial and less painful than chancroid, in which the causative *Ducrey bacillus* may be found on smear examination. Carcinoma and tuberculosis can be excluded by microscopic examination of excised tissue specimens should doubt exist as to their possibility although usually this is not necessary. *Syphilis* does not often produce lesions which resemble those of granuloma, and here, the finding of the Treponema and the results of blood examination would be of much diagnostic help. On the other hand, one must bear in mind the possibility of coexistence of the two diseases. Finally, lymphogranuloma inguinale must be stressed as the disease which may present the greatest difficulty in its differentiation from granuloma. The former, however, is characterized by the frequent occurrence of suppurative adenitis, by extensive and often destructive ulcerative lesions, and in later stages by cicatricial structure of the rectum. The absence of Donovan bodies in the smear and the positive Frei test obtained in lymphogranuloma will usually afford decisive information in questionable cases.

Treatment

In former years the treatment of granuloma consisted in the intravenous administration of antimony (tartar emetic) or Fuadin. Since the introduction of the antibiotics, however, their administration has completely superseded the older plans. Chloromycetin has thus far seemed the most effective, although Aureomycin and streptomycin have also been used. Usually 10 gm., either 1 gm. a day for 10 days or 2 gm. a day for 5 days,of the antibiotic will produce satisfactory result in the acute stage. In the chronic stages, such therapy is less effective and surgery may be necessary if the lesion is localized enough to permit removal.

Lymphopathia Venereum (Lymphogranuloma)

It is only in recent years that attention has been focused on this venereal disease, which is so widerly prevalent, especially in the south and chiefly among Negroes. The disease begins, after an incubation period of usually only a few days, as an initial lesion in the vagina, on the cervix, or on the external genitalia. This initial papule or pustule quickly disppears and is almost always overlooked.It is soon followed, however, be the appearance of the suppurative inguinal adenitis, or bubo. The condition appears, indeed, to be essentially a disease of the lympathics. associated with marked ulcerative and hypertrophic changes, these occurring in varying proportion.

If the ulcerative process dominates the picture. a large, ragged ulcer may be produced. always surrounded by fibrous induration and edema. On the other hand, when the hypertrophic process predominates, one sees enormous overgrowth of the connective tissue and great thickening and corrugation of the skin. producing the most common form of *elephariiasis*. although such rare entities as filariasis nay produce a similar picture. As with granuloma, extragenital sites are at times noted, as in the mouth and rectum. During the stage of bubo formation constitutional symptoms such as fever and malaise are commonly seen.

Mention has already been made in the preceding section that carcinoma has not infrequently developed on the basis of either preexisting lymphopathia or granuloma.

Diagnosis

Microscopically, the chief features are an extensive infiltration with polymorphonuclear, round, and plasma cells. Dilatation of the lymphatics, proliferation of endothelial cells, and later extensive fibrosis are likewise often seen with hyperkeratosis. The most striking feature is the proliferation and distortion of the epithelial *rete pegs* (*Pseudoepitheliomatous hyperplasia*). It is the spread of the causative virus along the lymphatics, with extensive inflammation and cicatrization of the endopelvic fascia, that brings about the extensive *rectal structure* so characteristic of this disease.

The cause of lymphogranuloma is a filterable virus, one of the largest of the known viruses. The diagnosis may be made by means of the Frei test, consisting of a positive cutaneous response obtained after injection of an antigen prepared from the sterilized pus of the buboes, or from the brain of the virus infected mouse. Unfortunately the test is per sistently positive and the acute lesion may be of another origin. The differentiation from granuloma has already been discussed in the previous section, and most of what has there been said as regards possible confusion with other vulvar lesions would apply to lymphogranuloma as well. Antibiotics have been beneficial for both diseases.

Treatment

Recently very satisfactory and at times striking results have been reported from sulfa therapy and even more from the antibiotics. *Chloromycetin*, *Streptomycin*, and *Achromycin* have all been used. The former, for exathple, can be given in doses offrom 250 to 500 mg. four times a day for from 5 to 10 days. Penicillin has been used effectively in many cases.

Surgical treatment is still occasionally called for, as in the excision of the enormous masses sometimes seen with an associated elephantiasis, or in the treatment of rectal strictures, in which colostomy may at times be necessary. With all granulomatous disease *multiple biopsy* should be performed to exclude concomitant malignancy.

WHITE LESIONS OF THE VULVA

Gross white appearance of the vulvar skin may be due to two general types of change namely: (1) absence or loss of pigment; and (2) increased keratinization (hyperkeratosis).

Absence of Pigment or Depigmentation

Vitiligo or leucoderma(congenital absence of pigment) appears most commonly in the late first or early second decade of life. There are rarely any symptoms associated with this condition, and it is usually found at various other areas of the body.

Scarring due to trauma or some chronic infections, as with x-ray burns and lymphopathia, may also result in depigmentation.

Increased Keratinization (Hyperkeratosis)

1. ***Chronic Infection.*** The end result of chronic infection may

be scarring, especially in those cases of the granulomatous diseases, however, the common dermatitides (eczematoid, neural, seborrhoeic, etc.) usually demonstrate thickening of the skin with whitish change. The edges of these lesions are often elevated with striking keratosis and linear excoriation. Obviously, this description fits that of gross "*leukoplakia*" and unfortunately the microscopic appearance also demonstrates the characteristics suggested in most texts as typical of leukoplakia.

2. *Benign Tumors.* Any of the papillomatous or verrucous lesions, in the chronic stages, may demonstrate areas of hyperkeratosis and whitish change.

3. *Leukoplakia and Leukoplakialike Lesions.* Controversy as to the pathogenesis, clinical course, and particularly the malignant potential of these so-called primary hyperkeratotic lesions, frequently described as the leukoplakias, has been a continuing issue in the study ofvulvar disease. *Schwimmer* in 1877 first applied the term *leukoplakia* to a whitish, premalignant, hyperkeratotic lesion of the buccal mucous membrane. Later. *Breiskv* in 1885 described a similar lesion on the vulva, however, microscopically the picture was that of a thinning of the epithelium and collaginization of the underlying tissue, commonly referred to as *"lichen sclerosus et atrophicus.* " Later Taussig described three developmental stages of the disease which he termed "chronic atrophic vulvitis". (1) erythema, edema, excoriation and dryness, associated with the microscopic findings of minimal hyperkeratosis. acanthosis. and mild inflammatory infiltrate: (2) thickening. with flattening of folds and whitish change in the skin microscopically demonstrating epithelial hypertrophy in addition to increased hyperkeratosis, acanthosis, and round cell infiltrate (hypertrophic leukoplakia) (3) cracking of the parchment-like skin with superficial ulceration and whitish or bluish white discoloration, now microscopically showing hyperkeraatosis, epithelial thinning, and dermal collagenization (atrophic leukoplakia). The author recognized little, if any, difference in the malignant potential between the atrophic and hypertrophic stages. In addition to these proposed progressive changes, Taussig recognized a primary "simple kraurosis" or shriveling, evidenced by constriction or stenosis of the vaginal outlet. This was considered to be a nonleukoplakic change, although, constriction admittedly could develop as the final result of "*chronic atrophic*" or "*leukoplakicvulvitis.*" Bonney, in general, agreed with Taussing's concept, although he did recognize a fourth, or quiescent, stage during which the malignant potential was essentially nonexistant.

The many terms that have been applied to these primary hyperkeratoses need some interpretation.

Leukoplakia has been used to describe a variety of whitish lesions since the term could be applied to any "white patch." More accurately, it should designate that hyperkeratotic, elevated, pruritic lesion which often demonstrates linear excoriations. As noted above, microscopically the problem is similarly confused in that the characteristic. features of leukoplakia, namely hyperkeratosis, acanthosis and inflammatory infiltrate, are also those of chronic forms of neurodermatitis, eczematoid dermatitis, and lichen planus. It would seem wiser to eliminate such descriptive terms as applied to specific disease for a designation which would relay information as to the malignant potential such as "hyperplastic vulvitis" with the modifying degrees, mi moderate, or marked to explain the degree of anaplastic activity to the clinician.

Lichen selerosus et atrophicus applies to a skin lesion which begins as a small bluish white papule. Frequently coalescence of these papules produces a picture of diffuse whitish change over the entire vulva and perianal region. In its terminal stage this disease stimulates *atrophic leukoplakia* and *kraurosis* in that there is loss of the subcutaneous tissue with flattening of the labial folds and constriction of the outlet. Actually *kraurosis* is simply a descriptive term meaning "shrinkage." The microscopic picture of atrophic leukoplakia. lichen sclerosus et atrophicus. and kraurosis are similar.

These lesions commonly appear in the early postmenopauşal years. Nevertheless, atrophy of primary type may be seen prepubertal, and patchy lichen selerosus selerosus et atrophicus is not infrequently seen in the fourth decade of life.

Although *atrophy* has been applied to these lesions, certain studies have indicated that the thinned epithelium is not metabolically inactive. Clark *et al.*, noted that the uptake of radioactive phosphorus is as great in these *atrophic* lesions as in carcinoma-in-situ. Similar findings have been recognized in our laboratory using other methodologies. Although, metabolic activity cannot be correlated directly with anaplasia, the changes do not justify the designation of atrophy. Furthermore, these lesions must be followed carefully as carcinoma can develop in this context. It is important to remember that any irritative lesion may become malignant although the thickened, elevated, hyperkeratotic type Seems to be more prone to anaplastic alteration. Of major importance in the study. and therapy of the lesions are the use of the biopsy and the elimination of scratching with the use of antipruritics, particularly hydrocortisones and antihistamines, intravaginal estrogens postmenopause, the treatment of specific vaginitis, the removal of local irritating medications, etc., and if necessary some variety of nerve block. Plastic procedures to increase the caliber of outlet are often necessary to eliminate the dyspareunia and allow for satisfactory coitus. Vulycetomy is of importance if anaplastic changes are noted in the tissue study.

Finally it must be recognized that *carcinoma-in-situ* and *invasive cancer* can and frequently do appear as whitish lesions. As a consequence any hyperkeratotic area must be biopsied and followed carefully Again therapy for the common symptomatology is imperative.

PRURITUS VULVAE

Pruritus, or itching, of the vulva is one of the most distressing and often one of the most baffling and intractable of gynecological symptoms. Although it is only a symptom and not a disease entity, it is often difficult to ferret out the underlying cause. It is believed that itching represents a subpain response, and that it has its origin in the epidermis rather than in the subcutaneous nerves. When the vulva is the seat of a definite dermatological lesion, such as eczema, dermatitis, or leukoplakia, it is easy to understand how itching would probably be a symptom, just as with a similar lesion elsewhere. In other cases the most meticulous general and local examination may fail to throw light on the cause. just as in some case of pruritus ani.

Local Causes

1. Any of the *common inflammatory skin diseases,* may be the cause of itching. Among these are intertrigo and other forms of simple dermatitis (vulvitis). eczema, herpes, and other skin lesions.

2. *Leukoplakia, Lichen Sclerosus etA trophicus, etc.* Among this group leukoplakia is of special importance, because it is usually the most common precursor of carcinoma of the vulva. The itching, characteristic of leukoplakia, must be treated vigorously and if medicinal therapy fails, surgery should be employed as suggested later in the discussion of leukoplakia.

3. *Ulcerative lesions of the vulva,* such as those associated with chancroid, granuloma inguinale, lyrnphogranuloma venereum, or cancer, are not infrequently associated with some degree of pruritus.

4. *Irritating discharges* from cervix, vagina, and urethra are common causes of vulvar itching. While some women with profuse

vaginal discharge maybe symptomatic, others with minimal leukorrhea have severe pruritis. These differences are not necessarily dependent upon the bacterial, parasitic, or fungous factors associated with the leukorrhea.

5. *Trichomonas and mycolic (yeast) infections* of the vagina deserve separate mention because of their frequency and the characteristic occurrence of itching as the chief subjective symptom. Injudicious use of various antibiotics which eliminate certain bacteria that live in synergistic fashion with vaginal fungi may allow massive overgrowth of the latter with the development of severe mycotic infections.

6. *Animal parasites,* such as pediculi, or the itch mite.

7. *Chemical irritation,* such as that due to strong soaps or irritating lotions and ointments.

8. *Uncleanliness,* which is likely to produce accumulations of sebaceous material, sweat, smegma, or urinary or even fecal deposits.

9. *The mechanical irritation of tight clothing* or of menstrual napkins.

10. *Masturbation, as* a result of the local congestion which it may produce.

General Causes

1. *Conditions of general physical debility,* as seen in undernutrition, vitamin deficiencies, anemia, tuberculosis, or cancer.

2. *Toxic conditions,* such as the use of various drugs (drug rashes). jaundice, and uremia.

3. *Certain constitutional diseases,* such as *leukemia* or *Hodgkin's disease*.

4. *Endocrine disorders* of one form or another. The most conspicuous example of this is seen in the form of the estrogen deficiency of the *menopause.* with not infrequently an associated *senile vaginitis,* and often characterized by troublesome itching. *Thyroid dysfunction* likewise may be a cause of this symptom.

5. *Diabetes mellitus.* While this might be included under one of the previous heads, it deserves separate mention because of the frequency of vulvar pruritus as a symptom. Indeed, one of the first steps in the study of the average case of pruritus should be examination of the urine for sugar. We have seen not a few cases in which gynecological examination has thus led to the discovery of previously unsuspected diabetes. In many and perhaps most cases of the diabetic

group, the immediate cause of the itching is an associated mycotic infection, as discussed under the heading (mycotic vulvitis).

6. *Allergy* may be due to food sensitivity manifested by local applications, synthetics in underclothing, anestehctic ointments, drugs, and possibly even to menstrual napkins. This is a not infrequent group, and the detection of the elusive allergic factor may call for meticulous investigation.

Treament

Causal

It goes almost without saying that the first essential in the cure of pruritus is a painstaking *search for the cause of the disorder.* From what has been said as to the etiology, this will often mean a very laborious investigation, and one which is not invariably crowned with success. In the majorityof cases, however, one or several factors of ostensible significance are revealed, and the correction of these brings relief to the patient. In many cases, as a matter of fact, the simplest gynecological examination will reveal the important factor. In other cases, however, extensive diagnostic studies, including varous laboratory methods, are called for. Such common local causes as *Trichomonas* and yeast infection are always to be borne in mind.

Estrogenic Therapy

Estrogenic therapy is often use for *pruritus vulvae,* but there is little rationale for its except in that group of cases associated with estrogen deficiency,and the resultant vaginal, as described for senile vaginitis.

Symptomatic

Stening and Elliott indicate that any patient with chronic pruritus and a vulvar lesion of any type deserves biopsy just as surely as postmentopausal bleeding warrants curettement. Regardless of the cause. there are certain *symptonratic measures* which can be resorted to in the treatment of almost all cases. Avoidance of overactivity. of clothing that is too binding or too warm, and of scratching should be insisted on, along with maintenance of general cleanliness: underclothing of synthetics, the use of strong soaps. and perfumed powders or lotions should be eliminanated. Various local anesthetic ointments are commonly used for symptomatic relief, but due to the possibility of sensitivity reactions may only complicate the problem. Cool boric acid compresses are strongly recommended for palliative purposes.

Antipruritic Substances

An endless array of local applications has been applications recommended for this purpose, and both patiant and physician will often turn from one to another in the effort to relieve pruritus. Measures which are of benefit to one patient seem useless in another. Calamine, various antihistamine, sulfur, tar, and vitamin preparations are frequently prescribed. These are now generally supplemented by ointments or sprays of hydrocortisone which are almost always, if not curative, of tremendous symptomatic value. The use of various sedatives and tranquilizers is of considerable assistance.

Alcohol Injections

The injection of 95 % alcohol subcutaneously by the technique recommended by Stone for pruritus am has been employed also for pruritus vulvae. and it is undoubtedly of help. This should obviously only be used in chronic conditions when medications have failed. Unfortunately, it may be followed by sloughing in the vulvar or anal region. Only 0.1 cc. of 95 % or absolute alcohol is injected beneath the dermis, needle punctures situated about 1 cm. apart. An anesthetic is required, but the resulting relief may continue for many months. Various plans of incising the labia with undercutting and disruption of the sensory nerves have been suggested by Mering but it is important to evaluate each case very critically as the author suggests. These have the value of preserving normal anatomy. Occasionally, however, vulvectomy is necessary to relieve severe degrees of pruritus, if hyperplastic changes are taking place in the skin.

Whatever the type of therapy, abolition of the scratch reflex seems desirable, for it is possible that this form of repeated mechanical trauma may be the stimulus that leads to carcinoma.

BENIGN TUMORS OF THE VULVA

CYSTIC

1. Bartholin duct cysts
2. Sebaceous cyst
3. Epidermal inclusion cyst
4. Wolffian duct cyst
5. Cyst of Canal of Nuck
6. Endometriosis

SOLID

1. Fibroma

2. Lipoma
3. Verrucous lesions (Condyloma acuminatum) 4. Angioma
5. Hidradenoma
6. Granular cell myoblastoma 7. Nevus

CYSTIC

1. Bartholin's Duct Cysts

These have been discussed under "Diseases of Bartholin's Glands," in this chapter.

2. Sebaceous or Atheromatous Cysts

These result from inflammatory blockage of the ducts of sebaceous glands, and are usually of small size. They are most commonly on the inner surfaces of the labia majors and minors. They contain a cheesy sebaceous material and aretprone to suppuration, with the formation of small furuncle-like abscesses. If very small and asymptomatic, no treatment is necessary, but if they are sufficiently large to be annoying, or if they are recurrently infected, simple excision under local anesthesia is indicated.

3. Epidermal Inclusion Cysts

Due to trauma or repeated infections, stratifed epithelium may be pinched off beneath the surface forming tiny cysts. These are filled with the castoff surface cells and are prone to infection. Surgery is necessary only in the latter condition.

4. Wolffian Duct Cysts

These occasionally arise from vestiges of the terminal portions of the Wolffian duct. They include the groups spoken of as (hymeneal cysts) and (cysts of the clitoris), but they may arise also from the libia minora close to the clitoris or from the periurethral region. They may be tiny or moderately large. and appear a thin walled sometines translucent structures. often pedunculated.

5. Cyst of Canal of Nuck (Hydrocele)

The round ligament inserts into the labium major and carries with it an investment of the peritoneum The latter is usually firmly attached to its ligament, but may at any point be divorced from its attachment and fluid may accumlate forming a cystic dilatation. Such may present in the labium at the point of insertion and corresponds to the hydrocele in the male.

6. Emdometriosis

Implants of endometrium in the vulva are rare and are most

commonly seen in the region of the Bartholin gland suggesting possible implantation at the time of surgery or drainage of a cyst or abscess. Cyclic recurrence of a painful nodule should suggest this possible diagnosis.

SOLID

1. Fibroma

Although not common, fibroma is not as rare as lipoma.Certain fibromas arise from the fibrous tissue of the vulva, and are usually of small or moderate size. They tend to become pedunculated, especially if rather large and heavy, and the pedicle may become so long that the growth dangles between the limbs like a pendulum. As a matter of fact, tumors of this sort have sometimes reached almost unbelievable size, the classical case reported by *Buckner (1851)* attaining a weight of *268* pounds. The microscopic structure is that if fibrous tissue, usually light textured and edematous, resembling myxomatous tissue. In some tumors there is an admixture of involuntary muscle elements (fibromyoma). Treatment is of course surgical.

2. Lipoma

In spite of the considerable amount of adipose tissue in the vulva, especially in the labia majora, lipoma is rare. It has the same clinical characteristics as those described for fibroma of vulvar origin, and the distinction is not always possible until microscopic examination. Such tumors are easily excised.

3. Verrucous Lesions

The most common form of vulvar verruca is that designated as condyloma acuminatum, to be distinguished from condyloma latum, the secondary syphilitic lesion in the vulva. Pathologically the coadyloma acuminatum is a.papilloma, with a typical treelike structure, and with a central core of connective tissue covered with a heavy mantle of epithelium. The stroma almost always shows some degree of chronic inflammation. The acuminate warts are often loosely spoken of as venereal warts, but such is a misnomer since they are of viral origin.

Clinically condylomata acuminate appear in the form of warty growths of various sizes which are usually multiple and which are discretely scattered over the vulva, especially its posterior portion, and often on the perineum, buttocks, and inner thighs. They are also found in the lower vagina, and more rarely in the upper vagina and even on the cervix

When numerous they tend to become confluent, forming large clusters. They undergo pronounced hypertrophy during pregnancy, sometimes forming huge cauliflower masses which may even offer obstacles to delivery (per vaginam). Actually, many may regress spontaneously postpartum if removal is not necessary during the pregnancy. Malignant degeneration may occur, but is rare, and only a few such cases have been seen in this country.

Formerly, the preferred treatment of condyloma was by excision, although fulguration or use of the high frequency current has been employed by some Topical application of 25% podophyllin in tincture of benzoin or mineral oil is quite effective in thektreatment of the smaller lesions, and this is the customary method of therapy. To avoid a chemical burn, care must be taken to wash off the treated area within a few,hours after application. Topical sulfonamides have been used effectively by some observers.

4. Angioma

Although angiomata are rare, the congenital type cause problems due to irritations of diapers, urine, and feces. However, it is important to take no action if possible, since most of these congenital types regress as the child grows.

5. Hidradenoma of Vulva

While this is a rare lesion, it is of some importance because it is so frequently mistaken for adenocarcinoma, not clinically but microscopically. The lesion arises from the vulvar sweat glands, and with rare exceptions it is benign. Clinically it appears as a small nodule usually raised above the surrounding surface. and having a fibroma-like appearance and consistency. In some cases to overlying skin may be reddened, granular, or ulcerated. In such cases there may be slight bleeding. Most frequently there are no symptoms, although occassionally itching is present. The usual location of the lesion is on the inner surface of the labia majora or the adjacent perineum. The treatment consists of simple excision. Only a rare malignancy is noted in the recent comprehensive review of Chung and Greene.

Supernumerary breast tissue may be found on the vulva and microscopically simulates the apocrine adenoma since the breast is a modified apocrine gland.

6. Granular Cell Myoblastoma of Vulva

This rather uncommon tumor, composed of irregular clumps of large pale staining cells with eosinophilic cytoplasmic granules, is most commonly found in the tongue, but has been found at many sites. Although called myoblastorna, the tumor is felt to arise from the myclin sheath of the nerve. Of interest is the pseudo-epitheliomatous change in the overlying epithelium suggesting epidermoid cancer. Rubin brings up to 23 the total number of such vulvar myoblastomas and, although these are included under benign tumors, he points out that incomplete removal may lead to recurrence.

7. Nevus

The nevus is an important lesions on the vulva since although the vulvar skin makes up only 1% of the entire body surface, 7 to 10% of malignant melanoma in the female occur on the external genitalia. This may be due to the many irritants which *affect* this area as well as the fact that juction activity is common in the vulvar nevus.

CARCINOMA OF THE VULVA

The most important of vulvar tumors is carcinoma, the third most common of all primary pelvic cancers, being exceeded in frequency only by uterine (Cervix and corpus) and ovarian cancer. Vulvar cancer accounts for 3 to 4% of all primary malignancies of the genital canal.

Carinoma-in-situ of the vulva is a definite entity, although far less common than intraepithelial cancer of the cervix. Intraepithelial cancer of the vulva has the same relation as the comparable cervical disease in its tendency to exist at the periphery of invasive cancer or to precede true infiltrative cancer. Indeed, some of the patterns of the so-called hypertrophic leukoplakia bear the same relation to early cancer that atypical cervical epithelium does to cervical intraepithelial cancer. By definition intraepithelial cervical cancer connotes full thickness replacement of the lining epithelium by undifferentiated abnormal cells, often of basal type; and similarly, intraepithelial cancer of the vulva shows abnormality of the lining epithelium with abormal mitotic activity. However, vulvar cancer is characteristically spinal in type, and some degree of differentiation of the component cells is often found despite undeniable intraepithelial anaplasia. It is important, however, to recognize that a pure cytologic type of in situ cancer of vulva is as rare as a similar pure lesion in the cervix. A variety of terms such as Bowen's disease, erythroplasia of Queyrat, etc.. have been used to describe types of in situ cancer. but basically the microscopic pictures are not sufficiently distinctive to be specific. Grossly the anaplasias may appear as granulomatous, leukoplakic, or variegated pigmented, whitish, slightly elevated lesions and are commonly multicentric in origin.

Paget's disease of the vulva is a specific form of *in situ* cancer characterized grossly by a reddish lesion interspersed with white epithelial islands and microscopically by the large pale "Paget" cells. While the similar lesion of the breast is usually associated with an underlying carcinoma, such is rare on the vulva.

Invasive carcinoma is preeminently a disease of elderly women, the great majority of cases occurring after the age of 50. The average age in taussig's large series was 59, and the decade between 60 and 70 shows the highest incidence. The exception occurs in those cases preceded by granulomatous disease where the average age is about 40 years as noted by Salzstein, Collins, and Alexander. The disease begins on any part of the vulva, most frequently the labia, the region of the clitoris, the vestibule, or the vulvovaginal gland. In all of these locations the cancer is of squamous cell or epidermoid variety, except that primary carcinoma in Bartholin's gland which may be either adenocarcinoma, transitional or epidermoid in character. In such instances a hard stony mass can be felt in the region of the gland.

The gross appearance may be whitish, ulcerated, or granulomatous depending on the primary lesion. As noted previously several authors have reported the premalignant nature of the granulomata and leukoplakic diseases.

Basal cell carcinoma is rare and appears as on the skin elsewhere as a superficial ulcer with "rolled" edges.

In the usual forms of vulvar cancer, the initial lesion becomes steadily larger, with increasing induration, ulceration, and surrounding edema. If neglacted, the destruction of the disease may involve most of the vulvar structure. Metastatic involvement of the superficial and deep inguinal glands, as well as the lymph glands at the femoral ring, soon develops, while the richness of the lymphatic communications with the pelvis leads to extension in that direction.

The symptoms in the early stage are apt to be very slight, consisting only of slight soreness and itching, although the latter is not invariably present. In many instances, however, there is a history of long standing pruritus antedating the appearance of carcinoma. As the ulceration and infiltration extend, the pain increases, and in the advanced cases it, may be persistent and intolerable unless controlled by narcotics.

Not uncommonly there is an unfortunate delay of 1'/, to 2 years between the appearance of symptoms and diagnosis of the disease. Much of this delay is due to reluctance of the older patient to seek medical consultation, however, in about one-third of the cases the physician is at fault as noted by Howson and Montgomery. In the early stage the patient *suffers* very little discomfort, and the lesion may seem even to the physician a rather unimpressive one unless he is familiar with its potentialities. *Biopsy and microscopic examination* are of decisive importance, and they should never be omitted when an ulcerative vulvar lesion is observed in elderly women. Upon this diagnostic procedure one must depend for the differentiation from other ulcerative lesions, such as syphilitic ulcers, or lymphogranuloma venereum.

Prophvlaxis is of considerable importance, for it has been noted that both leukoplakia and various granulomatous or other irritative lesions are frequent precursors of cancer. Fortunately these generally cause such intense pruritus and discomfort as to lead to medical attention, but haphazard use of various ointments, lotions, and sprays can only be condemned if biopsy of any suspicious lesion is not performed.

Treatment of Vulvar Cancer

There can be no doubt that the main treatment for carcinoma of the vulva is surgery. Vulvectomy is sufficient in those instances of in situ disease, however, thorough study of the removed tissue must be carried out to eliminate invasion. Radical vulvectomy is mandatory for invasive cancer. Lymphadenectomy is the rule, but there is considerable difference of opinion as to how extensive this should be. The presence of palpable nodes should not be the criterion; since in one-third of the cases in which nodes are enlarged the enlargement is not due to cancer but to infection. Likewise, in one-third of the cases in which there is metastatic disease to the nodes, the nodes are not clinically englarged.

Way emphasizes that vulvectomy must be so extensive as to disallow primary closure; and although we do not necessarily concur, we agree that *radical* removal of the vulva is the *essential part* of a surgical approach to this disease. The value of lymphadenectomy is less certain, for if the removed nodes show cancer. the salvage is markedly impaired. Nevertheless. Taussig's publications on the Bassett operation, i.e., radical vulvectomy with extensive lymphadenectomy, did result in a remarkably increased 5-year salvage. Perhaps this was by virtue of merely a more radical vulvar excision. for there is no doubt that if removed nodes contain cancer, recurrence may be delayed. but salvage approximated only 10%.

Green, Ulfelder, and Meigs perform a one-stage "crescent incision" to carry out simultaneous vulvectomy and bilateral lymphadenectomy. The New Orleans appeoach (Collins *et al.) is* more radical with an extended lymphadenectomy and freely utilizing exenteration if adjacent organs (vagina, urethra, or rectum)are involved without extrapelvic metastases. *McKelvey,* believing that complete excision of the local disease is paramount to salvage, feels that vulvectomy with superficial node dissection (one-stage under local anesthesia) is adequate treatment.

Collins has also pointed out that am·ability roughly parallels the extent of the lesion when seen, and he notes 3cm as the critical size below which cure is usual and above which, unlikely. A 5-year salvage of all patients should approximate 50% if adequate surgery is carried out. X-ray therapy is felt to be rarely indicated by most authors; however some Scandanavian schools have suggested extensive fulguration of the local growth and x-ray therapy to the nodes.

Although ultraradical surgery may be an unjustifably extensive approach for the age group usually affected and results in a rare salvage if the high nodes are involved, nevertheless operative therapy is generally accepted as the therapeutic approach of choice. The lesion is slow to metastasize and often does so in a superficial fashion. Wide local invasion and extension often precedes lymphatic or hematogenous dissemination. Such a disease process obviously deserves a wide local radical excision with some form of bilateral lymphadenectomy. The frequent crossover of lymphatics from one to the other side demands bilateral operation.

Other Vulvar Malignancies

Sarcoma of the vulva is exceedingly rare, only about 30 cases having been reported. *Malignant melanoma* is also rare; however, it is the second most common malignancy in the vulvar area. As in other parts of the body, its origin is usually in pigmented moles. Its tendency to widespread dissemination is known, and a fatal termination is common. Symmonds has reported improved results with early and radical surgery. A recent publication by Woodruff and Brack describes these and other unusual types of vulvourethal lesions.

URETHRA

Although the urethra is technically not part of the genital canal, the diseases that affect the area commonly involve the genitalia. Urethral infection is often gonoccocal, the vulvovaginal glands and cervix being also frequent sites of involvement. Actually the urethra may be the primary organ invaded by the gonococcus, however. the symptoms are usually vcrv transient. Residuae may remain in the urethral glands or Skene's ducts.

Many other organisms also involve the posterior portion of the urethra as well as of the trigone. The clinician must be mindful of the possibility that the suburethral gland infection may result in the formation of a diverticulum. This may be the cause of a recurrent cystitis. Palpation of the urethra may reveal a saclike outpouching from which pus can be "milked out, through the urethral meatus. Occasionally endoscopic examinations with urethrographic studies, as suggested by Davis and Cian, are necessary.

Although surgical excision of a diverticulum is the preferred treatment, simple urethritis, either acute or chronic, is frequently amenable to alkalinization of the urine and to the administration of sulfonamides or antibiotics. More helpful, particularly in the low grade, chronic infections, is the topical application of 2 to 5% silver nitrate. if the immediately adjacent Skene's glands are involved, as indicated by expression of pus on palpation, they may be easily fulgurated.

A real but frequently overlooked entity is the postmenopausal senile or atrophic urethritis. This frequently occurs in conjunction with a similar type of vaginitis as a sequel to estrogen deprivation. There is a reddening of the meatus as edema and exfoliation of the urethral mucosa lining occur, and the resultant appearance is much like a urethral caruncle. Local pain, terminal burning on urination, strangury, and even hematuria may occur, but prompt remission and relief are achieved by estrogen therapy Stilbestrol intravaginal suppositories, 0.5 mg., applied nightly for 2 to 3 weeks, are perhaps preferable to systemic steroid therapy. Fulguration, the preferred treatment for a caruncle, is not necessary in this form of urethral disease.

Benign tumors are uncommon, the most frequent being the caruncle. This small, reddish pedunculated lesion is occasionally tender and may bleed. Fulguration after biopsy is the treatment of choice.

The urethra may be the site of other pathological entities, such as stricture or fistula (frequently postirradiation or postoperative), granulomatous infection by lymphopathia or granuloma inguinale, prolapsed mucosa, and even carcinoma. The latter is rare and carries a poor prognosis, less than 50%. Treatment is generally radiation, as indicated by Brack and Farber, but occasionally radical surgical procedures are performed particularly in the radio resistant lesion.

9

VAGINAL DISEASES

VAGINITIS

Vaginitis (of bacterial or parasitic origin) comprises a sizable percentage of most gynecological practice. It is difficult for the clinician to be enthusiastic about such patients, whose complaints are truly valid, but the infection is never of serious import and is often difficult to eradicate. Since the histology of the vagina varies at different age periods, it is not strange that certain types of inflammatory involvement are characteristic of certain age periods. During reproductive life, for example, the vaginal epithelium is many layers thick. This fact, together with the absence of glands, makes gonorrheal infection very rare as compared to its incidence in the young child. In the latter, only a few layers of vaginal epithelial cells are seen, and the *Gonococcus* gains an easy foothold, so that gonorrheal vaginitis is most common in children. Again, in the senile phase of life, there is marked atrophy of the vaginal wall, so that infection by various organisms, including not infrequently the *Gonococcus*, occurs quite readily.

The normal, *flora* of the vagina may include many types of organisms (*Streptococcus*, *Staphylococcus*, *Doderlein's bacillus*, *diphtheroid* organisms, etc.) including some of pathogenic type, and not infrequently fungi of various sorts. The bacteriology of the vagina, however, is still very confusing. It seems clear, however, that the so-called bacillus of Döderlein, a normal inhabitant, plays an important role in maintaining the acidity which characterizes the normal vaginal secretion. This acidity is due to the presence of lactic acid formed from the splitting up of the glycogen present in the vaginal epithelial cells. The pH of the normal vaginal secretion averages from 4.5 to 5.

Causes

The *bacteria* most often responsible for vaginitis are the Gonococcus (more particularly in the infantile vagina, but not during reproductive life) and various strains of Streptococcus, the *Staphylococcus aureus,* colon bacillus, diphtheroid, and other organisms.

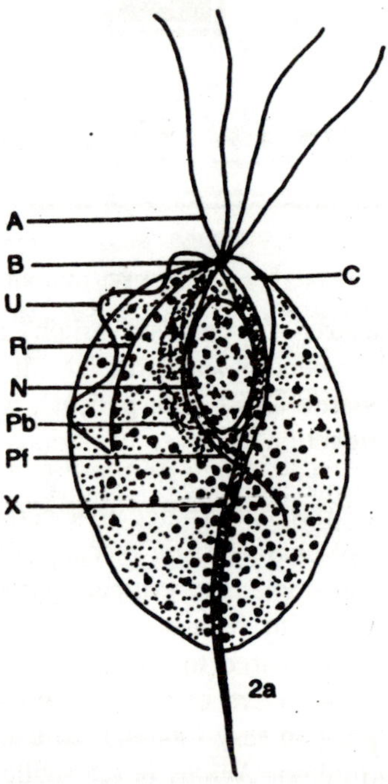

Fig. 9.1. T richomonas vaginalis. A, four antertorflagella; B-blepharoplast; U-undulating membrane; R-chronic basal rod; N-nucleus; Pb-parabasal body; pf-parabasal fibril; X-cytostome.

Other frequent causes are the *Trichomonas vaginalis, Hemophilus vaginalis,* and certain *yeast fungi,* especially the *Monilia* or *Candida albicans,* the same parasite which produces thrush in the oral cavity of the infant. These receive special consideration later in this chapter. Certain *general diseases* may, by the lowering of general vitality, predispose to the disease. Especially important in this connection is diabetes, which through the presence of large amounts of sugar in the blood and urine, may also predispose to the invasion and growth of yeast fungi. In the occasional case the presence of *foreign bodies,* especially neglected pessaries, may be followed by vaginitis, and a transient form of the latter may follow the use of *douches* which are too hot or which are chemically irritating. Another possible cause is infection by *discharges front the uterine* cavity or cervix. Finally, the acute *exanthematous diseases* may in rare cases cause vaginal inflammation.

Symptoms and Signs

The outstanding symptom of vaginitis, the one which as a rule leads the patient to seek advice, is *vaginal discharge,* which is commonly milky but in other cases thinner in consistency; and the addition of mucus from the cervix may make it mucopurulent. There is often much *local irritation* from the discharge, with vulvar and perineal *itching* and *burning,* especially on urination. The vulvovaginal mucosa is reddened and congested, and on speculum examination the entire vaginal mucous membrane likewise shows intense *redness* and *hyperemia.* In certain types the surface shows small reddish granular patches (follicular vaginitis).

Special types of vaginitis, especially those due to the Gonococcus in children, and the Trichomonas and yeast fungi in adults, present special characteristics, as will be described below.

Diagnosis of Nonspecific Form

While the diagnosis of vaginitis is made easily enough by simple *inspection* of the vagina, the assumption of its nonspecific nature is not permissible except by *exclusion of a more specific etiology.* In the adult this means especially exclusion of the Trichomonas, Hemophilus, and yeast fungus infections, which produce a clinical picture often not distinguishable from nonspecific vaginitis, except through demonstration of causative organism.

In the frequent cases of nonspecific vaginitis in children and virgins, speculum examination is not possible or desirable, but in these it is possible to inspect the vaginal surface by means of a vesical speculum of the Kelly type, the patient being placed in the knee-chest position.

Treatment

The nonspecific forms of vaginitis respond readily to simple measures of treatment. *Mild antiseptic douches* are useful, and frequently triple sulfa or Gantrisin cream is helpful.

TRICHOMONAS VAGINITIS

Although the organism known as the *Trichomonas vaginalis* was described by Donne as far back as 1836, its importance as the etiological factor in a frequent and troublesome form of vaginitis was not appreciated until recent years. As a matter of fact, there are still some who believe that it alone, without the presence of certain pathogenic bacteria, especially various strains of streptococci. cannot produce the vaginal inflammation with which it is often associated.

Incidence

The infection is an extremely common one, many looking upon the trichomonas variety as being the most frequent form of vaginitis. In a report of 5712 obstetrical and gynecological patients examined routinely for the Trichomonas, Peterson states that 24.6% of the smears were positive for this parasite. Bland and Goldstein, as well as others, have shown that the infection is exceedingly common in pregnant women.

Symptoms

The chief manifestation of trichomonas vaginitis is *leukorrhea, almost* invariably associated with *vaginal soreness, burning,* and often *itching*. The discharge may be rather thin and milky, but often it is very thick and whitish or yellowish white. When the patient is examined with a speculum, one often sees a pool of pus in the vaginal fornix, and characteristically this has a rather foamy or bubbly appearance. As might be expected, *dyspareunia* is a not infrequent complaint. The infection shows little tendency to involve the urethra or vulvovaginal glands, as does the gonococcal, although such infection may occur.

The appearance of the vagina is usually quite characteristic. The mucous membrane is reddened and inflamed, and the posterior fornix often presents a granular or *strawberry-like appearance* which is almost pathognomonic. Small petechial erosions may be seen on the cervix.

Diagnosis

The diagnosis is made by demonstration of the Trichomonas, and this is usually very easy if one uses the proper technique. The patient is cautioned to take no douche on the day of examination. A bivalve speculum is introduced without the use of a lubricant, as this destroys the activity of the parasite. A drop of pus is taken and a smear is then made on a warm slide, using a considerable amount of normal saline solution to dilute the pus and to avoid too rapid drying out of the smear. A cover glass may be used, but is not essential.

The slide is examined under a moderately high power, part of the illumination being cut off. The organisms, when present, are readily reconginable as motile, pear-shaped parasites, with long flagellae at the narrow end, and with an undulating cell membrane. They are intermediate in size between the ordinary pus cells and the pavement epithelial cells which are found in practically all vaginal smears. The active movements of the flagellae are readily seen, but must be distinguished from sperm cells.

Methods of Infection

There is still much uncertainty as to the source of vaginal infection with the Trichomonas. Infection from the rectum suggests itself as a possible source, and this view is held by many, although the recent studies of Allen and Butler do not support it. Contamination from bath water, or from towels, hands, and Instruments must all be considered, although in the individual case the explanation is rarely clear. The evidence that the organisms are not infrequently transmitted through coitus seems uncertain.

Treatment

An extensive literature has developed on the subject of the treatment of vaginal trichmoniasis, and a great variety of methods have been proposed. This in itself would indicate that none of these plans has been found altogether satisfactory, and such, in fact, is the view of those who have had the greatest experience in this field. There is general agreement that almost any of the many methods which have been employed will give good immediate results, the difficulty being in avoiding frequent recurrences of the condition, which are not uncommon.

Silver Picrate

One of the most popular, and apparently one of the most effective forms of treatment, is with silver picrate. About 5 gm, of the silver picrate powder preparation, readily available commercially and consisting of 1% silver picrate dispersed in kaolin, is blown into the vagina by some form of insufilator, after preliminary cleansing and drying. Following this the patient is instructed to insert a 2-grain suppository of silver picrate every night for 2 weeks, and then to return. Good results are reported.

β-Lactose Treatment

There has been some popularity of methods designed to promote the growth of the normal vaginal flora, especially the bacillus of Doderlein, which are looked upon as constituting the normal defense against the growth of pathogenic organisms. This they do by maintenance of vaginal acidity. For example, while the pH of the vagina averages about 4.5, it is often as high as 7 or more in cases of trichomonu infection. In such cases there is depletion of the normal glycogen content of the vaginal epithelium, and this may be prevented by the use of such carbohydrate substances as R-lactose, which has the further virtue of absorbing moisture very effectively. Frequent insuf lation is probably no more satisfactory than self-application of lactose powder in gelatin capsules (Butabs).

Floraquin Method

Diodoquin (Floraquin) is inserted into the posterior fornix. The patient is instructed to insert 1 moistened tablet into the posterior fornix night and morning thereafter for 7 days, then 1 at night only for 7 days, and finally 1 every other night for a week to 10 days.

Daily-morning douches of 3 tablespoon fuls of vinegar to 2 quarts of warm water may be used, followed in the active stage by the insertion of 1 tablet into the fornix. After 3 weeks of intensive treatment, a tablet should be inserted two or three times a week for about 3 months. A cure can be assumed if the parasites cannot be demonstrated after the third menstrual period.

Antibiotics

Although various types of systems and local antibiotic therapy have been suggested, we question whether they ever should be used. Although they may be effectively bactericidal, this very effectiveness may disrupt the synergistic relationship of vaginal fungi and bacteria. Thus, the patient may end up with a much more severe and intractable yeast infection and be even more symptomatic than she was before.

Other Methods of Treatment

Among other popular methods of treatment have been those employing arsenical compounds of one sort or another, chief among which have been such commercial preparations as carbarsone, acetarsone, Devegan, and Milibis. Although good results have been reported, it would seem that these substances are less widely used than formerly. Numerous other commercial trichomonacides have been introduced, especially to be mentioned is tricofuron.

Flagyl

In recent years, flagyl has been introduced and although there was a long delay in its acceptance by the F. D. A., it has been approved. The medication, given in doses of 250 mgm. three times a day by mouth for 10 days, offers an effective therapy especially for the stubborn cases resistant to local treatment. It has been extremely effective, nontoxic, and useful in the recurrent or recalcitrant cases which comprise a major nuisance in every day gynecological practice. The cure rate has exceeded 90 % in most reported series (Searle).

Treatment in Pregnancy

As already mentioned, trichomonas infection is extremely common in pregnant women. The methods of treatment are essentially the sane as in the nonpregnant condition, and they can be carried out with safety until the last month of pregnancy, when they should be discontinued.. The discontinuance of douches as early as possible seems advisable.

MYCOTIC VAGINITIS (FUNGOUS OR MONIAL VAGINITIS)

As with trichomonas infection, the frequency and importance of the mycotic form has been recognized only in recent years. Hesseltine states that about 10% of nonpregnant women who complain of vaginal discharge harbor fungi of the yeast group, and that in about one-third of pregnant women such fungi are to be found in the vagina, although only a small proportion have symptoms sufficiently troublesome to seek medical relief. The vulvoyaginal inflammation so often seen in diabetes is almost always due to the presence of fungi which thrive in the presence of the carbohydrate-rich environment characterizing that disase. It is most common in postmenopausal women.

The organisms responsible for this type of infection are fungi of the yeast group, similar to those which so often produce thrush in the oral cavity of the infant. There is still some confusion as to nomenclature, and various names are applied to the causative organism, *viz., Monilia albicans, Saccharontyces albicans, Oidium albicans,* but it is usually believed that the *Candida albicans* is the one most commonly involved.

Symptoms

The disease is characterized by *a discharge* which varies between a thin watery to a thick purulent character, *pruritus* which may be intense, *local irritation,* and marked *reddening* of the entire vaginal or vulvavaginal mucous membrane. In addition, there are often *thrushlike patches* on the vagina, vulva, or both. When the vulva is extensively involved, its surface may show large whitish or grayish areas of the apthous deposit, and itching may be exceedingly distressing, so that scratch marks are often present.

Diagnosis

While the above described clinical picture should at once suggest the probability of the mycotic etiology, the diagnosis is made positive by microscopic demonstration of the fungi. A smear is made from the exudate, and this is stained with the Gram stain. The fungi appear in the form of long threadlike fibers or *mycelia,* to which are attached the tiny buds or *conidia*. For confirmation, the organism may be cultured on Sabouraud's or Nickerson's medium.

Methods of Infection

As with Tiichomonas, the mode of contamination is rarely clearly explainable, although it seems certain that dissemination is by means of the hands, towels, coitus, clothing, bath water, or instruments.

Treatment

Although gentian violet used to be almost the specific treatment for yeast infection, it is so "messy" that it has been pretty well discarded. During the past few years the intravaginal use of Propion gel or Aci-gel has become very popular, and it is usually promptly effective in the relief of symptoms from monilial vaginitis. This jelly is introduced by the patient herself by means of a syringe applicator, usually twich a day for a period of several weeks. More recently even this has been more or less supplanted by the use of nystatin (*Mycostatin*) suppositories nightly for several weeks.

Hemophilus vaginalis Vaginitis

This agent as a sole or contributory cause to vaginitis has been noted by Gardner and Dukes, Brewer, Halpern, and Thomas, and others. Culture is taken with the use of Casman's blood agar medium as well as thioglycolate broth. The organism may be grown and identified, and although its importance as the sole agent in producing vaginitis is ucertain, it is frequently present.

The usual symptoms of leukorrhea, pruritus, and dyspareunia are produced, and it would seem that the Hemophilus must be considered a possible pathogenich cause in certain types of vaginitis that are recalcitrant to the usual treatment. Terramycin-polymyxin B was abandoned by Brewer despite success in eradicating the Hemophilus organisms, because of the frequent occurrence of *Candida albicans*. In its place he recommends the use of hexetidine, available commercially as Sterisil vaginal gel. Most methods of treatment lay be helpful at one time or another.

GONORRHEAL VULVOVAGINITIS IN CHILDREN

While the histological structure of the adult vagina, with its many layers of squamous eipithelium and its lack of glands, protects it from the attacks of the *Gonococcus*, this is not true of the immature vagina of the young child, with its thin mucous membrane covered with only a few layers of epithelial cells. *Gonorrheal vaginitis,* involving usually also the vulvar mucosa (*vulvovaginitis*) is not an uncommon disease. It is far less frequently encountered in private practice than in the dispensary type of patient.

Mode of Infection

The disease is spread through contact with infected persons. often other infected children, but the dissemination is usually an infirect one. through the medium of the fingers, towels, toilet seats, or bathtubs. While the method of spread can by proper investigation be explained in some cases, in many other this may be altogether impossible. In institutions like school, hospitals, or children's homes, the disease used to assume epidemic proportions. In a certain proportion of cases the infection is caused by rape, often incited by the superstition still prevalent among ignorant men that coitus with a child will 'cure gonorrhea.

Symptoms

The chief and often the only symptom is persistent vaginal discharge, often very slight, at times rather profuse, that the child's clothing is soiled with the whitish or yellowish or yell wish discharge. There is apt to be considerable local irritation, which at times lead to masturbation. The course of the disease if untreated is extremely chronic, with alternation of periods of remission and exacerbation, but the tendency is to disappearance of the vaginal inflammation and discharge with the onset of puberty.

Diagnosis

There is no question that many errors of diagnosis occur through failure to recognize the fact that other causes than the Gonococcus may be responsible for vaginal discharges in children. Among these may be mentioned pinworms, foreign bodies, and infection with such organisms as the *Alicrococcus catarrhalis,* Streptococcus, or colon bacillus. The only criterion of diagnosis is the microscopic demonstration of the Gonococcus, but even better is to obtain a positive culture; and here also there are pitfalls to be encountered and errors are not infrequent. The finding of the typical coffee bean, Grain-negative organisms within the cells (intracellular) is essential for diagnosis. Greenhill states that "there must be more than 10 typical Gram-negative diplococci intracellularly in the same slide and two or more within the same cell" in order to permit of positive diagnosis.

Treatment

Up to recent years there were few diseases so unsatisfactory to treat as the gonorrheal vulvovaginitis of children. Protracted treatment with all sorts of local antiseptics. such as silver nitrate. Argyrol, or Mercurochrome. was commonly employed, with notoriously unsatisfactory results. The introduction of the *estrogenic plan of treatment* in 1933 has now been largely replaced by intramuscular or even oral penicillin for 3 to 4 days. Results are uniformly good.

SENILE VAGINITIS

The atrophy of the vaginal mucosa which takes place normally at the time of the menopause makes it thin and pasty, and renders it very prone to infection. Frequently tiny superficial areas of granulation or ulceration develop, giving rise to slight vaginal staining. In seeking for the cause of slight postmenopausal bleeding, senile vaginitis, like the corresponding condition in the cervix and corpus uteri, must be borne in mind as a not infrequent one. The most characteristic symptoms, however, are discharge, itching, burning, and soreness in the vaginal region. The discharge is usually rather thin, and it may, as already mentioned, be blood-tinged. In later stages there may be contraction of the vaginal lumen, with dyspareunia or complete inability to carry on marital relations.

Treatment

Here again *estrogenic therapy* is often invoked with benefit, and this should always be local unless there is some other reason for oral administration. We usually prescribe nightly *vaginal suppositories of stilbestrol (0.5* mg.) for 3 to 4 weeks or some form of estrogenic vaginal cream combined with daily vinegar douces. It must be remembered that too vigorous estrogenic therapy may produce uterine bleeding, an undesirable occurrence because of the suspicion it may excite of adenocarcinoma of the uterus.

For the local pruritusand irritation, one may resort to any of the measures described in the siction on pruritus vulvae.

EMPHYSEMATOUS VAGINITIS

A rare variety of vaginitis is the so-called vaginitis emphysematosa. This condition has been found to be associated with pregnancy and also with cases of heart failure. It is characterized by the appearance ofbleblike, gas-filled cysts in the submucous layers of the upper vagina. There have been various hypotheses as to the source of the gas, but most authors do not think it is air. Foreign body giant cells may be found in the walls of the cysts.

NEOPLASMS OF THE VAGINA

Benign Tumors

The most common benign tumors of the vagina are the *cysts*. Aside from a few rare cases produced by distention of an anomalous blind ureter or of a rudimentary unfused Mullerian duct. cysts of the vagina arise in one of two ways.

Inclusion Cysts

These cysts, occurring at the lower end of the vagina and usually on the posterior surface, arise from inclusion beneath the surface of tags of mucosa resulting from perineal lacerations or from imperfect denudation in the course of surgical repair of the perineum. Such bits of mucosa become encysted, although the cysts are always small, rarely exceeding a few centimeters in diameter. They are not infrequently multiple. They are lined by a stratified squamous epithelium and the content is usually cheesy.

Gartner Duct Cysts

These arise from the vestigial remains of the Wolffian canals, which, as the so-called Gartner ducts,, course along the outer anterior aspect of the vaginal canal. The resulting cysts may be small, or they may become so large as to bulge from the vaginal outlet. They are always located- on the anterolateral aspect of the canal, as already mentioned. Microscopically they are lined with a varying type of epithelium, cuboidal or columnar, ciliated or noncdiated, and sometimes stratified.

Other benign tumors may occur, such as fibroma, fibromyoma, and adenymyoma, but they are rare. Condyloma acuminatum is not infrequently found in the lower portion of the vagina, usually in combination with similar lesions of the vulva. Endometriosis of the vaginal vault is likewise an occasional finding. Congenital hydrocolpos (or hematocolpos) must always be borne in mind.

Aside from the occasional large growth, there are usually no symptoms produced by the benign vaginal growth, which are generally found accidentally or because they can be felt by the patient. These neoplasms are properly treated by surgical excision.

A rarc form of ulcerative lesion may occur in the lateral fornices of the vagina, in association with adenomatous changes in the Wolffilan or mesonephrc duct vestiges located in this portion of thc vagina. Biopsy of such a lesion, which may be clinically suspicious of cancer, will show in the base of the ulcer the acinous or tubular elements derived from the mesonephric duct. A few of these cases were found in the group reported by Novak, Woodruff, and Novak.

Malignant Tumors

Of these by far the most common is *carcinoma,* which may be primary or secondary.

Primary Carcinoma is much less frequent titan in the vulva. and is almost always of the epidenmoid variety. although rarely adenocarcinoma may develop from aberrant glands or embryonic vestigial structures. Its usual location is on the posterior wall, where it develops as a papillary or indurated growth which soon ulcerated, with bleeding as a symptom. Its further extension may in late stages cause penetration into the rectum, with rectovaginal fistula as a result. The prognosis is extremely unfavorable. While there is a place for simple palliative surgical measures in some cases, the chief reliance in treatment must be upon radiotherapy, although the proximity of the bladder and rectum leads to limitations in the dosage. Salvage in most large series rarely exceeds 25%.

Carcinoma in situ. This may occur as (1) a primary vaginal entity;

(2) concurrent with or subsequent to intraepithelial carcinoma of the cervix; or (3) in conjunction with invasive cervical cancer. Copenhaven. Salzman, and Wright feel that the preferred treatment is surgery (including the necessary degree of vaginectomy) if the cervix is present. When the cervix has been removed, total vaginectomy seems radical if adequate irradiation results are obtainable. Thc authors feel satisfied with their techniques.

Secondary Carcinoma is common, chiefly because of the frequency with which carcinoma of the cervix extends to the surrounding vaginal wall. Adenocarcinoma of the corpus in its later stages may metastasize to the vagina, as may chorionepithelioma, and also carcinoma of distant organs.

Sarcoma is infrequent but may occur at any age. An interesting but very rare type is the *grapelike variety, sarcoma botryoides.* This highly malignant lesion was described by Spiegelberg as far back as 1879 as "sarcoma colli uteri hydropicum papillare." Until recently it had been

believed to arise from the uterine cervix and to be closely akin to uterine mixed mesodermal tumors. Due to the work of Daniel, Koss, and Brunschwig, it seems quite certain that the disease usually arises from the vagina, although there is certainly no reason why it cannot arise occasionally from the portio of the cervix. This is frequently involved secondarily. There is often close histological resemblace to uterine mixed cesoder mal sarcoma despite the different origin.

From a clinical standpoint this type of sarcoma occurs almost exclusively in infants, although a few young adults having a typical botryoid tumor are reported. The characteristic grapelike mass of pinkish. edematous polyps protruding from the vagina is almost pathognomonic. In advanced stages the whole vagina may be filled, with extension to the cervix. uterus. parametrium. and abdomen. The disease is almost uniformly fatal: irradiation affords at best only temporary palliation.

The recent study by Daniel points out the multicentric origin of this disease with multiple polyps springing up at various levels of the vagina. This emphasizes the necessity of total vaginectomy plus radical hysterectomy as a minimal surgical approach to this disease, and a handful of 5-year survivors are noted. In his own group at Memorial Hospital, Daniel notes 2 of 13 such salvages, but the author has informed me that one of the two has developed a recurrence at 6 years.

Few lethal tumors present such an innocuous microsopic pattern as may sarcoma botryoides. The squamous epithelium may be lifted up into multiple edematous papillae by subepithelium accumulations of fusiform tumor cells. Sometimes these are rather sparse, and since the individual cells themselves are not overly forbidding it is easy to see why a diagnosis of "benign vaginal polyp" is made, resulting in an unfortunate delay in treatment. There was in Daniel's series a complete absence of such mesenchymal structures as cartilage or glands elements as are noted frequently in uterine mixed mesodermal tumors, although striated tumor cells were seen on occasion.

Ovarian Tumors

There are a number of ovarian tumors, all of low grade (25 to 35 %) malignancy which may conveniently be discussed together because they have been thought to originate from some innate defect in the gonad, possibly during embryonic life, and because they may on occasion show evidence of functional activity. These tumors of the dysontogenetic group are (1) the *dysgerminoma,* which is generally hormonally inert, (2) the frequently estrogenic *granulosa-theca cell tumor,* and (3) the often androgenic *arrhenoblastoma.* Less common virilizing tumors are the hilus cell and adrenal neoplasms, and among the group of functionally active tumors we must include struma ovarii, a simple teratoma with an excess of thyroid tissue which leads to production of the thyroid hormone.

Of these functional or "special" tumors (so-called because a certain number are inert) the most common are the dysontogenetic lesions. Ten years ago the problem of these "special" tumors was a simple one. Dysgerminomas of neutral germ cell origin were almost always inert, arrhenoblastoma presumably derived from the undirected cords and tubules. which as a transitory effect even in the female are potentially virilizing, and granulosatheca tumors derived from the early mesenchyme were invariably thought of as feminizing. Today, however, due to the studies of Teilum, MacKinlay. Shippel, Nokes, and many others, the exact behavior of ovarian cells is subject to considerable disagreement.

The *dvsgerminoma,* of germ cell origin is of course an entity exactly similar and indistinguishable from the seminoma of the testis. On occasion it would appear that there are sex cord elements combined with these germ cells, as noted by Morris and Scully, who use the term *gonadoblastoma.* or by Teter. who has preferred to utilize *gonocytoma.* While the histopathology of such lesions is difficult it is perhaps not nearly air much of a problem to the gynecological pathologist as is the interpretation of the other special tumors.

In past years we have always emphasized the primary importance of the morphology of the tumor as the prime criterion in establishing a diagnosis. Yet it is becoming increasingly apparent to all gynecological pathologists that it is simply impossible to make the distinction between various neoplasms composed of poorly differentiated granulosatheca cells and certain arrhenoblastomas, just as it is not possible to distinguish between certain hilus cell lesions or luteinized granulosa-theca or adrenal tumors. Other similar problems of microscopic disagreement might be cited, despite the excellence of the pathologist (as noted in a recent review of Ovarian Tumor Registry material).

Suffice it to say that we are beginning to subscribe to Sandberg's doctrine that endocrine effect should be the method of classifying tumors of the functioning variety, and since he presents persuasive evidence that they all arise from mesenchyme, the generic term of *mesenchymoma or gonadal stromal* tumor would seem logical. We say this with full cognizance of the fact that certain embryologists might disagree as to the derivation of the so-called tubules and cords as regards its origin from mesenchyme or infolding germinal epithelium. We strongly subscribe to the former thesis.

In addition to pointing out the impossibility of distinguishing the histology of certain functioning ovarian tumors, Sandberg also points out that every histological type of endocrine tumor may at one time or another secrete the contrasexual hormone. Indeed, Novak and Mattingly have indicated that a virilizing hilus cell tumor may exhibit a bisexual hormonal response. Hirsutism, an enlarged clitoris, and amenorrhea, all suggestive of a virilizing stimulus, may coexist with endometrial hyperplasia, which is generally assumed to be due to an unopposed estrogen influence.

Our own impression is that the ovarian stromal cell is capable of profound differentiating possibilities into diffuse or cordlike tumors of the *granulosa-theca, theca-lutein*, or *Leydig cell* types. Very possibly it can be converted into such tubular structures as are present in the well differentiated arrhenoblastomas. Acceptance of this multiple potential differentiating capability of the ovarian stromal cells would seem to allow a delightfully simple approach to the nomenclature of the always difficult special ovarian tumors. It would simply allow the term of gonadal stromal tumor or mesenchymoma to be qualified by the endocrine effect, virilizing. feminizing, of inert. It should be understood that only such tumors as arrhenoblastoma and granulosa-theca cell tumors deserve this appellation, for dysgenninoma should be considered as having an origin from the primitive germ cells. which are generally neutral insofar as hormone effect is concerned. That there are certain exceptions to this latter premise is apparent, and will be discussed under the section on dysgenninoma.

HISTOCHEMICAL STUDIES

Because of the morphologic uncertainties in distinguishing between certain functioning ovarian tumors, it would seem that more recent methods of diagnosis might be utilized. Various histochemical techniques can be applied to cryostat sections of frozen ovarian tissue incubated with various substrates. Any resultant enzymatic activity may be considered highly suggestive (although not conclusive) of certain biosynthetic pathways necessary to steroid formation. For example, with dehydroepiandrosterone (DHA) as substrate, Goldberg, Jones, and Woodniff have indicated intense activity for steroid 3-(3-ol dehydrogenase in tissues normally producing progesterone (corpus luteum, placenta, or adrenal), but less appreciable activity in tissues or tumors producing estrogen or testosterone. Since DHA is an intermediate metabolite in the progression to estrogen and testosterone, enzyme activity is highly suggestive of steroid activity in morphologically equivocal tumors. Many substrates are available and useful in indicating precise cellular fimction, including steroidogenesis.

Other similar studies of enzyme histochemistry of the biosynthetic pathways are currently being utilized. Unquestionably they will add considerably to our knowledge of the behavior of various tumors, although interpretation of the biochemical data is often so complex that it may be beyond the scope of the average clinical gynecologist. Currently histochemical methods of absolutely distinguishing between estrogen and androgen producing cells by virtue of enzyme response are not perfected.

DYSGEMINOMA

Although Jakobovits notes occasional dysgerminomas that possess an estrogenic or androgenic effect, this is not regarded as an active tumor as far as endocrine effect is concerned. Since it is generally discussed with other functioning tumors which have been presumed to originate from some disorder in embryonic life (dysontogenetic). it seems logical to include it in this chapter.

Incidence

Morris and Scully note that dysgerminoma comprises 3 to 5% of all malignant ovarian tumors. Only about 540 cases have been reported, three-fourths of them occurring in the second or third decade of life.

Origin

This interesting tumor type is believed to arise from cells which date back to the early undifferentiated phase of gonadal development. In this phase the germ cells have not as yet acquired either male or female characteristics, so that, as might be expected, dysgerminoma has no effect on the sex characteristics of the patient. Such an origin, first suggested by Meyer, is given much support by the fact that an identical tumor occurs in the testicle, where it is commonly designated as seminoma or embryonal carcinoma. This is as one would expect with tumors which, as it were, lag behind the differentiating procession in gonads which later develop into either testes or ovaries.

The probable correctness of this theory of the origin of dysgenninoma is further indicated by the fact that in a considerable proportion of the reported cases the tumor has occurred in individuals showing some degree of gonadal deficiency, varying from minor degrees to actual pseudohermaphroditism. However, in such cases the tumor has no causal relation with the sex abnormality, which persists even when the tumor is removed. This is in contrast with certain other ovarian tumors which direct changes in sex characters with return to normal after removal tumors.

Because a small proportion dysgerminomas show various alien elements there are some who look upon these tumors as of teratomatous origin, but the prevailing concept is that most cases of dysgerminoma originate as described above. However, the presence of teratoid elements impairs the prognosis. An origin from the mature oocyte, as suggested by Hughesdon, seems to us implausible.

Pathology

Grossly, these tumors are of solid type, although when large, they often show degefter'tion and cystic cavities. They may be very small, measuring only a few centimeters in diameter, or they may reach such large size as to fill most of the abdominal cavity. They are, when small, surrounded by a rather dense capsule, which, however is often broken through as the tumor grows, with later infiltration of surrounding organs. The cut surface of the tumor is gray or grayish pink, but there are often areas of yellowish hue. The consistency is doughy but at times firm and rubbery. The growth is usually unilateral, although bilateral tumors have been noted in a few cases.

Microscopically, there are few tumors of the ovary which present such a distinctive picture, so that the diagnosis in most cases is easy, once one is familiar with this picture. The tumor is made up of rather large round or ovoid cells. arranged characteristically in alveoli separated by septa of partially hyalinized connective tissue which shows a characteristic infiltration with lymphocytes. The nuclei of the epithelial cells are large and rather deeply staining, and a varying number of mitoses are to be seen, although usually they are not numerous. Even in small tumors considerable areas of degeneration and hemorrhage are often present. Occasionally one finds large symplasmic giant cells, which have at times led to the mistaken diagnosis of associated tuberculosis. Morris and Scully have described *a "gonadoblastoma,"* a combined dysgerminoma-sex cord tumor, which has only recently been accepted as a specific entity. Teter notes various androgenic and estrogenic combinations with these primarily germ cell tumors which he attributes to sex cord portions. He utilizes the term *gonocytoma* but notes several types according to the endocrine effect observed and the cell elements contained.

Malignancy

This tumor undoubtedly belongs in the malignant group, but there is much variation in this respect in individual cases. Certainly the degree of malignancy is not to be compared to that of the common types of primary ovarian cancer, and cure has in many cases followed simple removal of the adnexa on the involved side. When the tumor is well encapsulated, the prognosis is in general good, but in the infiltrating variety, associated as it is with involvement of adjoining viscera and sometimes distant metastases, the outlook is very unfavorable. Estimates as to its degree of malignancy vary widely, but a recent extensive study of the Ovarian Tumor Registry by De Lima indicates a recurrence rate of 33 %, much lower than suggested by Pedowitz.

Clinical Characteristics

The incidence of these tumors appears to be about one-third of granulosa cell tumors, which in turn makes up something like 10 % of all primary malignant ovarian turnors (Fauvet). Dysgerminoma is characteristically a *tumor of early life* (carcinoma puellarum). It occurs not infrequently in very early childhood, and is common in the second and third decades of life. A number of cases have been associated in conjunction with pregnancy. In addition Neigus has commented on a positive A-Z test in the complete, proved absence of pregnancy, and he feels that this type of bioassay represents an ominous prognostic point due to combined trophoblastic elements.

As with so many other types of ovarian tumor, the first evidence of its presence is often the detection of a mass in the lower abdomen. There is no *characteristic effect on menstruation,* although it must be remembered that dysgerninoma often occurs in women who have. had amenorrhea as a result of gonadal deficiency. Where other marked sex abnormalities such as congenital pseudohenmaphroditism are present, the strong possibility of dysgerminoma should be considered when an ovarian tumor is diagnosed. On the other hand, the majority of cases have occurred in ostensibly normal women with often one or more pregnancies before the development of the tumor. *Ascites* has often been observed with these tumors, as with other solid ovarian growths. As already stated, the degree of malignancy varies, and the available reports on this point are still inadequate to permit of precise evaluation.

Treatment

While there is no difference of opinion as to the advisability of surgical treatment, there is still some uncertainty as to the extent of the operation in the individual case. Most of thesc patients are very young, so that there is a natural tendency to avoid radical operations if possible. In the case of young patients with well encapsulated unilateral tumors, conservative operation, consisting commonly of unilateral salpingo-oophorectomy, appears fully justified by the good results obtained in many reported cases. Rationalization suggests that if the tumor has exceeded the confines of the ovary, cure is unlikely. If the tumor is localized in the ovary, complete surgery is not necessary.

There is no question but that hysterectomy and bilateral adnexectomy is the proper procedure where there are no further procreative desires, irrespective of age. Thoeny et *al* have noted that patients undergoing conservative salpingo-oophorectomy have a higher incidence of recurrence (43 % of 14 patients) even with no apparent extension of the disease at the original operation. We are in complete agreement that any treatment less than total surgery with irradiation is not the *optimal* means of therapy, especially if there is any apparent local or lymphatic extension. We maintain, however, that the calculated risk (and not appreciably higher) is indicated with an intelligent patient's complete understanding. We know several such women treated conservatively who subsequently became pregnant, as reported recently by Ayerstand Johnson, and we do not feel women treated by conservative oophorectomy should routinely be subjected to radiotherapy (even with remaining ovary shielded as by Brody). If our suggested surgical approach to dysgerminoma be considered too conservative, we reiterate our belief that we are dealing with a tumor rather low malignant potential frequently involves youthful patients.

Where, on the other hand, the tumor is of the infiltrating variety, complete removal of the pelvic organs is indicated, and this should be followed by various forms of irradiation therapy. Today there is general agreement that dysgerminoma is usually quite radiosensitive, and recent studies by Brody and Thoeny *et al.* seem quite convincing, but we would not advocate irradiation therapy if only conservative unilateral adnexectomy is done. Not only may it defeat the purpose of conservatism, but Brody has indicated a high incidence of mental deficiency if pregnancy should occur.

GRANULOSA-THECA CELL TUMORS (FEMINIZING GROUP)

These neoplasms are properly discussed together, since it seems probable that they have a common origin and since their biological effects are so similar. They are given their special designations chiefly because of the different morphological patterns which they may assume. Not all authors, however, are convinced of the wisdom of any sharp separation, especially since mixed forms are not infrequent; indeed some admixture is almost the rule. Opinion today is that only the theca cells produce estrogen, and that granulosa cell tumors are feminizing only by virtue of any contained thecal cells.

Histogenesis

The exact histogenesis is far from certain, but the prevailing concept of the origin of granulosa cell tumors has been that they arise from cells of the early ovarian mesenchyme. The latter is the mother tissue of both granulosa and theca cells, so that tumors of such mesenchymal origin can assume the morphological characteristics of either granulosa or theca cell with occasional luteinization. In many tumors one finds mixtures of these various elements, and various studies have given substantial support to the concept of their common origin from the mesenchyme. There appears to be no acceptance of the hypothesis of McKay and his coworkers that granulosa cell tumors may have their origin from granulosa cells in atretic follicles and thecomas in cortical stromal hyperplasia.

Pathology of Granulosa Cell Tumors

Grossly these tumors vary in size from only a few millimeters in diameter to tumors filling a large part of the abdominal cavity and weighing over 30 pounds. As a rule they are of moderate, size. When small they are apt to be solid, but the larger tumors often show or many cystic cavities. The intervening solid tissue is of friable or granular consistency, and of grayish and sometimes yellowish hue.

Microscopically, the diagnosis of granulosa cell tumor is based upon the *granulosal character of the constituent cells* and upon the *growth characteristics* of these cells, which are quite like those of normal granulosa. For example. there is a tendency to the formation of tiny cystic areas of liquefaction, corresponding to the Call-Exner bodies so characteristic of the granulosa, especially in such rodents as the rabbit. The epithelial elements may dominate the picture in diffuse varieties of the tumor, with only a small amount of trabeculating connective tissue, often hyalinized. In such cases the epithelial cells have a tendency to arrange themselves in rosette-like or horseshoe-shaped clusters, resembling the primitive follicles. A very common variety is the cylindromatous, in which the presence of much larger amounts of connective tissue brings about an arrangement of the cells in columns or cylinders which often anastomose, and which in extreme cases gives the so-called moire pattern. A relatively uncommon type is characterized by large round masses of granulosa cells with often central cystic degeneration simulating very large follicles (von Kahlden type, formerly called *folliculoma inalignum).* Again the pattern may be gyriform or, less frequently, pseudoadenomatous, the latter being produced by cystic liquefaction of the connective tissue. Many different patterns may be found in a single tumor.

Pathology of Thecoma

Gross. In a considerable proportion of cases, a fibroma-like character may be given to the histological picture by the presence of large numbers of connective tissue elements. It is to this fibroma-like group that the term thecoma has been applied. Such tumors are commonly firm and fibrous in appearance and consistency, although they may, like the granulosal variety, show a tendency to cystic degeneration. The contralateral ovary may show evidence of profound overgrowth of stromal cells, the so-called "ovarian stromal hyperplasia" or "diffuse thecomatosis," and this is a frequent finding with many ovarian tumors, especially where there is apparent endocrine activity.

Microscopically they are described as distinguished especially by the presence of bundles of broad spindle cells, epithelioid in appearance, distributed in an irregular interlacing manner throughout the tumor, separated by varying sized bands of connective tissue and often hyaline plaques. Stress is laid also upon the presence of doubly refractile fat in large amounts within the cells and to a lesser extent in the surrounding connective tissue. Lipoid staining shows the presence of fat. practically always intracellular: this is only suggestive but not pathognomonic of steroid activity. In these thecal tumors. however. one often finds areas of what are apparently definite granulosa cells, so that one must question the advisability of too sharp a division between the granulosal and thecal tumors. especially in view of their identical endocrine effects.

Luteinization of Granulosa-Theca Cell Tumors

An interesting histological characteristic of this tumor type is that the constituent granulosa or theca cells may at times undergo a transformation into what are evidently typical lutein cells. We have seen a considerable group in which such a transformation is in progress, so that parts of the tumor have a lutein appearance, while others are still typically granulosal in character. It seems desirable to call these simply *"luteinized granulosa-theca tumors."* Although the term "luteoma" was formerly utilized, we feel it is misleading and leads to confusion, therefore, our own preference is to avoid it. The term *"folliculoma lipidigue" is* often applied to markedly luteinized granulosa cell tumors, often tubular, although Teilum has indicated that the origin is the Sertoli cell.

In at least a small group of reported tumors associated with luteinization, progesterone effects upon the endometrium have been noted in such transformed tumors, differing from the purely estrogenic effects which characterize granulosa cell tumors in general.

Occasionally an exaggerated progesterone effect with a frank decidual response may be noted. In other luteinized tumors, it would seem that the cells may be morphologically but not functionally like lutein cells, and that they are perhaps better to be spoken of as pseudolutein rather than lutein cells. In any case a feminizing effect is produced, rather than virilism which is so characteristic of the almost identical tumors of hilus cell origin. However, association of cell type and endocrine effect is inconstant.

PREGNANCY LUTEOMA

Sternberg describes a "pregnancy luteoma" as an ovarian enlargemen. (up to 12 cm.), which is generally solid, composed of eosinophilic, polyhedral cells, which are not a part of the corpus luteum of pregnancy, and may on occasion be bilateral. He is not certain whether this is a true neoplasm or merely a physiological response to pregnancy, similar to the theca lutein cysts so frequently seen in trophoblastic disease, and occasionally with normal pregnancy. Greene indicates that this particular picture should be regarded as a preexisting thecoma, which merely portrays the hormonal influences of pregnancy.

While we have seen a limited number of such ovarian enlargements, our own impression would be that it represents merely a profound exaggerated physiological response of the ovary to the increased endocrine stimulus of gestation. In the cases personally observed, it would lie extremely difficult to exclude a hilus cell tumor on a purely morphological basis., although the concomitant pregnancy and absence of Reinke crystalloids is helpful. Histochemical determination of steroid 3β-ol dehydrogenase might be expected in a progesteronesecreting tumoi as noted by Goldberg, Jones, and Woodruff.

Clinical characteristics of Granulosa-theca Tumors

These neoplasms of the ovary may be considered a fairly common tumor, comprising probably nearly 10 % of all solid malignant ovarian neoplasms. We have encountered more than 500 instances (including referred cases) of this neoplasm in our laboratory. The thecoma is much less common, although admixture is common. These tumors may occur at any age-before puberty, during the reproductive epoch, or after the menopause. While the larger tumors, like other ovarian neoplasms, may cause such symptoms as pain or discomfort, the more distinctive symptomatology is dependent upon the capability of the tumor cells to produce the estrogenic hormone. However, perforation of the tumor with intraperitoneal hemorrhage may lead to acute symptoms (French). Bilaterality is rare (approximately 5%).

When the tumor occurs *during rproductivd life,* as it does in a large proportion of cases, the clinical syndrome is not so striking as when it occurs against the background of the prepuberal or postmenopausal phase, during which there is normally little or no estrogenic hormone in the circulation. During the reproductive years, on the other hand, the tumor merely adds quantitatively to the cyclical hormonal content of the blood. No change would be expected in the secondary sex characters, for example, because these have long since been developed, while the effect upon menstruation would be merely a quantitative one, not unlike that which characterizes the relative hyperestrogenism which is associated with most cases of functional bleeding. Hyperestrgenism may be associated with normal menstruation, with hypermenorrhea, or with long periods of amenorrhea, as noted by Busby and Anderson, and these varying effects upon menstruation are noted with granulosa cell carcinoma. Nevertheless, pregnancy may concur with granulosa-theca cell tumors, and Diddle and O'Connor have noted this association in 37 of nearly 1200 reported cases of this type of lesion.

When, on the other hand, such tumors occur *in young children, long* before the inauguration of the normal estrogenic Function of the ovary, the clinical manifestations of precocious, puberty are evoked, viz., precocious menstruation and the premature appearance of secondary sex characters, such as hypertrophy of the breasts, the appearance of axillary and pubic hair, puberal development of the external genitalia, ansi also hypertrophy of the uterus. With the, removal of the tumor. these manifestations promptly regress. this constituting a crucial biological demonstration of the direct causal role of the tumor in the production of the symptoms. As a matter of fact, instances are recounted in which, after the removal of a unilateral tumor and disappearance of the abnormal symptoms, a recurrent tumor has developed in the remaining ovary, with again the production of precocious puberal symptoms and again their disappearance after the removal of the second tumor. It is of interest to note that the precocious menstruation of this syndrome is of the anovulatory, purely folliculartype, in which respect it differs from certain other types of precocious puberty and menstruation in which both ovulation and menstruation occur. In the latter group, insemination might theoretically bring about fertilization at abnormally early ages.

In the *postmenopausal* group of cases, again, occurring at a life phase at which little or no estrogenic hormone is found in the blood, the tumors may produce a reestablishment of periodic menstruation like bleeding, an estrogenic type of cytological specimen, and hypertrophy of the uterus with cases noted up to 84 years of age. No effect is seen upon secondary sex characters, presumably because of the higher threshold or unreceptivity of these at this phase of life. With the removal of tumors at this age, the abnormal menstruation of course ceases and, interestingly enough, the patient may experience a second menopause from the standpoint of the characteristic vasomotor phenomena.

It is generally accepted that estrogen is produced by associated theca cells. Our ideas in the past Pave always been that both granulosa and theca cells are capable of estrogenic production. More recently, however, Falck, utilizing intraocular transplants for study of various cell systems of granulosa and theca cells, has indicated that it is the *theca* interna cells that are actually responsible for the secretion of *estrogen,* but only where there is continuity with granulosa cells. Similarly his work would appear to indicate that the interstitial cells are capable of production of the estrogenic steroid if there is an association with granulosa or lutein cells. To further complicate this particular item we might simply mention the work of MacKinlay, whose review of granulosa cell tumors would seem to afford a strong suggestion that the granulosa and theca cells, normally estrogenic, may be converted into hilus or luteinized cells capable of androgen secretion. Such observations as the above would afford ample reason for accepting the possibility that any given endocrine-secreting tumor may excrete not a single but both types of sexual hormones. Our own feeling about the morphology of these tumors is well expressed in a recent study of the unclassified tumors of the Ovarian Tumor Registry. A number of pure thecomas have been observed with definite feminizing effects; however, Shippel, and Nokes, Claiborne, and Reingold report virilism as a sequel of thecomatous tumors.

Part of the confusion stems from the extreme problem in distinction of certain thecomatous tumors from certain undifferentiated arrhenoblastomas. Although it is agreed that cell morphology rather than endocrine effects should be the diagnostic criterion, the fact remains that some tumors are just too equivocal to allow for a specific diagnosis, even by the best pathologists. Perhaps differential stains, as yet undevised, might be helpful; histochemical techniques are valuable although they are more tedious.

Endocrine effect is uncertain and while not the sole means of diagnosis, it is gradually being recognized as the only practical method of distinguishing between various lesions. Certain tumors, histologically undistinguishable, seem to possess the faculty for either estrogenic or androgenic function, and Nokes, Claiborne, and Reingold have speculated on a potential bivalent response. Novak and Mattingly have also pointed out this possibility in attempting to reconcile the occurrence of endometrial hyperplasia, a presumed estrogen effect, with the clinically virilizing hilus cell tumors of the ovary. The androgenic function of the ovaries with convertibility of the steroids has.been reported fully by Vande Wiele.

Malignancy

In a review of 96 patients from the files of the Ovarian Tumor Registry, Busby and Anderson find a 25 % incidence of malignancy. Yet late recurrence, after more than 20 years, has been noted by Jones and Te Linde and by Sommers, Gates, and Goodof. Flick and Banfield indicate that thecoma is only about one-third as malignant as granulosa cell tumors and this accords with our own as well as other impressions. Since there is usually a combination of epithelioid and connective tissue-like components, it is difficult to make any precise statements.

Association of Endometrial Carcinoma with Feminizing Tumors

Various investigators have found that from 15 to 25 % of postmenopausal women with feminizing tumors of the ovary develop endometrical carcinoma. This association emphasizes the probable predisposing role of postmenopausal stimulation of the endometrium in the development of cancer.

In an earlier study of the subject, that of Ingram and Novak, 54 cases of combined feminizing tumors (feminizing mesenchymomas) and adenocarcinoma of the endometrium were collected. Similar recent studies include those of Mansell and Hertig, and of Greene. and there have been other corroborative reports.

A frequent observation is that a predominant thecoma apparently exerts a much stronger carcinogenic effect on the endometrium than does the tumor where there is a preponderance of granulosa cells, 29 of the reported cases of this combination involving thecoma and 25 granulosa cell tumor, in spite of the far greater general incidence of the latter. For example, in the first 500 cases of the Ovarian Tumor Registry, only 6 thecomas were encountered, as compared to 67 granulosa cell carcinomas. This would seem to support the view that theca rather than granulosa cells are the source of estrogen, as previously noted.

In making the diagnosis of endometrial carcinoma with feminizing ovarian tumors, one should bear in mind that benign hyperplasia may appear in a highly proliferative and atypical form which may simulate adenocarcinoma. There is no doubt that in at least some reported cases this error was made, although an effort was made to eliminate these in the collective study of Ingram and Novak. However, it has been noted by Morris and Scully, among others, that the stroma of many apparently inert ovarian tumors may assume thecal characteristics and thus act as a hypothetical focus for estrogen production and stimulation of the endometrium.

Treatment

Little need be said on the subject of treatment, which is of course surgical. When the tumors are small and unilateral, as they have been in practically all the prepuberal cases, unilateral salpingo-oophorectomy has frequently resulted in permanent cure. Preferable to *frozen* section at operation is removal of the total tumor so that the pathologist can select the most suspicious areas for microscopic evaluation; on the basis of this the clinician is in a better position to make a decision as to how radical the operation shall be. One should not, however, expect that 100 accuracy may be achieved, especially with dysontogenetic tumors where the microscopic pattern does not always parallel the clinical behavior.

In any case, one must realize that conservative operation is attended by some risk and periodic postoperative examinations are of obvious importance. In most of the cases occurring in adult women, complete operation would seem wise if the nature of the tumor is recognized at operation. Unfortunately this is usually not the case. therefore the problem not infrequently arises as to whether a unilateral operation should be followed by complete removal of the pelvic organs. In our experience with recurrences following conservative operation for granulosa cell tumors. the retained adnexa has not been involved by recurrent tumor, which is generally of diffuse intraabdominal nature. Considerable individualization should be practised, according to age, parity, extent of the tumor, whether encapsulated etc.

ARRHENOBLASTOMA AND ADRENAL OVARIAN TUMORS (MASCULINIZING GROUP

In contrast with the feminizing group, the masculinizing tumors are much less common, and we would estimate that they are perhaps one-fifth as frequent, according to the statistics of the Ovarian Tumor Registry. Estimates seem proper because of the extreme difficulty in making a diagnosis in many of these histologically complex tumors. The term "arrhenoblastoma" was originally applied by Meyer to a group of ovarian tumors whose common characteristic seemed an origin from the male gonadogenic structures at one phase or another of development, with differing histological pictures corresponding to the differing degrees of differentiation of these gonadogenic structures. Pedowitz's study of 1960 records 240 such tumors although they represent by far the most common type of virilizing gonadal neoplasm.

ARRHENOBLASTOMA

Histogenesis

As described previously, the early development of the ovary is identical with that of the testis, and in the later stages of female differentiation certain elements of male differentiating potency may be left in the medullary portion of the ovary. From these, tumors maydevelop in later life, and such neoplasnis may exhibit the capacity of producing the male hormone, with striking effects upon the sex characters of the woman. This, at any rate, was the view championed by Meyer and was accepted by most investigators, although today many students are speculating that the adult stromal cell (of mesenchymal origin) may be converted into an estrogenor androgen-secreting cell.

Scully among others prefers to consider arrhenoblastoma as a Sertoli-Leydig cell tumor; i.e., tumors of male cell type although possibly possessing bisexual endocrine influence, for the Sertoli cells are capable of estrogen secretion. With this later observation, we would not disagree, but at the same time we would welcome a stereotyped classification of ovarian tumors, especially of the functioning variety.

It would appear that the ultimate cell that evolves into most mature structures in the ovary is the *mesenchynte* or the gonadal stromal cell. Although the belief that persistent cell nests (Cohnheim) may later be the nucleus of certain neoplasms is passe. current ideas that various reserve or mature cells may undergo metaplastic changes is still a very real one. Our preference is to avoid such terminology as Sertoli cell for ovarian tumors, for this involves an element foreign to the female gonad. The *feminizing gonadal stromal tumor* would seem a more appropriate term, or virilizing, as the case may be. Likewise other lesions, not of the classically endocrine-secreting variety, might well be qualified by any overt hormonal action.

Pathology

Gross. These tumors, as encountered at operation, are usually of moderate size, and may be very small, although in a number of reported instances they have reached large proportions, up to 26 pounds (Hartz) in our current study. Pedowitz notes a number of tumors greater than 25 cm. in diameter and indicates that they are 96 % unilateral. Characteristically, especially when of small size, they are solid tumors, although they not infrequently exhibit one or more cystic areas, and in the larger tumors the cysts may be of large size. The color and consistency are variable, depending upon their widely differing histologic structure. They may be grayish, frequently with areas of definitely yellowish hue, but in some the cut surface is bluish, purplish, or reddish blue. The consistency may be quite firm in some cases, but degenerative changes are common, as is hemorrhage.

Microscopic

A description of the microscopic characteristics of arrhenoblastoma is not easy, because of the' extreme variations which may be encountered in different cases, and in different parts of the same tumor. At one extreme is the highly *d ferentiated* variety corresponding to the testicular adenoid described by Pick in 1905, and characterized by a very definite tubular structure. reproducing more or less perfectly the structure of normal testicular tubules. At the other extreme is the very *undifferentiated* variety which at first sight. may be considered a typical sarcoma. and in which only very careful study of many blocks may reveal the presence of structures like sex cords, or imperfect tubules, or lipoid-containing cells corresponding to interstitial cells. Finally, in the group designated by Meyer as the *intermediate,* one usually finds a varying number and distribution of definite tubular structures, interstitial cells, and of cell columns arranged in rather *zig-zag* fashion, quite like the sex cords seen in the early development of the gonads.

It is clear, therefore, that the microscopic recognition of these tumors presupposes some familiarity with the various phases of development of the seminiferous apparatus. As a matter of fact, the term arrhenoblastoma embraces a whole series of possible histological gradations, and no one stereotyped description of the microscopic appearance can be given. It is likely that the impetus to virilism is the interstitial Leydig cells, and it is interesting that these are uncommon in the highly differentiated "Pick's adenoma" which is rarely associated with an androgenic trend. The Sertoli cells found in the testis are thought to be potential producers of estrogen although histochemical studies in our laboratory suggest that they are relatively inert insofar as steroid excretion is concerned. In the male, Sertoli cells can produce feminizing tumors, as noted by Teilum, and the same author describes Sertoli cell tumors in the ovary.

Malignancy

While arrhenoblastoma is properly classified as a malignant tumor, there is no doubt that its degree of malignancy, like that of granulosa cell carcinoma, is much less than that of ovarian cancer in general. On the other hand, it must be remembered that many of the reports of this newly recognized and interesting tumor type have been made very soon after their observation, so that one cannot always be certain whether or not later recurrence had occurred. Even so, there are already available sufficient reports to indicate that in at least some cases the tumor may exhibit highly malignant characteristics. A recent review of the Ovarian Tumor Registry cases by Novak and Long would suggest a 33% recurrence note, and this would roughly correspond to the 22% figure on 122 cases reported by Javert and Finn.

Clinical Features

Arrhenoblastoma of the ovary occurs most frequently in relatively young patients, the decade between 20 and 30 showing the largest incidence; we have recently encountered a 30-month-old girl with this type of lesion. In our recent study, 75 % of the patients were less than 40 and 66 % less than 30, although women of 70, 67, and 64 were found to have an arrhenoblastoma.

The clinical course of these patients is characteristically divisible into two phases. There is first a stage of *defeminization* in which certain typical feminine characteristiee; are subtracted from the patient. and this is followed, with possible overlapping, by a stage of *masculinization, in* which certain positive masculine characteristics are added. Chief among the defeminization symptoms are amenorrhea. atrophy of the breasts. and loss of the subcutaneous fatty deposits which are responsible for the rounding of the feminine figure. Of the masculinization signs, the chief are hypertrophy of the clitoris, hirsutism, and deepening of the voice.

The first symptom noted by most patients is *amenorrhea,* which may come on abruptly. *Regression of the mammary glands* soon occurs. Changes in body contour may not be conspicuous and are often not noticed by the patient herself, or not at least until *hirsutism* has developed. The aberrant growth of hair, in our experience, does not usually reach the degree observed with adrenal cortical lesions, but it may be quite extensive.

A change in the patient's voice is often very noticeable, she herself often attributing this to a persistent "cold" or laryngitis. *A* normally soft, high-pitched feminine voice may be changed to a baritone or even to a basso, with often hoarseness or roughening of the voice. These vocal changes are due to lengthening of the vocal cords, while in marked cases there is overgrowth of the laryngeal cartilages with the development of a prominent "Adam's apple."

With reference to the *hypertrophy of the clitoris,* here again there are marked individual variations. In some cases it is only slight, in others the clitoris may assume the proportions of a miniature penis.

Hormone Studies. In these days of blood and urine hormone studies, the question arises as to the possible value of such investigations in the diagnosis of such tumors. In the present state of our knowledge it appears that by no means all cases have a definitely elevated level of 17-ketosteroids to the degree found in adrenal tumors. Scully points out that very small amounts of testosterone may be potently virilizing, although incapable of elevating the 17-ketosteroids. Other steroids, not nearly as androgenic, may feature an increased assay with no clinical evidence of masculinization. Nor does adrenocorticotrophic hormone *(ACTH)* or cortisone cause any appreciable change in the level of the 17-ketosteroids. Occurring in women who have, not infrequently, proved their sex by rearing children, the sexual chroniatin pattern will likely prove of little assistance.

Effects of Tumor Removal on Svmptoms. The crucial clinical test in the substantiation of a diagnosis of arrhenoblastoma is the regression of the abnormal masculinization symptoms after the removal of the tumor. Although this regression may not be complete in every case, it is usually striking in undoubted cases of arrhenoblastoma. The return of menstruation is the first manifestation of returning femininity, and in general the symptoms disappear in the order of their appearance. The positive manifestations of inasculinization. however. disappear much more slowly than those of defeminization, and often incompletely. Some degree of hirsutism and enlarged clitoris has persisted for over 10 years in the patient.

Treatment

The treatment of arrhenoblastoma is surgical, and conservatism appears to be fully justified in the case of young women in whom future pregnancies are important. *A* review of the Ovarian Tumor Registry material suggests that the 5-year salvage is in the nature of 65 % despite frequent conservative surgery. Where the true nature of these tumors is not recognized until after histological examination, an expectant plan of treatment is advisable, with periodic examination for several years. If there is any suggestion of pelvic recurrence of the tumor, radical removal of the pelvic organs is indicated. Postoperative radiation in such cases is probably advisable, although there is little knowledge of its effect on this group of tumors. Cytopathological methods of evaluating hormonal influence often substantiate the clinical impression.

ADRENAL TUMORS OF THE OVARY

The chief interest of this group lies in the fact that it gives rise to a clinical syndrome almost identical with that described above for arrhenoblastonia. Only a very small group of cases has been reported. The tumors are of small size, and are made up of tissue similar to that of the adrenal cortex. There has been much confusion in the literature with regard to the differentiation of these "lipoid-cell tumors." Our own preference is to avoid such terms as ovarian hypernephroma. luteoma, and masculinovoblastoma.

GYNANDROBLASTOMA

The name gynandroblastoma was applied by Meyer to a rare type of ovarian tumor which histologically shows components of both granulosa cell carcinoma and arrhenoblastoma. Only a small group of such cases has been described, and the dominant biological effect in most of these has been a masculinizing one, although at times such estrogen effects as endometrial hyperplasia with excessive bleeding have been noted. Although gynandroblastoma is excessively rare. and some cases are to be considered as a misinterpretation of the microscopic appearance, it is difficult to deny such a case as illtusrated by Morris and Scully.

We suspect that increasing awareness of the bisexual potential of normal and neoplastic cells. confirmed by histochemical techniques. may reveal that many tumors secrete both androgenic and estrogenie substances. If these be considered gynandroblastomas. the number *will* certainly increase.

VIRILIZING HILLS CELL TUMORS

A very small group of cases, numbering 18 at the present writing (and more recently set at 36 by Boivin and Richart), have been reported of tumors arising from the hilus cells of the ovary. Since all these tumors have shown masculinization effects, support is given to the prevailing view that the hilus cells are the homologues of the interstitial or Leydig cells of the testis, especially as the tumor cells have been found to show the Reinke albuminoid crystals so characteristic of the Leydig cells in some but by no means all cases. Plate, however, makes a very strong case for an estrogenic role; we believe either sexual trend is possible on various occasion. A recent review by Novak and Mattingly has indicated that these (18) tumors were always small (less, than 5 cm.), unilateral, benign, and virilizing (with one possible exception). An interesting if inexplicable association has been the presence of endometrial hyperplasia where uterine tissue was obtained.

A case report by Stewart and Woodard concerns the first malignant hilus cell tumor on record. Since the authors were kind enough to permit us to study their material, we can unanimously agree with their impressions of this clinically and histologically lethal tumor despite certain disagreement as noted in an addendum to the article by Boivin and Richart. In the material reviewed by us, Reinke crystalloids were plentiful. The concurrence of hilus cell tumors with gonadal dysgenesis. (Turner's syndrome) has been summarized by Warren, Erkman, and Cheatum.

Tumors with Functioning Matrix

It is becoming increasingly apparent to all pathologists that a certain number of ovarian tumors, not morphologically of the endocrinologically productive variety, possess hormonal activity. Indeed, these tumors may be of many types, both benign or malignant, and may produce either estrogenic or androgenic features.

It would appear that the ovarian stroma is capable of conversion into a steroid-secreting cell similar to a theca or Leydig cell. Consequently, a great many supposedly inert tumors such as Brenner, Krukenberg, and various carcinomas have appeared to exert a feminizing influence. Fewer androgenic tumors have been reported, but a recent review by Scully notes I 1 diverse tumors with virilizing tendencies.

From our own clinic Woodruff, Willams, and Goldberg have provided strong histochemical proof that certain tumour not usually recognized as endocrinologically active are capable of a hormonal effect. It would seem likely that increasing knowledge of biosynthetic pathways will suggest that many tumors regarded as inert will show evidence of an endocrine effect even though on occasion any estrogenic trend may be nullified by an equal androgenic effect. Such is a premature impression of various ovarian neoplasms that have been studied by certain histochemical techniques in our own laboratory.

HOMOLOGY OF CERTAIN OVARIAN AND TESTICULAR TUMORS

A provocative approach to the study of the dysontogenetic group of tumors has been suggested by Teilum, whose studies have led him to believe in the homology of certain tumor groups occurring in the ovary and testis. This concept seems fundamentally sound, but it would be premature to completely accept the homologous group described by Teilum or to use his studies as a basis for revamping our present system of classification, inadequate as it admittedly is. Those interested in the details of Teilum's studies are referred to his variouspublications on the subject.

A recent study by Warner et al. describes the production of certain dysontogenetic tumors in various fowls and rodents by a variety of methods. They point out (and their photomicrographs suggest) many structural similarities. The authors are inclined to feel that the tumors arise from "reserve" cells capable ofbipotential differentiation rather than from fetal rests, either androgenic or estrogenic. Although the "fetal rest" origin of various tumors is drawing more and more criticism in explaining tumorigenesis in general, and rightly so, we have always-been lukewarm towards evoking a frequently undemonstrable "reserve cell" origin for certain tumors. The same authors suggest a generic name for the androgen and estrogen secreting tumors, namely "gynandroblastoma," with "androblastoma" and "gynoblastoma" proposed for the subtypes. These terms have the obvious disadvantage of confusion with what the terms used to mean. Indeed it is becoming increasingly apparent that any observed endocrine effect should be incorporated into the diagnosis even though a decisive hormone effect is not always apparent. For example, Shippel, Nokes et al., and others report thecoma (usually regarded as estrogenic) as being associated with masculinization. Many other similar instances could be noted.

We might as well face the fact that certain tumors, classically of a certain type, may on occasion secrete the contrasexual hormone.

Yet if one will recall the very close chemical structure of the steroids. why should this be unexpected from a neoplastic tumor? The mere shift of a keto or hydroxyl group from one to another area in the steroid would be all that would be necessary, and actual conversion of these steroids has been observed and made to occur in certain animals. MacKinlay speaks of the convertible nature of granulosa and theca cells which may become producers of androgen or androgen-like substances.

Whether the suggestion of Warner et al. be followed we doubt. The way of a reformer in revising long accepted nomenclatures in always a diffucult one. Yet any proposal that might in any way improve the tremendously confused status of the classification and nomenclature of this tumor group deserves serious consideration.

UTERINE TUMOR

Sarcoma of the uterus is far less common than carcinoma; however, any precise statistics are difficult to assemble, for many clinics designate as low grade sarcomas what we personally would consider as merely cellular myomas. Obviously, this discrepancy affects not only salvage but also the incidence. hi a study from our own laboratory (Novak and Anderson) 59 instances of sarcoma were encountered in a period of 25 years, while during this same period 1263 cases of uterine cancer of all varieties (excluding only chorionepithelioma) were observed. Sarcomas therefore constituted less than 5 % of all uterine malignant tumors.

Pathology and Classifications

It is now generally accepted that sarcoma of the uterus may arise from any of the connective tissue elements of the uterine structure, and that it may be of myogenic origin as well. Thus it may arise from the myometrium, endometrium, blood vessels, or a myoma. Whether any lesion should be categorized as a leiomyosarcoma (of smooth muscle origin) or a fibromyosarcoma (of connective tissue variety) seems of purely academic interest as compared to whether it is malignant or benign.

Ober, as well as others, has attempted to classify sarcoma on a histogenetic basis, and he proposes the following scheme (which is presented here only in outline form).

1. Leiomyosarcoma
2. Mesenchymal sarcoma
   - (a) Pure homologus as endometrial sarcoma
   - (b) Pure heterologous as rhabdomyosarcoma
   - (c) Mixed homologous as carcinosarcoma
   - (d) Mixed heterologous as carcinosarcoma plus other heterologous elements
3. Blood vessel sarcomas
4. Lymphomas
5. Unclassified
6. Metastatic

There are numerous subclassifications which are not necessary for a simple workable means -of dividing these lesions. It is often difficult enough to distinguish them from various epithelial tumors without specific regard to their precise histogenesis.

SARCOMAS

Although *leiomyosarcoma* is a very infrequent complication of myoma, in the nature of 0.2 % or less, the prevalence of myomata still makes this the most common form of uterine sarcoma. Because of the rarity of malignant degeneration, however, the clinician tends to disregard this in his treatment of myomata. Sudden accelerated growth of a previously static tumor or postmenopausal enlargement will always suggest the possibility of sarcoma, and indicate surgery despite symptoms; actually most cases will ultimately show only degenerative changes, but the clinician cannot afford to procrastinate.

The diagnosis of this particular lesion is rarely made preoperative, because the symptoms and physical findings are attributed to the myomata; indeed surgery itself only rarely affords a clue, for in many instances the malignant change will involve only the central area of the tumor so that the surface is not abnormal. On occasion the myoma may be somewhat softer, cystic, and yellowish, and thus quite different from the firm nodular consistency usually found.

If the tumor be cut open after its removal, one will find an absence of the symmetrically whorled white, firm surface, the "raw pork" appearance described by Cullen, or when necrotic changes are marked, a more pultaceous appearance with cystic and hemorrhagic degeneration. Although this may represent merely degenerative phenomena, it should impel the surgeon to increase the scope of his operation; i.e., removal of, rather than ovarian conservation, hysterectomy rather than myomectomy, etc.

Endometrial sarcoma is less common and less malignant than leiomyosarcoma. It not infrequently assumes a polypoid architecture, and this is likewise true of growths originating from the mucosa of the cervix. However, benign polyps are generally smoother and less friable than these endometrial lesions, which histologically show complete overgrowth of abnormal stroma although an infrequent abnormal and distorted gland may be found. On occasion both connective tissue and epithelium are stimulated to malignancy with the development of a *carcinosarcoma*.

This should be regarded merely as a variant of endometrial sarcoma; Williams and Woodruff have discussed its relationship to benign polyp and endometrial adenocarcinoma.

Since this is a surface lesion, it frequently produces bleeding so that subsequent curettage may make the diagnosis, or if the lesion protrudes out the cervical os, simple biopsy may suffice. This of course is in contrast to leiomyosarcoma; if diagnosis is made, our preference is to employ preoperative irradiation, for it seems much more radiosensitive than leiomyosarcoma.

There are all degrees of histological and clinical malignancy with endometrial sarcoma. On occasion it may be very difficult to make a distinction between this and the locally invasive but nonmetastasizing *stromal endometriosis,* or *stromatosis* which may be a rather completely benign process or locally malignant with venous and lymphatic extension but rarely distant metastasis. (The rare hemangiopericytoma may histologically be a very difficult diagnostic problem.) More malignant degrees of stromal endometriosis or adenomyosis (stromatosis) merge imperceptibly into the patterns of an endometrial sarcoma.

The recent publication by Woodruff and Williams summarizes our own experiences with the rare highly malignant *mixed mesodermal tumor*. These have been considered to be of a teratomatous nature, containing a variety of mesodermal elements, such as cartilage, striped muscle, or mucoid tissue. Such tumors had been thought be many to be explained by the pulling down of mesodermal tissue by the Wolffian duct during the period of its embryologic descent.

More recently, Taylor has reemphasized that all of the elements are of stromal (Mullerian) origin, with abnormal differentiation being responsible for the component bone and cartilage formation. With this current view we are in complete accord. The frequency of *preceding irradiation* has been noted in most reports of these tumors. A recent case in association with bilateral thecoma has been reported by Laurian and Monroe. The prognosis is poor with, frequently, metastases to distant parts of the body, and Taylor has noted only 6 survivors in 40 patients studied.

Certain of these lesions seem to involve the cervix and vagina even in adults. There seems a close kinship between these and the *sarcoma botryoides* of vagina and cervix, seen primarily in children, although the histogenesis is not necessarily the same (see Vagina).

Mural sarcomas may at times also arise, as nodular and fairly circumscribed tumors, so that it may be difficult to be sure whether or not the tumor was preceded by a benign myoma. More often, however, they are much more diffuse in their growth, so much so that they may produce a fairly uniform enlargement of the uterus, which may even resemble an early pregnancy. The same thing is true of the diffuse varieties arising from the endometrial stroma.

Lymphomas. The various lymphoid malignancies are rare in the uterus, but still more commonly found than in the ovary. Ober and Tovell have noted occasional cases of lymphosarcoma which present primarily in the uterus with no apparent evidence of this disease in other areas of the body. Leukomoid deposits may likewise involve the genital tract, but generally in connection with an extensive spread of infiltrates so that the prognosis is very poor. In any case the outcome with any pelvic lymphoma is guarded.

Leiomyosarcoma

With reference to the much discussed question of the incidence of sarcomatous changes in myomas, the wide discrepancy of figures quoted suggests that there is as yet incomplete uniformity in recognition of the histological criteria of malignancy. The most common error is to mistake very cellular but benign myomas for spindle cell sarcoma, so that in some series an incidence of as much as 10 % of malignancy is reported. It would seem that mere cellularity in the absence of increased mitoses and abnormal and giant cells should not warrant the diagnosis of even a "low-grade sarcoma." Such is not the rule, however, and this might account for the high incidence of sarcoma in some clinics, as well as a high salvage, for these lesions rarely cause difficulties in the postoperative era. At least two mitotic figures per high power field should be encountered before considering a diagnosis of sarcoma. Such descriptive terms as round, giant, or spindle are occasionally utilized.

It is not always easy to be sure whether or not sarcoma is

secondary to benign myoma. The mere presence of myomas does not justify this assumption and, moreover, it must be remembered that sarcoma may arise as a rather nodular growth which might simulate a sarcomatous myoma. On the other hand, when a sarcoma is found developing in the interior of a myoma in which one can still find abundant evidence of the original benign tumor, the origin from such a tumor seems clear. In the late stages of the disease, however, such aids in determining the origin of the tumor are not available, and one can only speculate on this point.

In our own series of 59 cases, it was considered that in 39, or 66.1 %. the sarcoma. was secondary in myomas. This gives an incidence of 0.56 of sarcomatous degeneration in the 6981 myomas comprised in our material, a figure somewhat lower than the 1.2 % of Kelly, and Cullen in an earlier study from the same laboratory. Certainly, however, the incidence would seem less than I % according to accrued statistics, but one must always be mindful of "what constitutes a sarcoma." Such interpretation obviously dictates the salvage; for example, a recent article by Radman and Korman notes 17 of 19 patients alive following treatment for sarcoma. It would seem that their cases must include certain lesions of low grade activity, or else other figures are extremely pessimistic. The usual salvage lies in the 25 to 30% bracket, although Corscaden and Singh, in reporting at most a 0. 13 % incidence of malignant change in myomas, indicate that salvage with true sarcoma is very low.

In a group of 41 women who had all their treatment at the Mayo Clinic, Aaro and Dockerty note a surprisingly high 46% 5-year survival. It is likewise apparent from their study that mitosis count is a frequently helpful method of assessing the prognosis. A recent unpublished study from Johns Hopkins (Montague and Woodruf) on sarcoma arising in myoma suggests a nearly 50 % salvage of patients treated.

Clinical Characteristics

The disease most frequently affects women during the middle period of life, our own series showing the highest incidence during the fifth decade. On the other hand, the rare grapelike sarcoma of the cervix and vagina occurs characteristically in infancy. Any portion of the uterus may be the seat of the tumor, although the body is far more frequently involved than is the cervix. The greater frequency of corporeal as compared with cervical myomas will no doubt explain in part at least the predilection of sarcoma for the corpus uteri.

The *avmptontatology* is not distinctive, and is usually that of myoma in which most sarcomas arise. The diagnosis is not made until operation; or even more frequently, not until the pathological examination. *Abnormal bleeding* may be entirely absent, especially when the endometrium is not involved. On the other hand, it may be of great significance, especially when it occurs after the menopause, and particularly when in these postmenopausal cases the uterus is the seat of presumably myomatous enlargement. In younger women there may be either menstrual excess or intermenstrual bleeding. or both. Needless to say the hemorrhage is in any event only suggestive of possible malignancy, and carcinoma *will* more frequently be found to be its cause than sarcoma.

Certain tumors arise *retroperitoneallv*and. although they are generally not of pelvic origin. must be considered in differential diagnosis. Clinically they may present as a pelvic mass of considerable size with no associated menstrual abnormality. Pratt has pointed out the surgical difficulties with these lesions which are usually lymphomas or sarcomas.

Abnormal discharge may likewise be a symptom, as in carcinoma. In the earlier stages it is likely to be thin and watery, but sooner or later serosanguinous. Still later it may, as a result of necrosis and ulceration, become quite foul, and may even contain sloughing particles or shreds of tissue. *Rapid increase in the size of myomatous tumors,* especially when this is associated with bleeding, should likewise suggest the possibility of sarcoma. *Pain* may be a symptom, although often.not until the later infiltrative stages of the disease, when it may be intense and continuous. In these late stages, profound *anemia, cachexia,* and *weakness* may be noted, necessitating extensive preoperative preparation. Although recurrence and metastases with a fatal outcome are usually rapid, there are such exceptions as that noted recently by Drake and Dobben. They report a case with probable recurrence 18 years after complete operation and recovery, and their publication, with microscopic sections, would seem to suggest that it is a recurrent rather than a new malignancy.

Extension of the disease is by direct continuity, by the blood stream, and less commonly by the lymphaties. The hematogenous route is most important in metastasis, which therefore is more characteristically systemic rather than regional. Among the organs most frequently involved are the lungs and liver. Chest x-ray is routine when uterine sarcoma is diagnosed.

Treatment

Because of the difficulties of diagnosis, the treatment of sarcoma is often a matter of expediency rather than of deliberate planning. Surgery has been, and still is, the backbone of treatment, especially as so large a proportion of sarcomas are not discovered until operation for supposed myoma, or until the laboratory examination of such supposedly benign tumors. The possibility of sarcomatous change in myomas must always be borne in mind by the surgeon, and it is a wise precaution to cut into the tumor masses as soon as the utenis is removed, for a presumptive diagnosis of sarcoma can sometimes be made from the gross appearance of the cut surface.

Occasionally sarcoma is found after myomectomy has been performed or, more frequently in earlier days, when subtotal hysterectomy was the operation of choice. Although a secondary complete operation seems desirable in such instances, many patients were cured with no further treatment. It would seem that the patient's salvation lies in the fact that so many of the sarcomas developing in nn-omas are comparatively early and of a relatively low degree of malignancy. i.e.. cellular myoma.

Certainly we would hesitate to reoperate to remove a conserved ovary with an unsuspected sarcoma, preferring to believe that the adnexa retained will not be the sole site of infiltrative or recurrent disease.

Even the most extensive surgery and the most complete radiotherapy will fail to cure the more malignant types of sarcoma when these have reached an advanced stage, as they unfortunately often do, before the patient comes to operation. These advanced cases are poor operative risks as a result of such factors as extreme anemia, eachexia, and early extension and metastasis. The preferable plan of treatment is panhysterectomy followed by deep roentgenization, although there is considerable question as to how effective deep x-ray may be. As mentioned previously, endometrial sarcoma appears more radiosensitive. Chemotherapy is generally ineffectual.

12

OVARIAN CARCINOMA

Carcinoma of the ovary is a relatively frequent disease, ranking next to the various forms of uterine cancer insofar as the female reproducitve organs are concerned. It may be primary in the ovary or secondary to cancer in other organs.

Malignant ovarian neoplasms may be solid or cystic, and our own laboratory material would suggest that the latter is about twice as common. Due consideration must be given to the cystic degeneration which certain solid tumors undergo as well as the proliferative tendencies of the primarily cystic lesions. In other words, it is not easy to distinguish between certain cystic and solid ovarian neoplasms.

That malignant tumors often arise in bilateral fashion is true, but where there is evidence of generalized pelvic disease, it is sometimes impossible to be certain if there have been initial bilateral primary lesions or if a single tumor has spread to the contralateral ovary (and elsewhere) via direct extension or the richly communicating lymphatics.

At best only an approximate figure can be suggested, and our estimate would be that bilateral malignancy occurs in 25% of all cystic cancer, and slightly less commonly with solid carcinoma. Certain ovarian tumors as the gonadal stromal, mesonephroma, and Brenner varieties are only rarely noted as occurring in bilateral fashion (less than 10%).

The specific ratio between benign and malignant neoplasms must also represent an uncertain figure, even if we specifically delete such tumors as the simple functional lutein and follicle cysts, endometrial and tubo-ovarian lesions, and various related growths that are perhaps not true neoplasms. Certain laboratories will have different criteria as to what constitutes malignancy in a variety of pathological entities, such as papillary serous tumors. various cystic teratomas. and others. It is our own opinion that there is little purpose in even attempting to suggest a ratio between benign tumors and ovarian malignancies. Instead we should simply remember that most cystic tumors are benign, most solid ones are malignant, but any combination may be encountered with varying degrees of malignancy.

It is manifestly impossible to cite the actual *incidence* of carcinoma of the ovary, because of the varied interpretations between the benign and malignant. Randall, however, using figures from New York State where cancer is a reportable disease, estimates that at age 40 the probability of a woman's developing ovarian cancer is approximately 0.9%, although the actual incidence rises to a peak of 4% at age 70, after which it decreases.

The *clinical grouping* of ovarian malignancies has not been emphasized as strongly as in the case of uterine, and especially cervical cancer, nor has there been any uniformity in the classification of ovarian cancers. Yet it is obvious that the clinical stage must have an important bearing on prognosis, and this is indicated in reports in which cases are thus subdivided. The classification usually employed is that of Helsel. According to this, *Group* 1 comprises cancers limited to one ovary; *Group* 2, those cases in which the disease affects both ovaries or in which there is present a removable local extension; *Group 3,* cases in which there is locally irremovable extension or metastasis, or those in which there has been a rupture of the tumor at operation; and finally, *Group 4* would include the far advanced cases with a "frozen pelvis" or with distant metastasis. Other classifications do not differ materially from the above, and such descriptive terms as (1) completely, (2) incompletely operable, and (3) advanced would be as useful as any formal classification.

PRIMARY SOLID CARCINOMA OF OVARY

Types

The classification of solid primary ovarian cancer is also unsatisfactory from a pathological standpoint. We are obliged to have recourse chiefly to general pathological criteria of classification based chiefly on the growth pattern assumed by the tumors An exception to this is seen in the case of a certain group of teratomatous and dysontogenetic lesions. Aside from these the following variations of pattern may be noted in primary solid carcinoma.

(1) *Adenocarcinonta,* the most common form is characterized by its gland architecture. Like epidermoid carcinoma it may present various degrees of differentiation. In one type there is marked resemblance to endometrial adenocarcinoma. and Sampson has suggested that some of these tumors may actually arise from endometrial tissue in the ovaries. Such an origin is not easy to establish, but this has been done in certain case. In most of these, the adenocarcinoma arising in the endometrial cyst was of the type of adenoacanthoma, like a good many carcinomas arising in the uterine endometrium. Some adenocarcinomas are of papillary pattern and some nonpapillary.

(2) *Carcinoma,* also very frequent, is characterized by an absence of an adenomatous pattern. Various descriptive terms may be affixed, for example, medullary, alveolar, scirrhous, etc. Multiple. blocks and microscopic sections are necessary for a solid pattern may coexist with a predominantly cystic one.

Gross Characteristics

The size of solid ovarian carcinomas is very variable, although most of them give rise to symptoms which call for treatment before they have reached more than a moderate size. They may, however, attain sufficient size to fill the whole lower abdomen and to weigh many pounds. As a rule the external surface is smooth, but it may present many nodular thickenings or excrescences. On cutting into the tumor, the surface may be of grayish granular appearance, but often the tissue is brainlike and pultaceous, with not infrequently ragged looking cavities produced by extensive necrosis. In the smaller group of scirrhous tumours the consistency may be firm and fibrous. In the earlier stages the tumor is commonly unilateral, but there is an increasing tendency to bilaterality as the disease advances.

Mesonephroma of the Ovary

Schiller published several articles concerning a certain type of ovarian lesion that he believed originated from mesonephric duct remnants. These tumors were tubular, and the lumina were lined by a flat, hobnail. cuboidal epithelium, with occasional intraluminal projections, strongly suggestive of primitive glomeruli. This pattern was considered a specific entity, and was referred to as "Schiller's mesonephroma."

Somewhat later Saphir and Lackner reported a few cases of clear cell adenocarcinoma of the ovary which they believed were identical to renal tumors. These hypemepl comas or hypernephroid tumors of the ovary were thought to be of mesonephric origin. although we have never been able to find any cells in the primitive excretory system that might give rise to such tumors. Nevertheless this clear cell adenocarcinoma has been accepted by most gynocological has been accepted by most gynecological pathologists and was previously referred to as hypernephroma. although it is indistinguishable from adrenal tumors in the ovary.

Separate publications by Novak, Woodruff and Novak, and Novak and Woodruff appear to have established two very important points. (1) Certain tumors may show various admixtures of both the Schiller pattern and the clear cell architecture. (2) Such lesions are found exclusively in areas where there are remnants of the mesonephric apparatus, and the tumors are identical irrespective of the level at which they occur. Such sites as the vagina, vaginal fornices, and broad ligament may be affected. Similarly, the ovary may be the seat of mesonephroma, although the lesion actually arises from extraovarian vestiges of the mesonephric tubules, with subsequent involvement of the gonad. An early publication by Novak et al. noted 13 cases of mesonephromas occurring in the lower genital tract; a more recent article concerns 35 ovarian mesonephromas gathered from a files of the Ovarian Tumor Registry. Mesonephromas represent merely a variety of adenocarcinoma; they are usually partially cystic and solid.

Although histology is similar irrespective of the site at which they occur, ovarian mesonephromas appear to be considerably more lethal. Even where the lesion is confined to the ovary, mortality approximates 50 % despite any type of surgical and irradiation therapy. Where there is extraovarian extension there is practically no salvage. The high mortality rate, as compared to that of a similar tumor at a lower level, may well be a sequel of the intrapelvic location of the ovarian lesion where its presence is silent and not so apt to cause bleeding as vaginal and cervical mesonephromas. Wherever the tumor lies, it is endocrinologically inert.

Distinction of certain pure clear cell tumors of mesonephric origin from adrenal tumors is occasionally impossible; if there is any virilizing hormonal influence the lesion is apt to be adrenal. Certain other confused and confusing terms are often applied to these lipoid (or clear cell) growths, but we would suggest that such designations as masculinovoblastoma, hypernephroma, and luteoma should be reevaluated, with possibly the term "luteoma" being retained for such lesions as described by Scully and Sternberg. Distinction of such clear cell tumors as rnesonephroma, hilus cell, or adrenal depends both on morphology and any assistance the hormonal pattern may give. The papers of Novak and Woodruff are recommended for a more complete study of the tumors of mesonephric origin.

PRIMARY CYSTIC CARCINOMA OF OVARY

While a carcinoma of the ovary may arise as a cystic tumor it can unquestionably develop in a previously benign cystadenoma of the ovary. As to the frequent occurrence of secondary carcinomatous changes in cystadenomas there can be no doubt. It is not rare, for example, to encounter carcinoma at some portion in the wall of benign cysts which have been known to be present for many years. Again, in many carcinomas large areas of entirely benign cystadenonia may still be observed. In any event, the adenocarcinomas of the ovary are to be looked upon as the malignant prototypes of the benign cystadenoma, arising from the same elements which gave rise to the latter. On the above basis we may distinguish three chief varieties of primary cystic ovarian carcinoma.

Pseudomucinous Cystadenocarcinoma

This is the malignant prototype of pseudomucinous cystadenoma, or arises from the same tissue elements which give rise to the latter. Only about 5% of these undergo malignant degeneration; this occurrence is much less common than with the serous. The malignant disease may affect only a localized area of the cyst, but in most cases the latter is replaced by solid tumor.

The *microscopic* examination shows the typical picture of adenocarcinoma, but all degrees of differentiation are possible. The cells usually retain their mucoid tendencies to a greater or less extent, and hence one often finds large or small cavities filled with gelatinous material.

Serous Cystadenocarcinoma

This represents the malignant form of serous cystadenoma. It is much more common than the pseudomucinous variety, and is almost always characterized by a papillary architecture. The papillary growth is not infrequently present on the surface as well as within the cavity. All grades of transition may be seen between the picture of benign papillary serous cystadenoma and that characterized by almost solid papillary masses, with perhaps a ragged cystic cavity here and there. Indeed, Woodruff and Novak have indicated that one must recognize a borderline low grade type of papillary malignancy characterized histologically by a marked papillary growth and a tendency to implant on peritoneal surfaces with the production of ascites. They have likewise stressed the importance of repeated pathological sections from many areas of the lesion, for an ovarian tumor can show a highly variegated appearance, from the extremely benign to the highly malignant. The *microscopic examination* often presents considerable difficulty, especially in the cases in which the gross appearance is much like that of the benign serous cysts and in which the epithelial elements present only moderate stratification and increase, and only a moderate and perhaps doubtful anaplastic activity. Even in the absence of *very* clear-cut evidence of histological malignancy. such tumors often exhibit clinical malignancy, especially as regards peritoneal implantation. It is usually safer, therefore, to err on the side of safety, and to consider them in the malignant group, with correspondingly radical treatment, which will usually include the removal of the adnexa of the opposite side, as well as the uterus.

In the majority of cases, however, the malignant nature of this group of tumors is more clearly defined, with many layers of epithelium, showing disparity in size and shape of the cells and especially the nuclei, hyperchromatosis and marked mitotic activity. Invasion of the stroma by the epithelium is likewise often evident. The structure is definitely papillary, and the epithelial tissue may or may not show a definitely glandular pattern.

Secondary Carcinoma in Dermoid Cysts

This is rare, occurring in only 1 to 3% of dermoid tumors (Blackwell) and assuming usually the form of epidermoid carcinoma, since it develops from the skinlike elements in such tumors. On several occasions we have seen a genuine intraepithelial pattern.

SECONDARY OR METASTATIC CARCINOMA OF OVARY

Carcinoma of almost any type may occur in the ovary as a result of metastasis from primary sites in other parts of the body, especially in the latter stages of such malignant processes. A not in frequent variety of secondary ovarian cancer is that seen in association with carcinoma of the gastrointestinal tract or of the secondary organs of digestion. This may present the same histological pattern in the ovary as in the primary tumor, this usually being adenocarcinoma.

Krukenberg Tumor

There is one particular variety of secondary ovarian carcinoma, however, which assumes special characteristics, and to which the designation of Krukenberg tumor is applied. This may be an of accompaniment of primary carcinoma elsewhere, but especially in any portion of the gastrointestinal tract, most frequently the pylorus, but not infrequently the colon, rectum, small intestine, liver, or gall bladder. It should be emphasized that the term "Krukenberg tumor" should not be applied to any ovarian tumor secondary to a gastrointestinal lesion. The designation is purely on a histological basis.

Although it is generally believed that Krukenberg tumors are almost always metastatic. Woodruff and Novak have pointed out that about 20% *seem primarv* in nature. An origin from teratoma. pseudomucinous cyst. or mucoid degeneration in a Brenner tumor iNould appear to furnish the proper ovarian environment for a Krukenberg pattern to evolve. Prolonged salvage without gastrointestinal signs or symptoms, or autopsy on women dead from other causes, would leave little doubt as to a not infrequent primary ovarian origin. One or two cases have occurred during pregnancy as noted by Lawrence, Larson, and Hauge. and among the Ovarian Tumor Registry material utilized by Woodruff and Novak. The latter have found one 10 year salvage in a patient who had a characteristic unilateral primary Krukenberg tumor removed during pregnancy.

There has been considerable discussion as to the route by which carcinoma cells make their way to the ovary from such primary sites as the pylorus. Many believe that the cells after penetration of the stomach walls gravitate downward to the ovarian regions by way of the peritoneal fluid. There are many objections to this theory, and there is rcason to believe that retrograde lymphatic transplantation is the important factor. while in some cases the hematogenous route plays the important role.

The tumors are generally bilateral (over 50 %). They are solid and they have a tendency to retain the original ovarian contour, so that they are ovoid or kidneyshaped. The surface is smooth, although often nodular, and the cut surface of variegated appearance, with frequently areas of gelatinous consistency.

Microscopically, the pattern of the Krukenberg tumor is quite distinctive, and the diagnosis is dependent only on the histological pattern, not on an associated or prior gastrointestinal lesion. Small nests or acini of epithelial cells are distributed throughout a fibrous or myomatous stroma, and especially characteristic are the so-called *signet cells,* in which the mucoid accumulation in the cytoplasm displaces the flattened nucleus to one side of the cell. A marked stromal hyperplasia mimicking sarcoma may be present, and this stromal (thecal) reaction may lead to bleeding from a hyperplastic endometriur as noted by some authors. Although this type of estrogenic reaction is most commmonly found in these tumors with a functioning stroma, Ober et al. report a Krukenberg tumor with androgenic effects. For a more complete discussion of this tumor type the reader may be referred to the paper of Wood-ruff and Novak.

EXTENSION OF OVARIAN CARCINOMA

The other ovary becomes involved in more than one-half of all cases of ovarian carcinoma, while the tube and the uterus are not infrequently the seat of mmetastatic extension as one might expect from the richness of lymphatic intercommunication of these various organs. Even where the contralateral ovary appears grossly normal. cancer is found in the hilar h-mphatics in 25 to 50 %ofcases. Especially frequent is extension to the peritoneum. occurring in over 75 % of all cases. The lymphatic glands, especially those of the lumbar group, are involved in a very large proportion of the cases, especially in the later stages of the disease. Finally. metastases nay occur to such distant organs as the liver. pancreas. lungs. pleura, and long bones.

CLINICAL CHARACTERISTICS OF OVARIAN CARCINOMA

The most important symptoms of ovarian carcinoma are unfortunately rather late ones, as the onset of this disease is almost always very insidious and "silent" in nature. The presence of a mass in the lower abdomen is the first indication of the disease in a considerable proportion of cases, and unfortunately by this time other organs are often involved. Moderate heaviness or occasional pain may be noted, but are more apt to be absent. The same statement may be made concerning *menstrual disorders.* If the patient is in the childbearing age there may be menorrhagia or even occasional slight metorrhagia, but in the majority of cases no abnormality has been noted by the patient. In the postmenopausal cases, slight *bleeding* or a bloody discharge is noted in only a small proportion of the patients, and may be indicative of uterine metastasis. Thrombophlebitis, otherwise unexplained, may be due to silent tumor in proximity to the large veins. It has been amply demonstrated that the finding of tumor cells in the blood does not necessarily imply metastases.

Ascites is a relatively common accompaniment of ovarian cancer, especially of the papillary varieties. It is all too frequently indicative of peritoneal extension of the growth, but may he due merely to venous obstruction caused by partial torsion of the tumor, as in any other ovarian neoplasm. The ascites may be so extreme as to make palpation of the tumor impossible, and we have seen a number of instances in which only after paracentesis could the lower abdominal or pelvic masses be felt.

Ovarian Carcinoma in Pregnancy

This is a rather rare complication of pregnancy, albeit a rather serious one, for the symptoms and signs of pregnancy, may mask those caused by the ovarian tumor. Jubb suggests certain suggestive features, as lower abdominal pain and discomfort or disproportionate enlargement of the abdomen (out of keeping with the degree of gestation). Less common are such surgical emergencies as rupture or torsion of the pediele. and rarely obstruction to labor may occur. While the incidence of ovarian cancer in pregnancy is probably less than 0.5%. it is perhaps less commonly associated with the functioning ovarian tumors which Jubb has omitted from his case reports. Although his study would seem to support a conservative approach in the younger patient where the ovarian capsule is intact, this should depend upon the particular type and extent of the lesion. Conservative surgery can of course always be followed by more radical surgery whereas it is more difficult to replace removed organs.

Diagnosis

In a large proportion of cases the malignant nature of the tumors is not suspected before operation, and often not until the pathological examination is made. In many, however, a strongly presumptive diagnosis is possible, chiefly on palpatory findings. Vaginal smear rarely demonstrates exfoliated tumor cells, but Rubin and Frost note a frequent estrogenic effect in the maturation index. Preoperative culdocentesis may be helpful if the removed fluid is studied cytologically. This has been suggested as part of a routine "check-up" of even normal women, but we doubt if the usual patient would consent.

If pelvic examination reveals a mass occupying the position of the ovary, and if the mass is hard, fixed, and firm, ovarian carcinoma should be suspected, especially if the patient is in the cancer age. Benign solid tumors of the ovary, such as fibroma, give somewhat the same feeling, but they are less common. Benign cystic tumors, on the other hand, give a softer, elastic sensation to the examining hands, and are usually smoother in contour, as compared to the more nodular contour of most cancers. Many malignant tumors are partly cystic and partly nodular, and this very irregularity should be viewed with suspicion.

When such a tumor is associated with ascites, there can be little doubt as to its malignant nature. When the ascites is extreme, the tumor may be impalpable, and other causes of ascites, such as hepatic and cardiorenal disease or tuberculous peritonitis, may have to be eliminated. Occasionally paracentesis may be necessary to permit proper palpation of the pelvic organs, and a definite mass may then for the first time be felt. Microscopic examination of the centrifuged ascitic fluid may show typically malignant cells.

Peritoneal washing at laparotomy has been suggested by some as being of prognostic value, if performed prior to operative manipulation and immediately after entry into the abdomen. We are not impressed with this method, however, because of the vagarious nature of ovarian tumors. Sometimes an apparently localized lesion is followed by massive recurrence. In other instances extensive disease seems compatible with longevity.

The symptoms themselves are rarely of much value in diagnosis. Postmenopausal bleeding, however, always calls for complete gynecological examination. While the form of malignancy producing this symptom is generally cervical or corporeal carcinoma, ovarian malignancy is not a rare finding. Culdoscopy is occasionally helpful in differentiating between a harmless uterine or tubal mass and a true ovarian neoplasm. When, however, there is any doubt as to whether a pelvic mass might be ovarian or not, exploration is indicated because of the very deadly nature of ovarian cancer.

Even at the time of surgery, the exact nature of an ovarian tumor may be uncertain, and in such instances *a frozen section* may be helpful. It is perhaps preferable to remove the whole adnexal mass, and allow the pathologist to select likely areas for section rather than blindly remove one or two areas for evaluation. While this may minimize errors, permanent sections will on occasion show malignancy that had not been noted on frozen section, so that the trained gynecologist will also strongly consider the gross appearance of the lesion at surgery.

Prognosis

The outlook for the patient with ovarian carcinoma is very grave, especially if one omits from consideration the dysontogenetic group (granulosatheca cell tumor, arrhenoblastoma, and dysgerminoma) in which the results are far better. There are few writers who report a 5-year survival rate of much more than 20 %, and indeed in some areas such as New York, ovarian cancer accounts for more deaths than cervical malignancy due to improved detection of the latter disease. Unfortunately cytopathological techniques rarely are useful in detecting cancer of the ovary.

Meigs reports only 9.7 % of 72 patients with solid ovarian carcinoma to have survived for 5 years, although 21.9 %, of 82 patients with cystic carcinoma were still living. The entire series of 154 cases gave a 5-year survival rate of 15.5 %. Munnell, Jacox, and Taylor in a recent study of 343 cases of ovarian cancers, reported 27 % of 5-year survivals, but if certain special types of relatively low malignancy, like granulosa cell and low grade cystic tumors. were excluded from the series the salvage is only 12 %. Kent and McKay record a surprisingly good salvage of 36.4 %. but their cases comprise a large number of favorable cystic tumors.

Treatment

The proper treatment of ovarian carcinoma is *surgical.* Operation should be performed as early as possible. and should ideally comprise hysterectomy and bilateral salpingo-oophorectomy. Even when peritoneal involvement is disclosed, the primary lesions should be removed if this is safely possible, as there is rather general agreement that this retards the progress of the secondary extensions. Some degree of omentectomy decreases recurrent ascites, although it may predispose to intestinal obstruction.

Advanced Disease

Most gynecologists feel that ovarian carcinoma warrants exploration despite suggestive evidence of extrapelvic disease and even pulmonic or pleural spread. Admittedly the prognosis is poor but surgery is worthwhile (1) as a diagnostic measure, (2) in obviating incipient obstruction, and (3) as a palliative procedure by reducing tumor bulk, omental lesions, and ascites. Rarely there is profound regression following removal of the parent lesion, and modem methods of chemotherapy and irradiation often lead to prolonged remission although cure is minimal.

The postoperative employment of *irradiation therapy* has been almost universal, and is of undoubted value in prolonging life in many instances, with little regard as to tumor histology, as noted by Chu.

There is scant evidence, however, of any curative effect. More recently, radioactive colloidal gold or phosphate has been placed into the peritoneal cavity and seems of considerable aid in preventing the recurrent ascites which is such a frequent problem in the implanting papillary tumors although damage to the intestinal tract has been an occasional complication. It is of no assistance where there are large masses and of course is rarely curative, merely palliative in increasing the life span. Details are available in the papers of Kron and of Elkins and Keettel.

The varied methods of chemotherapy are still uncertain and equivocal, but occasional patients have prolonged remissions of 1 or 2 years following drug therapy, despite advanced disease. On the other hand, certain tumors are not arrested, and just as there are varying degrees of radiosensitivity, we must anticipate differences in drug sensitivity and resistance. Chlorambucil. triethylenemalamine (TEM), and thiotriethylene-phosphoramide (thio-TEPA), as reported by Navjoks, Crandall, and Treeter, are among the drugs utilized.

Parker and Singleton suggest increased longevity in certain drug-treated patients. and with this we would agree, although complete cure is unlikely. Severe bone marrow depression may ensue, but careful regulation of the drug may obviate this and other complications. We regard perfusion as a truly heroic and very dangerous procedure to be utilized only when there is no alternative type of therapy.

SARCOMA OF OVARY

Sarcoma of the ovary is far less common than carcinoma, its *incidence* as compared with carcinoma being about 1: 40. *It may occur at any age.* Most authors emphasize that it is frequent in children, but this is open to doubt, as so many ovarian tumors in children which were formerly diagnosed as sarcoma are now recognized as either granulosa cell carcinoma, dysgerminoma, or lymphomas.

Various types of sarcoma are found in the ovary, the spindle variety being more common than the round cell, although mixed forms often occur. The lymphomas, occasionally primary, and angiosarcoma are also described, but it appears that in the latter the perivascular arrangement of the cells is due to the fact that extensive degeneration has occurred except where the cells are near to their blood supply. Symptoms are identical to those of carcinoma.

TERATOMA

Teratoma of the ovary may be *cystic* or *solid*. The cystic form is represented by the benign dermoid, already described in the chapter on benign ovarian cysts. The *solid teratoma* differs from the simple dermoid not only in that it is a solid tumor, but also because it is malignant, and that it contains elements derived in from all three of the fetal layers. The term *embryonal carcinoma* is used by some for what we believe to be a typical teratoma; in other words, the lesion is the same despite the different terminology. Within recent years we have been convinced that a third and somewhat intermediate form should be recognized, *a benign solid teratoma,* as noted by Peterson. We base this assertion on the fact that we have encountered a small group of dominantly solid teratomas, made up of tissues derived from all the fetal layers, but all very mature. Some of these have been extremely large, and some have occurred in children, so that one might at first suspect such tumors to be the malignant types of teratoma seen chiefly in children and usually fatal. The particular group we are describing, however, have all been benign clinically.

The *histogenesis* of teratoma is not clearly known, the two chief theories being: (1) an origin from segregated blastomeres, and (2) an origin from unfertilized sex cells. According to the first of these, blastomeres may be segregated in early stages of embryonic development. lying dormant until later fife, when for some unknown reason they begin to differentiate into the tissues which they were originally designed to form. The weakness of this concept is that it does not explain why the ovary is such a seat of predilection for such teratomatous growths.

Perhaps somewhat more popular is the second theory. This is based on the fact that the ovary normally contains large numbers of germ cells, capable after certain preparatory changes of producing another human body if fertilized by the male element. Even without the latter, it is thought possible that a species of parthenogenetic development may occur because of certain stimulating if unknown factors which may arise, and that abortive and imperfect formation of various fetal tissues may thus occur.

According to this hypothesis, it will be seen that the histogenesis of teratoma is somewhat allied to the phenomenon of twinning. In this connection, it is worth noting that the chromosomal test for sex differentiation has been applied by Hunter, Lennox, and Durk to the study of a group of 21 teratomas. 12 occurring in females and 9 in males. All the teratomas borne by women were found to be female, but of those in males 4 were male and 5 female. No important lesson can be drawn from these findings in view ofour ignorance as to the histogenesis of teratomas.

Teratoma may occur at any age, but is *more common in younger individuals*. The tumors are usually of small or only moderate size. They are firm and solid, with often cartilaginous or bony areas, and not infrequently with small cavities produced by degeneration.

Microscopically almost any of the tissues or organs of the body may be reproduced in the tumor, although usually imperfectly. Cartilage, bone, teeth, brain tissue, intestine, and many other tissues may be found, although they are not always easy to differentiate, expecially as they are often of immature embryonic type. *Chorionepithelioma* of the ovarian tumor may occur with lung metastasis as commonly as with the usual trophoblastic lesion of the uterus. A limited experience with this rare lesion indicates that it responds less favorably to drug therapy than to the trophoblastic growths of the uterus.

A specific subdivision of teratoma is the so-called *strunia ovarii,* or thyroid tumor of the ovary. In this variety the thyroid tissue blots out other elements in large areas of the tumor, although usually at least some other teratomatous elements are found.

An interesting clinical feature of some cases of struma ovarii has been that the thyroid tissue is functionally active or even overactive, producing systemic manifestations of hyperthyroidism, with pronounced increase of the basal metabolic rate. Removal of such tumors has in a group of reported cases cured the hyperthyroidism (Woodruff).

The mere finding of a small amount of mature thyroid tissue does not justify the designation of stnnna ovary as such islands are not rarely seen in simple dermoids. The term should be used only when the thyroid tissue forms a dominating fraction of the tumor, although no mathematical rules can be laid down. Another interesting characteristic of teratoma is that in some cases there is a dominance of entodermic epithelium which morphologically resembles that so characteristic of pseudoinucinous cystadenoma. As a matter of fact, the commonly accepted theory is that the origin of most pseudomucinous cystadenomas is teratomatous, from the *entodermic* epithelium just described. Unquestionably, mucoid metaplasia of the germinal epithelium can occur and be a potential source of genesis for pseudomucinous lesions.

A small group of carcinoid tumors arising from argentaffine cells has been reported by Nissen to arise in teratomas; They are of low grade malignancy, but may, when extensive, produce a metabolite that may produce vasomotor changes.

The *symptoms* of teratoma are the presence of an *ovarian mass, occasionally slight bleeding* and not infrequently ascites. The course is definitely malignant, and metastases occur not only in various abdominal locations, but also in distant organs even where there is an intact capsule and no gross extension.

The *treatment* is of course surgical, but the prognosis is unfavorable in most cases. Breen and Neubecker in their study of 17 patients suggest complete hysterectomy and adnexectomy despite and average age of slightly more than 16 years. Our own preference would be to perform conservative surgery if the tumor capsule is intact, admittedly as a calculated risk, radiotherapy appears to be of little or no value. If, however, we include cases of solid but well differentiated tumors, the prognosis is much impoived. Out own preference is to use the term teratoma to indicate a malignant process, but to modify this by the prefix "*benign*" if there is an orderly arrangement of well differentiated cell patterns.

13

INFLAMMATORY GONADAL DISEASES

The rationale of separate chapters for acute and chronic pelvic inflammatory disease is that the former is (with certain exceptions) almost exclusively a medical problem, whereas most cases of chronic recurrent infection almost inevitably culminate in some type of surgical procedure.

The advent of the more recent and improved antibiotic agents has been attended by a significant decrease in the more serious forms and complications of infection of the generative tract. Probably pelvic infection is almost as frequent, but prompt treatment and response would seem to have led to a considerable reduction of such formerly frequent sequelae as tubo-ovarian or pelvic abscess, pelvic peritonitis, or even permanently closed tubes.

Pelvic inflammatory disease is usually secondary to infection and upward migration of various bacteria introduced at a lower level, although in its incipient form there may be remarkably little in the way of symptomatology. In any case the course of the disease is dependent on the strain and virulence of the particular organisms involved, as well as the individual body resistance to the offending bacteria. Although in most cases the tubes seem to bear the primary impact of the infectious process, there is a strong tendency for extension to the ovaries and pelvic peritoneum as a result of the propinquity of these structures to the uterus and tubes, and the intimacy of the lymphatic and vascular supply of all the pelvic organs.

Thus, the syndrome produced by genital infection is frequently a composite one, produced by various degrees of tubal involvement, with or without extension to the ovaries and pelvic peritoneum. As a rule the uterus itself is more or less immune to the inflammatory impact, for although there may be a very definite pathological involvement of the endometrial surface. this contributes little to the general symptomatology. This composite clinical syndrome is usually designated as pelvic inflammatory disease. and although there arc many exceptions. the usual tendency is to begin with a. rather acute episode, followed by either complete resolution or else gradual subsidence into a more chronic process characterized by not infrequent acute or subacute resurgence.

Etiology

From an etiological as well as from a clinical standpoint, one may distinguish three types of pelvic inflammatory disease.

1. *Gonorrheal,* due to infection by the Gonococcus, and comprising the largest proportion, about 60 % of all cases, although recent studies by Lukasik find the Gonococcus much less frequent than intestinal bacilli in tubal cultures. This should not imply any decrease in gonorrheal disease, for frequently culture is negative in cases of undoubted gonococcal tubo-ovarian abscess.

2. *Pvogenic,* due to infection by any one of a number of organisms, most frequently the Streptococcus (aerobic or anaerobic) or Staphylococcus. It is this variety of infection with which we are chiefly concerned in the frequent cases of puerperal and postabortive infection.

3. *Tuberculous,* the result of infection by the tubercle bacillus, and embracing approximately 5% of the cases of pelvic inflammatory disease in areas where poverty and malnutrition abound. This form of pelvic infection is of chronic nature.

GONORRHEAL TYPE

Pathology

The immediate focus in cases of infection of the upper genital tract is a gonorrheal involvement of the cervix, from which site the organisms make their way by surface invasion along the endoinetrium to the tubes and often beyond this to the peritoneum and ovaries. An acute gonorrheal infection of the urethra or vulvovaginal glands may constitute the primary focus.

Acute Endometritis of Gonorrheal Type

This form is rather rarely encountered in the pathological laboratory, inasmuch as both curettage and hystercetomy are usually contraindicated in the course of acute gonorrheal infections. It is characterized grossly by edema and hyperemia of the mucosa, and microscopically by hyperemia and infiltration by large numbers of polymorphonuelear leukocytes. Its tendency is toward spontaneous resolution, because of the usually good drainage of the uterine canal. and even more because of the monthly desquamation of menstruation with gradual attenuation in each cycle.

The endometrium may thus be completely purged of all infection even though there is extensive chronic tubal or tubo-ovarian infection. There are, however, numerous exceptions to this, because of the frequent occurrence of reinfection.

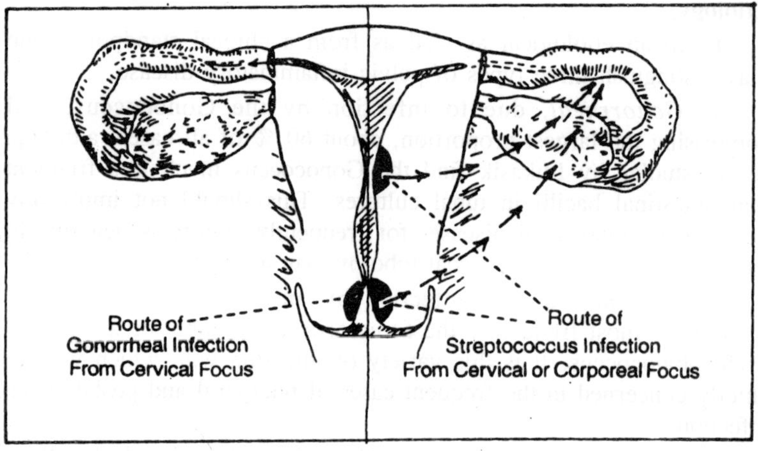

Fig. 13.1. Schematic drawing of two chief routes of pelvis infection.

Acute Salpingitis

This may be an almost immediate sequel of acute gonorrheal infection of the lower genital tract, or it may not occur until long afterward, perhaps many months or even years after the original infection. Since the organisms reach the tube by way of the mucous membrane, it is not surprising that the latter is the primary seat of the pathological changes. It becomes reddened and swollen, and soon gives forth an exudate which. except in the mildest cases, is purulent. This type of involvement is unfortunate for the patient, in that later occlusion and distention of the tube so frequently occur, with sterility a frequent result. The exudate may escape from the still open end of the tube, producing *acute pelvic peritonitis* and sometimes *pelvic abscess.*

The inflammatory process is rarely limited to the endosalpinx alone. the whole tube being swollen, hyperemic, and reddened, while acute *perisalpingitis* may manifest itself by a fibrinous exudate on the tubal peritoneum, with light adhesions to surrounding structures. Occlusion of the fimbriated orifice or of other parts of the lumen may occur. with the production of a pvosalpinx. although this is more often encountered in an acute exacerbation of the chronic form. As already mentioned. pelvic abscess may result from bacterial invasion or even escape of purulent exudate into the pelvis. Finally, and most frequently, the subsidence of the acute infection leaves a residue of chronic salpingitis of one form or another.

The *microscopic characteristics* of acute gonorrheal salpingitis are like those of acute inflammation in general. The chief features are infiltration with polymorphonuclear leukoeytes, hyperemia, and edema. In the milder cases the epithelium maybe intact, but in the more severe forms it shows degeneration and often is lost over considerable areas. The inflammatory reaction is rarely limited sharply to the mucosa, and commonly involves the muscular and serous coat to a greater or less extent.

A very important characteristic of acute gonorrheal salpingitis, and one which has great bearing on the practical treatment of such cases, is the tendency of the infecting organisms to disappear within a short time, ordinarily about 10 days. While, therefore, acute salpingitis may leave in its wake a pathologically wrecked tube, often distended with pus, and no longer of value from the standpoint of childbearing, the bacteriological examination of the tube and its contents often shows these to be sterile. This was pointed out years ago by the bacteriological studies of Curtis and others, and has been confirmed more recently by Blinick.

SEPTIC OR TYOGENIC TYPE

The pyogenic form of acute salpingitis usually follows *childbirth or abortion,* the latter especially of the criminal type. The infecting organism, generally the Streptococcus or Staphylococcus, reaches the tube by a route quite different from that followed by the Gonococcus, and the resulting changes in the tube are likewise quite different from those described for the gonorrheal variety. From portals of entry in the lower genital canal, usually the cervix, the organisms are disseminated outward through the veins and lymphaties of the broad ligaments. Thrombophlebitis and periphlebitis. lymphangitis and perilymphangitis. with cellulitis and even abscess of the broad ligaments are frequent results.

It might be appropriate to note that Sarma, writing from India, has tabulated a list of exotic diseases which may cause infection in the gravid or normal woman. Kala-azar, bilharziasis, malaria, and other diseases rarely seen in this country deserve consideration in various pelvic disorders seen in certain tropical areas.

Acute Endometritis

In the milder forms of infection. the endometrium may be merely hyperemic and edematous. but in the more virulent infections it may show extensive necrosis. The microscopic picture is that of acute inflammation, with varying degrees of necrotic change. With this one also finds in most cases degenerated villi and decidual tissue, and not infrequently extensive hemorrhage and thrombosis. On occasion a postabortal infection may be due to the *Clostridium welchii,* and women harboring this organism may be critically ill with general sepsis, shock, and renal failure. Massive antibiotics and such heroic measures as dialysis or an artificial kidney may not suffice; Rabinowitz *et alL* suggest the desirability of hysterectomy, and in a small group of cases this seemed to produce better results, especially if combined with a massive dosage of drugs.

Acute Salpingitis

As already stated, the infection reaches the tube from the outside, so to speak, and this explains why the resulting salpingitis is of predominantly interstitial type, with often little or no involvement of the mucosa. The cross section of such a tube characteristically shows an enormously thickened and infiltrated mesosalpinx, with great thickening of the tubal wall, but with a lumen which is quite normal and which is lined by an intact or almost intact mucosa. This is in sharp contrast to the gonorrheal form, in which the destructive force of the infection is vented upon the mucosa primarily, with frequent occlusion of the lumen and subsequent sterility.

On the other hand, the prognosis as to childbearing following pyogenic infection of the tubes is much better, and one not infrequently observes later pregnancies in cases of extensive pelvic inflammation of the pyogenic type. This is of course not always the case, for the'tubal orifices are sometimes closed by the extensive pelvic peritonitis which may accompany any acute infection of the pelvic organs.

The *microscopic picture* of acute pyogenic salpingitis, as might be expected from what has been said, is that of a normal or only slightly infiltrated mucosa with great thickening of the muscularis as a result of edema and leukocytic infiltration, and with usually some degree of acute fibrinous peritonitis of the tubal serosa.

Acute Ovaritis or Oophoritis

The ovary not infrequently participates in acute pelvic inflammatory processes. but rarely except as a penalty of its proximity to the tube. However, one only rarely observes oophoritis except in association with salpingitis: while on the other hand. the ovary is frequently uninvolved even in the presence of severe tubal inflammation. either acute or chronic.

The fact remains, however, that acute oophoritis, and even ovarian abscess, is at times found as a part of acute pelvic inflammatory disease. although abscesses are also often seen in association with long-standing chronic inflammation. Pelvic abscesses are often tubo-ovarian, representing the merging of tubal and ovarian cavities. Ovarian abscess with normal tubes is occasionally seen as a sequel to posthysterectomy infection which apparently spreads along lymphatic routes. Wilson and Black point out that this most commonly follows vaginal hysterectomy.

Acute Pelvic Peritonitis

In either the gonorrheal or pyogenic forms of infection acute pelvic peritonitis is a common concomitant. This manifests itself most frequently in the form of serous or fibrinous exudates with early development of adhesions between any of the adjoining pelvic structures, or between these and the small intestine, sigmoid, or rectum. In the acute stage these are light and fibrinous, but with increasing organization they later become dense and fibrous.

As a result ofexudation of infected material from the tube, or perhaps more frequently through the virulence of the peritoneal infection itself, pelvic abscess frequently results. It is not always easy to distinguish clinically between large abscesses within the tube or ovary (tuboovarian abscesses) and the extratubal variety, in which the pus is situated in the pelvic cavity proper, generally in the cul-de-sac, in which case its upper wall is usually formed by the matted and adherent intestinal coils. The usual location of the pelvic abscess in the region of the cul-de-sac points the way to its easy evacuation by incision through the posterior vaginal vault *(posterior colpotomy)*, the operation which is frequently indicated. Occasionally this is utilized in the postsurgical patient in whom there has been persistent slight bleeding; this may localize in the cul-de-sac and, if secondarily infected, may form a pelvic hematocele, amenable to drainage.

SYMPTOMS AND SIGNS

Gonorrheal Form

The gonorrheal form may follow this infection in the lower genital canal, or at times its nature can be assumed if there is a history of recent gonorrheal infection in the marital partner. In a large proportion of cases. however, the history is of little help, the assumption of gonorrheal causation being based chiefly on the absence ofany factor likely to produce pyogenic infection. such as recent childbirth. spontaneous miscarriage. criminal abortion. instrumentation. or operations upon the cervix.

In many cases, although not by any means all, the acute symptoms appear during or immediately after a menstrual period. This is explained by the greater vulnerability of the uterine cavity to gonorrheal invasion at the time of menstrual desquamation. Severe *pain* in the pelvic and lower abdominal region, *muscular rigidity, and tenderness, abdominal distention, nausea and vomiting, fever, leukoevtosis, rapid pulse,* with considerable *prostration* in the severe cases, are the common symptoms. The fever may reach 103° or even higher, with a marked leukocytosis and increased pulse rate. The abdomen is usually tense and tympanitic, with marked tenderness and rigidity in the lower quadrants. In the severe forms which are associated with the formation of large tubal or tubo-ovarian abscesses, it may be impossible to palpate even large masses on examination because of the tenderness and rigidity of the abdominal walls incurred by the pelvic peritonitis.

Pelvic Examination

This may be difficult and unsatisfactory, because of the patient's pain, tenderness, and rigidity, but usually the desired information is obtainable. When the uterus can be outlined between the examining hands, it is apt to be rather fixed, and *efforts* to move it by manipulation of the cervix or fundus cause much pain. There is extreme tenderness in both sides of the pelvis, but often in the acute stage no definite mass or enlargement of the adnexa can be made out. When the fever and pelvic pain persist, accompanied often by rectal pressure and pain, examination may reveal increasing induration, with later fluctuation and even bulging, in the region of the cul-desac, at times extending into the sides of the pelvis and perhaps downward along the posterior vaginal wall to a level which may be considerably lower than the cervix. Such findings leave no doubt as to the presence of a pelvic abscess, calling for evacuation through the posterior vaginal fornix (posterior colpotomy).

Postpartum and Postabortive Types

In these cases the patient is often very weak and septic. and there may be considerable local trauma in the perineum and vagina so that much gentleness is necessary in the examination, ideally performed with sterile technique. The cervix is apt to be lacerated and infected, especially if the pelvic infection follows full term delivery. The uterus in such cases is large and uninvoluted, while in the case of early criminal abortions, it is only slightly enlarged. Even gentle manipulation of the uterus may be . quite painful. One must always be cognizant of the possibility of uterine perforation and other trauma associated with criminal abortion.

Where the infection has invaded the broad ligaments the latter may be enormously thickened and infiltrated, so that the adnexa themselves cannot be made out *(broad ligament cellulitis)*. Where broad ligament abscesses are present, as they often are at a later stage, the lateral masses are even larger. In some cases, however, the broad ligaments show little involvement, and the enlarged and inflamed adnexa may be palpated as irregular, tender masses in the sides of the pelvis. Marked thickening, infiltration, and tenderness of the broad and uterosacral ligaments is a frequent manifestation of the *parametritis* so commonly present.

Pyometra

Where there is any blockage of the canal, as may occur particularly with senile changes in the cervix or upper vagina, pus may accumulate, with the formation of a pyometra. This is particularly common with a uterine malignancy, especially after irradiation, and is not a sequel to acute endometritis in the usual young woman. Surprisingly, despite the massive accumulation of pus, there may be little systemic reaction. Misdiagnosis is rather frequent for the overdistended softened uterus suggests an ovarian cyst.

DIAGNOSIS

Gonorrheal Infection

A history of gonorrhea in either the patient or her husband is of great value in diagnosis, but this aid is lacking in the great majority of cases. The occurrence of severe lower abdominal pain, usually bilateral, during or just after menstruation, with lower abdominal tenderness and rigidity, moderate tympanites, fever, often nausea and vomiting, rapid pulse, leukocytosis, leukorrhea, and marked pelvic tenderness on bimanual examination, will usually suffice to make the diagnosis reasonably certain. When acute cervicitis or urethritis is present. gonococei are occasionally demonstrable in the discharges.

In discussing the current status of gonorrhea, Simpson and Brown deplore the efficacy of past methods in detecting and treating gonorrhea. They suggest that use of the fluorescent antibody technique as noted by Deacon will disclose that a considerable number of promiscuous although ass1nptomatic women may harbor the Gonococcus. Due to varying degrees of drug resistance, massive dosage of penicillin is sometimes required to obliterate the disease.

Postpartum and Postabortive Infection

Here the history of onset following delivery or abortion is of obvious importance. The symptomatology is similar to that described for the gonorrheal group except that in the, more virulent cases, usually of streptococcal type, prostration is more marked, and chills not infrequently occur. The symptoms may manifest themselves within 6 or 8 hours or not for a number of days following the delivery or abortion. Where a definite history of criminal induction of abortion through instrumentation is obtained, the appearance of such symptoms as described leaves little doubt as to the origin of the infection. In many cases, even those of very virulent type, there is very little pain, although the systemic intoxication may be profound. There is a tendency to localization in the pelvis, with often a residue in the form of a large pelvic inflammatory mass or a broad ligament cellulitis or abscess. Unlike the gonorrheal cases, the fever in cases of this group is apt to be persistent, dragging along for weeks and even months. The importance of blood cultures, both aerobic and anaerobic, cannot be too strongly emphasized.

Many clinicians are beginning to feel that evacuation of the necrotic uterine contents will decrease the fever much sooner and thus avoid prolonged hospitalization. Massive dosage of antibiotics for less than 24 hours is followed by curettage, a procedure undreamed of for the febrile patient heretofore. Yet preliminary results indicate no ill effects, and make possible great financial and time saving to the patient. Considerable care must be exercised not to perforate the soft edematous uterus.

DIFFERENTIAL DIAGNOSIS

Acute Appendicitis

Although the initial pain in acute appendicitis may be diffuse, it soon tends to localize in the right lower abdomen, and this is even more true of the tenderness, which is sharply limited to the McBurney area. There is only slight fever, with a leukocytosis which in proportion to the fever is much higher than NNith pelvic inflammation. The problem is more difficult and sometimes impossible in the case of a perforative appendicitis with peritonitis. Under such conditions the abdominal pain, tenderness, and rigidity, like that of acute pelvic inflammation, involve the whole lower abdominal zone. Moreover, fever my be quite high and the pulse rapid. with considerable prostration. Nausea and vomiting are apt to be more severe than with pelvic inflammation and usually abdominal distention is much more pronounced. The history, especially that of an onset with original localization in the right lower quadrant as well as a record of previous attacks of appendicitis, is of the greatest value. Finally, while pelvic examination may show some tenderness even in cases of appendiceal peritonitis, it is rarely as clear-cut and pronounced as in the severe case of acute pelvic inflammation. while in some cases of the latter definite adnexal enlargement, or possibly even a pelvic abscess, may be palpable.

Acute Pyelitis

Although the kidneys are situated far above the pelvic level, the fact remains that severe acute pyelitis can at times produce a clinical picture not unlike that of acute pelvic inflammatory disease. High fever, accelerated pulse, abdominal pain, tenderness and distention, nausea and vomiting, and high leukocytosis are all frequent symptoms. The pain of pyelitis usually involves chiefly the upper abdominal zone, although sometimes it is general over the entire abdomen. Palpation over the kidney region may show marked tenderness in the costovertebral angle. With pyelitis there may be a high fever and some pain, but patients do not appear as ill or distressed as with salpingitis or appendicitis.

As a rule the abdominal pain of pyelitis is preceded or accompanied by pain in the lumbar region, radiating along the flanks, and there is likely to be increased frequency of urination, with some dysuria and tenesmus, although in a surprising proportion of cases such symptoms are not elicited. Of obvious importance is microscopic examination of the catheterized urine, which in pyclitis is likely to reveal large numbers of pus cells, often in clumps. Because of edema and ureteral blockage with poor drainage, however, the urine may be entirely negative for considerable periods of time.

Suppurating Ovarian Cyst

The occurrence of infection or torsion of an ovarian cyst gives rise to symptoms quite like those of acute pelvic inflammatory disease. but there may be a history of a previously existing tumor or on examination the rounded elastic unilateral tumor can be felt on pelvic and often on abdominal examination.

TREATMENT

Bed rest is preferable and usually easily enforced simply because the patient prefers this regimen and often spontaneously assumes a Fowler position because of the increased comfort due to relaxed abdominal muscle. This should be encouraged for it promotes gravitation of the infection to the pelvis: meals should be soft or liquid as determined by the presence of nausea or vomiting. and should these latter be pronunent intravenous fluids may be necessary. Fluids should be forced, the bowels regulated, and such analgesics or sedatives as aspirin and codeine or the barbiturates may be utilized.

Although there may be those individuals who consider douches or sitz baths inadvisable, we feel that heat in any form increases comfort and promotes resolution of the inflammatory process. Diathermy seems an expensive and cumbersome means of achieving the same effect, and this is rarely used.

In this day and age of high powered antibiotics it is well to remember that the much less expensive sulfonamides are frequently effective, and such drugs as Gantrisin or Kynex are usually tolerated well without toxic effects. A multitude of oral penicillin compounds are available, and these are also effective. A combination of the sulfonamides and penicillin seems of synergistic value, and this is frequently given for 4 to 7 days. Our own preference is to utilize these drugs initially, the more expensive broad spectrum antibiotics being held in reserve.

When strains of the disease resistant to sulfonamide-penicillin therapy are found, most of the antibiotics may be utilized with occasional good results. Streptomycin, chloromycetin, and tetracycline are a few of the many such agents available. Should there be no clinical response, the possibility of an acid-fast origin must he considered as well as such complications as a localized abscess or suppurative thrombophlebitis. Cortisone has been suggested by Collins for its antifibrotic tendencies.

Surgery during Acute Stage

Generally speaking, surgery should be avoided during the acute stage, but as mentioned previously there is a growing tendency to early curettage in conjunction with inassive antibiotic treatment where bleeding is a problem.

In other cases, especially of the Streptococcus variety most common after criminal abortions, examination may show enormous thickening and infiltration of the broad ligaments, with a continuing septic type of fever and, later, a suspicion of broad ligament abscess. Most of these cases are more safely drained through a gridiron incision just above Poupart's ligament than through the vagina, the latter carrying with it some risk of injury to the ureter or the uterine artery. A pelvic abscess, when sufficiently soft and pointing low in the rectovaginal septum. deserves posterior colpotomy. In rare instances, rupture of a tuba ovarian abscess may occur during this acute stage. and this may produce symptoms of shock which may even simulate those seen with rupture of a tubal pregnancy. When there is a strong suspicion of this complication. pelvic laparotomv is indicated; otherwise morbidity and mortality are high. Generally complete pelvic "clean-cut" is preferable to unilateral adnexectomy, as noted by Vermeeren and Te Linde. Pedowitz and Bloomfield note 100 % mortality in the early days of conservative therapy, with a current figure of less than 4% with mn extreme degree of surgery, combined with massive antibiotic therapy. It must be stressed that a ruptured tuboovarian abscess is a serious complication with considerable morbidity and some mortality.

Attention may also be called to the frequent simulation of mechanical obstruction in cases of acute pelvic peritonitis, associated as it may be with an adynamic or paralytic ileus. In most cases it is' advisable to institute such nonsurgical measures as intestinal decompression as promptly as possible, but one should not delay too long if improvement does not occur, because of the real possibility of obstruction of a mechanical type.

Finally, there is an occasional but inevitable case in which there is doubt between an acute salpingitis and an acute appendicitis. Although it should be an infrequent occurrence, it is better to err on the side of safety and to remove an occasional appendix unnecessarily than to run the hazard of appendiceal perforation and peritonitis.

Chronic Gonadal Diseases

Even a single attack of acute pelvic inflammation used to leave some residue of chronic disease and this was likely to be marked by repeated reinfection and exacerbations. The peritoneal involvement was indicated by the development of pelvic adhesions involving the uterus, tubes, and ovaries. Currently, it would appear that the newer antibiotics may completely cure salpingitis without the usual residue of "closed tubes" and sterility. Unquestionably, this is a factor in the increased Negro birth rate.

Chronic Endometritis

This is a relatively common lesion, although much less so than was once believed. Even in the presence of extensive chronic adnexitis, the endometrium may be entirely normal, due to the usually good drainage of the uterine canal, and also because of the monthly desquamation of menstruation. For example, the Gonococcus is a frequent invader of the endometrium, over which the infection travels upward to the tube. Acute forms of endometrial infection are rather rarely encountered in laboratory material, for as the endometritis becomes chronic it is attenuated with each menstrual desquamation, so that after two or three cycles the endometrium is rather completely purged of its infection. Reinfections from the cervix, however, are very frequent.

The *microscopic characteristics* of chronic salpingitis are similar to those of chronic inflammation„'elsewhere. The chief feature is a more or less extensive infiltration with round and plasma cells.

One of the most common forms of chronic endometritis is the *postabortive.* Retention of placental tissue is frequent after either full term delivery or abortion, especially the latter. Even in spontaneous abortion, the uterine cavity is soon invaded by organisms from the cervix and vagina, so that one may expect to find chronic endometritis in all the very numerous cases of incomplete miscarriage in which operative removal of the retained placental tissue is necessary. So frequent is this association that it is a good rule in all cases of chronic endometritis to examine the microscopic slides for chorionic villi and other evidences of recent pregnancy.

When villi are found they may be well preserved or they may show marked degeneration with fibrosis or hyalinization (ghost or shadow villi). Not infrequently the retained villi may form a polypoid mass of grumous material firmly attached to the uterine wall. The finding of villi is absolutely diagnostic of preceding pregnancy. Decidual cells are also often found. When they are well preserved, and have the typical appearance of large polygonal cells put together in mosaic fashion, there can be little doubt of preceding pregnancy. However, since decidual cells are of maternal origin, they cannot be considered as decisive in diagnosis as the fetal villi, and they may at times be simulated by other cells, such as those of certain types of epidermoid cancer. Some degree of myometritis may be a concomitant of endometritis.

Subinvolution of Uterus

Subinvolution of the uterus, as the term indicates, refers to the condition in which postpartum or postabortum involution is incomplete. The term, however, is not merely a clinical one, for Schwarz and his coworkers, as well as other writers, have shown that it is characterized by distinctive histological changes. Whereas normally involution is complete in 8 or 10 weeks after delivery, the subinvoluted uterus may show, many months later, a persistent moderate enlargement and congestion, especially when it is retrodisplaced, as it so commonly is. The syndrome of "pelvic congestion" as described by Taylor seems to us to be a rather nebulous dumping ground for all kinds of vague psychosomatic problems, and a frequent excuse in attempting justification of questionable hysterectomies before tissue committees.

The chief *microscopic* feature appears to be an increased amount of elastic tissue around the vessels and between the muscle bundles as a result of incompleteness of absorption of this tissue following delivery. Another characteristic finding is the formation of new blood vessels in the lumina of the degenerated and obliterated original vessels.

Chronic Salpingitis

This may be present either in the form of a diffuse chronic inflammation of the tubal wall (chronic interstitial salpingitis) or of certain sequelae of the inflammatory process. marked by overdistention of the tube with retained exudate (pyosalpinx or hydrosalpinx).

An interesting special variety of chronic salpingitis is the so-called *salpingitis isthtnica nodosa,* in which the residue of a sustained chronic inflammatory process is limited chiefly to the isthmic portion of the tube. In such cases marked modulation of the tubal isthmus is seen. the nodules being sometimes so large as to simulate small cornual fibroid tumors. The remainder of the tube may seem fairly normal, and the fimbriated end may be open, although in other cases the entire tube is thickened and the end closed and bulbous.

Microscopic examination in such cases presents a curious picture, in that there may appear to be many small lumina instead of just one. The original isthmic lumen may or may not be still recognizable, but in addition to this, many epithelium-lined glandlike cavities are scattered throughout the muscularis. Such cases are often mistaken for adenomyosis of the tube, but they differ from the latter in that the lining epithelium is tubal rather than uterine, that endometrial stroma is lacking, and that the muscle shows various degrees of round cell infiltration. Occasionally, however, distinction is very difficult.

Hydrosalpinx

Gonorrheal infection especially is prone to cause inflammatory obstruction at various points in the tube, especially the uterine and fimbriated ends. Purulent material is retained between the obstructed areas, with often enormous distention of the tube, constituting *pyosalpinx*. Mention has already been made of the fact that the invading organisms tend to disappear within a short time, with the ultimate formation of a *hvdrosalpinx;* and either may present as a large adherent mass frequently mistaken for an ovarian cyst. Various tubo-ovarian inflammatory masses may occur.

The microscopic picture of *pyosalpinx* is that of chronic inflammatory infiltration of the thickened walls, adhesions on the peritoneal surface, round and plasma cell infiltration of the tubal folds, degeneration and sometimes loss of considerable areas of the covering epithelium, and the presence of a large amount of pus within the lumen.

Two types of *hydrosalpinx* are described, *simplex* and *follicularis*. In the former the lumen on cross section is seen to consist of a single thin-walled cavity. In the follicular variety, on the other hand, it is divided into a number of, sometimes many, small compartments by *trabeculae* representing the fused tubal folds. In this variety, the overdistention of the lumen is preceded by a follicular salpingitis in which thus same matting together and fusion of adjacent folds takes place.

As to the cause of hydrosalpinx, there would seem to be little doubt that the condition is the frequent end result of long standing pyosalpinx, in which the purulent elements have been resorbed and a clear fluid left. This is confirmed by the fact that hydrosalpinx is rarely found unless the history indicates that the pelvic disease has been of long duration.

The *microscopic* appearance of hydrosalpinx simplex shows a clear cystic central cavity, with a flattened tubal mucosa whose folds have been ironed out and almost or entirely obliterated although, usually an occasional small fold can be seen here and there. The thinned-out wall of the tube often shows little or no evidence, in the form of inflammatory change, of the infection which had occurred perhaps many years previously.

In hydrosalpinx folliculans, as mentioned in the grass description, the distended lumen presents a multilocular appearance, each locule being a cross section of a gutter-like subdivision of the lumen. As in the simple variety, there is apt to be little microscopic evidence of the infectious storm which had passed over the tube long before.

Chronic Oophoritis and Perioophoritis

The ovaries may be extensively involved in chronic pelvic. inflammatory disease, but on the whole much less frequently than the tubes. In most cases the ovarian involvement is secondary to that of the adjacent tube. Infection may enter the ovary through the portals of ruptured follicles, and either a chronic oophoritis or an abscess thus result. In the former the ovarian stroma may show considerable inflammatory infiltration; in the latter large accumulations of pus may develop, not infrequently merging with an adjacent pyosalpinx to, form a *tuboovarian abscess*. The so-called cystic degeneration of the ovary is not infrequent, presumably from an exaggeration of the process of atresia folliculi as a result of the inflammatory hyperemia. Various "tubo-ovarian inflammatory cysts" may be formed.

Perhaps the most frequent of all ovarian lesions in chronic pelvic inflammatory disease is *chronic perioophoritis,* which is practically always found when the ovarian substance is involved, and in addition is often present when the ovary itself is comparatively normal. The surface involvement of the ovary is expressed through the presence of adhesions of light or dense fibrous texture. The germinal epithelium often extends to the undersurface of such adhesions, producing slitlike or glandlike spaces which may be mistaken for endometriosis, especially as the epithelium often becomes cuboidal or cvlindric as a result of the inflammatory stimulus.

SYMPTOMS OF CHRONIC PELVIC INFLAMMATORY DISEASE

In some cases a history of an initial acute attack of pelvic inflammation, with sometimes even the history of a definite gonorrheal infection or some other causative factor, such as infection after childbirth or criminal abortion, is obtainable, but in the majority of cases no such definite starting point in the symptomatology can be clearly established. As a rule the symptoms develop gradually, although at any time the clinical course of chronic pelvic inflammatory disease may be punctuated by acute exacerbations.

Pain may be so severe as to incapacitate the patient, but in a surprisingly large proportion it is of moderate or mild degree, even in the presence of extensive pelvic pathology. It is expressed generally as a *bearing-down or aching discomfort in the lower abdominal quadrants* and pelvic regions, but it is sometimes described as sharp and severe. Rather characteristically the pain is exaggerated just before or during menstruation. In the earlier stages the patient may complain of only occasional discomfort, especially on exertion or on prolonged standing. Later the discomfort may become constant and severe.

Backache and rectal discomfort or pressure are frequent complaints, explainable by the fact that the diseased adnexa impinge upon the back and rectum, to which they are not infrequently adherent. *Dvsmenorrhea* is the most common of the menstrual symptoms, and it may be so severe as to necessitate bed rest for a day or two each month. *Menorrhagia* is not uncommon, although rarely excessive, and *disturbances in menstrual rhythm* are also frequent, generally in the direction of a shortening of the intervals.

Bayly and Satlin point out that patients with chronic pelvic inflammatory disease are apt to have abnormal bleeding of one sort or another. We concur with their ideas as well as their impression that the mechanism of the bleeding is often uncertain.

Sterility is an unfortunate feature of many cases, particularly those of gonorrheal type. this disease being one of the most important of all causes of childlessness. Leukorrhea of some degree is almost always noted. It is not due to the adnexal disease *per se,* but is the result of the chronic cervical infection so commonly associated. Bladder irritability, with increased frcquent; of urination, dysuria, or tenesmus, may be observed even when there is no associated inflanunatory involvement of the bladder or urethra.

Various *secondary svniptons* may in the longstanding case be superimposed on the more directly pelvic manifestations already mentioned. Nervous irritability, loss of appetite and weight, insomnia, depression, and various other general symptoms may follow the constant nagging discomfort of which some patients complain. On the other hand it may again be emphasized that *many a woman who has undoubted chronic adnexitis suffers verv little or perhaps no discomfort whatsoever.*

DIAGNOSIS

When such symptoms as have been described develop following an acute attack of pelvic infection, or when there is a history of gonorrhea in either husband or wife, or a history of criminal abortion, the natural suspicion must be of chronic pelvic inflammatory disease. Even when no such history is obtainable, such an array of symptoms as those described in the previous section would be highly suggestive. One should remember that the Gonococcus does not respect social status.

More important than the history is the physical examination, and especially bimanual palpation of the pelvic organs. This reveals in the typical case a small or large, usually irregular, tender and rather fixed mass in both sides of the pelvis and sometimes filling the cul-de-sac. The uterus may be in normal position, but is often retroverted or retroflexed, and often much less movable than normally. Efforts to move it about by manipulation of the cervix or fundus may cause much pain, and drawing the cervix forward will also make the patient complain of pain, which not infrequently is referred to the rectum. The uterosacral ligaments are often thickened and sensitive. but not nodular as in endometriosis. Examination under anesthesia is frequently helpful, especially in the tense patient.

DIFFERENTIAL DIAGNOSIS

Among the pelvic conditions which may be mistaken for chronic pelvic inflammatory disease, and vice versa, is *ectopic pregnancy*. In the latter condition there is likely to be a history of slight delay, in menstruation, followed by persistent slight bleeding of a "spotting" character. Sometimes. on the other hand, the flow may be anticipated by a number of days. In pelvic inflammatory disease the menstrual rhythm ectopic pregnancy the pain is likely to be colicky, severe, and one-sided, with not infrequently associated nausea and attacks of faintness. The latter are lacking in chronic pelvic inflammation, and the pain is most often bilateral and of heavy bearing-down or aching character. Pelvic examination in cases of tubal pregnancy shows a unilateral tender mass. with no tenderness in the opposite side. Culdoscopic examination is generally decisive. and this simple cndoscopic method of visualizing the pelvic organs is highly recommended in the study of many pelvic complaints.

Evaluation of tubal disease is often facilitated by examination under anesthesia along with curettage which may on occasion reveal a tuberculous disease. We likewise feel that a Rubin's test may be of assistance in the distinction of inflammatory disease and endometriosis. Sweeney rightly emphasizes the possibility of false negative or positive tests, but gives us the impression that insulation is just about as useful as hysterograms, especially if proper techniques and interpretation are not to be had. We feel that evaluation of hysterosalpingograms is not always completely reliable; for examplc, a recent patient with an apparent complete cornual blockage in her only remaining tube subsequently became pregnant.

Pelvic endometriosis is another condition which may be difficult to distinguish from chronic pelvic inflammatory disease. In either, there may be a history of pelvic pain, increasing dysmenorrhea, dyspareunia, and involuntary sterility, and in either the pelvic examination may reveal the adnexa to be enlarged and adherent to the posterior surface of a retroplaced uterus. The presence of one or more nodules in the uterosacral ligaments is always highly suggestive of endometriosis, but this physical sign is often absent. Of circumstantial value is the fact that endometriosis is more likely to occur in the higher types of patient, while pelvic inflammatory disease is more apt to be seen in the dispensary group. In the presence of severe symptoms of the type enumerated above, surgery is likely to be indicated with either disease, so that failure to make an accurate preoperative diagnosis works no hardship on the patient.

Ideopathic retroperitoneal fibrosis is placed in this chapter with certain misgivings, for it is by no means certain that this represents an inflammatory process. Actually it is a rather new entity in gynecological journals, and it is only in the last 5 years that this ill defined disease has been recognized by us, although such urologists as Ormond noted it earlier.

Clinically the symptoms are rather vague, consisting primarily of nondescript pain with occasional nausea, anorexia, low grade fever, and urinary symptoms. Pelvic examination may suggest varying degrees of induration or the presence of a mass, and pyelography often shows bilateral ureteral obstruction with a tendency towards medial displacement of the ureters.

The cause is highly speculative; infections of various types including tuberculosis, collagen disorders, hypersensitivity reaction, and a host of other etiological factors have been suggested. That it is an infection of the pelvis (admittedly retroperitoneal) with subsequent lyinphangitis and fibrosis seems most likely. Treatment has generally consisted of lysis of the obstructed ureter. occasionally with intraperitoneal fixation, although x-ray and cortisone have also been suggested as therapeutic measures.

TREATMENT

The trend of recent years in the management of chronic pelvic inflammatory disease has been definitely a conservative one, although there are still many cases in which surgery must be invoked. It should be remembered, first of all, that the disease is rarely a life-endangering one, so that efforts at conservative treatment are not fraught with any real danger to the patient, as is the case with certain other gynecological diseases.

In women with large tubo-ovarian masses and with often a retrodisplaced uterus firmly fixed to the rectum, and with troublesome symptoms which can not be relieved by palliative measures, surgery is fully justified. This is true even in the case of younger women, especially when repeated tubal patency tests have shown the tubes to be closed. If pregnancy is to be denied such women, the next best thing is to restore them to health, as can be done in most cases by surgery. The results of plastic procedures to restore tubal patency are notoriously poor, but they are justified if the patient is exceedingly anxious for even the slightest possibility of success, and if the slimness of her chances in this respect is honestly put before her.

It must also be remembered that women with chronic pelvic

inflammatory disease must run the risk of acute exacerbations as a result of reinfection from the cervix or from an infected sex partner. This is probably the usual explanation of such exacerbation, rather than the assumption of a flare-up in a dormant tubal infection (Curtis). In any event, if exacerbatioxis occur rather frequently in spite of treatment of lower genital foci and efforts to prevent marital reinfection, surgery may be indicated, but it should be done in a quiescent period of the disease. Abdominal operation is always contraindicated in the acute stage, and should ordinarily be deferred for a number of weeks after subsidence of the acute symptoms.

On the whole, however, conservative treatment is indicated when the patient gets along quite comfortably, with perhaps no discomfort other than slight dysmenorrhea or occasional slight bearing- down in the pelvic region, or perhaps not even these symptoms. Even if the symptoms are much more pronounced, there is no urgency in recommending surgical treatment, and conservative treatment should be given a trial. This consists of such simple measures as enforcing a reasonable amount of rest. moderation in sexual intercourse. the eradication of any foci of infection in the cervix, urethra, or vulvovaginal glands, the avoidance insofar as possible of reinfection, and the use of hot douches or sitz baths. Some have advocated the use of some form of cortisone (for its antifbrotic effect) in conjunction with antibiotics.

When, on the other hand, the patient becomes increasingly miserable because of pain in the lower abdomen, severe dysmenorrhea, menstrual irregularities, and sometimes even a condition of semiin-validism, elective operation is ordinarily indicated. In the same way, the nature and extent of the operation must be decided on an individual basis. In most cases, unfortunately, both tubes are involved and both must often be removed. If one tube is still patent and the patient exceedingly anxious for children, she will usually be willing to run the risk of a possible second operation later on, if she can be honestly told that she has at least some chance of pregnancy.

Even if both tubes are closed, some form of plastic operation such as salpingostomy, resection and tubouterine anastomosis, or cornual implantation of the ovaries is justified in the occasional case in which the woman is desperately anxious for motherhood, with full explanation of the very small percentage of successful results in such cases, probably not over about 5%.

Results with tuboplastic surgery following tubal sterilization are somewhat better, for one is not dealing with a basically diseased tube. Indeed operation on infected closed tubes may often restore patency but not the vital physiological and peristaltic action of the oviduct. Siegler and Hellman have recently reviewed the prerequisites for and results with tubal plastic surgery in 50 patients. Hanton, Pratt, and Banner report 18 pregnancies among 75 women treated by a variety of tuboplastic procedures; however, 74% of those studied had patent tubes immediately postoperative although in those studied later, tubal patency was present in 55%.

When both tubes are so hopelessly involved that their removal is necessary, opinion is uniform that hysterectomy is advisable. There is no reason to preserve the uterus when pregnancy cannot ensue, but of course the woman should be advised as to what hysterectomy will entail. The true facts are apt to be very different from what she had heard in the beauty parlor or her bridge club. Only in the youthful. unrealistic woman who cannot be convinced of the unimportance of continued menstruation should the uterus be preserved. Total hysterectomy is the operation of choice. but it is preferable to leave the cervix should removal pose a threat to the integrity ofureter. bladder. or bowel. When the discriminating surgeon suspects he may have a difficult operative case, he will perform office biopsy and smear. If these are negative the decision to abstain from removal of the cervix is made much more simple.

Finally, the *importance of conserving ovarian tissue* whenever possible cannot be too strongly emphasized. Practically all operations for pelvic inflammatory disease are done on women in the reproductive age for the cessation of menstruation seems to uniformly end the stimulus to "flare-ups" even when infection has been present. Entirely aside from the question of pregnancy, and even when this is obviously impossible, the retention of ovarian tissue may spare the woman many of the possible discomforts of an artificial menopause. It is perfectly true that oven complete ablation of both ovaries in young women may cause only slight menopausal disturbance, but in a small proportion the symptoms are sufficiently severe that, in the woman's own mind, her lot is far worse than before operation. Where one tube is closed but not hopelessly distorted, it seems preferable on occasion to preserve the entire adnexa. Removal of the tube alone, especially where adherent, is often attended by marked cystic changes in the ovary. In any case preservation of some ovarian tissue can usually be accomplished.

15

FAILURE OF MENSTRUATION

Amenorrhea is not a disease but a symptom and may be arbitrarily defined as the absence of menses for 3 months or longer. *Primary amenorrhea* is defined as the failure of menses to appear initially and should not be diagnosed before the patient has reached the age of 18 years. *Secondary amenorrhea* implies the cessation of menses after an initial menarche. *Physiological amenorrhea* is the normal absence of menses before puberty, during pregnancy and lactation, and after the menopause. *Cryptomenorrhea* signifies that menstruation actually occurs but does not appear externally because of obstruction of the lower genital canal. *Oligomenorrhea* is defined as a reduction in the frequency of . menses; the interval must be longer than 38 days but less than 3 months. This must not be confused with the term *hypomenorrhea,* which is used to designate the reduction in the number of days or the amount of menstrual flow.

Incidence

It is difficult to arrive at a statistical evaluation of the occurrence of amenorrhea and oligomenorrhea in a general gynecological practice but it probably comprises less than 5% of patients. This figure will, of course, vary with the socioeconomic status of the patients as well as the geographical location. Kaeser finds the incidence of primary amenorrhea among 15,000 gynecological patients, over a 10 year period, to be 0.65%.

Classification

As indicated, amenorrhea and oligomenorrhea are symptoms which may be caused by a variety of etiological factors. A single individual with a constant etiological background may show at various times any or all of the pathological manifestations of menstruation. including dysfunctional utc.ine bleeding. oligomenorrhea. amenorrhea. infertility and habitual abortion. It is most satisfactory, therefore, whenever possible, to make the classification of these symptom complexes on the basis of the underlying etiological disturbance. The following outline shows the etiological classification of amenorrhea to be used in the discussion. Etiological Classification of Amenorrhea

I. Lesions of central origin

A. Neurogenic

1. Organic
2. Idiopathic hypothalamic dysfunction - Stein syndrome
3. Inhibition of the prolactin inhibition factor-Chiari-Frommel

B. *Pituitary disturbances*

1. Insufficiency
   (a) Destructive processes (Sheehan's and Simmonds' disease)
2. Tumors
   (a) Chromophobe adenoma (Ahumada-del Castillio)
   (b) Acidophilic adenoma (acromegaly)
   (c) Basophilic adenoma (Cushing's disease)
3. Congenital defects (?)
   (a) Hypogonadotrophic eunuchoidism

C. Psychogenic amenorrhea

1. Major and minor psychosis
2. Emotional shock
3. Pseudocyesis
4. Anorexia nervosa

II. Lesions of intermediate origin

A. Chronic illnesses

B. Metabolic diseases

1. Thyroid
   (a) Hypothyroidism and hyperthyroidism
2. Pancreas

(a) Diabetes mellitus

3. Adrenal

(a) Congenital adrenal hyperplasia, adrenogenital syndrome, and related disturbances

(b) Cushing's disease and "stress obesity"

C. Nutritional disturbances

1. Malnutrition
2. Exogenous obesity

D. Excretory and metabolic disease

1. Liver cirrhosis
2. Chronic nephritis (?)

III. Lesions of peripheral origin

A. Ovarian amenorrhea

1. Insufficiency

(a) Congenital developmental defects-hermaphroditism and related conditions

(1) Gonadal dysgenesis (Turner's syndrome)

(2) True hermaphroditism

(3) Male hermaphroditism

(4) Testicular feminizaticm syndrome

(b) Premature menopause

(c) Destructive lesions-abscesses, neoplasms, irradiation, and surgical trauma

2. Tumors

(a) Arrhenoblastoma, hilus cell, adrenal rest (b) Granulosa cell, thecoma

B. End organs-cryptomenorrhea

1. Congenital defects

(a) Imperforate hymen

(b) Absence or atresia of vagina

(c) Septum of vagina

(d) Absence of uterus (congenital absence of Mullerian ducts)

2. Traumatic

(a) Stenosis of vagina

(b) Stenosis of cervix

(c) Sclerosis of uterine cavity

IV. Physiological amenorrhea

A. Delayed puberty

B. Pregnancy

C. Postpartum amenorrhea

D. Menopause

V. Etiology undetermined

DIAGNOSIS AND TREATMENT

As oligomenorrhea and amenorrhea are symptoms of a great variety of difficulties, from organic brain disease to localized disorders in the pelvis, it is obvious that extensive tests and examinations may be required in order to make a correct etiological diagnosis. Optimal success in the therapy of amenor hea usually depends upon such a diagnosis. An outline of the clinical methods presently available is shown in Figure. The most careful observer is occasionally confronted with a patient in whom no etiological factor is demonstrable. It is undoubtedly incorrect to classify all such cases as of psychogenic origin, but such a practice is not uncommon and, until additional evidence is available, no more satisfactory solution can be suggested.

The endometrial findings among a group of amenorrheic and oligomenorrheic patients will show, in the main atrophic or nonsecretory patterns. However, there will be a moderate number of hyperplastic patterns, a few with endometritis, including tuberculosis and other forms of inflammatory and sclerotic processes, a few with abnormal secretory patterns, and, only rarely, normal secretory patterns.

Investigative Procedures

There is no substitute for a good history. This must include a careful reconstruction of the setting of the amenorrhea, emphasizing such factors as relate to emotional stress; gain or loss of weight; acute or chronic illnesses; accidents or injuries; relationship to pregnancy or possibility of unsuspected pregnancy; symptoms of characteristic metabolic diseases, such as polyuria and polydipsia or diabetes; susceptibility to temperature changes, changes in bowel habits and energy for thyroid disease; and the family history relating to menstrual characteristics, fertility, metabolic disease, or tuberculosis. In the case of primary amenorrhea the early developmental history, as well as a notation of possible birth trauma, is important.

Although a complete investigation for primary amenorrhea need not be undertaken until after the age of 18 years, a history should be obtained and a physical examination, including a pelvic or rectal examination, should be made whenever the patient, or her family, is concerned enough to consult a physician. If this is done one can detect congenital anomalies at an early age. when the best psychological adjustment of both child and parents is possible.

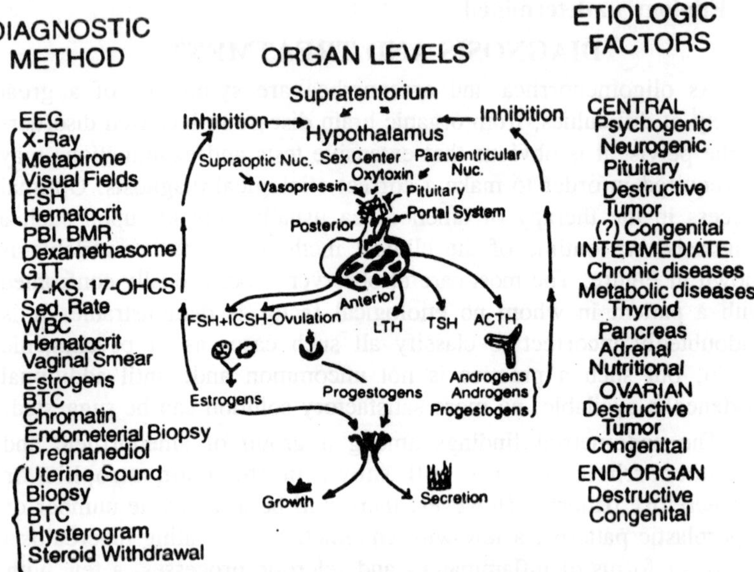

Fig. 15.1. Diagnostic methods correlated with anatomical levels at which defects responsible for amenorrhea may occur.

In the investigation of secondary amenorrhea an endometrial biopsy and, if any suspicion of tuberculosis exists, an acid-fast culture should be taken at the initial visit unless the possibility of an intrauterine pregnancy is present. This test is often a diagnostic shortcut and will indicate immediately (1) the ovarian status, (2) the possibility of pregnancy complications, and (3) end organ factors such as tuberculous endometritis and traumatic amenorrhea. A Papanicolaou smear with maturation index and cervical mucus study will also help in the evaluation of ovarian function and should be obtained at the preliminary examination. In all patients with primary amenorrhea a buccal smear for sex chromatin should be taken to exclude problems of intersexuality, including the triplo-X syndrome.

Other examinations will depend upon the specific problems involved and may include special examinations such as neurological and opthalmological examinations: culdoscopic examination or gyneeography; x-ray of the sella turcica and chest: electroencephalogram: hematology with sedimentation rate included: liver and kidney function studies: thyroid function studies; a glucose tolerance test; hormonal analysis, such as 17-ketosteroid, 17-hydroxysteroid, urinary estrogen, and gonadotrophin assays; basal body temperature charts; and steroid withdrawal tests.

General Considerations for Therapy

Each patient must be treated according to the etiological factors involved and such specific therapy will be outlined under the specific headings. Only general considerations will be discussed in the following paragraphs.

Amenorrhea *per se* is not necessarily an indication for therapy. Although the production of a regular menstrual flow is possible whenever there is a functioning end organ with no obstruction of the lower genital passage, the production of ovulation is quite a different matter. Because the treatment of anovulation is often unsatisfactory and usually involves long continued endocrine therapy, and the simple initiation of menstrual bleeding is rarely justifiable, a careful analysis must be made of each individual patient to determine if her symptoms warrant treatment. In patients with oligomenorrhea there is usually no necessity for any treatment other than reassurance and general measures, since fertility is usually not appreciably impaired. This is, of course, especially true if the patient is approaching the 40's, or if childbearing is unimportant.

On the other hand, there are certain patients in whom efforts at treatment are indicated. These include the following groups.

1. Young women, married or unmarried, in whom the possibility of future pregnancies is of the greatest importance. As a matter of fact, it is the commonly associated sterility rather than the amenorrhea which often prompts the married woman to seek medical advice.

2. Women who, in spite of the physician's reassurance, are depressed and upset because of absence of menstruation.

3. Patients who have some associated medical problem.

Primary amenorrhea is notoriously much less responsive to treatment than the secondary variety. Not a few girls who later menstruate normally exhibit late puberty, so that ovarian organotherapy is rarely justifiable in patients under 17. On the other hand, it seems to be true that patients whose first menstruation does not appear until perhaps the age of 17 or 18 are more prone to later irregularities than those who reach puberty at the expected age of 14 or thereabout. The advice to abstain from organotherapy in girls below 17 does not apply to those patients who present clear evidence of endocrinopathy of one sort or another. nor does it mean that such general measures as rest and proper food should not be advised whenever necessary regardless of the patient's age.

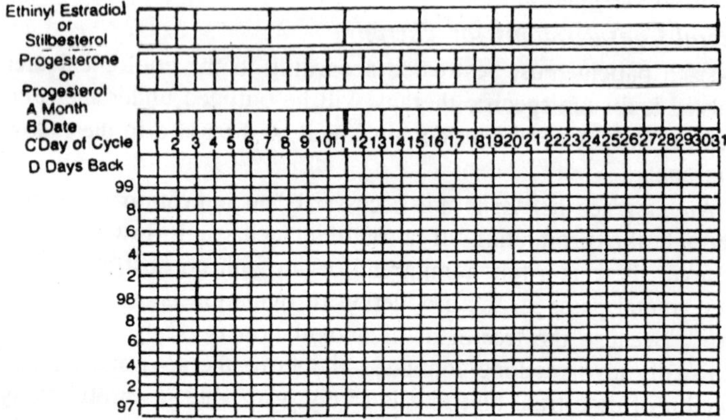

Fig. 15.2. One schedule for cyclindrical steroid therapy. This has been designed to reproduce, as far as possible, the normal hormonal findings. The correlation wi th tha basal temperature is valuable in judging the effectiveness of the therapy. (Progestoral is a trade name for ethisterone or pregneninolone).

There are several general methods advocated for the production of ovulation when the amenorrhea is due to factors located in the nervous system, e.g., psychosomatic, neurogenic, or hypothalamic. (1) steroid therapy designed to trigger pituitary function; (2) gonadotrophic therapy designed to replace pituitary function; (3) synthetic steroid therapy designed to suppress completely the pituitary and produce a rebound phenomenon; (4) irradiation therapy of the ovary according to the Kaplan method which apparently affects the pituitary secondarily by producing an initial estrogenic flood (Rakoff); and (5) clomiphene therapy which apparently stimulates pituitary activity via the hypothalamus. As clomiphene is an antiestrogenic drug, its action on the hypothalamus may be to block the estrogen inhibitory effect.

There are many steroid schedules which can be used in an effort to trigger pituitary function. Intravenous estrogens have been proposed in lieu of cyclic steroid therapy. but the results are no better than those obtained with oral preparations and as the theoretical risk of complications is always increased with intravenous medication, it should not be advocated when other methods are equally satisfactory. or unsatisfactory, as is usually the case.

Gonadotrophin Therapy

The successful use of gonadotrophin therapy has heretofore been handicapped by sensitivity reactions, due to a foreign protein, and loss of responsiveness, presumably due to the formation of anti-hormones. Both of these adverse reactions apparently arose from the use of animal gonadotrophins. With the availability of human gonadotrophin these two most troublesome problems have been overcome. There still remains the problem of proper dosage and, although progress has been made, it has been handicapped by the lack of truly purified hormone preparations; all of the currently availabe gonadotrophins are a mixture of both FSH and ICSH. However a menopausal urine gonadotrophin has been purified to a satisfactory degree to be clinically useful as an FSH source and human chorionic gonadotrophin, HCG, from pregnancy urine has proved to be a satisfactory substitute for pituitary ICSH (LH).

For the proper use, rather than abuse, of these new therapeutic tools, it is necessary (1) to make an etiologic diagnosis in order to select the proper patients for therapy, (2) to arrive at a proper dose schedule, and (3) to be familiar with possible complications which may arise.

Any lesion of central origin will respond to gonadotrophic therapy. However, the classic indication is hypogonadotrophic eunuchoidism. It is obvious that pituitary tumors should be carefully excluded and, in consideration of the treatment of patients with psychogenic amenorrhea or Sheehan's disease, factors other than gynecologic should play a major role in the selection of suitable patients. Although clomiphene is the treatment of choice in hypothalamic amenorrhea, if one elects to use gonadotrophins it is especially important that the urinary gonadotrophin assay be below 6.6 mp124 hours. If the patient has a detectable pituitary function of her own this will invalidate the dosage calculation and complications due to overdosage, which are multiple cysts and multiple pregnancies, will arise. The Stein-Leventhal syndrome is also specifically excluded as the polycystic ovary is peculiarly sensitive to gonadotrophin stimulation.

The dosage schedule which has been found satisfactory is 1500 to 2000 mg. equivalents of FSH, standardized against die European Standard menopausal urine preparation (IRP-HMG) given daily for approximately 10 to 14 days. When a rapid urinary estrogen assay is not available, the clinical evaluation suggested by Igarashi and Matsumoto can satisfactorily be used. A daily vaginal smear for a maturation index, and observation for the occurrence of cervical dilatation and estrogenic mucus. will indicate when a full estrogenic response has been obtained. This usually occurs between 10 and 14 days and, if no response has been obtained by 14 days, treatment should be discontinued. At the full estrogen response, following a 1-day rest period, 2500 IU of HCG are given for 4 days. In our experience this has been an adequate dose schedule to induce ovulation in the hypogonadotrophic, amenorrheic patient, and still low enough to obviate the complications of overdosage.

The major complications of gonadotrophin therapy are superovulations with multiple cyst formation and subsequent multiple pregnancies. These complications have led to death through rupture of the cysts, or rupture of the uterus during pregnancy. Therefore, it cannot be emphasized too strongly that, prior to treatment, an etiologic diagnosis must be established and a proper selection of patients must be made to insure that they do not have endogenous gonadotrophic function. A proper exogenous dosage must be employed and frequent pelvic examinations made; the maximum ovarian size is reached between 7 and 10 days after the initiation of the chorionic gonadotrophin which triggers the ovulation.

Pituitary suppression therapy in the production of ovulation as suggested by Garcia, Pincus, and Rock is usually as disappointing as cyclic steroid therapy. A synthetic progesterone with estrogen added is the most efficient therapy, and, beginning on the 5th-cycle day, 5 mg. daily are given for 24 days each month during a 3- to 6-month period. Treatment is not infrequently complicated by irregular bleeding during the first cycle. Following suppression, the gonadotrophic rebound may, on occasion, induce an improved ovarian function. As there is evidence that, at least, some progestational agents also have a direct effect upon the ovary caution must be used in the selection of the progestogen.

Although low dosage irradiation of the ovaries for the correction of menstrual abnormalities has been repeatedly demonstrated to be therapeutically effective, the radiation biologist and geneticist have been so emphatic in their caution against the use of therapeutic x-rays that most gynecologists have abandoned this form of treatment. The viewpoint is summarized by Glass in his review on radiation hazards.

Clomiphene

A number of years ago, a weak synthetic estrogen, tri-para-anisylchloroethylene (Tace) was developed as an antiestrogenic, and possibly an antifertility. drug. Many derivatives were synthesized in an effort to derive an antiestrogenic compound which would block gonadotrophin secretion. Experimental evidence indicated that clomiphene was satisfactory in the rat as it produced pituitary inhibition, blocked estrogen activity. and inhibited pregnancy. Subsequent clinical trials proved that in the human the reverse effect was produced; gonadotrophin secretion was increased and stimulation of ovarian function and excessive estrogen production ensued.

Although clomiphene is still classified as an experimental drug there have been so many successful clinical trials, with so few and such relatively mild complications, that it is reasonable to believe the drug will soon be commercially available. Its mode of action is apparently to block estrogen at the hypothalamic level, thus removing the inhibition to pituitary gonadotrophin production and allowing a gonadotrophic flood. The increased gonadotrophic secretion causes excessive ovarian stimulation with excretion of urinary estrogen, ovulation, and normal corpus luteum function.

The success rate of such therapy, as with any drug, depends upon the care and skill used in making an etiologic diagnosis when selecting patients suitable for therapy. The classic indication for clomiphene treatment is hypothalamic hypogonadotrophism. The inclusion of the Stein-Leventhal syndrome as a hypothalamic disease can be justified on the basis of experimental evidence and analogy with other endocrine metabolic disease states.

The most serious complications reported are the occurrence of multiple ovarian cysts with rupture, and multiple pregnancies. As the pathologic picture is similar to that seen with pituitary gonadotrophin administration, it seems clear that these effects are the results of a pituitary stimulation.

Transitory blurring of vision and hot flushes are not infrequent symptoms and an occasional patient notices some loss of scalp hair. This alopecia, however, has not been severe and regression occurs rapidly after cessation of treatment. If care is taken in using an initial low dosage over a short period and the patient is observed for evidence of ovarian stimulation and not retreated until the initial reaction has subsided, these complications of over stimulation can usually be avoided. Liver function studies should he made if there is a history of any liver disease. since clomiphene is excreted by way of the bile ducts.

Although many dosage schedules have been reported, it would seem that 50 mg. daily for 5 to 10 days. repeated after 30 days if necessary is a good standard procedure to start with. The lowest dosage should be used in patients with the Stein- Leventhal syndrome. If no effect is observed after 3 cycles, the dosage can be increased to 100 ing. daily for 5 days. It is recommended that the total dosage in any single case not exceed 600 mg. in 1 month.

Although no adverse effects on the fetus have been reported in humans treated during early pregnancy, clomiphene has produced fetal anomalies in experimental animals. It is therefore recommended that treatment be avoided during pregnancy.

Thyroid

Thyroid has long been advocated as of therapeutic value in the correction of menstrual disorders; however, its empiric and indiscriminate use should not be encouraged. It will prove useful only when there is evidence of a low thyroid function as reflected in the basal metabolic rate, blood cholesterol, proteinbound iodine, or I'll uptake. When such evidence exist adequate thyroid dosage must be used and overdosage avoided; 0.2 to 0.3 mg. of sodium levothyroxine daily is usually sufficient and 3 months is the shortest possible therapeutic trial period. A repeat basal metabolic rate should show some improvement at this time. If there is none, however, this is not necessarily an indication for increased dosage, and reevaluation is advisable. There is no evidence that triiodothyronine is more efficient in hypothyroidism than are thyroid hormones; however, a therapeutic effect can be obtained more rapidly. If this drug is used it must be remembered that one cannot rely upon the protein bound iodine as a standard for judging adequate replacement. The protein-bound iodine will be suppressed as a result of depression of pituitary production of thyro- trophic hormones and resultant thyroid inactivity. Under these circumstances a basal metabolic rate serves as a guide. Triiodothyronine is indicated when the hypometabolic state exists; this condition is characterized by a normal proteinhound iodine and lowered basal metabolic rate.

Nutrition

A good nutritional status is mandatory for the ultimate success of any treatment and must not be overlooked in our zeal for less mundane therapy.

LESIONS OF CENTRAL ORIGIN

Lesions of central origin can be subdivided into three major groups: (1) neurogenic, (2) psychogenic, and (3) pituitary. Neurogenic amenorrhea may be further subdivided into organic brain disease and idiopathic hypothalamic failure; psychosomatic amenorrhea into major and minor psychosis. emotional shock. anorexia nervosa. and pseudocyesis: and pituitary amenorrhea into pituitan insufficiency. tumors and congenital deficiency of gonadotrophic hormone production.

Neurogenic Lesions and Organic Brain Disease

Organic

The diagnosis of organic brain disease is made with the help of the physical examination and history of encephalitis or related infections. accidents, injuries, or exposure to toxic substances such as lead or carbon monoxide. Laboratory findings are characterized by a low, or low normal, urinary gonadotrophin excretion, lowered urinary estrogen excretion and a moderately atrophic vaginal smear. Depending upon the severity, or the position, of the neurological lesion, there may be associated abnormalities of laboratory findings related to thyroid, adrenal, or pancreatic functions. The electroencephalogram is a valuable diagnostic aid.

Kinnunen and Kauppinen, in a survey of 78 patients who had amenorrhea following brain injury, indicate that the duration of unconsciousness is a fairly good index of the possibility of amenorrhea. The prognosis in patients with neurogenic amenorrhea is poor except for those following acute trauma. Under these circumstances recovery may occur.

Adequate pituitary hormone therapy should be successful in bypassing the neurological lesions. In our series of 352 patients with amenorrhea, 9 had organic brain disease; 3 were related to central nervous system syphilis, 3 to traumatic epilepsy (probably from birth injuries), and 2 to cerebral accident; in 1 case there was a history of carbon monoxide poisoning and in the other a motor accident; 1 patient had multiple sclerosis.

Idiopathic Hypothalamic Insufficiency

In hypothalamic failure either the hypothalaiic cells are defective in their secretory ability or they are excessively sensitive to inhibitory stimulation. In either case there is a lack of stimulation to the pituitary gonadotrophic cells.

The cardinal symptom of idiopathic hypothalamic failure is infrequent, but usually ovulatory, menstruation; the menstrual irregularity dates from the menarche and is often associated with a family history of menstrual irregularities. On physical examination there are no detectable neurogenic or psychogenic factors, and despite a normal encephalogram the laboratory findings are similar to those in patients with organic brain disease.

There is usually no indication for therapy among this group of patients as pregnancy frequently occurs without difficulty. However, if infertility is a problem, regular menstruation with a reasonable expectation ofensuing pregnancy can usually be initiated with clomiphene. As this dnig is still quite new patients should be followed carefully, with frequent repeated pelvic examinations, to be sure that ovarian cysts have not been induced. Dosage should not be over 600 mg. total per month to avoid possible complications of alopecia, flushes, and visual symptoms mentioned in the preceding section on clomiphene.

Among our 352 amenorrhea patients, 9 were diagnosed as having idopathic hypothalamic failure. The prognosis in the group of patients is good and 4 of 6 patients adequately followed became pregnant.

The Stein-Leventhal Syndrome

The Stein-Leventhal syndrome is characterized by bilateral polycysic ovaries in association with infertility and anovulatory menstrual irregularities. These are manifest as either amenorrhea, oligomenorrhea, or functional uterine bleeding. A mild or marked degree of hirsutism is usually present. The one single criterion which must always be present to substantiate the diagnosis is bilaterally enlarged ovaries. Therefore the diagnosis cannot be made without some form of visualization of the ovaries. Stein has for many years advocated gynecography; however, culdoscopy is another method of visual diagnosis.

The differential diagnosis must often be made between the Stein syndrome and mild adrenal hyperplasia. A prolonged cortisone suppression test is sometimes helpful in this regard. A sufficient amount of adrenal hormone is given to maintain a suppression of 17-ketosteroid secretion to 6 mg. per 24 hours, or below, over a 6-month period; 25 to 50 mg. of cortisone acetate or its equivalent daily is usually satisfactory. The classic response in a patient with the Stein-Leventhal syndrome is a single ovulation usually within the first 6 weeks of treatment followed thereafter by a reversion to her previous state of anovulation. If continued ovulatory menses do not ensue or suppression cannot be sustained, a Stein syndrome is suspect. An adrenal tumor, however, may also be associated with these laboratory findings, and if the ketosteroid excretion is remarkably elevated, especially if there is also a high dehydroepian-drosterone excretion, this is most likely.

The ovaries of a patient with the Stein-Leventhal syndrome should be 1-1/2 to 2 times enlarged. They are often the size of the uterus which is frequently small, allowing one to feel three structures of equal size in the pelvis. Macroscopically. the ovaries are pearly white in appearance with multiple cysts beneath the capsule. Microscopically, they are characterized by a capsule formed by hyalinization of the interstitial tissue of the cortex directly beneath the germinal epithelium. This hyalinization may engulf the primordial follicles. There are numerous follicular cysts which characteristically have a thin granulosal lining and a marked luteinization of the theca interna. There are no corpora lutea present, although there may be evidences of old corpora albicantia (occasionally, however, even in a typical Stein-Leventhal syndrome a sporadic ovulation can occur). As all of these elements are present at times in the normal ovary and the findings represent simply an exaggeration of the normal, there is no diagnostic pathologic picture. Comparison of the "Stein-Leventhal ovary" and the ovary removed with hysterectomy performed for recurrent anovulatory bleeding would suggest that histological differentiation is impossible except for the marked bilateral enlargement of the "S.L." ovary; in other words, the difference is merely quantitative.

Therefore, the diagnosis cannot be made as a pathologic entity and one can only report the ovarian findings as "compatible with" those seen with the Stein-Leventhal syndrome. Contrariwise, however, although a positive finding is not diagnostic, a negative correlation, e.g., "not compatible with," is good evidence that one is not dealing with a Stein-Leventhal syndrome.

The excessive follicle maturation and hyperluteinization are indications of excessive gonadotrophic stimulation and excessive steroid production. Laboratory investigations indicate that this is indeed the case. *Ingersoll* and *McArthur* demonstrated that total urinary gonadotrophins are elevated, and, if a fractionation study is carried out, it is the ICSH which is responsible for the elevation. In patients who show endometrial hyperplasia and hyperestrogenism (25% of all cases), the urinary estrogen excretion is above normal while in patients who show hirsutism, the 17-ketosteroid excretion is usually slightly elevated or in the high normal range indicating excessive androgen secretion. This has been proved by the demonstration that in the polycystic ovary the ovarian vein blood contains excessive amounts of testosterone, as well as by *in vitro* experiments of *Sandor* and *Lanthier*. These authors have shown that slices from ovaries of patients with the androgenic form of the Stein-Leventhal syndrome transform A,-androstene-3,17-dione into testosterone at a more rapid rate than do slices from ovaries of normal women.

Other laboratory tests such as the vaginal maturation index, and the endometrial biopsy vary depending upon whether or not the ovary is producing excessive androgen or excessive estrogen. In the variety associated with excessive androgen production. the maturation index shows a complete shift to the left or a midzone shift *vti* ith atrophic endometrium, while in the estrogenic variety, the maturation index may be completely shifted to the right and the endometrium may show marked adenomatous hyperplasia.

Stein recognized many years ago that it was impossible to treat the syndrome with suppressive doses of steroids. *Keettel, Bradbury,* and *Stoddard* reported apparent hypersensitivity of the Stein- Leventhal ovary to pituitary gonadotrophins and described a remarkable ovarian enlargement which occurred following the use of these substances. *Crooke et al.* extended this work and indicated that under gonadotrophic stimulation polycystic ovaries could, be made to produce excessive amounts of estrogen and to ovulate with the production of normal or high amounts of progesterone. In our own experience it was found that ovarian cyst formation was produced only if pituitary gonadotrophins (predominantly FSH) were given and not if human chorionic gonadotrophin was given alone.

In resume then, the whole picture represents a patient with the paradoxical finding of *excessive gonadotrophin production* and ICSH predominance over FSH, in association with *excessive ovarian steroid formation* either androgen or estrogen. Additional *estrogens do not suppress the excessive gonadogrophin* production and stimulation with pituitary *gonadotrophins causes a hyperresponse* with multiple cyst formation.

Although the exact pathogenesis of the Stein-Leventhal syndrome is still not completely documented, the existing evidence establishes it as a isease of the neuroendocrine homeostatic control mechanism and places it in the same category as Cushing's syndrome and perhaps Gr ves'-disease, hyperthyroidism. These diseases are characterized by excessive pituitary activity in the paradoxical presence of excessive target organ hormone formation, hyperresponsiveness to pituitary stimulation and lack of response to pituitary suppression in the absence of a pituitary tumor. The explanation.for these aberrations of physiology is a block in the hypothalamic center or centers which control the pituitary secretion and release of trophic hormones.

The exact nature of the agents which block the hypothalamic centers in the case of the Stein-Leventhal syndrome is unknown but it would seem. from a review of case histories, that this may be of varied origin. Experiments in the rat by Barraclough indicate that gonadotrophic centers can be blocked by androgen given within ; days of birth. That some stimulation early in life may often be responsible for (lie condition in the lrunian is indicated by the fact that many patients exhibit their symptoms from the onset of the menstrual function. In addition to the possible effect of steroids as blocking agents for the hypothalamic nuclei, one would have to consider emotional stress and other factors in the external environment such as drugs and illnesses. These stimuli, through their effect upon the hypothalamus, alter the secretion and release of the pituitary gonadotrophins, changing the ratio of FSH:ICSH. It is probably the changing ratio which determines the enzymic mechanism of the ovarian theca cells and sets the equilibrium in favour of either estrogen or androgen production. The high ICSH in relation to FSH also inhibits ovulation and corpus luteum formation. By using human pituitary gonadotrophins in amenorrhoeic, hypogonadotrophin patients, Diezfalucy has shown that if the ICSH value is too high in relation to the FSH value, ovulation does not occur. When additional FSH is given, as in our experiments and those of *Crooke et al.,* ovulation does occur in Stein-ovaries, further substantiating the theory.

Although the pathogenesis is uncertain, the treatment is well documented. A bilateral wedge resection operation will cure the menstrual irregularities in 85% of the patients and pregnancy can be expected in 75% of the married women. The rate of recurrence is low if patients are carefully selected. The explanation for the success of the wedge resection is problematical. Reports in the current literature seem to substantiate the fact that clomiphene is also a successful therapeutic agent in the Stein-Leventhal syndrome. The therapy was first suggested by *Kistner* with MRL-25, an early analogue of the drug. At the present time, the optimum dosage is still uncertain but is in the range of 50 mg. daily for 5 days. given at monthly intervals. A small dosage is preferable as with larger dosage it is possible to produce ovarian cyst formation. It is also wise to preclude a pregnancy until the cycle has been satisfactorily regulated.

One would have to surmise that with both methods of therapy, surgical and clomiphene. one is shifting the gonadotrophic ratio in favor of FSH against ICSH. It is easy to explain this syndrome if one accepts the *hypothesis* that there is an ICSH inhibitory center in the hypothalamus. If this center is blocked (and it is this one that controls the cyclic release of ICSH), then the tonic center, which is constantly stimulating ICSH production. predominates and a constant high ICSH prevails with relatively normal FSH values. This abnormal ratio inhibits ovulation. Therapy, by some neurohumoral mechanism, unblocks the ICSH inhibitory center.

The indications for treatment in Stein- Leventhal syndrome are infertility. functional uterine bleeding and in the rare instance hirsutism. Functional uterine bleeding is an important indication for therapy: as mentioned in the chapter on carcinoma of the fundus, there is certain evidence that this condition may precede endometrial carcinoma. Hirsutisin would constitute an indication in a young girl who was rapidly developing an extreme amount of hair. Under these circumstances, operation would be done only with the full knowledge of the patient that the hirsutism already present may not regress and with the hope that progression will be forestalled. In the absence of functional uterine bleeding or marked hirsutism, it is wise to postpone surgical treatment until such a time when fertility is of importance. Medical treatment can, of course, be used with fewer reservations. In our series of amenorrheic women there were 23 with bilateral polycystic ovaries. Nine of these patients had a wedge resection operation and all 9 were cured of menstrual irregularities; 4 of 5 married women became pregnant.

Inhibition of the Prolactin Inhibiting Factor (PIF)

Occasional, after a pregnancy one observes persistent lactation and failure of menses to reappear. These symptoms are characteristic of the *Chiari-Frommel* syndrome and are associated with an atrophic vagina and uterus and a low urinary gonadotrophin excretion. Theoretically, the condition represents an inhibition of the prolactin-inhibiting factor of the hypothalamus. Although usually due to physiologic causes, it may be associated with a tumor causing destruction of the center or tracts involved. The results of treatment are often unsatisfactory; however, continuous high dosage ofprogestene and clomiphene citrate have both been reported as occasionally successful.

Pituitary Amenorrhea

Pituitary Insufficiency (Sheehan's Disease)

The most common cause of pituitary insufficiency is necrosis of the anterior lobe due to a traumatic labor or delivery, as classically described *by Sheehan. Nassar* has inferred from experimental work that the use of ergot may predispose to pituitary thrombosis. However, the pituitary is normally enlarged during pregnancy and may, on occasion, thrombose spontaneously. Depending upon the severity of the thrombosis, there is postpartum collapse and hyperpyrexia. After an immediate recovery there is an absence of lactation and amenorrhea. The initial physical signs are uterine and vaginal atrophy with a slight. or occasionally marked, gain in weight. Signs characteristic of the late stages are loss of axillary andpubic hair, lowered blood pressure. and loss of weight. Thus the final stage is that initially described by Simmonds for pituitary eachexia. Such patients are susceptible to infections and other forms of stress and thus live in a precarious state. Sheehan describes acquisition of pigment due to intermedin, and although theoretically this is possible since the intermediate and posterior lobe of the pituitary are supposedly unaffected by the venous thrombosis, in our experience this finding is certainly unusual.

It is reported that some patients, over a period of years, tend to have an amelioration of the disease probably due to a compensatory hypertrophy of the remaining pituitary cells. If satisfactory temporary replacement therapy can be obtained, patients have been reported to have become pregnant, and *Murdoch* and *Govan* say this is the best treatment of the condition as, under the pregnancy stimulation, the pituitary gland hypertrophies. On the other hand, *Israel* and *Constan* warn that this can be an extremely dangerous situation for, as a result of the stress of labor and delivery, collapse and death may occur.

The laboratory findings are characteristic of panhypopituitarism: a lowered or absent gonadotrophin excretion, a low 17-ketosteroid and 11-corticosteroid excretion, a low protein-bound iodine and basal metabolic rate, a flat glucose tolerance test, and anemia. .

The treatment is replacement therapy, with 25 mg. of cortisone acetate, or its equivalent, daily. On occasion it may be necessary to use in addition 96 mg. of desiccated thyroid a day to give these patients a general feeling of well-being. Although replacement steroid therapy will induce menstruation, it is certainly not indicated except for psychological reasons. When sterility is a problem, pituitary gonadotrophin therapy is the treatment of choice if one has the temerity to care for the pregnancy which may ensue under such precarious conditions. In the last decade we have seen an even dozen patients fulfilling the criteria for Sheehan's disease.

Pituitary Tumors

Although pituitary tumors are uncommon in any series of amenorrhea patients, the reverse is not true, in that amenorrhea is an extremely common symptom among women with pituitary tumors. In a series of 15 young women who had pituitary tumors. all had amenorrhea as one of the presenting symptoms (Jagiello). Thus it is most important to keep this etiological factor in mind and to make the diagnosis when it does occur.

A history of headache and visual disturbances with amenorrhea is suggestive of an intracranial difficulty. However. these may be late symptoms and a slow growing lesion can exist for years prior to their onset. The specific laboratory diagnostic aids are (1) an x-ray of the sella turcica. and (2) a color visual field examination, as the firm diagnostic sign may be the encroachment of the tumor on the optic tracts with an ensuing defect in red perception.

Any type of pituitary tumor can produce amenorrhea. The most common type. the *chromophobe adenoma,* usually has no specific endocrine symptoms and produces amenorrhea through gross destruction of pituitary tissue. However, prolactin-producing chromophobe adenomas which are assoociated with *theAhumada-del Castillio syndrome*. This is characterized by persistent lactation in the absence of a previous pregnancy, extreme atrophy of the uterus and vaginal mucosa, small ovaries, and a copious milky secretion from the breasts bilaterally. Breast secretion may, on occasion be enough to cause the patient annoyance and embarrassment, whereas in other instances it may be noticed only by the physician during the breast examination. When an associated defect in the sella turcica is present, the diagnosis is assured. However, in our experience, only about a quarter of the patients show this defect. A case has been reported by *Bricaire et alL* with complete laboratory data including a prolactin assay which was reported as high, 20 pigeon units per 100 ml. of serum.

Two patients in the series reviewed showed a chromophobe adenoma without associated endocrine symptoms. One was cured of the adenoma surgically and the other died postoperatively. If the pituitary has been destroyed, amenorrhea, of course, persists following operative therapy, and the only curative treatment would be substitution gonadotrophic therapy.

The *basophilic adenoma* is associated with *Cushing's syndrome* which will be discussed in the section on adrenal, under "Lesions of Intermediate Origin." The *acidophilic adenoma* is associated with the signs and symptoms of *acromegaly,* and 85 % of young women with acromegaly are said to have menstrual disturbances. The physical appearance of the patient with this condition is usually the best diagnostic aid. There is excessive growth of hands and feet and an increase in coarseness of all of the features. This is associated with an increase in the size of the nose and prognathous of the lower jaw. There may be unusual muscular weakness, polyuria. and polvdipsia in the later stages. The laboratory findings are characterized by the absence of urinary gonadotrophins and the presence of a diabetic type of glucose'tolerance curve and an increased metabolic rate or protein-bound iodine. It is important to recognize these tumors prior to the occurrence of severe visual field defects as pressure on the optic nerves may cause blindness. These adenomas are ordinaril% radiosensitive. and some form of radiation therapy should be employed. When the condition is arrested, amenorrhea is usually corrected. However, if pressure necrosis of the pituitary has occurred, the amenorrhea may be permanent.

Congenital Deficiency of Gonadotrophic Hormones (Hypogonadotrophic Eunuchoidism)

This condition is extremely rare. It is theoretically due to a specific failure of the pituitary to produce gonadotrophic hormones. However, there is no pathology available on the pituitaries of any of these individuals to date.

The diagnosis is made when primary amenorrhea occurs with a eunuchoid stature in the absence of urinary gonadotrophins. A familial occurrence is reported. The pathology of the ovary shows follicles in all stages of evolution but no evidence of cwulation or corpus luteum formation. Again, the treatment of choice in these cases is substitution gonadotrophin therapy. Because of the familial occurrence a chromosomal defect might be suspected.

Psychogenic Amenorrhea

Psychogenic amenorrhea can be further subdivided into (1) major and minor psychosis, (2) emotional shock, (3) pseudocyesis, and (4) anorexia nervosa.

Major and Minor Psychosis

The diagnosis is made on the basis of the patient's psychiatric symptoms. The endocrine assays have been reviewed by *Ray, Nicholson-Valley,* and *Grappl* and are found to show low normal values within the range seen in patients having neurogenic disturbances. This would indicate, as one might expect, that the final common pathway for the production of the amenorrhea is through a depressed pituitary function. The most common major psychosis associated with amenorrhea is a depressive state. However, according to *Kroger* and *Freed,* amenorrhea may also occur in the less profound psychiatric disturbances and may be a manifestation of emotional immaturity, overtly expressing the patient's subconscious attitude of a distaste for intercourse, a fear of pregnancy, or of promiscuity.

Some of these conditions are relatively easy to diagnose, as the amenorrhea immediately follows an unfortunate emotional experience. In other patients the diagnosis is made on an exclusion basis in that no other etiological factor can be found and the patient is emotionally unstable.

The treatment consists of psychiatric care. and. with the present psychiatric approach, the prognosis is poor. It is unusual to be able to induce ovulation with cyclic steroid therapy, but gonadotrophic therapy is usually successful. However, it is questionable whether such patients should be treated in this substitution fashion until psychiatric care has been administered.

There were 7 patients among our series with this diagnosis and the course of the amenorrhea seemed to parallel the course of the psychiatric disturbance. Two were improved psychiatrically and these were cured of their amenorrhea.

Emotional Shock

Any traumatic experience may be followed by amenorrhea and the history is the diagnostic criterion. Amenorrhea is usually temporary, and menses may be expected to resume within 6 months. The laboratory investigation, according *toaFaierman,* indicates lowered pituitary function. *Bass* reported that amenorrhea occurred in 50% of women interned in concentration camps during World War II; the onset was within 4 weeks of internment and spontaneous remission occurred in 94% of the women in spite of deteriorating food supplies. A nutritional basis would therefore seem to be excluded. A number of such reports have been reviewed by *Randall and McElin.*

The experience with shock treatments for various psychiatric disturbances has been interesting in this regard; Liepelt reports that 84.7% of 300 patients receiving such therapy have some period of amenorrhea, ranging from 6 weeks to 13 months. The treatment of amenorrhea secondary to emotional shock or trauma is largely reassurance followed by gonadotrophin substitution therapy if necessary.

Pseudocyesis

This condition is characterized by (1) an obsession of pregnancy, (2) weight gain, (3) normal secondary sexual characteristics and pelvic organs, (4) lactation, and (5) an impaired ovulatory mechanism. Since secondary sexual characteristics and pelvic organs are normal, it may be assumed that the estrogenic function is maintained at least to some degree. The lesion would therefore' scem to be localized to a disturbance of the FSH:ICSH ratio. A corpus luteum cyst or ectopic pregnancy may be associated with similar symptoms and these diagnoses, as well as the possibility of a missed abortion, must be excfuded.

The laboratory findings are characterized by a low normal gonadotrophin excretion. estrogens within the normal range and a midzone shift in the vaginal smear pattern. A negative serum chorionic gonadotrophin assay *will* also assist *in* the differential diagnosis.

Endometrial biopsy or curettage should be considered only if an intrauterine pregnancy can be excluded.

As the basis of this disturbance is often due to the patient's desire to become pregnant and inability to do so, the problem can frequently be handled by a gynecologist without psychiatric help. A discussion,aiid explanation of her problems, together with the initiation of an infertility investigation, will often suffice.

There were 4 patients with this diagnosis in our series. None received psychiatric care but were handled entirely by a gynecologist and all have had a return of regular menstrual periods. There have been 3 subsequent pregnancies. As cited by Rakoff, the prognosis among this group of patients is apparently good.

Anorexia Nervosa

Anorexia nervosa is characterized by severe malnutrition with no associated lethargy or inanition. This persistent feeling of well-being, in spite of profound weight loss, distinguishes the condition from the pituitary cachexia seen with Simmonds' disease. The other characteristic of the syndrome is that the patient is unable to give an accurate account of her food intake and, either willfully or compulsively, falsifies the record. This preoccupation with weight and the inability to eat is the overt manifestation of a severe psychological disturbance. The associated loss of weight is secondarily responsibe for the amenorrhea. The physical examination is characterized by emaciation, a fine lanugo type of hirsutism, normal axillary and pubic hair, and atrophy of internal and external genitalia.

The laboratory findings in our experience are compatible with a low or absent total pituitary function. This is in accordance with *Emanuel* 's findings, although *Bliss* and *Migeon* report only a lowered go dotrophic function. The differential diagnosis between anorexia nervosa and panhypopituitarism of Simmonds' disease is made on the appearance of the patient in conjunction with the history.

As the etiology is psychogenic the treatment is psychiatric rather than endocrine. However, because of the very cleverly concealed personality problems, it is often difficult to persuade the family that psychiatric care is necessary, or desirable. If the patient accepts advice and weight gain is accomplished, menses recur within 3 months after a minimal ideal weight is regained. *Daily* and *Sargeant* have advocated a hospital regimen of combined chlorpromazine and insulin. Chlorpromazine is given in massive dosage increasing *from 150* mg. a day to as much as 1000 mg. a day. Insulin is started with 5 units and progressively increased to drowsiness, the average morning dose in the reported series being 60 units. The courses are interrupted for three large meals a day. This regimen serves to restore the patient's nutritional status to such an extent that she is able to accept treatment for her psychological problems. The condition is not to be taken lightly, as 10 to 20 % of patients with anorexia nervosa develop irreversible, fatal malnutrition.

There were 12 women in our series with this disturbance, 6 of whom have been adequately followed. Only 1 patient accepted treatment and gained weight. Her menses returned promptly and she has since become pregnant.

LESIONS OF INTERMEDIATE ORIGIN

Intermediate problems concerned with the production of amenorrhea are those factors whic: exert their effect somewhere between the central stimulatory and pituitary gonadotrophic functions and the ovarian or end organ levels. These maybe divided into chronic illness, metabolic disease, nutritional factors, and disease of organs concerned with the excretion and metabolism of the steroid hormones.

Chronic Disease

Although any chronic disease process associated with inanition can be associated with amenorrhea, by far the most common one is tuberculosis. Tuberculosis may exert its influence through constitutional factors or specifically by destruction of the ovary or endometrium. These latter causes have been discussed under the organs involved. Diagnosis of a chronic disease process is made on the basis of an increased sedimentation rate, elevation of white count, and the presence of a low grade fever. Normal menses reappear when the disease process is arrested or cured. Only 2 patient in the reported series had amenorrhea associated with tuberculosis.

Metabolic Disease

Disturbances of the pituitary and ovarian function are discussed under these specific headings and metabolic disease is herein divided into three categories: disturbances of the thyroid, the pancreas, and the adrenal.

Thyroid

Both *hypo-and hvperrhvroid* states may be associated with menstrual irregularities and amenorrhea. These diagnoses must be made by some specific test for thyroid function such as the basal metabolic rate, the protein-bound iodine. or an "I uptake. To confirm the diagnosis of hypothyroidism the basal metabolic rate should be -10 or below, and the protein-bound iodine under 4 pg. per 100 ml. of serum; two or more tests should be made. It must also be remembered that the diagnosis of hypothyroidism cannot be made in the presence of malnutrition, as lowered thyroid function invariably exists under these conditions. The diagnosis of hyperthyroidism cannot be made unless the basal metabolic rate is consistently +20 or above and the protein-bound iodine is 8 pg. per 100 ml. of serum or above. In either case some clinical signs and symptoms of hypo- or hyperthyroidism should be present. The classic signs of hypothyroidism are sensitivity to heat and cold, a tendency to constipation, dryness of the skin and hair, and slow reaction time. Hyperthyroidism is characterized by an elevation of the pulse rate, a fine tremor, some loss of weight, excessive perspiration, a lid lag, and occasionally exophthalmos.

The treatment of hypothyroidism is the administration of desiccated thyroid. The usual dosage is between 96 and 128 mg. daily. Therapy must be continued for at least 3 months and as long thereafter as necessary to maintain the basal metabolic rate or the protein-bound iodine at normal levels or both. Therapy should be interrupted periodically and patients checked for remissions. There is usually no indication for the use of triiodothyronine in patients with simple hypothyroidism. If or when it is given it must be remembered that the protein- bound iodine is no longer of value as a guide to therapy, and a basal metabolic rate must be used. Either severe hypothyroidism to the point of myxedema or hyperthyroidism warrant medical consultation. In the treatment of hyperthyroidism antithyroid drug therapy is usually to he desired, and some form of propylthiouracil, administered over long periods of time, will usually result in a euthyroid state. Unless there is a suspicion of malignancy, or unless there is resistance to antithyroid drug therapy. thyroidectomy is usually not advisable. Radioactive iodine treatment carries the theoretical possibility of late carcinogenic effects and in addition may produce permanent amenorrhea, perhaps through its effect upon the ovary. Therefore, especially in women of the childbearing age, this type of therapy is not recommended.

In our own series of amenorrheic patients there were 34 with hypothyroidism and 2 with hyperthyroidism. The prognosis is relatively good; of 30 patients adequately treated and followed 28 were improved and 8 became pregnant.

When a euthyroid state is achieved in Graves disease, the menstrual abnormalities are usually promptly corrected and fertility is restored. Among our own patients. however. the 2 women with this condition who were treated with radioactive iodine have remained amenorrheic despite apparently normal thyroid function.

Pancreas

Although *diabetes mellitus* is more apt to be associated with functional bleeding. amenorrhea is occasionally present. There are at least three theoretical causes for the menstrual disturbance. First, the difficulty may be due to the diabetes *per se,* resulting from the insulin deficiency; second, it can be caused by associated nutritional deficiencies; or third, it can be caused by the emotional disturbances which occur so frequently with this disease, especially if the diabetic control is poor.

The classic signs and symptoms are obesity followed by weight loss, polyuria, polydipsia, and nocturia. Often it is the monilial vulvoyaginitis, commonly associated with diabetes, which brings the patient to the doctor; therefore the gynecologist may be the first who has the opportunity of making the diagnosis. It should be unnecessary to state that in the presence of these symptoms a determination for urinary sugar must be obtained.

The important laboratory finding is an elevated fasting blood sugar. It has been our experience that when the diabetes is satisfactorily controlled, the menstrual periods become regulated. Although some observers have advocated the use of estrogen therapy in the menopausal type of diabetes. this rather unorthodox form of treatment is certainly not applicable to most patients, and the interesting observations of Houssay tend to shed 'light on the physiological defects of the disease rather than to serve as a practical aid to therapy.

An interesting experimental approach to the problem led *Foglia et al.* to conclude that the pancreatectomized rat exhibits alterations of the estrous cycle and disturbances of fertility prior to the development of frank diabetes. As there is some evidence that anatomical changes can be detected in the prediabetic human, these findings are of additional importance.

There were 6 women with amenorrhea and diabetes in the series reported by us and although there were no pregnancies, 4 were symptomatically improved with good diabetic control only.

Adrenal

The two outstanding adrenal syndromes associated with menstrual abnormalities are the *adrenogenital syndrome and Cushing's disease.* Addison's disease is occasionally associated with amenorrhea in its late stages and under these circumstances it is impossible to say that the cachexia is not the major factor rather than the adrenal insufficiency.

Congenital Adrenal Hiperplasia

Probably the most dramatic form of the adrenogenital syndrome has been classically described by *Glvnn* as female pseudohermaphroditism, and the laboratory aspects have been elaborated upon by *Wilkins*. The characteristic features are the deformity of the external genitalia, precocious virilism, short stature, deep skin pigmentation, and an absence of menses. There are all transitions between marked congenital adrenal hyperplasia and postpubertal virilization.

The disease is a heritable one, caused by a specific enzyme deficiency which prevents the adrenal from synthesizing cortisol. Depending upon the specific enzyme deficiency which the patient has inherited certain specific urinary metabolistes will be increased. In the classic form the urinary ketosteroid excretion is markedly elevated, usually being in the range of 50 mg. per 24 hours. An elevated pregnanetriol excretion indicates an insufficiency of the 21-hydroxylase enzyme and blockage of adrenal production of cortisol at the 17-

hydroxyprogesterone step. The hypertensive form of congenital adrenal hyperplasia has an increased urinary excretion of pregnan-3 a, 17a, 21-triol-20-one (THS) indicating defective 11-0-hydroxylation. This form of the disease may be unassociated with an increased 17-ketosteroid excretion.

The adrenal pathology is characterized by a hyperplasia of the zona reticularis and either anatomical absence, or a failure of fat accumulation in, the zona fasciculata.

In the severe forms of congenital hyperplasia the deficiency of cortisone causes excessive pituitary adrenocorticotrophin (ACTH) production, which in turn produces the abnormally stimulated adrenal. The steroids which are secreted by the adrenal, in lieu of cortisone, suppress the pituitary gonadotrophins, and ovarian insufficiency and amenorrhea ensue.

There is reason to believe that certain patients with postpubertal virilization also have the same, or a related, problem but to a milder degree. This is evidenced by the course of the disease and the clinical and laboratory findings, and substantiated by the adrenal histology. There are, however, a majority of hirsute patients with many similar clinical findings who apparently do not have a true enzymic insufficiency, as in the congenital form of adrenal hyperplasia, but rather are suffering from a physiologic insufficiency induced by stress. There is some evidence that in a predominately Mediterranean population, where hirsutism is relatively common, the rate of adrenal *androgen to cortisol* production is increased. Blackman, in morphological study of the adrenal of hirsute women. noted an increase in the size of the *zona reticulata* regardless of the cause of the hirsutism. Both observations substantiate the belief that in women with a hirsute tendency there is a "variation" of normal adrenal function.

Dorfman *et al.* have demonstrated that A_4androstenedione inhibits 11 f3-hydroxylase activity in the adrenal. If a patient has a tendency to synthesize adrenal androgens excessively, under *stress* the increased rate of synthesis of androstenedione might be sufficient to start a vicious circle.

Bush and *Mahesh* have published a fascinating case report of twins, one of whom developed hirsutism under particularly stressful circumstances. Both twins exhibited a high androgen cortisol ratio following ACTH stimulation. The authors postulate that chronic stress constituted a prolonged ACTH test for the one twin who thereby produced enough androgen to initiate the hirsutism. There maybe many such women in the general population who have either a very slight congenitally defective adrenal cortex or simply represent the extreme of the nonnal variation in the rate of adrenal androgen production. If the adrenal secretion rate is accelerated by stress, symptoms such as hirsutism, acne, oligomenorrhea and infertility appear.

The treatment for congenital adrenal hyperplasia, postpubertal virilization and related disturbances is cortisone substitution therapy; 50 mg. of cortisone acetate or its equivalent, daily by mouth, is usually adequate to maintain a ketosteroid excretion suppression of about 5 mg. per 24 hours, which is the desirable level. If it is impossible to maintain the suppression, one must suspect a tumor of the adrenal or ovarian pathology as discussed in this chapter under "The Stein-Leventhal Syndrome."

In the relatively mild forms it is often possible to maintain a suppression with as little as 25 mg. of cortisone acetate daily (or its equivalent) after the initial suppression has been well established. In the congenital form, which is due to a genetic deficiency of a specific adrenal enzyme, therapy will need to be continued throughout life. However. in the form induced by stress, once the vicious circle has been interrupted. steroid therapy can be discontinued until the next stressful situation develops.

There were 46 women in this category in our series of amenorrheic patients. Four had severe forms of congenital adrenal hyperplasia and 42 were cases of related dysfunctions. Of 27 patients adequately treated and followed. 23 were improved and 8 of 13 married patients achieved a pregnancy.

Cushing's Disease

In contrast to congenital adrenal hyperplasia. *Cushing's disease* represents a hyperfunction of the entire adrenal cortex including the cortisone-secreting zona fasciculata. The pituitary-adrenal homeostatic mechanisms are out of control as there is excessive ACTH production in the presence of excessive cortisol. *Cushing* in his initial publication believed that the syndrome was always the result of a pituitary tumor or pituitary basophilism. Since the initial paper, however, it has become clear that bilateral adrenal hyperplasia may occur without a demonstrable pituitary lesion and adrenal tumors are not infrequently responsible for the condition. In addition to these possibilities, Heinbecker has implicated the hypothalamus as the primary disease site. Thus, when Cushing's disease exists, the differential diagnosis must be made among a pituitary tumor, bilateral hyperplasia of the adrenals, or adrenal tumor. In addition to the three principle primary sites of origin for the syndrome, there is a fourth unusual one. Two reports have appeared in the literature of Cushing's disease resulting from an adrenal rest tumor in the ovary *(Kepler et al.* and *Rottino* and *AfcGrath)*. In this era of corticosteroid therapy for many diseases, the physician should also be alerted to the possibility of an iatrogenic factor in the production of a Cushing-like picture.

The subject of etiology has been extensively reviewed by *Plotz,* and according to autopsy findings in 97 cases, carcinoma of the adrenal occurred 16 times, adenoma 11 times, benign hyperplasia 58 times. A pituitary adenoma was associated with adenomatous hyperplasia 40 times and with carcinoma and benign adrenal adenoma once. There were changes in the paraventricular nucleus in 8 instances, and these 8 instances were distributed evenly among the adrenal carcinomas, hyperplasias, and pituitary adenomas.

Cushing's disease is characterized by obesity. ame orrhea, moon face. hirsutism, hypertension. purple striae, erythemic acne, and easy bruisability. The pelvic organs are usually normal and there is no enlargement of the clitoris or marked vaginal atrophy. When the fullblown picture exists the syndrome is so striking that the diagnosis is blatant: however, in the early stages it may be extremely difficult. The laboratory findings are characterized by an elevation of the urinary and blood corticoids: The urinary 17-ketosteroid assay is usually nonnal or only moderately elevated: if an adrenal tumor is present it may be markedly elevated. There is a polycythemia. diabetic glucose tolerance curve. and x-ray evidence of osteoporosis. The typical response to ACTH stimulation is an over-reaction 'yith at least a 3-fold increase of the urinary and blood corticoids. It is usually impossible to suppress the urinary corticoids below 10 mg./24 hours by cortisone. When an adrenal tumor is present there is usually no response to ACTH stimulation or cortisol suppression. Unfortunately, however, not all tumors are autonomous and some do show a response.

The treatment of the disease depends upon its etiology. *Sosman* recommends irradiation of the pituitary for those patients without adrenal tumors. Certainly this is the method of choice if a pituitary tumor can be demonstrated. However, most authorities have recommended adrenal extirpation for bilateral adrenal hyperplasia. The decision between pituitary irradiation and adrenalectomy is further complicated by the difficulty in excluding the possibility of an adrenal tumor. This may be attempted by perirenal carbon dioxide insufflation, by laminography, by simple intravenous pyelograms with attention to the adrenal shadow; or by adrenal angiogram. In our experience none of these is completely satisfactory.

It is often possible to decide at operation, by the appearance of one adrenal whether or not there is 'a tumor in the other. If at operation the exposed gland is atrophied, it should be left in situ with a presumptive diagnosis of a contralateral tumor. If, however, the exposed adrenal is hypertrophied it is removed with all or 90 % of the opposite gland. When the partial operation is performed there is always a possibility that a second operation will be necessary; however, this seems like a worthwhile risk to take in an effort to prevent lifelong invalidism with dependence upon prolonged, expensive replacement therapy.

Stress Obesity

A borderline clinical picture with moderately elevated urinary corticoids occurs more frequently than true Cushing's disease. It is thought that this picture represents the response of certain individuals to the *"stress* of *obesity."* There were 7 such patients in our series of amenorrheic women, and the treatment was simple weight reduction. The one patient who cooperated and reduced to a normal figure had a remission of all her symptoms.

Nutritional Amenorrhea

One of the basic influences which determines how any endocrine gland may act, or indeed any substitution therapy, is the diet. *Richter* has ably demonstrated this clinical factor in a laboratory animal, by using self-selective diets in rats. Adrenalectomized, parathyroidectomized and pancreatectomized animals can all adjust to their deficiencies if allowed a sufficient choice of diet.

In the human the importance of malnutrition in reproductive function has been demonstrated. Disturbances of reproductive functions can be caused in animal experimentation by specific caloric deficiencies, protein deficiencies, or vitamin deficiencies with special reference to vitamins A, B, and C. Whether one or all of these factors operate in nutritional amenorrhea of the human is undetermined. There is a relatively large literature by European authors on the occurence of nutritional amenorrhea during World Wars I and II but it is generally difficult for the authors to separate nutritional from psychogenic factors. Heynemann was of the opinion that nutrition played an important part in war amenorrhea, as he observed an increase in the incidence in Germany after 1944 when the deterioration of food supplies occurred. *Plotz* believed that the protein deficiency aspects were most important and reported that 17 of 19 women with nutritional amenorrhea of over 1 year's duration responded to an amino acid preparation. The first vaginal bleeding occurred after an average of 31 days of therapy and permanent success was achieved in almost every case.

It is the general opinion, quoted by Seitz, that nutritional amenorrhea is usually reversible; 80% of the patients reviewed recovered with improved nutrition. However, the prognosis is graver when the nutritional damage occurs at or just prior to puberty. This is in keeping with the experience in animal experimentation, reviewed by *Asdell,* which indicates that the younger the animal when nutritional damage occurs the more difficult it is to repair. There is also some evidence that residual damage may result; *Klebarow* reports a 75 % incidence of infertility among concentration camp victims of World War II who suffered severe malnutrition, in contrast to a 25 % incidence of infertility in the general population. He further states that this may be attributable to damage of the germinal cells, as impaired spermatogenesis, under similar circumstances, was found among males. Stalko, in an examination of ovaries of 120 women who died of starvation, found an absence of primordial follicles and replacement of the cortical layer with scar tissue indicating that the amenorrhea might be primarily due to ovarian damage. The occurrence of amenorrhea in patients with exogenous obesity is somewhat more difficult to explain but may be based on some relative dietary imbalance associated %with the abnormal caloric intake.

The treatment of both malnutrition and obesity is directed toward general dietary habits-either weight gain or weight reduction, with a well balanced high protein diet. Of 16 recent patients with exogenous obesity and amenorrhea, only 9 were adequately treated and followed.

Seven were improved with regular menses when a normal weight was acquired, and 1 became pregnant. Two were unimproved. There were 9 patients with malnutrition and 6 were followed. Only 3 showed a satisfactory weight gain and all 3 responded with regular menses.

Disturbances of Steroid Excretion and Metabolism

Liver Cirrhosis

The 'onjugation and metabolism of estrogens and progesterone takes place in the liver; the excretion is accomplished to a large extent through the bile and hepatic portal system to the bowel. In cirrhosis of the liver, impairment of conjugation of estrogen leads to an excess of circulating active estrogens. This may result in functional bleeding interspersed with periods of amenorrhea. Although this is certainly the most common menstrual cycle aberration associated with cirrhosis, *Green and Rubin* report 18 patients havi^g amenorrhea as the menstrual symptom. The diagnosis is made on the basis of the physical findings and liver function tests.

The treatment is medical and the prognosis is poor.

LESIONS OF PERIPHERAL ORIGIN

Ovarian

Ovarian causes for amenorrhea can be classified as follows.

1. *Ovarian insufficiency.* (a) congenital defects, gonadal dysgenesis, and related conditions; (b) the premature menopause, congenital and acquired.

2. *Ovarian dysfunction:* Stein-Leventhal "syndrome (possibly hypothalamic in origin).

3. *Ovarian tumors:* (a) arrhenoblastoma, hilus cell tumor, and adrenal rest tumor; (b) granulosa cell tumor; (c) dysgerminoma.

All of these conditions, with the exception of the ovarian tumors, are characterized by the laboratory finding of an elevated urinary gonadotrophin assay. Although the values in the patients with the Stein-Leventhal syndrome may be lower and more variable than those found in other types. they also tend to be moderately elevated.

Congenitally Defective Gonads

Gonadal agenesis (Turner's Syndrome). In 1938 Turner described a syndrome of"infantilism." congenital webbed neck, and decubitus valgus. *Albright. Smith,* and *Fraser,* demonstrated the association of this syndrome with an elevated urinary gonadotrophin titer. and Wilkins and Fleischmann in 1944 described the pathology which was characterized by absence of gonads and the presence of normally developed but immature Miillerian ducts. The gonads are represented grossly by a primitive streak of white or yellow, and microscopically by stroma only or by stroma and Leydig cells. In 1954 a number of investigators independently reported that a majority of these patients had a negative or male type chromatin pattern, and in 1959 *Ford* and *Jones* reported that at least some of these patients with negative chromatin patterns represented not an XY but an XO configuration of sex chromosomes. These contributions provided the building stones for a satisfactory explanation of the syndrome. Those patients who show an OX or a fragmented XX chromosomal configuration can be explained on the basis of nondysjunction ofthe sex chromosomes associated apparently with other chromosomal abnormalities to account for the concomitant congenital defects. Patients who have a normal XX chromosome pattern may represent the result of embryonic gonadal damage prior to the 8th week of development. Under these circumstances, in the absence of the embryonic gonadal organizers, the Mullerian ducts are retained and the external genitalia develop in a female manner, according to the experimental embryological investigations of *Jost*.

Every stage of developmental anomaly can be seen in the negative chromatin patients-from gonads with a few Leydig cells associated with female genitalia and hypertrophy of the clitoris only. to almost normal testicular development and male external genitalia except for hypospadia. For a complete summary of this abnormal development.

The clinical features of a typical Turner's syndrome are so characteristic that one can recognize such a patient as she walks into the consultation room. There is shortness of stature, webbing of the neck, deformity of the carrying angle, a shield type chest with nipples placed far laterally, no breast development, and scanty or absent axillary and pubic hair. From this typical picture of Turner's syndrome and dwarf stature there are all gradations through the normal stature with eunuchoid proportions to gigantism with or without other stigmata. In addition a number of other associated congenital defects have been described, the most important one being coarctation of the aorta.

The laboratory findings are characteristic in that there must be an elevated urinary gonadotrophin level, and most of the patients exhibit a negative chromatin pattern: the buccal smear therefore is often the most rapid and least expensive way to make a diagnosis. Thyroid studies arc normal. The urinary 17-ketosteroid excretion is normal or low.

Until such a time when transplantation of organs is feasible, the treatment of this condition will remain as substitution therapy only. Estrogen is given in interrupted dosage, depending upon the amount of drug necessary to induce vaginal bleeding: 0.5 to 2 mg. of stilbestrol, or its equivalent, daily through the 25th day of each month, discontinued and resumed the 1st day of the following month.

In cases of dwarfism, if the patient is pubertal and epiphyseal fusion has not occurred, smaller dosages of estrogen over longer periods of time should be tried in an effort to induce a maximal growth spurt prior to epiphyseal closure which will occur with estrogen stimulation. Whitelaw *et al.* report a growth of 9.5 cm. in a year in a patient treated with an anabolic steroid and suggest that this form of therapy should be given until epiphyseal closure or failed response occur. They advise liver function tests and observation for androgenicity.

Therapy may be expected to induce normal breast development, vaginal cornification, and menstruation. The induction of menstruation is usually desirable for psychological reasons. Pregnancy, of course, cannot be expected to occur, and axillary and pubic hair will usually remain scanty or absent unless an androgenic stimulus is supplied. This is possibly due to an associated adrenal insufficiency but might also be indirect evidence for the normal occurrence of an ovarian androgen. If coarctation of the aorta is present surgical correction wherever possible should be advised, and if webbing of the neck is deforming, plastic surgery can offer excellent cosmetic results. It is well to have a psychological evaluation, and therapeutic consultations if necessary, to insure that the patient is adjusted to her limitations and will thus be able to live a completely normal life except for ability to bear children.

There were 20 patients with gonadal agenesis among our series of 352 women with amenorrhea.

True Hermaphroditism

True hermaphroditism is extremely rare. A summary of the 58 cases reported in the literature up to 1955 can be found in the textbook on this subject by Jones and Scott. Most true hermaphrodites are raised as men and this was the case in 39 of the 58 patients reported. This indicates, of course, that in a majority of instances the external genitalia are masculine rather than feminine in appearance. The condition should be suspected in patients who show some ambiguity of the external genitalia, associated with breast development. Minimal hirsutism may occur but has been absent in the majority of the reported cases.

These cases are interesting from the point of view of experimental embryology, as they indicate that the male gonad exerts a strong influence on the development of external genitalia. Thus, even in the 16 patients in the literature who showed an ovary on one side and an ovotestis on the other, only 8 had been raised as females. The Mullerian duct must be more positively influenced by the ovarian organizer, since a normal uterus was present in about half of the patients. Almost all of these individuals menstruated; thus, in contrast to gonadal dysgenesis, the ovarian tissue present in true hermaphrodites is functioning.

The diagnosis can be suspected by the physical findings, and the laboratory data are of very little assistance. The chromatin pattern can be positive or negative and the 17-kctosteroid and gonadotrophin assays are within normal range. The diagnosis therefore is made by thc pathologist at the time of operation, and the treatment is surgical correction.

Male Hermaphroditism

Male hermaphrodites show ambiguous external genitalia, no breast development, minimal hirsutism, and a negative chromatin pattern. There was 1 such congenital abnormality among our series of patients.

Testicular Feminization

This interesting form of hermaphroditism is characterized by a normal female appearance with excellent breast development and completely normal female external genitalia. However, in about a third of the cases there is either no axillary or pubic hair, or the axillary and pubic hair is extremely scanty. There is a short or absent vagina and no cervix. The differential diagnosis must be madc between this condition and that of congenital absence of the Mullerian ducts. A negative chromatin pattern is confinnatory of a diagnosis of testicular feminization.

The laboratory findings are bizarre and can vary widely. Some patients show an elevated urinary gonadotrophin. Others show urinary gonadotrophins in the normal range. Most patients have a 17-ketosteroid excretion compatible with a normal male, and estrogen excretion compatible with a normal female. *Morris* has recently reported a comprehensive survey of his experience with this condition. The assumption is that this is a heritable developmental enzymatic defect of the testosterone target organs.

The treatment is opcrative removal of the testes after the age of puberty and vaginal plastic procedure if indicated. One patient among the 252 with amenorrhea %%as found to have this condition.

Ovarian Insufficiency

Premature Menopause, Congenital

The idiopathic premature menopause can be familial or sporadic. The description, in 1959 by Jacobs and Baikie, of a patient with a premature menopause who showed a triplo-X chromosomal pattern associated with multichromocenters in cells from a buccal smear, indicates that this condition may also be associated with nondysjunction of chromosomes or a disturbance related to gonadal dysgenesis. The ovaries of such individuals may appear small and deformed or almost normal grossly. Microscopically, the appearance is indistinguishable from that of a normal ovary.

Acquired defects

In addition to the congenital types of ovarian defects, ovarian destruction can occur in association with (1) tuberculous pelvic inflammatory disease, (2) irradiation, or (3) operative procedures. Very occasionally, primary amenorrhea results when pelvic tuberculosis occurs in a prepubertal child. Such a case has been described by *Reiss*. Under these circumstances, of course, eunuchoid proportions and gigantism are associated.

The diagnosis of a premature menopause can be suspected when the patient gives a history of hot flushes; but the laboratory finding of an elevated urinary gonadotrophin is the absolute criterion. There is no cure for a premature menopause, and therapy must be substitutional only. There were 24 patients, among the series reported, who had a premature menopause.

End Organs: Uterine and Vaginal Cryptomenorrhea

The conditions embraced under this heading are: traumatic occlusion of the vagina; the imperforate hymen; congenital absence or atresia of the vagina; vaginal septa; congenital absence of the Miillerian ducts; traumatic occlusion of the cervix; and destruction of the endometrium.

Occlusion of the Vagina and Cervix

The term *gynatresia* is applied to occlusion of any part of the genital canal. It may be of congenital or.acquired origin.

"Congenital Anomalies of the Female Generative Organs." The most important is imperforate hymen, although occasionally the congenital block involves the cervical or vaginal segment of the canal.

Symptoms

When atresia of the cervix or any part of the vagina is present, or when the hymen is imperforate, the menstrual discharge. if it occurs, is retained behind the obstruction. Of these causes. imperforate hymen is much the most common. The retained blood distends the vagina *(hematocolpos)* while with succeeding periods there is distention of the cervix *(hematotrachelos)*, uterine cavity *(hematonzetra)*, and finally even of the tubes *(hematosalpinx)*.

With each succeeding period there is increasing pain and

discomfort. When the uterine distention becomes marked. a bulging enlargement of the lower abdomen develops, and the patient's discomfort may be extreme, especially at the time of the periods. Difficulty in voiding is a common symptom.

Diagnosis

The diagnosis in such cases is usually easy, especially in the case of imperforate hymen. The distended hymen actually bulges forward from the pressure of the retained blood, and fluctuation can be felt both through the hymen and on rectal examination. In the less frequent cases in which the obstruction is higher up, the diagnosis is not always so obvious, but a history of regularly recurring menstrual molimina, with increasing menstrual discomfort without external menstrual flow, together with the finding of a fluctuating mass on bimanual abdominorectal palpation, will leave little doubt as to the nature of the condition.

Treatment

The treatment in the case of imperforate hymen is simple, consisting simply in slow evacuation of the blood through a crucial incision in the hymen. Strict asepsis must of course be observed, and most writers, whether justifiably or not, warn of the especial proneness of such patients to infection. After evacuation of the blood, the hymen may be excised, or as some prefer, gently but widely divulsed, to avoid agglutination and secondary closure.

In the case of obstruction higher up, the problem is not so simple. If the lower vagina is involved, and the septum thin, somewhat the same plan may be followed as with imperforate hymen. But if the obstruction is higher and the intervening mass of tissue thick, much care is necessary in evacuating the blood, and the later treatment may involve some form of plastic operation for what is'essentially absence of the vagina.

Acquired Gynatresia

Gynatresia is by no means always due to congenital factors, and as a matter of fact the acquired variety is more frequent. The portions of the genital canal which by their occlusion may cause retention of thegenital discharge-are the cervix and the vagina. Especially frequent is the cervix, the canal of which is normally much the narrowest portion of the uterovaginal tract.

Causes

The most important causes of acquired gynatresia are the following.

Senile Contraction

Although atrophy of the genital canal. including its mucosa, occurs normally after the menopause, it may in some women be so extreme as to cause blockage of the cervix and occasionally to the vagina. This is especially true because of the proneness of the thin, senile mucous membrane to secondary infection and ulceration. As a result of complete occlusion of the cervical canal in the woman who is no longer menstruating, the retained discharge consists of pus rather than blood, although there may be a bloody admixture because of the presence of granulation tissue in the wall of the retention cavity. Such retention of pus in the uterine cavity is called pyometra. It is very gradual in development, with often no symptoms for many months. Attention is called to the condition in many cases by the seepage of slight amounts of blood from the granulation tissue in the cervical canal, whereas in other cases there may be pelvic discomfort or even the development of a mass.

Malignant Disease

One of the most common of all causes of gynatresia is malignant disease, usually of the cervix. Either epidermoid or adenocarcinoma may be responsible, and in most cases there has been an antecedent history of bleeding from the cancer. A not uncommon occurrence, especially in older women, is to encounter the pyometra in the course of diagnostic curettage performed because of postmenopausal bleeding. In other cases the pyometra develops in the late stages of carcinoma whose existence has long been known.

Radiotherapy and Cauterization

As a result of the radiotherapy universally employed for carcinoma of the cervix, stricture or complete -atresia of the cervical canal may occur, with pyometra as the usual result. Such postradiation strictures may not develop until a long time, even several years, after the application of radium. The widely prevalent and sometimes injudicious or improper use of the cautery in the treatment of cervicitis has left in its wake a definite incidence of strictures of the cervix and even complete atresia of the canal. The same result may follow the use of chemical caustics, such as strong solutions of nitrate of silver, within the cervix.

Surgical Operations

An occasional result of operations upon the cervix is the occurrence of stricture or atresia. This may follow even simple dilatation when this is associated with laceration of the tissue, but is more likely to occur after cervical cauterization, conization, or such plastic operations as the Sturmdorf tracheloplasty or cervical amputation.

Symptoms

When a previously normal woman ceases to menstruate, but suffers severe colicky pain at the time of the expected period, the possibility of gynatresia should be suspected. especially if there is a history of one of the causative factors enumerated above. The pain recurs at each menstrual date, and pelvic examination will usually, within a month or two. reveal evidence of distention of the uterus, if as is most common, the obstruction is in the cervix. The latter becomes large and broad, and develops a peculiar elastic feel, with sometimes distinct fluctuation. Later the body of the uterus likewise becomes large and fluctuant.

When the gynatresia occurs in postmenopausal women, its development is much more insidious and its recognition more difficult, because the retained genital secretion is far less in amount than the normal menstrual flow. In a large proportion of cases pyometra is found accidentally, as already mentioned. The retained secretion commonly undergoes secondary infection, and there may be fever or chills, in addition to increasing pelvic discomfort and slight bleeding.

Diagnosis

When such symptoms as have been described lead to the suspicion of cervical occlusion, the diagnosis can be made reasonably certain by direct exploration of the cervical canal by the uterine sound, always under strict aseptic precautions. When the occlusion is light, the probe itself may be followed by a telltale trickle of blood or pus. When the blockage is tight even a very fine probe will fail to enter the uterus. In such cases the diagnosis can be made by passing a large caliber aspirating needle through the cervical wall into the distended cavity.

Treatment

The treatment of the common forms of acquired gynatresia consists of dilatation followed by drainage. The dilatation may be a comparatively simple office procedure, although it must be repeated from time to time, as most strictures of the cervix have a tendency to contract down. Small olivepointed metal dilators are ordinarily most useful.

Congenital Absence of the Mullerian Ducts

This condition is characterized by a normal development and

normal endocrine findings, with absence of the uterus and upper third of the vagina. As mentioned previously, it must be differentiated from testicular feminization and this can be done by the buccal smear which is positive. or feminine, in type. Once the diagnosis is made it must be determined as accurately as possible whether there is absence of the uterus as well as a congenital absence of the upper third of the vagina. In rare instances there is simply a vaginal constriction band and a normal uterus is present above. In this case. of course. a surgical procedure will assure normal reproductive function. whereas. if the uterus is absent. the only procedure required is either a vaginal plastic operation or the use of a Frank tube to produce a vagina by pressure as described in 1928. One patient in the present series had a transverse vaginal septum and was cured bN simple incision.

Destruction of the Endometrium and Traumatic Strictures of the Cervix

This condition has been classically described by Ashermam. Although usually associated with secondary amenorrhea, the condition can, very occasionally, be the cause of primary amenorrhea, as when pelvic tuberculosis has involved the endometrium extensively prepube-rtally. Aside from tuberculosis, cervical stenosis and endometrial sclerosis are almost always secondary to a dilatation and curettage or some other intracervical or intrauterine procedure which has been unduly traumatic or associated with an inflammatory process. A postpartum or postabortion curettage, as well as procedures associated with criminal abortions, classically predispose to this type of scarring.

Diagnosis of amenorrhea associated with destructive or congenital lesions of the end organs is made on the basis of an examination and curettage which demonstrate a vaginal or cervical obstruction or scarring of the endometrium. The basal temperature chart indicates ovulation in the absence of menstruation, and after the administration of adequate amounts of estrogen withdrawal fails to induce menstr-uation. Although frequently advocated as a diagnostic aid in this condition, the hysterogram is usually unsatisfactory.

The treatment of the condition is repeated dilatation of the cervix and curettage. Although this seems paradoxical, the therapeutic effect is probably due to the "freshening up" of the scar tissue, allowing the remains of the basalis layer of the endometrium to regrow. Various operative procedures, originating with that of Strassman, have been advocated for the correction of the condition. These differ mainly only in the use of different materials to substitute for the endometrial lining. The success obtained with any of these procedures can probably be attributed to the regenerative powers of the endometrium when the cervix is patent.

There were 6 patients with cryptomenorrhea in our series of amenorrheic women,, and 2 have become pregnant after repeated curettages.

PHYSIOLOGICAL AMENORRHEA

Physiological types of amenorrhea need only be mentioned briefly as associated with puberty, pregnancy, and the menopause.

Delayed Puberty

The diagnosis of delayed puberty might be best included under lesions of the nervous system, as it is now our concept that puberty is initiated by maturation of the hypothalamus rather than of the pituitary.

Statistically speaking, the diagnosis cannot be made until after the age of 17 years, although any delay of menstruation after 14 years is considered delayed over the average age. The diagnosis is made when the history, physical findings, and laboratory data are all within normal limits, and it is facilitated if there is a family history of a delayed menarche. The causes are numerous, the most important being poor general health, nutrition, or hygiene.

A careful follow-up examination should be made yearly until one is sure that the correct diagnosis has been established. There were 3 patients among our group with this diagnosis and all 3 are menstruating regularly at the present time.

Pregnancy and Postpartum Amenorrhea

Any patient presenting with amenorrhea is presumed to be pregnant until proved otherwise. If the physical examination is equivocal, a pregnancy test can be performed to exclude the diagnosis. Postpartum amenorrhes is usual, especially if the patient nurses tier baby. The normal duration of this amenorrhea is between 6 weeks and 3 months if the patient does not lactate. If the patient has nursed, menses usually return within 6 months of delivery, or 6 weeks after cessation of lactation; any period of amenorrhea longer than this can be considered as prolonged, lactation amenorrhea. A differential diagnosis must be made between this physiological condition and true Sheehan's disease, pituitary necrosis caused by the destruction of the gland at the time of the traumatic delivery. If there is a history of a postpartum dilatation and curettage, the possibility of endometrial sclerosis must also be entertained. The diagnosis of postpartum amenorrhea is made on the basis of a history of an uncomplicated delivery and normal laboratory findings. However, this differential diagnosis is not to be made didactically for, if destruction of the pituitary (Sheehan's disease) has not been complete, the findings may be identical with those of postpartum lactation amenorrhea. The Chiari-Fronunel syndrome is another variant.

Time will usually suffice to cure the condition but cyclic steroid therapy will often suppress the pituitary prolactin and predispose to a more rapid resumption of regular menses.

In the series of amenorrheic women reported there were 16 with prolonged postpartum amenorrhea. Fourteen patients were followed adequately and 8 have had subsequent pregnancies: an additional 3 have menstruated regularly and 3 remain amenorrheic.

INDEX

A

a benign solid teratoma, 275
a bipartite 102
A corona glandis 27
a corpus luteum 88
a frozen section 272
a germinal epithelium, 79
a gonadoblastoma 238
a medulla 79
A paradidymis, 3
a perivitelline space 99
a second polar body 87
a testis 3
A urinary bladder 4
a zona pellucida. 99
Abnormal bleeding 261
Abnormal discharge 261
Abscess 199
acidophilic adenoma 319
acromegaly, 319
acute 199
acute pelvic peritonitis 281
Adcnocarcinonta, 265
afford 199
albuginea nea 80
Albumen glands 162
Alicrococcus catarrhalis 229
Alicrococcus catarrhalis 199
all higher 154
Alytes 150
amenorrhea 250
Amphigonopeterus aurora 37
amplexation 148
ampulla 91, 157
ampullar glands 157
ampullary gland 3
ampullary glands 10
anal, inguinal, perinaeal, 160
androgen to cortisol 326
anemia, cachexia 261
Anguilla, 167
antrum 81
appendix epididymidis 165
appendix epididymis 3
Ascites 239, 271
Asdell, 330
atrophic 208
atrophic leukoplakia 208
atrophy 208
avmptontatology 261

B

Bacillus crassus, 201
bacteria 222
baculum 23
baculurn or os penis 4
Bartholin's glands 159

basophilic adenoma 319
Bass 320
becoming 199
bicornuate uterus: 102
Blarina; 25
bleeding 270
Bliss 322
breeding season. 166
Breiskv 207
broad ligament 164
bulbus penis 4, 23
burning, 223
Bush 326

C

Callorhycnhus antarcticus, 46
Candida albicans 227
Candida albicans 222
Candida albicans 229
Candida krtvcei 184
capacitation 70, 180
capacity 61
caput epididymis 8
Carcinoma 265
carcinoma 232
carcinoma-in-situ 209
carcinosarcoma. 258
cauda epididymis 8
centrosome 86
cervical glands 158
cervix 155
Cetorhinus maximus 46
Chiari-Frommel 316
childbirth or abortion, 281
Chorionepi-thelioma 276
chromophobe adenoma, 318
chronic perioophoritis, 294
Ciliated Cells. 92
Citellus 33
clinical grouping 264
clitoris 157
clitoris, 155
cloacal glands 160
Clostridium welchii 282
coelomi 1
colliculus seminalis 165
colliculus seminalis 3, 22
conidia. 228
Constan 317
copulatory 13
corona radiata, 98
corpora cavernosa, 153
corpora cavernosa penis 22
corpora cavernosa. 4
corpus albicans. 88
corpus epididymis 8
corpus hemorrhagicum. 88
corpus luteum spurium 88
corpus luteum verum; 88
corpus spongiosum 4, 22
cortex. 79
Coturnix coturnix 42
Count per milliliter: 179
Cowper's glands 159
Crooke et al. 314
crura 4, 22
Cryptomenorrhea 300
Cryptoti, 25
Cryptotis parva. 25
Cushing 327
Cushing's syndrome 319
Cymatogaster aggregata 46
cystic 274
cysts 200

D

Daily 322
dartos tunic 7
decapacitation factor 70
defeminization 250
diabetes mellitus 324
diagnosis 202

Didelphis marsupialis, 25
Didelphys, 155
discharges front the uterine 223
double cloacal organs 151
douches 223
ducluti efferentes. 8
ductuli aberrantes 164
ductus deferens. 3
ductus epididymidis 9
ductus epididymis 3
dvsgerminoma, 235
Dvsmenorrhea 294
dysgerminoma, 234

E

Echidna. 159
ectopic pregnancy. 296
Eczematoid 197
Edema 198
efforts 284
ejaculatory duct. 10
Elephantulus intufi, 147
elephariiasis. 205
embryonal carcinoma 275
embryonic bisexuality). 72
Endometrial sarcoma 258
endometrium 104
entodermic 276
epididymis. 3
epoophoron 164
equatorial plate 86
Erinaceus, 157
essential part 218
estrogen, 245
estrogenic therapy 230
estrus 105
et al. 100, 177, 182, 326, 333, 208
etiological agent 201
Eunice viridis, 168
Eurycea lucifuga 47
Evaluation 296
exanthematous diseases 223
external spermalic fascia, 7
external urethral orifice. 22
extragenital sites. 203

F

Fallopian tube, 160
familiaris) 27
ferentiated 249
fimbriae. 90
first polar body. 87
Foglia et al. 325
follicularis 293
folliculitis 197
Ford 331
foreign bodies, 223
Freed, 320
frozen 247
fructolysis 58

G

Gaertner's duct, 164
general diseases 222
genital ridges 1
germinal epithelium, 1
Girardinus, 151, 161
glands of Littre, 159
glans, 27
glans penis. 4, 23
gonadoblastoma. 235
gonocytoma 238
Gonorrheal, 279
Govan 317
granulosa-theca cell tumor, 234
Green and Rubin 331
growth characteristics 241

H

hemipenis 151
Hemophilus ducrevii 201

Hemophilus vaginalis 194
Herpes genitalis 197
hilus. 79
Hippocampus, 162
hirsutism 251
histogenesis 275
Horaichthys setnai 46
hvdrosalpinx; 292
hymen. 156
hyperemia. 223
hypomenorrhea, 300
hypothesis 316

I

Ideopathic retroperitoneal fibrosis 297
in situ 217
In vitro 98
in vitro 61, 314
in vivo 126
incidence 264, 274
incomplete cyclers. 146
inediastinuin testis, 5
infundibulum, 90
Ingersoll 313
inguinal canal is 4
inspection 223
intermediate, 249
Interstitial cells of Leydig 7
interstitial cells. 3
intertrigo 197
invasive cancer 209
Invasive carcinoma 217
irradiation therapy 273
Israel 317
isthmus. 91
itching 223
itching. 224

J

Jones 331
Jost 332

K

Keettel, Bradbury, 314
Kistner 315
Klebarow 330
kraurosis 208
Kroger 320

L

labia majora, 157
labia minora, 156
Lanthier. 314
late diestrus, 105
leiomyosarcoma 257
Leukoplakia 208
leukoplakia 207
leukorrhea, almost 224
liquor folliculi, 81
lobules, 3
local irritation 223
local irritation, 227
longa glandis. 27

M

Macroscelides proboscideus), 147
Mahesh 326
Malignant melanoma 219
mammary glands, 160
marsupial. 156
McArthur 313
medullary cords; 73
membrana granulosa, 81
membrana propria, 81
menopause 168
Menorrhagia 294
menstrual disorders. 270
menstrual flow. 170
mesenchyme. 3
mesenchynte 248

mesonephros 1
mesorchium 1
mesosalpinx 89
mesotubariuni superius 89
Micrococcus catarrhalis 194
Micrometrus minimus 37
Microscopic 292
microscopic 267, 292, 293
microscopic characteristics 281, 291
microscopic examination 268
microscopic picture 203, 283
Microscopically 276
Microscopically, 238, 241, 269
Microtus arvalis 21
Microtus townsendii, 136
Migeon 322
mixed mesodermal tumor. 258
Monilia 222
mons Veneris. 157, 165
Morris 334
Motility 61, 179
Moyo-castor coypus 9
Mullerian duct 4
Mullerian ducts 3, 4
Mullerian ducts. 3
Muller's tubercle. 3
multiple biopsy 206
Mural sarcomas 259
Murdoch 317
mycelia, 228
myoepithelial cells. 118

N

nests, 120
nidamental glands, 162
normal, Jlora 221
Nototreina pygmaeum, 162

O

oestrous cycle, 168
Oligomenorrhea 300
oogonium 81
oophorus, 87
optimal 240
Orycteropus 161
os penis 23
os priapi, 154
ostium abdominale, 162
oulbourehtral glands, 159
ovarian bursa 90
Oxyuris vermicularis. 194

P

Pain 261, 294
pain 284
pampiniform plexus, 8
paradidymis 164
parametritis 285
parietal layer 5
paroophoron 164
pars bulbus glandis 27
pars cavernosa. 21
pars longa glandis; 27
pars spongiosa 21
pathological changes 200
pelvic abscess. 281
Pelvic endometriosis 296
penis, 150
per se 305
per se, 295, 324
Perameles, 155
periovarial sac 90
periovarial sac. 79
perisalpingitis 281
phallus. 154
Physiological amenorrhea 300
Plethodon cinereus 40
Plotz 330

postabortive. 291
postmenopausal 245
preceding irradiation 258
preputium. 154
Primary amenorrhea 300
Primary Carcinoma 232
Primary infertility 172
primary or Secondary. 200
primary sex cords 1
primordial germ cells 1
Procavia capensis 43
processus urethrails. 154
procreation. Infertility, 172
Proechimys semispinosus, 44
prostaglandin may 65
prostate gland, 159
prostatic ulricle. 4
pruritus 227
pruritus vulvae, 211
Psoriasis 197
puberty, 49
pyosalpinx 292
pyosalpinx. 292

R

radical 218
Ray, Nicholson-Valley, 320
rectal strcture 206
reddening 227
redness 223
Reiss. 335
rete cords 3
rete pegs 205
rete tubules, 3
retroperitoneallv 261
Rhinoderma darzvini 162
Richter 329
Rottino 328
rudimentary organs 164

S

Salamandra atra 151
salpingitis isthtnica nodosa, 292
Sandor 314
Sarcoma 219, 232
sarcoma botryoides 259
Sargeant 322
Schwimmer 207
Sciurus 33
Sciurus carolinensis. 33
Sciurus. 33
Sciurus; 33
scrotal raphe. 4
scrotal sac. 4
scrotal swellings 4
Seborrhea 197
seborrheic dermatitis 197
Secondary amenorrhea 300
Secondary Carcinoma 232
secondary infertility 172
secondary oocyte; 87
secondary svniptons 295
seem primary 269
semen, 159
seminal vesicle, 10, 157
seminiferous tubules 3, 5
seminiferous tubules. 73
senile vaginitis, 210
septula, extend 5
septum scroti. 7
Sertoli's 6
simplex 102, 293
smegma. 160
solid teratoma 275
solid. 274
Sosman 328
spermatic fascia, 7
spermatogenic cells 6
spermatophores, 151
spermatozoon 50

spinbarkeit 183
Spindle fibers 86
Staphylo-coccus aureus, 222
steatopygy. 157
Stein 314
Sterility 172, 295
stigma 87
Stoddard 314
strawberry-like appearance 224
stress 326
stromal endometriosis, 258
stromatosis 258
strunia ovarii, 276
submaxillary glands 160
suffers 218
surgical. 273
sustentacular cells. 6
symptoms 277
Syngnathus, 162

T

T pallidum 202
Tachyglossus aculeatus) 145
testes, 5
The scrotum containing 154
theca 245
theca externa. 81
theca folliculi, 81
theca interna 81
thrushlike patches 228
Thvroid dysfunction 210
trabeculae 293
Treatment 202
treatment 277
Trichomonas vaginalis 199, 224
Tuberculous 279
tuboovarian abscess 293
tubuli contorli 6
tubuli recti 6
tunica albuginea 5, 22
tunica albuginea 3
tunica vaginalis 5
Tyson's glands 160

U

undifferentiated 249
urethra 4
urethral process 27
Urocyon) 27
urogenilal folds 4
urogenital sinus 4
uterine glands 158
uterus, 155, 160
utriculus prostaticus, 22

V

vagina 155
vagina masculina, 165
vagina. 150
vaginal discharge, 223
vaginal plug 13
vaginal soreness, burning, 224
vesiculase. 17
vestibular glands, 158
vestibule, 155
vitelline membrane 99
vitro 71

W

weakness 261
Wilkins. 325

Y

yolk sac. As 1

Z

zig-zag 249
zona pellucida, 81
zone reticulata 326